FIFTH ■ EDITION

BEHAVIOR CHANGE
in the
HUMAN
SERVICES

To Dorothy Rish

and

to the memory of Marvin A. Rish

FIFTH·EDITION

BEHAVIOR CHANGE
in the
HUMAN SERVICES

Behavioral and Cognitive Principles and Applications

MARTIN · SUNDEL
SANDRA · S. · SUNDEL

SAGE Publications
Thousand Oaks · London · New Delhi

For information:

Sage Publications, Inc.
2455 Teller Road
Thousand Oaks, California 91320
E-mail: order@sagepub.com

Sage Publications Ltd.
1 Oliver's Yard
55 City Road
London EC1Y 1SP
United Kingdom

Sage Publications India Pvt. Ltd.
B-42, Panchsheel Enclave
Post Box 4109
New Delhi 110 017 India

Printed in the United States of America

Library of Congress Cataloging-in-Publication Data

Sundel, Martin, 1940–
Behavior change in the human services: Behavioral and cognitive principles
and applications / Martin Sundel, Sandra S. Sundel.
5th ed.
    p. cm.
Includes bibliographical references and indexes.
ISBN 0-7619-8870-X (pbk.)
    1. Behavior modification—Textbooks. I. Sundel, Sandra Stone, 1948– II. Title.
BF637.B4S89 2005
153.8′5—dc22   2004009277

04   05   06   07   10   9   8   7   6   5   4   3   2   1

Acquiring Editor:	Arthur T. Pomponio
Editorial Assistant:	Veronica Novak
Production Editor:	Diana E. Axelsen
Typesetter:	C&M Digitals (P) Ltd.
Cover Designer:	Janet Foulger

Contents

Preface

Has this ever happened to you? It's 3:00 a.m., and you are frantically cramming for tomorrow's exam. You are fighting off sleep, trying to fool your body with food and caffeine while trying to keep your mind alert. You have 5 hours to read 10 chapters, and you swear that you will never do this to yourself again. Next term will be different. You will keep up with your reading throughout the class, so next time you will only have to review the night before the final.

Somehow you get through the night, and you do manage to pass the exam. Then, before long, you find yourself in the exact same situation, in the wee hours of the night before another exam—perhaps for a different class and a different professor—cursing yourself for this self-inflicted torture. You wonder why you allow this to happen repeatedly. What prevents you from making a change in your study habits? If this scenario sounds all too familiar, then you have experienced the power of positive reinforcement. Each passing grade reinforces your current study habits, and the cycle repeats itself with every class. What would happen if you failed the exam? You would probably evaluate what went wrong and do your best to prevent it from happening again. You would make sure that you keep up with the reading and are fully prepared for each lecture.

Study habits, like other behaviors, can be changed. Also, the changes do not have to involve negative consequences or pain. Whether you are a student with bad study habits or a client seeking professional help with any of a variety of problems, the behavior change approach presented in this book can help you to decrease undesired behaviors and increase desired behaviors. In this book, you will learn about behavior change principles that can be applied to a wide range of problems and situations encountered in the human service professions. In the chapters that follow, we present a problem-solving framework through which you can apply behavior change principles to the real-life situations that you and your clients confront. We present the basic principles of behavior change within a practice context that relates them to assessment, intervention, and evaluation.

This book continues in the spirit and tradition of the previous four editions of *Behavior Change (Modification) in the Human Services*. In the period since the first edition was published in 1975, we have witnessed tremendous growth and development in the application of behavior change principles in the human services.

This trend continues to the present, and the changes since the fourth edition was published in 1999 attest to the continuing need for students and practitioners to acquire a basic foundation for practice before pursuing advanced study and application in specialized areas. Mastery of the content of this volume requires focus and discipline in acquiring requisite knowledge of principles, procedures, and intervention techniques and relating them to situations encountered in fieldwork, internships, professional practice, and everyday life.

We believe that we have made several improvements in this new edition, including the introduction of new concepts, suggested activities for each chapter, and updated references. We have integrated the two chapters that appeared in previous editions on positive reinforcement contingencies and schedules of reinforcement into one (Chapter 4) and have combined two chapters from previous editions on behavioral assessment into one more efficient chapter as well (Chapter 13). We have also included goal setting in the intervention and planning chapter (Chapter 14). Finally, we have updated the chapter on intervention techniques and expanded it to include current developments in the field, such as the movement toward evidence-based practice (Chapter 15).

This book is designed for students and practitioners in social work, psychology, counseling, special education, nursing, and allied health and human service professions. Teachers, clergy, parents, and others will also find the principles, techniques, and examples in this book relevant to situations they encounter. The examples presented are drawn from diverse areas to illustrate the range and versatility of the behavioral approach in an increasingly multicultural society.

This new edition builds on the strengths of the previous editions and contains a number of features designed to make learning the behavior change approach interesting and rewarding. You need have no prior course work or background in psychology to use this book. Each chapter includes objectives, suggested activities, and a list of references and resources, and chapter pretests and posttests appear in appendixes. The objectives that begin each chapter specify what you can expect to learn from studying that chapter. We present behavioral principles so that the content of each chapter builds on the knowledge and skills covered in the preceding chapters. Charts, graphs, and other illustrations serve as aids in the analysis of case material and examples. The chapter pretests and posttests allow you to evaluate your own ability to apply and integrate the course content. They also enable you to apply the principles discussed in the book to specific case material and to compare how much you know before you study the chapters with your level of knowledge afterward. The suggested activities presented at the end of each chapter allow you to apply concepts covered in the chapter to everyday situations and classroom activities.

The material in this book has been classroom tested. The course materials included here have been used extensively with many students and practitioners from diverse cultural and educational settings. We have continually revised the content of the materials and the order in which we present them, as well as the test questions and answers, based on the performance and feedback of these students and practitioners.

Chapters 1 through 12 discuss the basic principles of operant and respondent conditioning, including observational learning. Beginning with Chapter 1, we define behavior to include measures of either overt or covert (cognitive) actions. We address issues and topics related to ethics and cultural diversity throughout the text. The chapters on behavioral assessment (Chapter 13) and intervention planning and evaluation (Chapter 14) are presented after coverage of the basic principles. In the final chapter, on intervention techniques, we discuss additional applications of behavioral and cognitive-behavioral techniques to selected target behaviors. We also address some current issues and trends, including the movement toward empiricism, evidence-based practice, and practice guidelines.

We have updated the lists of references and suggested readings throughout the text while retaining many of the works included in earlier editions because of their classic contributions to the field. Although psychologists have been prominent in the development and application of behavioral and cognitive principles, many of the important new additions to the "References and Resources" sections reflect the contemporary contributions of researchers in social work, special education, psychiatry, and other helping professions.

The numerous case examples we present throughout the book are drawn from practice settings. In all case materials and examples, the names of the individuals are fictitious. The case examples are not meant to be complete records. Rather, they are intended to provide basic information that will help you to relate specific principles to real-life situations.

This book has benefited from the challenging comments and suggestions of our students and colleagues, including those in our courses, workshops, and continuing education programs. We are indebted to our many colleagues, too numerous to mention individually here, who have provided conceptual, empirical, and clinical foundations for the body of knowledge incorporated in this text. Many of their names appear in the lists of references and suggested readings that accompany the chapters.

Arthur Pomponio, our editor at Sage Publications, and Veronica Novak, editorial assistant, gave support during all phases of preparing this new edition. Diana Axelsen, senior production editor, guided the editing of the book, which included skillful copyediting by Judy Selhorst. Donald Sloane (Washington University) and Frank Sparzo (Ball State University) made valuable comments and suggestions in their reviews of the book. Stephen Wong (Florida International University) provided us with helpful resources and informed perspectives on several issues. Bruce Thyer (Florida State University) and Joseph Himle (University of Michigan) contributed useful reference materials.

We hope that reading this book will be positively reinforcing for you, and that you will be stimulated to further develop your knowledge and expertise in this exciting field of practice. If you do, we will have achieved our purpose in writing this book.

To the Student:
How to Use This Book

Course Materials

This book contains the following materials:

- *Case examples:* Eight case examples demonstrate the application of behavioral principles to practice problems. We present many of these case examples over the course of the various chapters; they also appear together in Appendix 1 for your convenience.
- *Chapters:* This volume's 15 chapters present behavioral and cognitive concepts, principles, and applications. Each chapter begins with a set of specified learning objectives. Chapter pretests and answers to the pretest questions are provided in Appendixes 2 and 3, respectively. Chapter posttests and answers to the posttest questions appear in Appendixes 4 and 5, respectively. You should consider the chapter pre- and posttests to be integral parts of the chapters, as they allow you to assess your mastery of the content. Each chapter builds on content from previous chapters; therefore, we recommend that you work through the chapters in the order in which they are presented.
- *Suggested activities:* Suggestions for activities related to chapter content are included at the end of each chapter. These exercises and questions provide you with the opportunity to apply concepts covered in the chapter. Many of the activities require interaction or discussion with others in a classroom or other group setting.
- *References and resources:* Each chapter ends with a list of the works cited in the chapter along with other suggested readings.
- *Course posttest:* A posttest for the entire text, consisting of 33 questions, appears in Appendix 6 (the answers are provided in Appendix 7).
- *Notational symbols appendix:* A summary of the notational symbols and behavioral diagrams used throughout the text is provided in Appendix 8.
- *Glossary:* The glossary contains definitions of technical and specialized terms, which are introduced in boldface type in the text.

Case Examples

We use eight case examples throughout the text to illustrate applications of the behavioral and cognitive principles. To answer the questions on the course posttest, you will need information found in these case examples. You will also need information from the case examples to answer many of the questions on the chapter pretests and posttests.

In all of the case studies and examples presented in this volume, the names of the individuals are fictitious. The case examples are not meant to be complete records. Rather, they are intended to give you basic information that will help you to apply behavioral and cognitive concepts to real-life situations.

The Chapters

Objectives are stated at the beginning of each chapter to indicate the results you can achieve after completing the chapter. Chapter pretests (in Appendix 2) will orient you to the chapters, and by scoring the pretests (using the answers provided in Appendix 3), you can assess your familiarity with the content. You are not expected to achieve criterion score on the chapter pretests.

Taking the chapter pretests will give you practice with the types of questions and answers you will find on the posttests. If you achieve criterion score on a chapter pretest, you can take that chapter's posttest without reading the chapter. If you also achieve criterion score on the chapter posttest, you can skip that chapter and go on to the next chapter pretest. If you achieve less than criterion score on a chapter pretest, you should study that chapter.

Each chapter covers the content necessary to achieve the listed objectives. After you have studied a chapter, you should take the chapter posttest (in Appendix 4) and score it by comparing your answers with those given in Appendix 5. If you do not achieve criterion score, you should review the chapter and retake the test, repeating this procedure until you achieve criterion score.

Suggested activities are included at the end of each chapter. These exercises and questions provide you with opportunities to apply the concepts covered in the chapter, to ensure that you have a solid grasp of the material. Some of the activities require interaction or discussion with others in a classroom or other group setting.

The "References and Resources" section at the end of each chapter includes both the works cited in the text and suggested additional readings. The references, which represent only a small sample of the available literature, have been selected based on their relevance for specific principles or applications. You may want to consult these books and articles—which discuss theoretical foundations, present case studies, and report on empirical research—for further clarification and elaboration of the various concepts and applications presented in this volume.

The Course Posttest

You should take the course posttest, which appears in Appendix 6, after you have completed your study of the 15 chapters, and score it using the answers given in Appendix 7. If you do not achieve criterion score, you should review the chapters related to your incorrect answers. When you achieve criterion score on the course posttest, you have demonstrated mastery of the content of this text.

Scoring the Pre- and Posttests

Many of the questions in the pre- and posttests ask for examples that demonstrate the application of particular concepts; therefore, a number of different correct answers may be possible for individual questions. For these questions, criteria for correct answers are delineated. If your answer to a given question meets all of the criteria stated, you receive the maximum number of points. If your answer includes two out of three correct parts, for example, you receive two points for the question. If your answer does not meet any of the stated criteria, you receive zero points for that question.

The tests incorporate many open-ended questions that require you to formulate answers based on your analysis of the content covered. These questions are designed to help you develop skills in applying the principles rather than merely identifying which of two or more answers is correct. Sample answers are given for each open-ended question that meet the criteria specified for a correct answer.

You can use the following guidelines in scoring certain kinds of questions that appear frequently throughout the tests:

1. When a question asks for a description of a procedure, the answer must list the operations or steps required to carry out that procedure.

2. When a question asks for an example that describes a procedure or technique, the answer must include a specific application of that procedure or technique.

3. When the question asks for a diagram of a procedure or technique, the answer must include the correct symbols and notations. If the question asks for a diagram showing an example, the symbols of the diagram must be drawn correctly and explained in relation to a specific example.

4. When a question asks for a description of the effect of a certain procedure, the answer must describe the expected outcome of using that procedure.

5. When a question asks for an example that describes the effect of a certain procedure, the answer must state the outcome of that procedure in relation to information based on a specific example. When a case example is given, the answer must be stated in relation to information obtained from that example.

   6.When a question asks for an evaluation of the effectiveness of a certain procedure or technique, the answer must state a specific criterion for determining whether or not the procedure or technique produced its intended outcome.

Below we present examples of correct, partially correct, and incorrect answers to the same question to illustrate some of the points noted above:

Question: Describe the positive reinforcement procedure and its effect on the strength of a response. (2 points)

Correct answer: The presentation of an object or event following a response (procedure) that increases the strength of that response (effect). (2 points)

Partially correct answer: Present a positive reinforcer to someone immediately after performance of the target behavior (procedure). Its effect is to modify that behavior. (1 point)

Incorrect answer: (a) Indicate reinforcer before desired behavior to entice person to act in desired way. (b) Give positive reinforcer immediately after behavior as a reward. (0 points)

The point value stated after each question reflects the number of components required for a complete answer. In this example, a total of 2 points is possible for a correct answer: 1 point for the correctly stated procedure and 1 point for the correctly stated effect. The first answer received 2 points. The second answer was only half correct; therefore, it received 1 point. The third answer was incorrect and received 0 points.

The acceptable score for each test is established as 90% of the questions answered correctly. This is indicated as the criterion score shown at the end of each test.

Recommendations for Instructor Use of This Book

A variety of instructional formats can be used with this book. The instructor may use the book by itself or in conjunction with supplementary readings. We recommend that the instructor assign chapters in sequential order to be completed by the students prior to class sessions. In some cases, however, instructors may choose to assign chapters in a different order. For example, some instructors prefer to teach negative reinforcement immediately after positive reinforcement. Because negative reinforcement is often a difficult concept for students to learn, we present it in Chapter 10, after other basic principles have been discussed. In our experience, this order provides an effective way of teaching the principles and avoids encouraging the common erroneous conception among students that negative reinforcement is the opposite of positive reinforcement.

The instructor may use class time to clarify, elaborate, and discuss the content of the chapters and other readings as well as for demonstrations and practice skill sessions that allow students to participate in role plays involving applications of principles and techniques. The instructor may want to employ some of the suggested activities provided at the end of each chapter to help students practice their knowledge of chapter content.

The instructor may want to have students report their pretest and posttest scores each week and chart them over the period of the course, retaking each deficient posttest until 90% criterion or better is achieved. The course posttest, or selected items from this test, can be used in a final exam for the course, to be taken in class or completed at home.

In an alternative format, students might be required to complete the chapter pretests and read the chapters outside of class. They then take the chapter posttests in class, scoring their own papers, exchanging papers for scoring, or handing them in for scoring by the instructor.

The instructor may assign additional readings in both basic and applied research to supplement this book. The lists of suggested readings at the end of each chapter include many classic works in the field as well as current literature related to the topics covered.

Introduction

In a parent training group, Carla's mother, Juanita, told the practitioner that almost every time she told Carla to put her toys away, Carla screamed. Juanita would attempt to placate Carla by promising to buy her new clothes and by putting the toys away herself.

On the basis of the behavioral assessment, the practitioner suspected that Juanita was reinforcing Carla's screaming by putting the toys away and promising to buy Carla new clothes. The practitioner showed Juanita how to use extinction to decrease Carla's screaming. The procedure involved withholding the positive reinforcers for Carla's screaming.

The practitioner instructed Juanita to stop making promises, to stop putting away the toys, and to walk away from Carla when she screamed about putting away her toys. The practitioner told Juanita that Carla's screaming might get worse before it got better, but that if she held firm, Carla's screaming would gradually decrease. Juanita carried out these instructions for 7 days, during which time Carla's screaming gradually decreased, after an increase on the second day. By the sixth day, Carla no longer screamed when told to put her toys away.

The practitioner also instructed Juanita to praise Carla and give her tangible reinforcers, such as gum or cookies, when she put her toys away. Juanita followed these instructions, and Carla began putting her toys away more frequently.

This case example illustrates how the behavioral approach can be used to improve a parent-child relationship. In this book, we present the basic principles of behavior change derived from the experimental analysis of behavior and provide examples of their application to a wide range of problems and situations encountered by human service practitioners. We also provide a method for applying these principles within a problem-solving framework to allow the practitioner to do the following:

- Develop a collaborative and mutually reinforcing relationship with the client
- Assess the client's problem or target situation and develop a hypothesis regarding the controlling conditions of the target behavior

- Formulate behavior change goals
- Design an intervention plan
- Implement a behavior change program based on the intervention plan
- Monitor and evaluate the effects of the behavior change program

We present behavioral and cognitive principles within this problem-solving framework to facilitate their application in human service settings.

Origins of the Behavioral and Cognitive-Behavioral Approaches

Behavior change approaches, including **behavior therapy** and **cognitive behavior therapy,** have become increasingly popular during the past decade and have produced the majority of empirically supported psychosocial intervention techniques available to practitioners (Chambless and Ollendick, 2001; Chambless et al., 1996). Their historical roots, however, can be traced to the early and middle 20th century. Names such as Pavlov, Watson, Thorndike, and Skinner are associated with early contributions of classical and operant conditioning to the study of human behavior. Basic principles of behavior change called *behavior modification, behavior therapy,* and *applied behavior analysis* were derived primarily from learning theory and the experimental analysis of behavior with nonhuman organisms. The principles were then extended to the analysis and modification of human behaviors.

Principles of behavior change have been applied to a wide range of human problems (e.g., Baer & Pinkston, 1997; Barlow, 2001; Beck & Rector, 2001; Jason & Fries, 2004; Thyer & Myers, 2000; Wolpe, 1990). In this book, we focus on the principles of operant conditioning (e.g., Skinner, 1953), respondent (classical or "Pavlovian") conditioning (e.g., Pavlov, 1927), and observational or vicarious learning related to modeling and imitation (e.g., Bandura, 1969, 1977). We also introduce related developments in the cognitive approach, particularly those that have become associated with the behavioral approach. Especially noteworthy are the contributions of Beck's cognitive therapy (e.g., Beck, 1976; Beck & Emery, 1985), Ellis's rational emotive therapy (e.g., Ellis, 1962, 1984), and Meichenbaum's self-instruction training and stress inoculation training (e.g., Meichenbaum, 1977, 1985, 1994).

Many practitioners consider the individual's cognitive or covert processes to be a logical extension of the behavioral paradigm. The cognitive approach is based on the premise that negative thoughts, images, feelings, and beliefs produce undesired or maladaptive behaviors. Modification of such private or covert events is thought to diminish and thus help to resolve a client's psychosocial or emotional problems. The practitioner shows the client how to modify irrational, unproductive, or self-defeating cognitions and replace them with more constructive expectations and self-appraisals.

Comparing the Behavioral and Cognitive Approaches

Behavioral interventions are used to modify target behaviors by directly influencing their controlling conditions, and they rely on behavioral changes to influence related covert behaviors (e.g., Gelernter et al., 1991; Newman, Hofmann, Trabert, Roth, & Taylor, 1994). For example, Stuart's target behavior was watching television instead of looking for a job, and he frequently told himself, "What's the use of trying to get a job? No one will hire me." When Stuart initiated a job search by reading the classified ads and sending résumés to potential employers, these behaviors were positively reinforced with job interviews. Stuart's self-talk changed from "No one will hire me" to "If I interview at enough companies, I'll get a good job."

In contrast, cognitive interventions focus on modification of client cognitions as the target events and rely on cognitive changes to influence overt behavior change. In this case, Stuart's target behaviors were self-statements such as "No one will hire me," "I'm a failure," and "Nothing good ever happens to me." With cognitive intervention, Stuart changed his self-talk to positive statements, such as "I have some good abilities and someone will want to hire me" and "I just have to get my foot in the door with some job interviews to get hired." Cognitive therapy assumes that the alteration of such cognitions will lead to the desired behavior change, such as Stuart's initiation of job-seeking behaviors.

Many practitioners combine behavioral and cognitive approaches (e.g., Beck, Rush, Shaw, & Emery, 1979; Cautela & Ishaq, 1996; Dobson, 2001; Ellis, 1993; Hollon & Beck, 1994; Lazarus, 1976; Linehan, 1993; Mahoney, 1974; Meichenbaum, 1977) and regard behavior therapy to be more broadly defined as the application of behavioral and cognitive sciences to human problems. Bandura's (e.g., 1969, 1977) social learning theory influenced the conceptual development of this movement. Cautela's (e.g., 1966) covert conditioning, Meichenbaum's (e.g., 1977, 1994) self-instructional methodology, and D'Zurilla and Goldfried's (1971) problem-solving training provided further extensions and elaborations of attempts to combine cognitive and behavioral approaches. Multimodal behavior therapy, developed by Arnold Lazarus (e.g., 1976), is an example of the eclectic use of cognitive, behavioral, and social learning techniques.

The cognitive-behavioral approach combines the use of behavioral and cognitive interventions with the intention of improving efficacy. A practitioner can start with a behavioral intervention and then add a cognitive intervention or vice versa. For example, the practitioner assigns Stuart the task of sending his résumé to prospective employers and praises him after he sends it (behavioral intervention). Stuart, however, still tells himself, "I'll never get a call from anyone. No one is interested in me." The practitioner can then add a cognitive intervention that focuses on changing Stuart's negative self-statements to positive ones. Alternatively, the practitioner might begin with a cognitive intervention to help Stuart change his self-talk. The practitioner can then add behavioral assignments for Stuart to perform at home, such as selecting job possibilities from classified ads and submitting his résumé to prospective employers.

In a chapter titled "The Place of Feeling in the Analysis of Behavior" in his book on issues in behavior analysis, Skinner (1989, p. 25) argues, as he had previously (Skinner, 1974), that behaviorists acknowledge feelings (and other covert phenomena) but do not accept them as the sole explanation for behavior. Behaviorists almost always view verbal behavior that refers to unobservable events as a reaction to some aspect of behavior or the environment. According to Skinner (1989):

> We do not cry *because* we are sad or feel sad *because* we cry; we cry *and* feel sad because something has happened. . . . It is easy to mistake what we feel as a cause because we feel it while we are behaving (or even before we behave), but the events which are actually responsible for what we do (and hence what we feel) lie in the . . . past. The experimental analysis of behavior advances our understanding of feelings by clarifying the roles of both past and present environments. (pp. 4–5)

Characteristics of Behavior Change Approaches

The behaviorally oriented practitioner uses a helping approach that emphasizes the following characteristics:

- Active participation of the client in problem solving
- Assessment of the client's behaviors and their controlling conditions in measurable terms
- Individualized behavior change programs
- Use of empirically tested procedures and practice guidelines to increase desired behaviors and decrease undesired behaviors
- Short-term, time-limited intervention programs for many target behaviors
- Evaluation procedures that allow the client and practitioner to determine the effects of the behavior change program

The behavioral approach provides human service practitioners with a framework from which to address problems that require sensitive, practical, and ethical interventions. Issues of effectiveness and cost are paramount to sponsors of social services, mental health, mental retardation, education, corrections, health, and other human service programs. Decreased governmental funding for human service programs has been accompanied by increased reliance on managed care programs operated by insurance companies and other for-profit enterprises. These funding sources have placed great emphasis on practitioner accountability in providing cost-effective services. Behavioral practitioners use measurable criteria to evaluate their services and can educate program sponsors to better understand cost and treatment considerations related to behavior change.

Cultural Diversity

Behavioral approaches have often been viewed as value-free and culture-free (e.g., Blechman, 1984; Paniagua, 1998), but in reality they are subject to the same cultural biases evident in any given society. The behavioral literature has addressed issues of cultural diversity, including empirically based practice with culturally diverse clients, such as members of ethnic minority groups, older adults, gay men, lesbians, and individuals with disabilities (e.g., Fudge, 1996; Iwamasa & Smith, 1996; Kassinove & Uecke, 1991; Purcell, Campos, & Perilla, 1996). Some scholars have called for a greater emphasis on diversity issues in the literature (e.g., Iwamasa, 1997; McCrady, 2001; Nelson-Gray, Gaynor, & Korotitsch, 1997). More research is needed to examine the extent to which behavioral interventions are appropriate and effective with diverse populations, the role of culture in assessment, and how cultural issues influence the behavior of both the practitioner and the client in multicultural settings (e.g., Iwamasa, 1997; McCrady, 2001). Issues of multiculturalism, and their effects on both client and practitioner behavior, can be identified and studied to establish empirically validated intervention techniques with individuals from different cultural backgrounds.

Applications of Behavior Change Approaches

Behavioral principles and intervention techniques have been applied to the entire spectrum of age groups, from infants and children to younger and older adults. They have been used in residential and outpatient treatment settings and in prevention programs, such as parent training, classroom management, cardiovascular risk reduction, and promotion of healthy lifestyles. The current trend in self-help books based on the behavioral approach has expanded the resources available for individuals who wish to modify their own behaviors.

Behavioral analysis has been used to examine a broad range of human problems, such as anxiety, depression, phobias, overeating, smoking, drug abuse, alcoholism, stuttering, enuresis and encopresis, marital discord, family violence, nail biting, posttraumatic stress disorder, sexual abuse, and sexual dysfunction. Relaxation methods based on the behavioral approach, including biofeedback, are often used for stress management and tension reduction (Schwartz & Andrasik, 2003). Behavioral medicine (e.g., Blechman & Brownell, 1998; Graves & Miller, 2003) has developed as an interdisciplinary field for the treatment and prevention of health problems such as asthma, insomnia, headaches, hypertension, colitis, ulcers, and physical pain. An increasingly informed public has also become cognizant of the use of behavioral approaches in self-management programs related to overeating, substance abuse, social competence, time management, exercise, and other concerns.

Behavioral approaches have been used in a variety of institutions and environments, including family service agencies, psychiatric hospitals, community health and mental health centers, group homes and institutions for persons with mental retardation, criminal justice programs, child guidance clinics, child welfare agencies, nursing homes and other programs serving older adults, industrial/business settings, schools, neighborhoods, and other community settings. Once concentrated primarily in closed institutions, behavioral practitioners can now be found in almost every kind of agency, organization, institutional, and community setting as well as in private practice. This increased range of applications has been accompanied by greater sophistication and sensitivity of practitioners to ethnic diversity and gender issues, as well as to organizational and community standards and norms relevant for integration and optimal use of the behavioral approach. Behavior therapy has been viewed as an advantageous approach to providing mental health services in the current pervasive managed care environment (e.g., Hayes & Gregg, 2001; Mash & Hunsley, 1993).

New directions within the behavioral approach include greater consideration of environmental and contextual variables, application of computer technology, and development of innovative behavioral psychotherapies. Researchers have effectively applied computer-generated virtual reality technology in the treatment of phobias and panic disorder (e.g., Calbring, Westling, Ljungstrand, Ekselius, & Andersson, 2001; Gilroy, Kirkby, Daniels, Menzies, & Montgomery, 2003; Gruber, Moran, Roth, & Taylor, 2001). Computer technology is also providing new ways of serving clients, through "virtual therapy" (Bobicz & Richard, 2003).

The behavioral approach seeks to improve the human condition and to advance the base of scientific knowledge concerning human behavior. That accumulated body of knowledge and its applications constitute the state of the art in the field, the basic features of which are encompassed in this book.

In a recent article, Carr and Britton (2003) report on comparative citation frequencies for the leading applied behavioral psychology journals. According to their research, the nine journals cited most frequently in 2000 are as follows, in rank order:

1. *Behaviour Research and Therapy*

2. *Journal of Applied Behavior Analysis*

3. *Behavior Therapy*

4. *Journal of Behavior Therapy and Experimental Psychiatry*

5. *Behavior Modification*

6. *Behaviour Change*

7. *Child and Family Behavior Therapy*

8. *Cognitive and Behavioral Practice*

9. *Journal of Organizational Behavior Management*

A variety of other behavioral journals are available as well, including some that are not primarily behavioral but sometimes publish behaviorally oriented articles. Among these journals are the following:

The Behavior Analyst

Behavior and Social Issues

the Behavior Therapist

Behavioral Analysts for Social Action

Behavioral and Cognitive Psychotherapy

Behavioral Assessment

Behavioral Counseling Quarterly

Behavioral Residential Treatment

Behavioural Psychotherapy

Clinical Behavior Therapy Review

Cognitive Therapy and Research

Journal of Behavioral Education

Journal of Behavioral Medicine

Journal of Child and Family Behavior Therapy

Journal of Consulting and Clinical Psychology

Journal of Evidence-Based Social Work

Journal of the Experimental Analysis of Behavior

Journal of Psychopathology and Behavioral Assessment

Journal of Rational-Emotive & Cognitive-Behavior Therapy

Psychophysiology and Biofeedback (formerly *Biofeedback and Self-Regulation*)

Research in Developmental Disabilities

Research on Social Work Practice

Information about membership, conferences, and literature is available from the following professional organizations:

Association for the Advancement of Behavior Therapy
305 Seventh Avenue, 16th Floor
New York, NY 10001–6008
www.aabt.org

Association for Behavior Analysis
1219 South Park Street
Kalamazoo, MI 49001
www.abainternational.org

Society of Behavioral Medicine
7600 Terrace Avenue, Suite 203
Middleton, WI 53562
www.sbm.org

References and Resources

Baer, D. M., & Pinkston, E. M. (Eds.). (1997). *Environment and behavior.* Boulder, CO: Westview.

Baer, D. M., Wolf, M. M., & Risley, T. R. (1968). Some current dimensions of applied behavior analysis. *Journal of Applied Behavior Analysis, 1,* 91–97.

Bandura, A. A. (1969). *Principles of behavior modification.* New York: Holt, Rinehart & Winston.

Bandura, A. A. (1977). *Social learning theory.* Englewood Cliffs, NJ: Prentice Hall.

Barlow, D. H. (Ed.). (2001). *Clinical handbook of psychological disorders* (3rd ed.). New York: Guilford.

Beck, A. T. (1976). *Cognitive therapy and the emotional disorders.* New York: International Universities Press.

Beck, A. T., & Emery, G. (1985). *Anxiety disorders and phobias: A cognitive perspective.* New York: Basic Books.

Beck, A. T., & Rector, N. (2001). Cognitive therapy of schizophrenia: A new therapy for the new millennium. *American Journal of Psychotherapy, 54,* 291–300.

Beck, A. T., Rush, A. J., Shaw, F. B., & Emery, G. (1979). *The cognitive therapy of depression.* New York: Guilford.

Beck, J. G. (1997). Introduction [Special series: Mental health in the elderly: Challenges for behavior therapy]. *Behavior Therapy, 28,* 1–2.

Blechman, E. A. (Ed.). (1984). *Behavior modification with women.* New York: Guilford.

Blechman, E. A., & Brownell, K. D. (Eds.). (1998). *Behavioral medicine and women: A comprehensive handbook.* New York: Guilford.

Bobicz, K. P., & Richard, D. C. S. (2003). The virtual therapist: Behavior therapy in a digital age. *the Behavior Therapist, 26,* 265–270.

Calbring, P., Westling, B. E., Ljungstrand, P., Ekselius, L., & Andersson, G. (2001). Treatment of panic disorder via the Internet: A randomized trial of a self-help program. *Behavior Therapy, 32,* 751–764.

Carr, J. E., & Britton, L. E. (2003). Citation trends of applied journals in behavioral psychology: 1981–2000. *Journal of Applied Behavior Analysis, 36,* 113–117.

Cautela, J. R. (1966). Treatment of compulsive behavior by covert sensitization. *Psychological Record, 16,* 33–41.

Cautela, J. R., & Ishaq, W. (Eds.). (1996). *Contemporary issues in behavior therapy: Improving the human condition.* New York: Plenum.

Chambless, D. L., & Ollendick, T. H. (2001). Empirically supported psychological interventions: Controversies and evidence. *Annual Review of Psychology, 52,* 685–716.

Chambless, D. L., Sanderson, W. C., Shoham, V., Johnson, S. B., Pope, K. S., Crits-Christoph, P., et al. (1996). An update on empirically validated therapies. *The Clinical Psychologist, 49,* 5–18.

Chambless, D. L., & Williams, K. E. (1995). A preliminary study of African Americans with agoraphobia: Symptom severity and outcome of treatment with in vivo exposure. *Behavior Therapy, 26,* 501–515.

Cooper, Z., Fairburn, C. G., & Hawker, D. M. (2003). *Cognitive-behavioral treatment of obesity: A clinician's guide.* New York: Guilford.

Dobson, K. S. (Ed.). (2001). *Handbook of cognitive-behavioral therapies* (2nd ed.). New York: Guilford.

D'Zurilla, T. J., & Goldfried, M. R. (1971). Problem solving and behavior modification. *Journal of Abnormal Psychology, 78,* 107–126.

Ellis, A. (1962). *Reason and emotion in psychotherapy.* New York: Lyle Stuart.

Ellis, A. (1984). *Rational-emotive therapy and cognitive behavior therapy.* New York: Springer.

Ellis, A. (1993). Changing rational-emotive therapy (RET) to rational-emotive behavior therapy (REBT). *the Behavior Therapist, 16,* 257–258.

Fudge, R. C. (1996). The use of behavior therapy in the development of ethnic consciousness: A treatment model. *Cognitive and Behavioral Practice, 3,* 317–335.

Gelernter, C. S., Uhde, T. W., Cimbolic, P., Arnkoff, D. B., Vittone, B. J., Tancer, M. E., et al. (1991). Cognitive-behavioral and pharmacological treatments of social phobia. *Archives of General Psychiatry, 48,* 938–945.

Gilroy, L. J., Kirkby, K. C., Daniels, B. A., Menzies, R. G., & Montgomery, I. M. (2003). Long-term follow-up of computer-aided vicarious exposure versus live graded exposure in the treatment of spider phobia. *Behavior Therapy, 34,* 65–76.

Graves, K. D., & Miller, P. M. (2003). Behavioral medicine in the prevention and treatment of cardiovascular disease. *Behavior Modification, 27,* 3–25.

Gruber, K., Moran, P. J., Roth, W. T., & Taylor, C. B. (2001). Computer-assisted cognitive behavioral therapy for social phobia. *Behavior Therapy, 32,* 155–165.

Hayes, S. C., & Gregg, J. (2001). Factors promoting and inhibiting the development and use of clinical practice guidelines. *Behavior Therapy, 32,* 211–217.

Hollon, S. D., & Beck, A. T. (1994). Cognitive and cognitive-behavioral therapies. In A. E. Bergin & S. L. Garfield (Eds.), *Handbook of psychotherapy and behavior change: An empirical analysis* (4th ed., pp. 428–466). New York: John Wiley.

Iwamasa, G. Y. (1997). Behavior therapy and a culturally diverse society: Forging an alliance. *Behavior Therapy, 28,* 347–358.

Iwamasa, G. Y., & Smith, S. K. (1996). Ethnic diversity in behavioral psychology: A review of the literature. *Behavior Modification, 20,* 45–59.

Jason, L. A., & Fries, M. (2004). Helping parents reduce children's television viewing. *Research on Social Work Practice, 14,* 121–131.

Kassinove, H., & Uecke, C. (1991). Religious involvement and behavior therapy training: Student conflicts and ethical concerns. *the Behavior Therapist, 14,* 148–149.

Lazarus, A. A. (1976). *Multi-modal behavior therapy.* New York: Springer-Verlag.

Linehan, M. M. (1993). *Cognitive-behavioral treatment of personality disorder.* New York: Guilford.

Mahoney, M. J. (1974). *Cognition and behavior modification.* Cambridge, MA: Ballinger.

Mash, E. J., & Hunsley, J. (1993). Behavior therapy and managed mental health care: Integrating effectiveness and economies in mental health practice. *Behavior Therapy, 24,* 67–90.

Mattaini, M. A., & Thyer, B. A. (Eds.). (1996). *Finding solutions to social problems: Behavioral strategies for change.* Washington, DC: American Psychological Association.

McCrady, B. S. (2001). Introduction [Special series: Behavior therapy perspectives on the American Psychiatric Association practice guidelines]. *Behavior Therapy, 32,* 209–210.

Meichenbaum, D. H. (1977). *Cognitive behavior modification: An integrative approach.* New York: Plenum.

Meichenbaum, D. H. (1985). *Stress inoculation training: A clinical guidebook.* New York: Pergamon.

Meichenbaum, D. H. (1994). *A clinical handbook/practical therapist manual for assessing and treating adults with post-traumatic stress disorder.* Waterloo, ON: Institute Press.

Middleton, M. B., & Cartledge, G. (1995). The effects of social skills instruction and parental involvement on the aggressive behaviors of African American males. *Behavior Modification, 19,* 192–210.

Nackerud, L., Waller, R. J., Waller, K., & Thyer, B. A. (1997). Behavior analysis and social welfare policy: The example of Aid to Families with Dependent Children (AFDC). In P. A. Lamal (Ed.), *Cultural contingencies: Behavior analytic perspectives on cultural practices* (pp. 169–184). Westport, CT: Greenwood.

Nelson-Gray, R., Gaynor, S. T., & Korotitsch, W. J. (1997). Commentary on "Behavior therapy and a culturally diverse society: Forging an alliance." *Behavior Therapy, 28,* 359–361.

Newman, M. G., Hofmann, S. G., Trabert, W., Roth, W. T., & Taylor, C. B. (1994). Does behavioral treatment of social phobia lead to cognitive changes? *Behavior Therapy, 25,* 503–517.

Paniagua, F. A. (1998). *Assessing and treating culturally diverse clients: A practical guide* (2nd ed.). Thousand Oaks, CA: Sage.

Pavlov, I. P. (1927). *Conditioned reflexes: An investigation of the physiological activity of the cerebral cortex* (G. V. Anrep, Trans.). London: Oxford University Press.

Plaud, J. J., & Eifert, G. H. (1998). *From behavior theory to behavior therapy.* Boston: Allyn & Bacon.

Purcell, D. W., Campos, P. E., & Perilla, J. L. (1996). Therapy with lesbians and gay men: A cognitive behavioral perspective. *Cognitive and Behavioral Practice, 3,* 391–415.

Rothbaum, B. O., Hodges, L. F., Kooper, R., Opdyke, D., Williford, J. S., & North, M. (1995). Effectiveness of computer-generated (virtual reality) graded exposure in the treatment of acrophobia. *American Journal of Psychiatry, 152,* 626–628.

Schwartz, M. S., & Andrasik, F. (Eds.). (2003). *Biofeedback: A practitioner's guide* (3rd ed.). New York: Guilford.

Sisson, L. A., & Lyon, S. R. (Eds.). (1995). Community integration for persons with the most severe disabilities: Innovations in school, employment, and independent living settings [Special issue]. *Behavior Modification, 19*(1).

Skinner, B. F. (1938). *Behavior of organisms: An experimental analysis.* Englewood Cliffs, NJ: Prentice Hall.

Skinner, B. F. (1953). *Science and human behavior.* New York: Macmillan.

Skinner, B. F. (1974). *About behaviorism.* New York: Knopf.

Skinner, B. F. (1989). *Recent issues in the analysis of behavior.* Columbus, OH: Merrill.

Thorndike, E. L. (1931). *Human learning.* New York: Century.

Thyer, B. A. (1994). Social learning theory: Empirical applications to culturally diverse practice. In R. R. Greene (Ed.), *Human behavior theory: A diversity framework* (pp. 133–146). New York: Aldine.

Thyer, B. A., & Myers, L. L. (2000). Approaches to behavioral change. In P. Allen-Meares & C. Garvin (Eds.), *Handbook of social work direct practice* (pp. 197–216). Thousand Oaks, CA: Sage.

Watson, J. B. (1930). *Behaviorism.* Chicago: University of Chicago Press.

Wilson, G. T., & Fairburn, C. G. (2002). Treatments for eating disorders. In P. E. Nathan & J. M. Gorman (Eds.), *A guide to treatments that work* (2nd ed., pp. 559–592). New York: Oxford University Press.

Wolpe, J. (1958). *Psychotherapy by reciprocal inhibition.* Stanford, CA: Stanford University Press.

Wolpe, J. (1990). *The practice of behavior therapy* (4th ed.). Elmsford, NY: Pergamon.

CHAPTER 1

Specifying Behavior

Shortly after the midterm grades came out, a teacher referred Robert to the school social worker, describing Robert as "inattentive in the classroom, poorly motivated, and having low self-esteem." The social worker wondered what Robert did or said that led to this description.

Hayley told the therapist that she felt "nervous all the time." Her nervousness increased as it came closer to the time her husband, Jason, came home from work each day.

Objectives

After completing this chapter, you should be able to do the following:

- Distinguish between vague and behaviorally specific statements.
- Describe events according to observable or measurable behaviors or responses.
- Rewrite vague statements into behaviorally specific ones.
- Specify measures of response strength using rate, duration, and intensity.

Overt and Covert Behaviors

This book presents a behavioral approach to assessing and changing human behavior. An essential skill in this approach is the ability to state problems and situations in clear, specific language. The behavioral practitioner strives for specificity in describing the movements and actions of individuals. These activities are called **behaviors** or **responses,** terms that we use interchangeably throughout this book. A behavior is defined as any observable or measurable movement or activity of an individual. Behavior can be verbal or nonverbal, overt or covert. Overt responses are observable and measurable. Covert or private responses are measurable but are not observable. Examples of overt verbal responses are screaming, stuttering, saying "thank you," lecturing to an audience, and laughing. Overt nonverbal responses include smiling, trembling, throwing a baseball, and raising an eyebrow.

Covert responses are private or unobservable events that can be cognitive, emotional, or physiological. Cognitive behaviors include thoughts, perceptions, attitudes, and beliefs. Much of this behavior is described as "self-talk," the things that people say to themselves (or "think") in response to antecedent and consequent stimuli. "I'll never pass this test," "My mother always blames me," and "If I speak up in class everyone will think I'm stupid" are examples of negative **self-statements.** "I'm as smart as anyone else in this class" and "If I study the material all week I'll be able to pass the exam" are examples of positive self-statements.

Emotions are covert behaviors that influence, and are influenced by, cognitions. For example, if you believe that flying in an airplane is dangerous, you may feel anxious just reading an airline schedule. Alternatively, if you believe that flying is a safe and efficient way to travel, boarding an airplane to go on a vacation may evoke pleasant feelings. Practitioners have access to these private events through an individual's self-reports and through physiological measures. Measurement of a covert behavior consists of a self-report of its rate, intensity, and duration. Physiological behaviors include heart rate, blood pressure, pulse rate, and brain waves, and are measured by instruments such as heart rate monitors, stethoscopes, sphygmomanometers, and electroencephalographs (EEGs).

The approach that we take in this book is consistent with the position that covert behaviors are subject to the same principles of behavior change as overt behaviors (e.g., Homme, 1965; Thyer & Myers, 1997). Covert behaviors can be operantly conditioned or classically conditioned through association with individuals or other stimuli. Covert behaviors are treated as appropriate targets for assessment and intervention.

Human service practitioners frequently encounter problems that are presented in vague, nonspecific language. For example, Tina complained that her boyfriend was "hard to get along with because of his emotional insecurity." The behavioral practitioner attempted to delineate the problem in words that clearly specified verbal and nonverbal behaviors. Thus the practitioner asked Tina to describe her boyfriend's speech and nonverbal behaviors that were related to his "insecurity." She specified his behaviors as follows: statements such as "You'd be better off without me" and "Everyone is getting ahead except me" and nonverbal behaviors such as walking slouched, with his head down, and writing 25 letters each week in response to job advertisements in the newspaper.

Mr. Madison remarked to a practitioner that his 14-year-old daughter was not acting feminine enough. The practitioner asked him to describe his daughter's verbal and nonverbal behaviors related to her "not acting feminine enough." Mr. Madison said that his daughter wore only pants, never skirts or dresses, and that she frequently wore jackets and ties. She also sometimes used profane language and stayed out past her 11:00 p.m. curfew. Whether or not you agree with Mr. Madison's definition of "feminine behavior" and his desire to change his daughter's behaviors are issues that might be appropriate for discussion in a counseling situation. The point here is that the practitioner can obtain a clear picture of the client's concerns through behavioral specification of vague terms.

To clearly specify an event, the individual's behavior is described in *positive, observable* terms. A negatively stated description such as "Robert does *not* turn in his class assignments" is insufficient because it fails to describe what Robert is doing in the problematic situation. An appropriate description of Robert's problematic behavior might be "Robert plays video games instead of writing his assignment."

A description of an individual's behavior in observable terms specifies what the person *says* or *does*. Unobservable constructs, such as "ego impairment," "low self-esteem," and "underlying hostility," are insufficient descriptions of behavior. The use of such terms does not contribute essential information about the behavior, and the constructs are not measurable. If such terms are used, they should be accompanied by behaviorally specific descriptions of what the individual says or does.

For example, if 19-year-old Paul is described as "exhibiting underlying hostility" we still do not know exactly what he says or does, and his behavior is open to many interpretations. The label "underlying hostility" could be an interpretation or a conclusion drawn, for example, on the basis of Paul's having set three fires. In a counseling situation, the treatment issue could be formulated in terms of whether to modify behaviors related to the fire setting or to explore the "underlying hostility." Robert's teacher described him as having low self-esteem. The following are some of the behaviors that might have led her to use this description: Robert says, "I'm not smart enough to do this math homework," he buys drugs and gives them to his friends, or he turns in blank papers instead of completing his assignments.

Hayley complained of feeling "nervous all the time." The behaviors that led her to describe herself this way included heart palpitations and a racing pulse. She also reported excessive worrying about her marriage; for example, she told herself, "I will never be able to please Jason and he will wind up leaving me."

The following are some common examples of vague language, along with a behaviorally specific measure of each example:

Vague Statement	Behaviorally Specific Measure
She has low self-esteem.	She says, "I'm not as smart as my sister."
He exhibits hostility.	He throws dishes at his wife.
He doesn't love me.	He answers the phone during dinner.
She is intelligent.	She reads the *New York Times* every day.
He is really depressed.	He stays in bed 12 hours a day and says, "Life isn't worth living."
He is not reliable.	He arrives late to work.
She is a cheapskate.	She buys gifts for friends at the dollar store although she has a high-paying job.
I try to give my mother lots of support.	I call my mother three times a week to ask if she needs anything.

In this book, we focus on the specification and analysis of an individual's behaviors and their controlling conditions so that intervention plans can be formulated on the basis of observable or measurable events. This approach avoids or minimizes the use of hypothetical, unobservable constructs and vague inferences. If labels are used, they are accompanied by behavioral descriptions. Covert behaviors are measured through self-report or instrumentation. The following case example illustrates the benefits of behavioral specification compared with the use of vague, nonspecific language.

CASE EXAMPLE 1

Behavioral Assessment of Drug Abuse

Robert is a 13-year-old junior high school student who started drinking beer 6 months ago at a party given by one of his friends. He liked the feeling of acceptance from the older kids at the party and continued his experimentation with other drugs, including crack cocaine. During the past 2 months, Robert has turned in incomplete class assignments, sometimes handing in blank sheets of paper. His midterm report card showed four Fs and one C in an art course. Robert's parents were concerned that he would drop out of school or not pass to the next level. Last week, his mother found crack and some of her diet pills in Robert's desk drawer. When confronted with this evidence, Robert admitted to taking drugs but argued that his drug use did not interfere with his functioning in school or at home.

Shortly after the midterm grades came out, a teacher referred Robert to the school social worker, describing him as "inattentive in the classroom, poorly motivated, and having low self-esteem." He was failing most of his classes.

Robert complained to the school social worker that his parents frequently grounded him, nagged him, withheld his allowance, and denied him privileges such as watching television and going out with his friends. Upon further questioning, Robert said that his parents disciplined him because of his poor grades. Robert admitted that he might flunk out of school but denied that his drug taking was interfering with his studying. When the social worker asked him to describe his use of drugs and alcohol, Robert stated that he drank beer every weekend with his friends and smoked crack once a month. Robert said that when he started studying, his friends often invited him over to listen to music and drink beer and that this happened about three times a week. He also spent an average of three evenings per week at his girlfriend's home, and they usually began these evenings by drinking beer or wine. When he was home alone, Robert typically looked in his notebook for class assignments, took a drink or two before beginning them, and completed only parts of his assignments or none of them at all. The baseline rate of Robert's drug use, including alcohol, was 7 days per week. The baseline rate of Robert's drinking before beginning homework assignments was 4 days per week.

Note: All names used in the examples in this book are fictitious.

Clarifying Vague Terms and Fuzzy Language

In Case Example 1, the teacher complained that Robert was "inattentive and poorly motivated" in class. The social worker wanted to know in specific terms how Robert was inattentive and poorly motivated. Did he stare out the window? Did he walk around the room? Did he throw papers on the floor? Did he laugh at the teacher? Did he make faces? The social worker wanted a more specific description of Robert's behavior, such as "Robert stared at the ceiling in class and completed only 1 out of 10 math problems." Thus a stranger reading this description is provided with a concrete, observable, and measurable instance of Robert's inattentive and poorly motivated classroom behavior.

Similarly, statements such as "Greg refused to take his medicine as prescribed" or "Jane denied spreading the rumor about Carol's affair" fail to describe exactly what these individuals said or did in those situations. Refusing to take his medicine could mean that Greg said, "I refuse to take my medicine," or that he emptied the bottle of pills into the trash. When Jane "denied" spreading the rumor, this could mean that Jane said, "You're a liar," or that she walked away from the person who accused her of spreading the rumor.

Vague language referring to an individual's actions can be defined in behaviorally specific terms. This usually requires the reporting of actual observations of the individual's behavior in the given situation. An adequate description provides enough detail about the form or appearance of the response so that other individuals can accurately identify the response.

Target Behavior

The **target behavior** is the behavior to be observed and measured; it is the focus of change. Depending on the desired behavior change, a practitioner can specify one of four outcomes or directions in which a target behavior can be modified: Behavioral interventions can be applied so that a behavior is (a) newly developed, (b) increased or strengthened, (c) maintained at a particular rate or pattern of occurrence, or (d) decreased, weakened, or suppressed. *Elimination* of a behavior is not included as an outcome because it is possible, in various circumstances, for a behavior that has been weakened or suppressed to recur.

Measuring Response Strength

A precise description of a response includes a measure of **response strength.** The strength of a response is measured by (a) how often the response occurs within a given time period (response rate or frequency per time unit), (b) how long the response lasts (duration), and (c) the severity of the response (intensity).

Response rate or **frequency** per time unit is the primary measure of response strength—for example, "Phil washed his hands eight times in the past hour," or "Andre came home from school crying three times last week." Examples of **duration** are "Tiffany held her breath for 20 seconds" and "Corrine remained in her house for 4 weeks without going outside." **Intensity** can be measured electronically or mechanically, such as with an audiometer (which measures loudness) or through the use of a self-rating scale. A client might use a self-rating scale to describe the intensity of his or her anxiety on a scale ranging from 0 to 100. For example, Hayley rated her nervousness (anxiety) as 90 on a 100-point scale. Sometimes, two or more measures of response strength may be used to describe a particular response; for example, "Candace cried in her room for more than 30 minutes [duration] three times this week [rate]." We discuss measures of response strength in later chapters.

The Behavioral Assessment Approach

The behavioral assessment approach presented in this book can be applied to a wide variety of situations. The first step in behavioral assessment is to specify the target behavior in behaviorally specific terms. The second step is to collect **baseline data**—that is, specific measures of response strength prior to intervention. Practitioners use baseline data to set goals and formulate intervention plans. These data also provide measurable criteria for evaluating behavioral change.

Obtaining Baseline Data

Response rate, or frequency of the response (per unit of time), is the most common baseline measure; for example, "Robert drank beer with his friends three times per week for the past 6 weeks," or "Alice called her ex-boyfriend six times per day for the past 10 days." These data are obtained during assessment; in the cases of Robert and Alice, the data indicate the baseline rate of Robert's beer drinking and Alice's calling her ex-boyfriend—that is, the rates at which these behaviors occurred prior to the implementation of any intervention plans.

A chart showing a week of baseline data for Robert's beer drinking might appear as follows:

Daily Chart of Baseline Data for Robert

Description of Response: Robert drinks beer with his friends

Days	Response Strength[a] (frequency per day)
Monday	0
Tuesday	0
Wednesday	0
Thursday	0
Friday	l
Saturday	l
Sunday	l
	Total: 3

a. Specify the measure of response strength to be used, in this case, frequency per day. Place a vertical mark (l) in this column to indicate each occurrence of the target response.

Another way of charting Robert's baseline rate of drinking beer might be on a weekly rather than a daily basis:

Weekly Chart of Baseline Data for Robert

Description of Response: Robert drinks beer with his friends

Week	Response Strength (frequency per week)
1				
2			
3				
4			
5					
6	ЖЖ
	Total: 19 Average: 3 times/week

The behavioral assessment framework will be elaborated in Chapter 13.

Summary

1. A response, or behavior, is defined as any observable or measurable movement or activity of an individual, whether overt or covert, verbal or nonverbal.

2. Covert responses are private or unobservable events that can be either cognitive or physiological. Cognitive responses include thoughts, emotions, attitudes, and beliefs. Physiological responses include heart rate, blood pressure, and pulse rate. A covert response can be measured through the individual's self-report of its rate, intensity, and duration. A physiological response can be measured through the use of an instrument such as a heart rate monitor.

3. An observable response specifies what the individual says or does in positive terms.

4. If vague terms are used in labeling unobservable events, they should be accompanied by behaviorally specific measures.

5. The target behavior is the behavior to be observed or measured and is the focus of change. Behavioral interventions can be applied so that a target behavior is (a) newly developed, (b) increased or strengthened, (c) maintained at a particular rate or pattern of occurrence, or (d) decreased, weakened, or suppressed.

6. Three measures of response strength are rate (frequency/time unit), duration, and intensity. Response rate is the most common measure of response strength.

7. The first step in behavioral assessment is to specify the target response in behaviorally specific terms. The second step is to collect baseline data. Practitioners systematically record baseline data to analyze measures of response strength prior to intervening.

Suggested Activities

1. Listen for vague statements that you or your friends typically use to describe people and their behaviors. List three of these vague statements and identify at least one behaviorally specific measure for each.

2. Using your list from activity 1 above, identify each behavior as overt (specifying verbal or nonverbal) or covert (specifying cognitive, emotional, or physiological).

3. Pick a behavior of yours as a target behavior and describe it in behaviorally specific terms. Record the baseline data for that behavior, specifying the measure of response strength to be used.

4. Pair up with a classmate and decide which of you will play the role of client and which will play the role of therapist. Role-play an initial interview in which the therapist is explaining the rationale for asking the client to use behaviorally specific language.

References and Resources

Anderson, C. M., Hawkins, R. P., & Scotti, J. R. (1997). Private events in behavior analysis: Conceptual basis and clinical relevance. *Behavior Therapy, 28,* 157–179.

Baer, D. M., Wolf, M. M., & Risley, T. R. (1987). Some still current dimensions of applied behavior analysis. *Journal of Applied Behavior Analysis, 20,* 313–327.

Hawkins, R. P. (1986). Selection of target behaviors. In R. P. Nelson & S. C. Hayes (Eds.), *Conceptual foundations of behavioral assessment* (pp. 331–385). New York: Guilford.

Hersen, M., & Bellack, A. S. (Eds.). (1988). *Dictionary of behavioral assessment techniques.* New York: Pergamon.

Homme, L. E. (1965). Perspectives in psychology: Control of coverants, the operants of the mind. *Psychological Record, 15,* 501–511.

Mager, R. F. (1962). *Preparing instructional objectives.* Palo Alto, CA: Fearon.

Peterson, L., Tremblay, G., Ewigman, B., & Popkey, C. (2002). The parental daily diary: A sensitive measure of the process of change in a child maltreatment prevention program. *Behavior Modification, 26,* 627–647.

Thyer, B. A., & Myers, L. L. (1997). Behavioral and cognitive theories. In J. R. Brandell (Ed.), *Theory and practice in clinical social work* (pp. 18–37). New York: Free Press.

Wood, S. J., Murdock, J. Y., & Cronin, M. E. (2002). Self-monitoring and at-risk middle school students: Academic performance improves, maintains, and generalizes. *Behavior Modification, 26,* 605–626.

CHAPTER 2

Positive Reinforcement

Social worker:	One of my clients keeps arriving late for his appointments. It's ruining my schedule.
Supervisor:	What are you doing about it?
Social worker:	When he arrives, I tell him how glad I am to see him and then I add on extra time at the end of the session.
Supervisor:	No wonder he keeps coming late!

Objectives

After completing this chapter, you should be able to do the following:

- Give an example of the positive reinforcement procedure and its effect on the strength of a response.
- Describe how baseline data are used to determine whether or not a stimulus acts as a positive reinforcer.
- Indicate when a positive reinforcer should be delivered to maximize its effectiveness.
- Draw a diagram showing how positive reinforcement can be used to increase the rate of a response.

Reinforcing Stimuli

A **stimulus** (plural, *stimuli*) can be any object or event. It can include physical features of the environment (e.g., a cell phone ringing, a television commercial) or an individual's behavior (e.g., a smile, a request for directions, a child crying). A stimulus can precede or follow a response. In this chapter, we are concerned with the **positive reinforcer,** the stimulus that follows a response and increases its strength or likelihood of occurrence.

Stimuli can be unconditioned (primary) or conditioned (secondary). **Unconditioned stimuli** are intrinsically or naturally effective (e.g., as positive reinforcers) because of their importance for survival or biological functioning; they do not require prior association with other stimuli to be effective. Food, sex, sleep, water, and tactile stimulation are examples of unconditioned stimuli. **Conditioned stimuli** acquire their effectiveness through pairing or association with other stimuli. Money, points, fines, attention, and threats are examples of conditioned stimuli. Unconditioned and conditioned stimuli can be positive or negative, reinforcing or punishing. We address these topics in other chapters.

A positive reinforcer is a stimulus presented after a response that increases the strength of the response—usually its **rate** or frequency of occurrence during a specific time period. The positive reinforcer is presented *contingent* on performance of the response—that is, the response must be emitted or performed for the positive reinforcer to be delivered. Thus the principle of positive reinforcement states that the strength of a response can be increased by certain consequences—namely, presentation of a stimulus that acts as a positive reinforcer. A response that is positively reinforced is more likely to be performed again under similar conditions.

Positive reinforcers can be unconditioned or conditioned stimuli. An **unconditioned positive reinforcer** is sometimes called a *natural reinforcer* because it increases the strength of a response it follows without requiring prior association with other positive reinforcers. For example, food and sex are unconditioned positive reinforcers. A **conditioned positive reinforcer** increases the strength of a response because of its association with other positive reinforcers. Money and praise are conditioned positive reinforcers for most people because they have been associated with a variety of positive reinforcers.

Behavioral diagrams using notational symbols can be used to depict relationships between stimuli and responses. We use behavioral diagrams in this book to provide schematic representations of behavioral concepts and procedures. Practitioners can use such diagrams to analyze client problems in behavioral terms. They visually depict relationships that may not be readily apparent from verbal descriptions.

The symbol for an unconditioned positive reinforcer is S^{R+} (note the uppercase R). The symbol for a conditioned positive reinforcer is S^{r+} (note the lowercase r). In this book, when a positive reinforcer is known, the appropriate notation is used: uppercase for an unconditioned reinforcer and lowercase for a conditioned reinforcer. If the positive reinforcer is not known, however, the notation S^{R+} will be used as a generic term.

A behavioral diagram can be used to depict the procedure of positive reinforcement. A response (R) is performed and followed by ($\rightarrow$) a stimulus (S) that increases (+) the strength of the response.

Positive Reinforcement Diagram

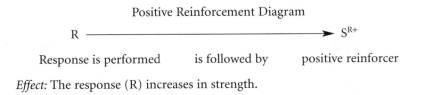

Response is performed   is followed by   positive reinforcer

Effect: The response (R) increases in strength.

For example, if rate is the measure of response strength, the effect of positive reinforcement is an increase in response rate.

Behaviors conditioned or strengthened in this manner are called **operant behaviors.** An operant behavior is controlled or governed by its consequences, such as positive reinforcement. The individual operates or acts on the environment to produce those consequences through the process of **operant conditioning**, or instrumental learning. In contrast, **respondent behavior** is elicited by a specific antecedent event through **respondent conditioning,** also called **classical conditioning**. We discuss respondent behavior in Chapter 11.

Examples of Positive Reinforcement

When someone performs a behavior that is followed by a positive reinforcer, the person will likely perform that behavior on similar occasions in the future. For example, Ken told jokes to his friends last week, and his friends laughed. The next time Ken saw his friends, he told jokes again. Their laughter had served as a positive reinforcer for Ken's joke telling. In diagram form, this example would appear as follows:

Positive Reinforcement Diagram for Ken's Joke Telling

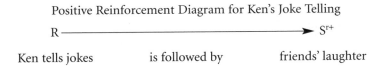

Ken tells jokes   is followed by   friends' laughter

Effect: Ken's joke telling increases in strength—that is, the likelihood is increased that Ken will tell jokes to his friends in similar circumstances in the future.

Another example shows how parents can use positive reinforcement to increase the toothbrushing of a child with poor dental hygiene. For the past 3 months, 10-year-old Gary has brushed his teeth an average of once each week. His parents' previous attempts to influence his toothbrushing by reasoning with him or warning him of negative consequences, such as more cavities, were unsuccessful. A plan is arranged whereby each time Gary brushes his teeth he receives 50 cents. The money serves as a positive reinforcer for toothbrushing if the rate of Gary's toothbrushing increases. The response in this example is Gary's toothbrushing. As long as the money serves as a positive reinforcer, Gary will continue to brush his teeth. In Chapter 4, we examine some of the factors involved in maintaining response strength without having to present the reinforcer each time the response occurs.

In the example presented at the beginning of this chapter, the social worker positively reinforced the client for arriving late for appointments. By greeting him warmly and adding extra time to the session, the social worker unintentionally increased the likelihood that the client would arrive late again. The supervisor pointed out the reinforcing effect of the social worker's behavior on the client's late arrivals. The social worker had identified the client's late arrival as a problem because it affected his appointment schedule for the rest of the day. When the relationship between the client's behavior and the social worker's reaction to it was analyzed behaviorally, the social worker decided to change the situation by asking the client to arrive on time and ending all appointments at their scheduled times. (See Chapters 3, 5, and 9 for discussion of techniques to decrease undesired behaviors.)

Some common positive reinforcers include food, water, and sex (unconditioned) and attention, praise, and money (conditioned). Although stimuli may differ in their ability to serve as positive reinforcers for different individuals, almost any object or event can act as a positive reinforcer for specific responses under certain conditions. Even stimuli that appear to be unpleasant can serve as positive reinforcers. Sometimes, undesired behaviors can be inadvertently reinforced with such stimuli. For example, Ed and Charlie jumped up and down on the bed. Their grandmother shouted, "Boys! Don't jump on that bed! You'll get hurt." Ed and Charlie laughed and jumped faster. Their grandmother repeated her warning and shouted at them, but they continued to jump faster and faster. In diagram form, this example appears as follows:

Reinforcement Diagram for Jumping on the Bed

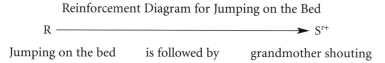

$$R \longrightarrow S^{r+}$$

Jumping on the bed   is followed by   grandmother shouting

Effect: Jumping on the bed increased in rate. The likelihood is increased that this behavior will be performed again under similar conditions.

The two preceding examples demonstrate how undesired behaviors can be positively reinforced unintentionally. Identifying positive reinforcers for undesired behaviors is an important step in the assessment of target behaviors. Following are some examples of responses and possible positive reinforcers:

Response	*Positive Reinforcer (S^{R+} or S^{r+})*
Ken tells jokes	Friends laugh (S^{r+})
Gary brushes his teeth	He receives 50 cents (S^{r+})
Client arrives late	Social worker greets him warmly, adds extra time onto the session (S^{r+})
Ed and Charlie jump on the bed	Grandmother shouts (S^{r+})
Bud whines	Mother gives him a cookie (S^{R+})
Madison catches the ball	Father hugs her (S^{R+})
Student completes assignment	She goes to a movie with a friend (S^{r+})

Reinforcers and Rewards

The term *reward* has been used incorrectly as synonymous with the term *positive reinforcer*. A **reward** is an object or event identified by a person as pleasant, satisfying, or desirable and that the individual will seek out or approach. Rewards can, and frequently do, serve as positive reinforcers. A stimulus is called a positive reinforcer, however, only if it is demonstrated to increase the strength of a response it follows. For example, suppose Gary's toothbrushing did not increase over the baseline rate of once per week after he was paid 50 cents each time he brushed his teeth. His mother could correctly conclude that the money was not a positive reinforcer for Gary's toothbrushing.

The following diagram shows a response followed by a stimulus that fails to serve as a positive reinforcer. The stimulus is neutral in regard to increasing the strength of the toothbrushing response.

Diagram for Toothbrushing Followed by Neutral Stimulus

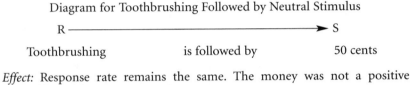

Effect: Response rate remains the same. The money was not a positive reinforcer for Gary's toothbrushing.

When Gary's mother followed his toothbrushing with praise, however, Gary's rate of toothbrushing increased during a 2-week period. Praise served as a positive reinforcer for Gary's toothbrushing:

Positive Reinforcement Diagram for Toothbrushing

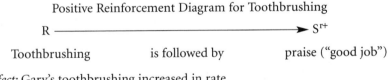

Effect: Gary's toothbrushing increased in rate.

Factors That Influence Reinforcer Effectiveness

Many factors can influence the effectiveness of a positive reinforcer: timing, deprivation, satiation, size, amount, type, and quality.

When to Deliver a Positive Reinforcer

A positive reinforcer is most effective when delivered or made available *immediately* after the target response. If we give Nathan an ice cream cone *before* he washes the car, it is less likely that he will wash the car than if we give him the ice cream cone *after* he washes the car. If we wait too long to give Nathan his ice cream cone for washing the car, however, he might be less willing to wash the car in the future. A delay in reinforcement could also result in the unintentional strengthening of a behavior occurring at the time reinforcement is delivered rather than the strengthening of the desired behavior. For example, when Nathan finished washing the car, he played his guitar. If the positive reinforcer was given to Nathan while he was playing his guitar, guitar playing could be the response that was reinforced rather than car washing. Therefore, to maximize the effectiveness of a positive reinforcer, the reinforcer should be presented not only *after* the response has occurred but *immediately after* it is performed.

Deprivation and Satiation

Deprivation refers to a condition in which a reinforcer has not been available to or experienced by an individual for a period of time—for example, Sam has not had dessert for 8 days and Sheila has gone without sleep for 24 hours. **Satiation** refers to a condition in which a reinforcer has been consumed or experienced by an individual until it loses its reinforcing effect. For example, we can offer Nathan an ice cream cone for washing the car after he has eaten a triple-scoop ice cream cone. It is unlikely, however, that he will wash the car at this time to get another ice cream cone, as he is probably satiated on ice cream. If Nathan has not eaten ice cream for several days, however, it is more likely that he will wash the car for an ice cream cone because his deprivation level in regard to ice cream is higher.

In general, a positive reinforcer is most effective when a high level of deprivation exists and less effective during a low level of deprivation. A positive reinforcer is ineffective when an individual is satiated on that reinforcer. Deprivation and satiation levels are changing conditions that need to be evaluated at the time a reinforcer is selected.

It is inadvisable for a helping professional to use any form of deprivation that restricts client rights. On rare occasions, a trained professional might determine that the benefits of using deprivation clearly outweigh the risks and potential side effects of another procedure. In such a case, the client, or his or her guardian, would have to give written consent. It is usually more desirable, however, to use naturally occurring periods of deprivation, such as the time before a meal, when no food has been consumed for several hours, or early in the morning, when there have been no activities since the previous night.

Size, Amount, and Type of the Reinforcer

The effectiveness of a stimulus as a positive reinforcer may be related to its size, amount, type, or quality. A candy bar may increase the rate of 7-year-old Ariel's pulling weeds, but it probably will not increase the weed-pulling rate of 14-year-old Jenny. The type of reinforcer that is appropriate for a 7-year-old may not be appropriate for a 14-year-old. By the same token, a $10 bonus may be an effective reinforcer for doing extra work for someone earning $10,000 per year but would be less likely to act as a reinforcer for someone earning $75,000 per year.

The importance of size or amount of reinforcement becomes evident when we observe that Ariel pulls weeds for a candy bar, but one candy bar will not serve as a positive reinforcer for harder jobs such as raking and bagging leaves or shoveling snow from the driveway. For $15, however, the likelihood is greatly increased that Ariel will rake leaves or shovel snow. An individual's estimate of the effort required to perform a response can influence the effectiveness of the reinforcer. For example, most people probably would not walk from North Miami to Coconut Grove for $25, although many would eagerly attempt to do so for $15,000. A cross-country runner, however, might accept $25 to traverse this route.

How to Identify Potential Reinforcers

Before a practitioner attempts to increase the strength of a behavior through positive reinforcement, he or she must determine what stimulus to use as a positive reinforcer. There are several ways to identify stimuli that could act as positive reinforcers for an individual: (a) Observe what the individual does when allowed to choose an activity, (b) ask the individual what stimuli have served as positive reinforcers in the past, and (c) have the individual complete a reinforcement survey (e.g., Cautela, 1977; Cautela & Kastenbaum, 1967). Reinforcement surveys list specific stimuli that have served as positive reinforcers for individuals, such as various foods, activities, sports, and hobbies. The person is asked to rate the attractiveness of each item on the reinforcement schedule. The practitioner then considers these ratings in selecting stimuli that are likely to serve as positive reinforcers for the individual. *A stimulus is not a positive reinforcer, however, until it can be demonstrated to strengthen a behavior and increase its likelihood of occurrence.*

Reinforcer Sampling

It is sometimes difficult to identify a reinforcer that will be effective for a particular person. In such a case, the practitioner can create a reinforcer by giving the individual an opportunity to experience the reinforcer noncontingently—that is, without requiring the performance of a response. Once the individual experiences the reinforcer, a response would be required for further presentation of that reinforcer. For example, many stores give free samples. This is usually a tiny bit of a product that, if you want more, you have to buy in larger quantities. A bakery, for instance, may put out small pieces of cake or cookies to allow customers to sample the products. If customers want more, they have to buy the products. Cosmetics companies and grocery stores also provide free samples to encourage customers to try and then purchase products. Similarly, some music stores allow customers to listen to parts of CDs over headsets so that they will purchase the CDs if they like what they hear.

How to Evaluate the Effect of a Stimulus as a Positive Reinforcer

The effect of a stimulus as a positive reinforcer on a target behavior can be evaluated through a comparison of the baseline rate of the behavior with its rate after delivery of the reinforcer. For example, Donna was instructed by the physical therapist to exercise her leg five times per day to help her regain full use of the leg after surgery. Because exercising her leg was painful, Donna had been exercising it only once or twice each day. To increase Donna's exercising, the medical social worker designed a program that Donna's mother could implement at home. Donna's mother would give Donna stars on a chart as reinforcers for doing her leg exercises. Donna could trade these stars for various items, such as crossword puzzle books, CDs, or magazines.

To determine whether the stars were positive reinforcers for Donna's exercising, the social worker compared Donna's baseline rate of exercising with her exercise rate after she received stars. The baseline rate indicated that Donna exercised her leg once a day for a 7-day period. The following chart shows a week of baseline data recorded for Donna's exercising:

Daily Chart of Baseline Data for Donna's Exercising

Description of Response: Donna exercised her leg

Day	Response Strength (frequency per day)
Monday	|
Tuesday	||
Wednesday	|
Thursday	0
Friday	|
Saturday	|
Sunday	|
	Total: 7

After Donna received stars for exercising, her response rate increased to an average of five times a day during a 3-week period. These data provided measures of the effectiveness of stars as positive reinforcers for Donna's exercising. A daily chart of Donna's exercising after she began receiving stars for doing so for 1 week appears as follows:

Daily Chart of Donna's Exercising With Positive Reinforcement

Description of Response: Donna exercised her leg

Day	Response Strength (frequency per day)
Monday	卌
Tuesday	‖‖
Wednesday	卌 ‖
Thursday	卌
Friday	卌
Saturday	‖‖
Sunday	卌
	Total: 35 Average: 5 times/day

A weekly chart of Donna's exercising with positive reinforcement during a 3-week period appears as follows:

Weekly Chart of Donna's Exercising With Positive Reinforcement

Description of Response: Donna exercised her leg

Week	Response Strength (frequency per week)
1	35
2	30
3	40
	Total: 105 Average: 35 times per week

The above charts indicate that the stars served as positive reinforcers for Donna's exercising her leg.

In another example, Kara was told by her therapist to increase aerobic exercise as part of her treatment program for depression (e.g., Tkachuk & Martin, 1999). She routinely walked on a treadmill at the health club for 5 minutes once or twice a week (baseline rate). Kara told the therapist that she liked to play a certain video game that was available at the health club. The therapist told Kara not to play that particular game until after she had walked on the treadmill for 15 minutes. Every time Kara spent 15 minutes walking on the treadmill, she would immediately go and play the video game. After 6 weeks of following the program, Kara's walking on the treadmill at the health club increased to 15 minutes five times per week. The video game served as a positive reinforcer for Kara's walking on the treadmill.

Reinforcement of Behavior:
Social, Tangible, and Self-Administered

Some people positively reinforce their own behaviors with praise (e.g., "I did a good job") or make other positive statements about themselves (e.g., "That was a difficult task, but I did it."). For others, completing a job is the most important reinforcer. These individuals appear to require fewer external reinforcers than others to maintain desired behaviors. They are often described as self-starters or high achievers, or as being highly motivated or deriving great satisfaction from their work.

Other people seem to require frequent external approval or tangible demonstrations of their worth, or their productivity decreases. For example, some children pay little attention to their teachers in school. Points, privileges, praise, and tangible positive reinforcers, such as food or stickers, can be used to increase children's attending to their teachers and performing assigned tasks. Other children find schoolwork positively reinforcing, so for them task completion and grades are major reinforcers. These differences in reinforcer effectiveness for various behaviors may be related to the reinforcement practices of parents and others as well as individual differences among children.

Interpersonal relationships may involve combinations of social, tangible, and self-administered reinforcement. For example, Jed begged his parents for a car. After saying "No" for several months, they gave in and bought him a car. Jed received social reinforcement from the approval of his friends, tangible reinforcement from driving the car, and self-administered reinforcement when he told himself, "I really handled my parents just right." Jed's begging was reinforced by social, tangible, and self-administered reinforcement.

In another example, Theresa lived alone in an assisted-living facility. The facility's activities director called Theresa every day to invite her to join one of the programs, but Theresa always said, "No." One day, however, she gave in and went to a music program, participated in the sing-along, and had some refreshments with the other residents. Theresa received social reinforcement in the form of attention from the activities director and the residents when she attended the activity. The tangible reinforcers she received were the refreshments and the singing. Theresa told herself, "That was fun after all," which was self-administered reinforcement. Although Theresa's earlier refusals may have been reinforced by the attention of the activities director, she received social, tangible, and self-administered reinforcement for attending the activity.

Summary

1. A stimulus can be any object or event. It can include physical features of the environment and an individual's own behavior or the behavior of others.

2. Stimuli can be unconditioned, such as food and sex, or conditioned, such as money and attention.

3. A positive reinforcer is a stimulus presented after a response that increases the strength of the response. Rate or frequency per time unit is the most common measure of response strength. A response that has been strengthened through positive reinforcement is more likely to be performed again under similar conditions.

4. A stimulus that serves as a positive reinforcer for one person's behavior may be ineffective when used with someone else. Stimuli identified as rewards may not serve as positive reinforcers even though they appear to be attractive. Stimuli that appear aversive or unpleasant, however, may unintentionally act as positive reinforcers.

5. The effectiveness of a stimulus as a positive reinforcer is influenced by the following factors: timing, deprivation, satiation, size, amount, type, and quality.

6. Some people seem to be highly responsive to social or tangible reinforcers, whereas others are responsive to self-administered reinforcement, such as task accomplishment or self-praise.

Suggested Activities

1. List five stimuli that can act as positive reinforcers for you or someone you know. How do you know these stimuli are positive reinforcers? Give an example.

2. Team up with another member of your class and discuss one target behavior for each of you that you want to increase. Be sure to pick a behavior that is easily observable, such as raising your hand in class, eating certain kinds of food, reading a given number of pages in your textbook, or answering questions in the posttests. Chart the baseline rate of the behavior for each other.

3. Use one of the reinforcers you listed in activity 1 above to increase the target behavior you identified in activity 2. Continue to chart the rate of the response as it increases. (Hint: If the target response does not increase, perhaps the stimulus you have chosen is not a positive reinforcer.)

4. Discuss the results of activity 3 with your class partner. Your instructor might also ask you to present your results in class.

References and Resources

Bachrach, J., Erwin, W. J., & Mohr, J. P. (1965). The control of eating behavior in an anorexic by operant conditioning techniques. In L. P. Ullmann & L. Krasner (Eds.), *Case studies in behavior modification* (pp. 153–163). New York: Holt, Rinehart & Winston.

Cautela, J. R. (1977). Children's Reinforcement Survey Schedule (CRSS). In J. R. Cautela (Ed.), *Behavior analysis forms for social intervention* (pp. 52–62). Champaign, IL: Research Press.

Cautela, J. R., & Kastenbaum, R. A. (1967). A reinforcement survey schedule for use in therapy, training and research. *Psychological Reports, 20,* 1115–1130.

Gewirtz, J. L., & Baer, D. M. (1958). Deprivation and satiation of social reinforcers as drive conditions. *Journal of Abnormal and Social Psychology, 57,* 165–172.

Haughton, E., & Ayllon, T. (1965). Production and elimination of symptomatic behavior. In L. P. Ullmann & L. Krasner (Eds.), *Case studies in behavior modification* (pp. 94–98). New York: Holt, Rinehart & Winston.

Hupp, S. D., Reitman, D., Northup, J., O'Callahan, P., & LeBlanc, M. (2002). The effects of delayed rewards, tokens, and stimulant medication on sportsmanlike behavior with ADHD-diagnosed children. *Behavior Modification, 26,* 148–162.

Kelley, M. E., Piazza, C. C., Fisher, W. W., & Oberdorff, A. J. (2003). Acquisition of cup drinking using previously refused foods as positive and negative reinforcement. *Journal of Applied Behavior Analysis, 36,* 89–93.

O'Donahoe, J. W. (1998). Positive reinforcement: The selection of behavior. In W. O'Donohue (Ed.), *Learning and behavior therapy* (pp. 169–187). Boston: Allyn & Bacon.

O'Donohue, W., Plaud, J. J., & Becker, J. E. (1992). The possible function of positive reinforcement in home-bound agoraphobia: A case study. *Journal of Behavior Therapy and Experimental Psychiatry, 23,* 303–312.

Salzinger, K. (1996). Reinforcement history: A concept underutilized in behavior analysis. *Journal of Behavior Therapy and Experimental Psychiatry, 27,* 199–207.

Skinner, B. F. (1938). The differentiation of a response. In B. F. Skinner, *Behavior of organisms* (pp. 308–340). Englewood Cliffs, NJ: Prentice Hall.

Skinner, B. F. (1953). Shaping and maintaining operant behavior. In B. F. Skinner, *Science and human behavior* (pp. 91–106). New York: Free Press.

Terri, L., & Lewinsohn, P. (1982). Modification of the pleasant and unpleasant events schedules for use with the elderly. *Journal of Consulting and Clinical Psychology, 55,* 444–445.

Tkachuk, G. A., & Martin, G. L. (1999). Exercise therapy for psychiatric disorders: Research and clinical implications. *Professional Psychology: Research and Practice, 30,* 275–282.

Williams, J. A., Koegel, R. L., & Egel, A. L. (1981). Response-reinforcer relationships and improved learning in autistic children. *Journal of Applied Behavior Analysis, 14,* 53–60.

CHAPTER 3

Extinction

Sharon met Dwayne at a party, and he called her the next day to ask her on a date. She told him she had a boyfriend and wouldn't go out with him. Dwayne began e-mailing her, asking why she wouldn't go out with him. The first day he sent 3 e-mails, and the next day he sent 5. Sharon answered the first 3 of the e-mails, then decided to stop answering. Dwayne sent her 10 e-mails on the third day and another 10 on the fourth day. On the fifth day, he sent 12 e-mails.

Sharon was tempted to reply, to tell Dwayne to stop bothering her, but she resisted. On the sixth day, he sent 8 e-mails, and on the seventh day he sent 5. He sent 2 e-mails on the eighth day and 2 on the ninth day and one last e-mail on the tenth day. Sharon never heard from Dwayne again after that.

Objectives

After completing this chapter, you should be able to do the following:

- Give an example of an extinction procedure used to decrease the strength of a behavior.
- Determine whether a given stimulus serves as a positive reinforcer for a specific response.
- Identify the positive reinforcers for desired and undesired behaviors, given a case example.
- Describe the effect of extinction on the rate of a target response.
- Describe how spontaneous recovery can be addressed in an intervention plan.

Decreasing Response Strength

In Chapter 2, we described how positive reinforcement can be used to increase the strength of a response. This chapter is concerned with how the strength of a response is decreased by the application of a procedure called **extinction**, an example of which is given in Case Example 2 (see p. 34). Like positive reinforcement, extinction alters the **consequences** of a behavior. By systematically withholding the positively reinforcing consequences of a behavior, we can decrease its frequency.

The extinction procedure consists of withholding the positive reinforcer each time the target response is performed. The contingency between the response and the positive reinforcer is discontinued. The extinction effect is a decrease in the rate of the response to zero or to a prespecified rate. A response that decreases to zero has been extinguished and has a low probability of occurring again under similar conditions. The extinction procedure is shown in diagram form as follows:

Extinction Diagram

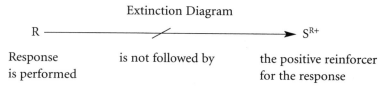

R		S^{R+}
Response is performed	is not followed by	the positive reinforcer for the response

Effect: Response decreases in strength to zero or a prespecified rate.

The slash through the arrow in the above diagram indicates that the positive reinforcer (S^{R+}) is withheld (discontinued or no longer presented) until the response (R) decreases in strength to the designated rate.

The effect of the extinction procedure is that the target response decreases in strength to (a) zero or a prespecified rate or (b) its **baseline rate** or **baseline level**—that is, the rate prior to intervention. For example, in Chapter 2, we determined that the baseline rate of Donna's exercising was one time per day. When Donna received stars contingent on her exercising, the rate increased to an average of five times per day. The positive reinforcement diagram for Donna's exercising is as follows:

Positive Reinforcement Diagram for Exercising

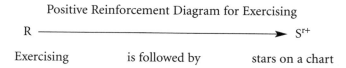

R		S^{r+}
Exercising	is followed by	stars on a chart

Effect: Donna's exercising increased in rate over its baseline.

After 3 weeks of this program, Donna's mother ran out of stars and stopped giving them to her. The rate of Donna's exercising decreased to its baseline rate of one time per day. In diagram form, this extinction procedure can be depicted as follows:

Extinction Diagram for Exercising

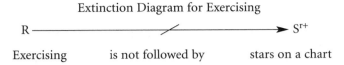

| R | is not followed by | S^{r+} |

Exercising   is not followed by   stars on a chart

Effect: Donna's exercising decreased to its baseline rate.

This example demonstrates the effect of extinction in decreasing the rate of exercising.

In another example, Kara's walking on the treadmill increased when she played a video game for every 15 minutes of walking. When the video game was broken for a week, Kara's walking on the treadmill decreased to its baseline level of 5 minutes two times that week. The week the game was broken demonstrates the effect of extinction on Kara's walking on the treadmill.

Following are examples of extinction and its effect applied to some behaviors:

Behavior	Extinction	Effect
Kara walks on a treadmill	Video game broken	Rate of walking on treadmill decreases
Sally giggles in class	Other students withhold laughter	Rate of giggling decreases
Carla screams about putting toys away	Mother stops putting toys away and ignores screaming	Rate of Carla's screaming decreases
Jordy whines for more TV	Father withholds attention and ignores whining	Rate of Jordy's whining decreases
Jack bangs his head against the wall	Teacher withholds attention	Rate of head banging decreases
Bella makes appropriate conversation in a group	Social worker withholds praise	Rate of appropriate conversation decreases

Single-Subject Evaluation Designs

Single-subject evaluation designs are also called single-case experimental designs or single-system research designs (SSRDs). The basic evaluation design is the AB design, where A refers to the baseline and B refers to the intervention. The only two requirements for this design are (a) the collection of baseline measures and (b) the collection of data after an intervention has been introduced. In Case Example 2, the baseline rate of Bella's speaking on topic in the group averaged zero times per group meeting. After the introduction of positive reinforcement in the form of praise by the social worker and group members, the rate of her speaking on topic increased to an average of five times per group meeting.

CASE EXAMPLE 2

Developing Appropriate Conversation

Bella and Cliff were older adults with memory impairment in a group conducted at a senior center. In social situations, they often asked questions and made comments that were unrelated to the topic being discussed. For example, when several group members were discussing a recent film, Cliff asked the person speaking if he was going grocery shopping that afternoon. The baseline rate of Bella's speaking on topic was zero. In addition, Bella and Cliff were frequently observed talking continuously for 5 minutes or more without pausing for responses from others. These speech patterns resulted in their being ridiculed and excluded from conversations held by other group members.

The social worker devised a conversational exercise for the six members of a group in which Bella and Cliff participated. The social worker began the exercise by making a statement and then asking each of the group members to add a statement to her introduction. Each new statement was required to bear logical connection to the preceding statement. For example, the social worker began speaking about how to cook dinner for oneself. At first, Bella and Cliff both added inappropriate statements, such as "You should see my grandson. He is so smart," or "You know, when I was selling cars in New York I always was the top salesman of the month." On these occasions, they were stopped by the social worker or group members, who asked them to make appropriate statements and complimented or praised them for doing so. Group members prompted Bella and Cliff, offering hints and suggestions for correct statements.

As they practiced this exercise on subsequent occasions, both Bella and Cliff made fewer inappropriate remarks and increasingly more appropriate ones. The rate of Bella's speaking on topic increased to five times per group meeting after six group sessions. The frequency of Bella's and Cliff's appropriate remarks during conversations outside the group was also observed to increase. Staff members and relatives reinforced Bella's and Cliff's appropriate speech.

Figure 3.1 is a graph of Bella's speaking on topic. We can readily observe the change in behavior from A to B; the data indicate an improvement after the intervention was introduced. The AB design, however, does not allow us to state empirically that the intervention "caused" the behavior change. We cannot rule out other factors that may have been responsible for the observed change, such as a new drug that improved Bella's concentration.

Another design, ABAB, is more rigorous in controlling for factors influencing behavior change. The first A (A_1) is the baseline condition. The first B (B_1) refers to the intervention. The second A (A_2) refers to a return or reversal to the baseline condition—that is, the intervention is removed. The second B (B_2) refers to reinstatement of the intervention. The **ABAB design,** also called a **reversal design,** is used to evaluate the effectiveness of an intervention in producing behavior change. The behavior will reverse as the phases are altered if the reinforcer is effective in producing the behavior change. The baseline and intervention phases are alternated

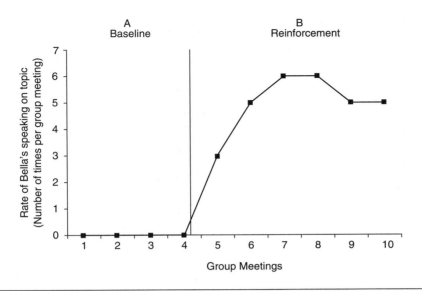

Figure 3.1   AB Graph of Bella's Speaking on Topic

to demonstrate that the intervention was responsible for the behavior change. ABAB designs have a built-in replication feature.

In Figure 3.2, A_1 is the baseline rate of Bella's speaking on topic in the group. B_1 refers to her response rate after positive reinforcement was delivered contingent on her speaking on topic. The rate of Bella's speaking on topic increased. A_2 is a return to baseline conditions when a new staff member took over the group and no longer praised Bella for speaking on topic. This resulted in extinction of Bella's speaking on topic, which returned to its baseline rate. B_2 refers to reinstatement of positive reinforcement contingent on her speaking on topic when the original social worker returned. The rate of Bella's speaking on topic again increased. These data demonstrate the effectiveness of praise by the social worker as a positive reinforcer for Bella's speaking on topic in the group. Because the social worker's praise was the positive reinforcer, withholding that praise decreased Bella's speaking on topic. Restoring praise by the social worker, therefore, was effective in reinstating Bella's appropriate speech.

Applying Extinction to Decrease Undesired Behaviors

Behavioral practitioners do not always have the opportunity to develop a behavior, extinguish it, and reinstate it. Often, we are asked simply to eliminate or decrease an undesired behavior to a desired, prespecified rate—for example, Sally's excessive giggling in class. In this situation, we must determine the reinforcing consequences for Sally's giggling.

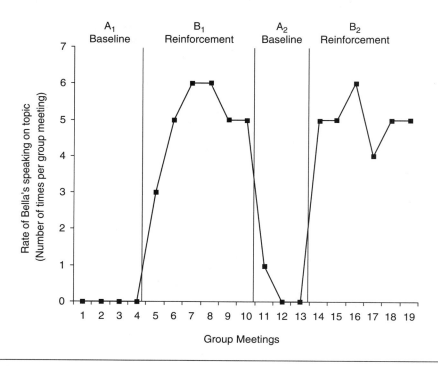

Figure 3.2   ABAB Graph of Bella's Speaking on Topic

We follow three basic steps in applying extinction to decrease a response. The first step is to observe what happens when Sally giggles in class to identify the positive reinforcer for giggling. We observe that other students laugh when Sally giggles, which could indicate that their laughter is a positive reinforcer for her giggling.

Second, we count the number of times Sally giggles during a given time period to determine her rate of giggling. We decide to count each occurrence of giggling as a separate giggling response if it lasts 1 to 5 seconds. Averaging baseline data, we find that Sally giggles an average of six times an hour.

Third, we remove the consequences of her giggling in class. We instruct the other students to continue working, to turn their faces away from Sally, and to remain silent when she giggles. If our initial observation that the students' laughter positively reinforced Sally's giggling is accurate, removing this positive reinforcer should result in a decrease in giggling. If the children's laughter is not a positive reinforcer for Sally's giggling, its removal will have little or no effect on her rate of giggling.

In Figure 3.3, A_1 is the baseline rate of Sally's giggling and B_1 is the intervention, extinction. During B_1, the rate of Sally's giggling initially increased and then gradually decreased to zero. A_2 is a return to the baseline condition—that is, removal of the intervention and allowing positive reinforcement for giggling. During A_2, the rate of Sally's giggling increased toward the baseline rate of A_1. B_2 refers to reinstatement of the intervention. During B_2, Sally's giggling again decreased to zero.

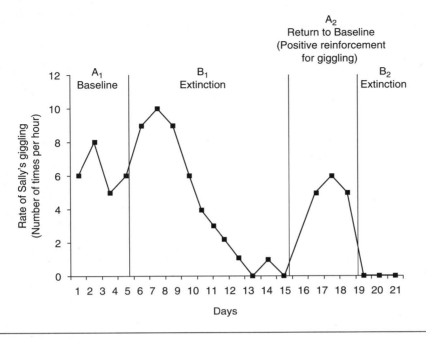

Figure 3.3   Graph of Sally's Giggling in Class

These data show that the removal of the positive reinforcer, the children's laughter, was effective in decreasing Sally's giggling.

The following steps will enable you to determine whether a given stimulus serves as a positive reinforcer for a specific response:

1. Determine the baseline rate of the response.

2. Identify the potential positive reinforcer for the response.

3. Withhold the stimulus that you have identified as the potential positive reinforcer for the response.

4. Measure the rate of the response. If it decreases (even after an initial increase), it is likely that the stimulus you identified is the positive reinforcer for the response.

5. If it is important to demonstrate that the stimulus is in fact the positive reinforcer, reinstate the stimulus following the response.

6. Measure the rate of the response. If it increases again, the stimulus has served as the positive reinforcer for the response.

The following shows the steps you could use to determine whether the students' laughter is the positive reinforcer for Sally's giggling. The steps are listed on the left, and the examples of Sally's giggling are listed on the right:

1. Determine the baseline rate of the target response.	1. Sally giggled six times per hour.
2. Identify the potential positive reinforcer for the target response.	2. The students' laughter followed Sally's giggling, indicating it could be the positive reinforcer for her giggling.
3. Withhold the stimulus that you have identified as the potential positive reinforcer for the response.	3. The teacher told the students to turn away from Sally and remain silent when she giggled.
4. Measure the rate of the response.	4. Sally's giggling increased at first to ten times per hour and then decreased to zero times per hour.
5. Reinstate the stimulus following the response.	5. The students laughed when Sally giggled (as instructed by the teacher).
6. Measure the rate of the response.	6. Sally giggled six times per hour.

The procedure described above demonstrated that the students' laughter was probably the positive reinforcer for Sally's giggling. To extinguish Sally's giggling again, the teacher would tell the other students to turn away from Sally and remain silent when she giggled.

In practice, AB designs are the most common. ABAB designs are more appropriate for research programs that require careful testing of treatment effects. The ABAB design in this case demonstrated that the students' laughter, not some other event, was controlling Sally's giggling. Because Sally's giggling is an undesired behavior, however, it would be inappropriate to reinstate giggling by asking the students to reinforce it.

CASE EXAMPLE 3

Decreasing Tantrum Behaviors

In a parent training group, Carla's mother, Juanita, told the social worker that almost every time she told 5-year-old Carla to put her toys away, Carla screamed. The baseline duration of Carla's screaming averaged 5.5 minutes per episode. Juanita would attempt to placate Carla by promising to buy her new clothes and by putting the toys away herself.

The social worker suspected that Juanita was positively reinforcing Carla's screaming by putting the toys away and promising to buy Carla new clothes. She showed Juanita how to use extinction to decrease Carla's screaming. The procedure involved withholding the positive reinforcers for Carla's screaming.

The social worker instructed Juanita to stop making promises, stop putting away the toys, and walk away from Carla when she screamed about putting away her toys. She told Juanita that Carla's screaming might get worse before it got better but that if she held firm, Carla's screaming would gradually decrease. Juanita carried out these instructions and the duration of Carla's scream-ing gradually decreased, after an increase on the second day of extinction. By the sixth day of the extinction intervention, Carla no longer screamed when told to put her toys away.

The social worker also instructed Juanita to praise Carla and give her tangible reinforcers, such as gum or cookies, when she put her toys away. Juanita followed these instructions, and Carla began putting her toys away more frequently.

Figure 3.4 is a graph showing extinction of Carla's screaming when she was asked to put her toys away. To obtain baseline data, the social worker told Juanita to record how long Carla screamed when asked to put her toys away for 2 days *before* beginning the extinction intervention. Carla screamed for 5 minutes the first day and 6 minutes the second day. On the first day Juanita implemented the extinction intervention, Carla screamed for 5 minutes. She screamed for 9 minutes on the second day, 5 minutes on the third day, 3 minutes on the fourth day, and 1 minute on the fifth day; Carla did not scream when asked to put her toys away on the sixth and seventh days.

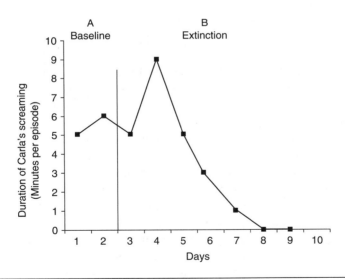

Figure 3.4   Graph of Extinction of Carla's Screaming

Ethical Considerations

The use of some single-subject designs raises the ethical issues of reinstating posi-tive reinforcement for undesired behaviors (e.g., Sally's giggling) and removing positive reinforcement for desired behaviors (e.g., Bella's speaking on topic in group meetings). In practice, undesired behaviors, especially those that are harmful to the individual or others, should not be reinstated after extinction to demonstrate effectiveness of the procedure. Similarly, behaviors that are beneficial to the individual or others should not be extinguished.

It might be appropriate to remove and reinstate reinforcement using an ABAB design in a carefully controlled research study that attempts to develop new knowledge about the effects of certain stimuli on behavior, determine the effects of novel interventions, or assess the effects of interventions on different behaviors. In such research studies, the informed consent of the individuals involved, or their legally responsible significant others, should always be obtained. The researchers should clearly state the rationale of the studies, indicating the benefit for the individuals or future clients. Other evaluative approaches, often used in research studies, do not involve returning to baseline conditions. Multiple-baseline designs, for example, do not require reversal to baseline (see Chapter 13). Other experimental designs that do not involve reversal to baseline include changing criterion, simultaneous treatment, and multielement designs. Detailed treatments and examples of these alternative designs can be found elsewhere (e.g., Bloom, Fischer, & Orme, 2003; Royse, 1995).

Effects of Extinction

In extinction, the target response may not disappear immediately. In fact, the initial effect of extinction is often a response burst or sharp increase in the strength of the target behavior. For example, during the first 3 days that students ignored Sally's giggling, her average hourly rate of giggling increased from 6 to 10 times per hour (see Figure 3.3). Disruptive or "emotional" responses, such as kicking, hitting, or complaining, might also be observed. For example, when you put money in a vending machine for a soft drink and nothing comes out, you might hit or kick the machine, especially if you have been positively reinforced previously for such behavior by getting the desired item or your money back from the machine. Similarly, the first day Bella did not receive praise for speaking on topic, she might have complained or mumbled under her breath. If reinforcement is continuously withheld, however, the target behavior will gradually decrease until it reaches its baseline or a prespecified rate. Our measure for effective reduction of Sally's giggling would be the teacher's estimate of a reasonable rate for that behavior in appropriate circumstances. Extinction, therefore, is judged to be effective when the target behavior decreases to a prespecified rate.

Many behaviors are reinforced by social consequences such as attention, praise, recognition, conversation, and expressions of interest or concern from other individuals. The withholding of such **social reinforcers** to extinguish undesired behavior might include turning away from the individual, avoiding eye contact, and refraining from conversation. In withholding social reinforcement, it is important to avoid scowling, grimacing, or exhibiting other facial or verbal behaviors that could unintentionally reinforce the response to be extinguished.

Consistency and Control of Reinforcement

Two practical difficulties might be encountered in implementing an extinction procedure: (a) ensuring that reinforcement is consistently withheld for undesired behaviors and (b) preventing delivery of reinforcement by others for undesired behaviors. In applying extinction, it is necessary to consistently withhold the reinforcer for the response. The pressure to "give in" or reinstate the reinforcer must be resisted, especially during the period of increased responding or disruptive behavior that can occur at the beginning of extinction. Reinstating the reinforcer for the undesired response makes the response more difficult to extinguish in the future.

For example, the social worker told Juanita (see Case Example 3, p. 38) to extinguish Carla's screaming by ignoring her and walking away when Carla screamed about putting her toys away. The social worker also warned Juanita that Carla's screaming might increase in intensity when the extinction intervention first began, and that Carla might kick the furniture or throw her toys around the room. If Juanita were to respond by putting Carla's toys away and promising to buy her clothes as before, Juanita would reinstate the positive reinforcers for the undesired behavior, making it more difficult to extinguish.

In the example at the beginning of this chapter, Sharon extinguished Dwayne's e-mailing behavior when she stopped answering his e-mails. Before his e-mailing extinguished, however, Dwayne's rate of e-mailing Sharon increased. Although Sharon was tempted to answer Dwayne's e-mails, she continued to withhold her response. If she had given in to the temptation, she would have reinforced Dwayne's e-mailing, thereby making it more difficult to extinguish.

The second major difficulty in implementing an extinction program is that of preventing the delivery of reinforcement by others for the undesired behavior. When we are not in control of the individual's reinforcing environment, someone else could reinforce the behavior that we are attempting to extinguish. For example, Carla's grandmother might put Carla's toys away when she screams, making the response more difficult to extinguish. Such unauthorized reinforcement for undesired behavior has been referred to as "bootleg reinforcement" (Ayllon & Michael, 1959).

Positive Reinforcement of Appropriate Behaviors

As we have shown above, extinction is used to decrease the strength of a response. For example, Donna's exercising decreased when her mother stopped giving her stars, Kara's walking on the treadmill decreased when she stopped playing the video game after walking on the treadmill, Sally's giggling decreased when her classmates stopped laughing, and Bella's speaking on topic decreased when she no longer was praised by the social worker. In each of these cases, the target response decreased when the positive reinforcer was withheld. When we extinguish an undesired behavior, however, it may also be important to positively reinforce appropriate behaviors in the problematic situation. When we extinguish Sally's giggling, therefore, we also positively reinforce appropriate classroom behaviors, such as reading quietly, talking at appropriate times to other students and to the teacher, reading aloud for the class, and answering the teacher's questions. Sally can be positively reinforced for these responses by teacher attention, praise, points, or extra privileges. Similarly, when extinguishing Carla's screaming, Juanita was instructed to positively reinforce appropriate behaviors Carla performs, such as reading a book, playing with her dolls, or helping her mother put groceries away.

Spontaneous Recovery

A feature of extinction that is important to the behavioral practitioner is **spontaneous recovery.** After a behavior has been extinguished, it might recur even though it has not been reinforced for some time. The behavior could recur when the individual is in a situation similar to the one in which the behavior was originally reinforced. Individuals conducting the extinction procedure are instructed to continue to withhold the reinforcer if the response recurs.

For example, at bedtime 3-year-old Jordy whined for more television time, and his father usually gave in. Jordy's bedtime got later and later, and it became difficult to wake him in the morning. Jordy's parents tried to get him to bed earlier, but Jordy always got his way. To extinguish Jordy's whining, his father was instructed to turn off the TV at the same time every night, to tell Jordy there would be no more TV that evening, and to ignore his whining. At first, Jordy's whining increased in intensity (volume), frequency, and duration, and he threw his toys on the floor. Jordy's father continued to turn off the TV at Jordy's bedtime each night, and Jordy's whining began to decrease in frequency, duration, and intensity. On the seventh night, when his father turned off the TV, Jordy went immediately to his room and prepared for bed. Jordy's father continued this procedure successfully for 2 weeks, and Jordy stopped whining at bedtime. One evening the following week, Jordy's mother turned off the TV at his bedtime. Jordy whined, but the TV remained off. This incident of spontaneous recovery of Jordy's whining was handled effectively—that is, Jordy's mother reinstated the extinction procedure.

In anticipation of the possible spontaneous recovery of Jordy's whining, Jordy's parents were instructed to remain firm in turning off the TV at bedtime. They were also told to inform anyone else who would be responsible for turning off the TV at Jordy's bedtime to ignore his whining should it occur.

In implementing the extinction procedure, we identify all individuals who have control over the availability or delivery of positive reinforcement for the target behavior in the person's environment. These individuals are instructed to follow the extinction procedure consistently. In Jordy's situation, both his mother and father, as well as babysitters and relatives, were instructed to turn off the TV and leave it off at the designated time so that Jordy's whining would not be positively reinforced.

During the course of extinction, Jordy's parents were instructed to positively reinforce Jordy's appropriate behaviors at bedtime. Such behaviors included picking out his clothes for the next day, asking for a story, kissing his parents good night, and saying good night to his parents.

Summary

1. Extinction is a procedure for decreasing response strength or the likelihood that a response will be performed again under similar conditions.

2. The extinction procedure consists of withholding the positive reinforcer for a response until the response decreases to a prespecified rate or to its baseline rate. The contingency between a response and a positive reinforcer is terminated. The positive reinforcer is withheld each time the response is performed.

3. Positive reinforcement involves the presentation of a positive reinforcer contingent on performance of a response; extinction involves withholding the positive reinforcer contingent on performance of a response.

4. The extinction procedure can be used to determine whether a stimulus has served as a positive reinforcer for a specific response.

5. To extinguish a response, one must determine (a) response strength, (b) the positive reinforcer for the response, and (c) whether withholding the positive reinforcer results in a decrease in response strength.

6. The AB and ABAB experimental designs are used in the evaluation of case studies. Ethical concerns with the ABAB design include reinstating positive reinforcement for undesired behaviors and removing positive reinforcement for desired behaviors.

7. The initial effect of extinction may be a response burst or sharp increase in the strength of a target response, along with disruptive or "emotional" responses.

8. Lack of consistency in withholding positive reinforcement and the inability to prevent delivery of positive reinforcement by others ("bootleg reinforcement") are two practical difficulties encountered in implementing an extinction procedure.

9. When a target behavior is extinguished, it may also be important to positively reinforce appropriate behaviors in the problematic situation.

10. The possible spontaneous recovery of an extinguished response can be anticipated and a plan can be arranged for continued extinction of the response.

Suggested Activities

1. Divide the class into groups of three. In each group, appoint one person to be the "client," one to be the "therapist," and the third to be the observer. The therapist will provide positive reinforcement in the form of eye contact, head nodding, and saying, "mm hmm," when the client begins to speak about any topic. This will continue for 2 minutes, at which time the therapist will no longer provide the positive reinforcement. Instead, the therapist will look away, remain silent, and even turn his or her body away from the client. The

observer records the results, including the frequency and duration of the client's speaking about the selected topic, rate of speaking about other topics, and other behaviors.

2. Repeat activity 1 with each group member in a different role.

References and Resources

Ayllon, T., & Michael, J. (1959). The psychiatric nurse as a behavioral engineer. *Journal of the Experimental Analysis of Behavior, 2,* 323–334.

Bloom, M., Fischer, J., & Orme, J. G. (2003). *Evaluating practice: Guidelines for the accountable professional* (4th ed.). Boston: Allyn & Bacon.

Iwata, B. A., Pace, G. M., Cowdery, G. E., & Miltenberger, R. G. (1994). What makes extinction work: An analysis of procedural form and function. *Journal of Applied Behavior Analysis, 27,* 131–144.

Kelley, M. E., Lerman, D. C., & Van Camp, C. M. (2002). The effects of competing reinforcement schedules on the acquisition of functional communication. *Journal of Applied Behavior Analysis, 35,* 59–63.

Lerman, D. C., & Iwata, B. A. (1996). Developing a technology for the use of operant extinction in clinical settings: An examination of basic and applied research. *Journal of Applied Behavior Analysis, 29,* 345–382.

Lerman, D. C., Iwata, B. A., & Wallace, M. D. (1999). Side effects of extinction: Prevalence of bursting and aggression during the treatment of self-injurious behavior. *Journal of Applied Behavior Analysis, 32,* 1–8.

Pinkston, E. M., Reese, N. M., LeBlanc, J. M., & Baer, D. M. (1973). Independent control of a pre-school child's aggression and peer interaction by contingent teacher attention. *Journal of Applied Behavior Analysis, 6,* 115–124.

Rincover, A. (1978). Sensory extinction: A procedure for eliminating self-stimulating behavior in autistic children. *Journal of Abnormal Child Psychology, 6,* 299–310.

Royse, D. (1995). *Research methods in social work* (2nd ed.). Chicago: Nelson-Hall.

Williams, C. D. (1959). The elimination of tantrum behavior by extinction procedures. *Journal of Abnormal and Social Psychology, 59,* 269.

Wolf, M., Birnbrauer, J., Lawler, J., & Williams, T. (1970). The operant extinction, reinstatement, and re-extinction of vomiting behavior in a retarded child. In R. Ulrich, T. Stachnick, & J. Mabry (Eds.), *Control of human behavior* (Vol. 2, pp. 146–153). Glenview, IL: Scott, Foresman.

CHAPTER 4

Positive Reinforcement Contingencies

Lenora frequently invites her friends for coffee in the morning, but she rarely gives her children breakfast. Lenora can increase the rate of giving her children breakfast if inviting her friends over is made contingent on her making breakfast for her children.

Objectives

After completing this chapter, you should be able to do the following:

- Give an example of a positive reinforcement contingency.
- Compare self-control reinforcement contingencies with accidental reinforcement contingencies.
- Define and give an example of the Premack Principle.
- Compare resistance to extinction for a response maintained on a continuous schedule of reinforcement versus an intermittent schedule of reinforcement.
- Describe how to schedule the delivery of reinforcement to maintain a response after it has been established, given a case example.

Behavioral Contingencies and Positive Reinforcement

In the preceding chapters, we have discussed positive reinforcement and extinction—two procedures for modifying a response by altering its consequences. In positive reinforcement, the positive reinforcer is presented *contingent on* performance of the response. In extinction, the positive reinforcer is withheld *contingent on* performance of the response.

A **behavioral contingency** specifies the behaviors to be performed for certain consequences to follow. A positive reinforcement contingency is one type of behavioral contingency. **Self-control reinforcement contingencies, accidental reinforcement contingencies, punishment contingencies,** and **negative reinforcement contingencies** are other types of behavioral contingencies.

A **positive reinforcement contingency** indicates that a behavior must be performed for a positive reinforcer to follow. The contingency is stated in positive terms, with clear specification of the behavior, the positive reinforcer, and the circumstances in which reinforcement will occur. Examples of positive reinforcement contingencies include the following: "If you trim the hedges, we will go fishing"; "After you finish your piano lesson, Diane, you may go shopping with Sherry"; and "If you want to have sex with me, you must put on a condom." The positive reinforcer is more likely to be effective when it immediately follows the desired behavior than when it is delayed.

The following example from our own experience illustrates the use of a positive reinforcement contingency:

Monsters in the Closet

Years ago, we faced a difficult problem with our daughter, Jenny, when she was 5 years old. Jenny was afraid of monsters in her room, and she had trouble falling asleep every night. What was worse, she woke up in the middle of the night—every night—and came to our bedroom for comfort. For five nights in a row, one of us had to take her back to her own bed at 4:00 a.m. after she woke us up or just curled up in our bed.

Frustrated and exhausted, we devised an intervention to address the problem. Jenny would get a quarter every morning she slept through the night and would have one taken away from her if she awakened us. Three sleepless nights later, it was clear that this plan did not work. It appeared that quarters were not reinforcing for Jenny. Plan B involved buying barrettes of different colors and shapes to use as positive reinforcers for Jenny's sleeping through the night. We showed Jenny a few of the barrettes before she went to bed and told her that she could pick two the next morning if she slept through the night and did not wake us up. We placed the barrettes on the nightstand in our bedroom.

The first night—no visitor! The next morning, Jenny ecstatically picked out two purple barrettes, and we laid on the praise and kisses. The second night—no visitor! The next morning, Jenny was again delighted with the blue barrettes she chose and the hugs and kisses we gave her. One more night and she could get the pink ones. The third night—once again a peaceful night of undisturbed sleep. Total cost of the program thus far: $2.99 for the barrettes.

After a few more nights of uninterrupted sleep and a few more mornings of wonderful reinforcers, we told Jenny that now she would have to go two nights in a row before she would get a "surprise." No problem. We then stretched it to three nights. Piece of cake! Jenny had no more trouble staying asleep at night, and everyone felt better in the morning. The barrettes were faded out while Jenny continued to receive hugs, kisses, and lots of praise. Interestingly, her talk of monsters in the closet disappeared along with the sleep problem.

Positive reinforcement contingencies can be stated explicitly, as in the example of Jenny and the barrettes, or they can generate rules that control behavior with or without the person's awareness or ability to describe them. In a marital relationship, for instance, one or both partners may be unaware of the positive reinforcement contingencies that exist between the behaviors of one partner and the affection (or other reinforcers) provided by the other. For example, Jean is more likely to have sex with Timothy after he cooks dinner for her, or washes her car, or brings her flowers.

Contingency Contracting

Behavioral contracts are written agreements between individuals that state the contingencies between behaviors and their consequences. A behavioral contract specifies the desired behaviors and the reinforcers to be given for performing them. The contract also states the negative consequences, or punishers, to be presented for not fulfilling the terms of the contract. Practitioners use behavioral contracts in intervention plans to help their clients develop desired behaviors.

Contingency contracting is the practice of establishing behavioral contracts between individuals. Behavioral contracts have been used with a wide range of target behaviors, such as increasing positive interactions between delinquent teenagers and their parents; reducing disruptive classroom behaviors of students and increasing their on-task performance; decreasing smoking, overeating, and drug abuse; and increasing positive marital interactions.

A major requirement of contingency contracting is the participation of all parties involved in a behavior change program. Terms of the contract are discussed to promote each party's commitment to abide by them. Typically, the practitioner negotiates the conditions of a behavioral contract so that they are satisfactory to all parties and signed by all parties.

For example, Mr. and Mrs. Geary would like for Sue, their 14-year-old daughter, to arrive home by 10:00 p.m. each weeknight. They have been arguing about this issue for 6 weeks, because Sue frequently arrives home after midnight. The practitioner who has been counseling this family helped negotiate a behavioral contract that focused on Sue's curfew. The parents wanted Sue home by 10:00 p.m. on weeknights—that is, Sunday through Thursday nights. Sue wanted extra spending money and permission to invite her girlfriends to her house more often.

Figure 4.1 shows the behavioral contract Sue and her parents signed. According to the terms of the contract, each night Sue arrived home by 10:00 p.m. she would give herself a check mark on a chart. At the end of the week, she would receive $2.00 for each check mark. Thus Sue could earn a total of $10.00 per week. The contract

SUE AGREES TO:
Be in the house by 10:00 p.m. each
weeknight (Sunday through Thursday).

Put a check mark on a chart for each night
she is home by 10:00 p.m.

MR. and MRS. GEARY AGREE TO:
Give Sue $2.00 for each check mark.

BONUS: If Sue compiles 10 check marks in 2 weeks, Mr. and Mrs. Geary will allow her to
have a girlfriend stay over one Friday or Saturday night.

PENALTY: For every weeknight Sue comes home after 10:00 p.m., she will have to be in the
house by 6:00 p.m. for the next two nights.

SIGNED:

Sue Geary   _____

Helen Geary   _____

Fred Geary   _____

DATE: _____

Figure 4.1   Behavioral Contract Between Sue and Her Parents

also included a bonus clause, which stated that if Sue compiled 10 check marks in 2 weeks, she could have a girlfriend stay over one Friday or Saturday night. For every night that Sue came home after 10:00 p.m., she would not be allowed to leave the house after 6:00 p.m. for the next two nights.

A behavioral contract can be an effective aid to behavior change because the desired behavior and the consequences—reinforcers and punishers—are specified in advance. All parties involved know what to expect as a result of performing the designated behaviors. The behaviors and consequences need to be monitored, however, to ensure that the terms of the contract are being carried out. If difficulties arise, they should be discussed and the contract renegotiated, if necessary.

A protective services case plan is another type of behavioral contract. Figure 4.2 shows the behavioral contract (case plan) for Lenora Jackson. Lenora is a single mother with three children under the age of 10. Jerry James, a social worker with the State Protective Services Office, was sent to work with Lenora after her children were reported absent from school for 5 weeks. When he visited Lenora's home, he observed poor hygiene and housekeeping as well as behavioral problems with the children. Lenora's case plan specifies the behaviors she must perform for the children to remain in her home, such as bathing and dressing the children in clean clothes every day, feeding them breakfast before school, getting them to school on time every day, and attending parenting classes. If Lenora performs these behaviors, she will continue to receive assistance from the state; if she fails to perform these behaviors, her children could be placed in foster care. As part of the contract, the social worker agrees to provide Lenora with names and phone numbers of places she can call for help with transportation, clothing, and school supplies. He will also make weekly visits to monitor the children's school attendance, their cleanliness, and their behavior and to discuss any problems Lenora might have.

PARENT (LENORA) AGREES TO:	WORKER (MR. JAMES) AGREES TO:
Attend parenting classes at XYZ agency twice each week for 12 weeks and receive certificate of completion.	Give Lenora names and phone numbers to call for information on transportation, school clothes, and school supplies.
Bathe the children each night before bed.	Visit the home weekly for 4 weeks to monitor conditions in the home, the relationship between Lenora and her children, and Lenora's attendance at the parenting classes; discuss any other issues or problems Lenora wants to discuss.
Dress the children in clean clothes for school.	
Feed the children breakfast before they leave for school.	
	Look into Lenora's eligibility for other services, such as the Homebuilders program.

If Lenora works on the goals stated in her case plan, Mr. James will continue to visit her weekly and provide services to help keep her children at home.

NOTE: If Lenora stops working on her goals, the possibility of removing the children from the home will be discussed, and they could be removed to foster care.

SIGNED:

Parent _____

PS Worker _____

DATE: _____

Figure 4.2   Behavioral Contract Between Lenora Jackson, Parent, and Jerry James, Protective Services Worker

Accidental Reinforcement Contingencies

A response can be established or operantly conditioned by accidental reinforcement, in which the reinforcer is not functionally related to performance of the response. If we flip a light switch on and off, our response is functionally related to the onset or removal of light. **Superstitious behavior**, however, is usually the result of an accidental or coincidental relationship between a response and a reinforcer. The response is followed by an unplanned or noncontingent reinforcer that coincidentally strengthens the response. The delivery of the reinforcer is not functionally related to performance of the response. For example, a gambler twirls his "lucky" ring while playing blackjack and is dealt a winning hand. He attributes his win to the twirling of the ring. An event other than twirling the ring produced the reinforcer of winning, but the ring-twirling response accidentally became associated with the reinforcer. The gambler twirls his ring again while playing blackjack, although this behavior cannot produce the reinforcer. Winning is not contingent on ring twirling. The gambler would have drawn the winning cards on the reinforcing occasion whether or not he twirled his ring.

Many strange behaviors have been reinforced by gamblers and others on the basis of accidental contingencies between behaviors and reinforcers. Anecdotes include a woman who ate marshmallows while playing bingo because eating them was previously associated with her winning a jackpot, a man who pulled on his ear during a horse race after winning a bet on a previous race while pulling on his ear, and a football player who wore the same unwashed "lucky" socks every game after he scored the winning touchdown wearing those socks.

Self-Control Reinforcement Contingencies

Positive reinforcement contingencies can be applied in a self-control or self-management program (e.g., Watson & Tharp, 1997). In this way, the individual can increase the strength of desired behaviors by providing self-administered reinforcement. For example, Jon was in danger of flunking statistics because he had completed only a few of his assignments. He spent much of his time playing basketball. By arranging to play basketball only after completing his statistics homework, Jon increased the frequency of his completing those assignments. After Bonita followed her diet for 4 weeks and lost 12 pounds, she bought herself a new dress. Annemarie, a social worker, made sure that she recorded a client interview before taking a coffee break. In all these situations, the individuals arranged for self-administered positive reinforcers to follow their desired behaviors.

Self-control reinforcement contingencies are preferable to accidental reinforcement contingencies because the individual can arrange conditions so that the reinforcer predictably follows the desired behavior. Self-reinforcement can be covert as well as overt. Individuals can positively reinforce themselves by making positive statements to themselves following desired behaviors, or they can imagine a pleasant, relaxing scene, such as lying on a beach, as a positive reinforcer. For example, after Gwen worked out on the treadmill for 30 minutes, she told herself, "That was really good. I am on my way to a healthy body!" Tony completed a difficult assignment and then imagined himself lying on a beach in Hawaii, feeling completely relaxed and content.

The Premack Principle

The **Premack Principle,** which is named for its originator (Premack, 1959, 1965), applies to a specific kind of positive reinforcement contingency. The Premack Principle states that a response, R_1, occurring more frequently (with higher probability) than another response, R_2, can serve as a reinforcer for the R_2 response that occurs less frequently (with lower probability). In other words, the high-probability response, R_1, can increase the strength of the low-probability response, R_2. One accomplishes this by allowing R_1 to occur only after R_2 has been performed. R_1 is made contingent on performance of R_2.

For example, watching television is a high-probability behavior and raking leaves is a low-probability behavior. By arranging the contingency so that watching television is contingent on raking leaves, you can increase the probability that the leaves will be raked. If eating snacks is a high-probability behavior and reading journal articles is a low-probability behavior, you can increase your reading rate by making snacking contingent on reading a certain number of pages or for a certain amount of time. Any high-probability behavior can be used as a reinforcer, such as drinking a cup of coffee or taking a bathroom break. For example, Sal, a bill collector, made five telephone calls before he drank a cup of coffee. Allison completed the first draft of a press release before taking a bathroom break.

You can identify high-probability responses for yourself by monitoring and recording how you spend your free time. Your high-frequency responses are potential reinforcers for low-probability responses you wish to strengthen. For example, Jane frequently e-mailed her friends but rarely practiced the flute. According to the Premack Principle, e-mailing her friends could serve as a reinforcer for Jane's practicing the flute if e-mailing is made contingent on her practicing the flute. Lenora frequently invited her friends over for coffee in the morning, but she rarely gave her children breakfast. The Premack Principle indicates that inviting her friends over for coffee could act as a reinforcer for Lenora's making breakfast for the children, if inviting her friends is made contingent on her making breakfast. In these examples, using the Premack Principle increased the frequency of practicing the flute for Jane and Lenora's making breakfast for her children.

It is probable that the effectiveness of the Premack Principle is influenced by response deprivation. The high-probability behavior is prevented from occurring until after the low-probability behavior occurs, thereby creating a state of deprivation with regard to the high-probability behavior (Timberlake & Allison, 1974). Thus the high-probability behavior is likely to act as a reinforcer for the low-probability behavior.

Continuous and Intermittent Reinforcement

In the preceding chapters on positive reinforcement and extinction, we noted that the behavioral contingencies for increasing or decreasing a behavior specified that the positive reinforcer would be presented or withheld continuously—that is, each time the behavior occurred. According to these contingencies, the behavior was strengthened on a **continuous reinforcement (CRF) schedule** and weakened or extinguished on a continuous schedule of nonreinforcement. A **schedule of reinforcement** is a behavioral contingency that specifies how often and under what conditions reinforcement is delivered for a response.

In Chapter 2, we discussed the use of continuous reinforcement to increase the frequency of Donna's exercising her leg. After a response is well established, however, it is not always necessary to deliver a positive reinforcer each time the response occurs. The response can be maintained on a less than continuous schedule of reinforcement; this is called **intermittent reinforcement.**

It is advantageous to use continuous rather than intermittent reinforcement to establish a behavior or to strengthen one that occurs with low frequency. A continuous reinforcement schedule is used to establish the functional relationship between the response and the reinforcer. After the response is established and performed consistently, reinforcement can be shifted gradually from a CRF schedule to an intermittent reinforcement schedule. If intermittent reinforcement is applied after the response is established but before it is performed consistently, the response may extinguish. Intermittent reinforcement schedules are used to maintain responses that have been acquired and occur consistently.

Intermittent reinforcement has four advantages over continuous reinforcement:

- Fewer reinforcements are required to maintain the behavior, resulting in more efficient use of available reinforcers.
- A response maintained on an intermittent schedule of reinforcement is more resistant to extinction. **Resistance to extinction** refers to the number of responses performed during extinction of the response. A response maintained on an intermittent schedule of reinforcement will take longer to extinguish than a response maintained on a continuous schedule of reinforcement, as shown in Figure 4.3 (Skinner, 1948). The graphs in Figure 4.3 show that the response maintained on a CRF schedule is extinguished in 10 sessions, whereas the response maintained on an intermittent schedule of reinforcement is extinguished in 100 sessions.
- The reinforcer is effective for a longer time because satiation occurs gradually.
- Intermittent reinforcement more closely resembles reinforcement patterns that occur in the individual's environment. For example, we are not reinforced every time we go to a party or ask for a raise.

There are three types of intermittent reinforcement schedules: ratio, interval, and duration. Ratio schedules require a certain number of responses for reinforcement. Interval schedules require the performance of a response after a certain amount of time has passed for reinforcement. Duration schedules require that the response occurs continuously for a certain period of time for reinforcement. Each type of schedule can further be segmented into fixed and variable subtypes.

Ratio Schedules

Fixed-ratio (FR) schedules of reinforcement require a prescribed number of responses to be performed for a positive reinforcer to be presented. For example, in an FR 2 schedule, two responses are required before a positive reinforcer will be presented, and an FR 10 schedule requires that 10 responses be performed for reinforcement. A CRF schedule is the same as an FR 1 schedule, because the reinforcer is presented after each response.

The FR schedule typically generates high rates of responding with minimal hesitation between responses until the ratio is completed. For example, a worker with developmental disabilities at a sheltered workshop is paid on a piecework basis, $5.00 for every 10 boxes of batteries packed. An individual on this schedule typically performs at a high, consistent rate, taking little time off until the ratio is completed (packing 10 boxes, in this case). After reinforcement is obtained, the worker rests for a brief period. This brief period of rest is called a *postreinforcement pause*, which is a characteristic of

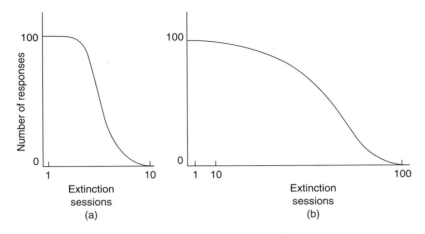

(a) Response maintained on a continuous reinforcement schedule.
(b) Response maintained on an intermittent reinforcement schedule.

Figure 4.3   Comparison of Resistance to Extinction Under Continuous and Intermittent Reinforcement

the FR schedule. The length of the postreinforcement pause increases with the size of the ratio; for example, an FR 20 schedule for a behavior will produce a longer postreinforcement pause than will an FR 5 schedule for that behavior.

When an FR schedule is used, the ratio, or number of responses required for reinforcement, should be increased gradually. If the response does not receive adequate reinforcement, it will extinguish. The more drastic the increase in the ratio, the more likely it is that the response will extinguish. For example, in teaching a child with Down syndrome to dress herself, the teacher initially gave the child a raisin each time the child pushed a button through the correct buttonhole on her shirt. This initial CRF schedule is the same as FR 1. The teacher, wanting to strengthen the buttoning response, increased the ratio to FR 2, then to FR 3, and then to FR 4. FR 4 required the child to button four buttons to receive the raisin. If the teacher had shifted from CRF immediately to FR 4, the child probably would not have buttoned four buttons, the reinforcer would not have been presented, and the response would have extinguished. Such a rapid shift from CRF to an FR that is too large to support the response is called **straining the ratio.** The same effect could have occurred had the teacher shifted from FR 2 to FR 8. The eight responses required on the latter reinforcement schedule could have been too many to maintain the response, and the response would have extinguished.

Variable-ratio (VR) schedules of reinforcement require a random number of responses to be performed for a positive reinforcer to be presented. Reinforcement is programmed for delivery on a schedule that varies around an average (mean) number of responses. The ratio is randomly varied so that the individual cannot predict the number of responses required from one reinforcement to the next. Thus the individual never knows which response will lead to presentation of the reinforcer; he or she knows only that any response could be followed by the reinforcer.

For example, on a VR 10 schedule, reinforcement will be presented after an average of 10 responses. This means that reinforcement can occur after 1 response, after 10 responses, or after 20 responses or more, as long as the average number of responses producing reinforcement is 10.

VR schedules, like FR schedules, generate high rates of responding with minimal hesitation between responses. The VR schedule generates the highest response rate because, unlike the FR schedule, there is no (or minimal) postreinforcement pause. Slot machines are programmed to deliver reinforcement on a VR schedule. Because gamblers never know exactly what ratio is required for reinforcement, they insert money and pull the machine handle or push the button at a high rate, with minimal hesitation between responses. Unfortunately for the gambler, the slot machine is programmed on a high VR schedule to take more of the gambler's money than it pays out.

Scheduling reinforcement. When teaching a new behavior, such as Todd's completing math problems, the best method involves beginning with a CRF schedule and then shifting to a small FR schedule—for example, FR 2—after a consistent rate of responding is established. The FR schedule is gradually increased to larger ratios, such as FR 3, FR 4, FR 6, and FR 9. After a consistent rate of responding is achieved with higher FR schedules, reinforcement can be shifted to a VR schedule, which more closely approximates the reinforcement usually available in the natural environment, such as the classroom or the home. Because VR schedules generate the highest response rates, new behavior can be strengthened effectively through the gradual shifting of the schedule of reinforcement in progression from CRF to FR to VR.

Interval Schedules

In **fixed-interval (FI) schedules,** reinforcement becomes available for the first response performed after the passage of a specified period of time. For example, in an FI 2-hour schedule, 2 hours must pass before a response can be reinforced. The FI schedule requires that not only must the time interval pass but also the response must be performed after this period of time has elapsed. If the reinforcement required only the passage of time, any behavior occurring at the end of the interval could be inadvertently reinforced.

Fixed-interval schedules generate response patterns with an initial low rate of responding and a terminal high rate of responding. This means that as the interval draws to an end, the frequency of responses increases. FI schedules also generate postreinforcement pauses.

Many behaviors in our daily schedules revolve around fixed intervals. For example, a train arrives at a station at precisely 7:00 p.m. every day as its last run of the day. Any response of looking for the train at the station prior to 7:00 p.m. is not reinforced; the train is not there. The response of looking for the train at 7:00 p.m. or later is reinforced by the presence of the train.

In another example, your response of shopping for shoes at a store that is open from 10:00 a.m. to 9:00 p.m. is reinforced only if you go to that store after 9:59 a.m.

and before 9:00 p.m. You are unlikely to go to that store at 6:00 a.m., more likely to go at 9:55 a.m., and most likely to go after 10:00 a.m. A greater number of responses occur after 9:59 a.m. than before. Once you have gone to the store and are reinforced by buying shoes, you will most likely not go to that store again (postreinforcement pause) until you want another pair of shoes. A similar behavior pattern can be found in situations involving deadlines. For example, if exams are scheduled for the end of the month, a student might exert little effort on studying during the first few days of that month and somewhat more near the middle of the month, but by the last few days before the exam the student's study behaviors would increase up to the day of the exam. In this case, the reinforcer is completion of the exam.

Limited hold. Interval schedules can also include a limited hold (LH). This refers to situations in which the reinforcer is made available for only a limited time after the interval has elapsed and the response has occurred. The fixed-interval example of shopping for shoes is really an FI 13-hour/LH 11-hour schedule. The interval of time between the closing of the store and the time it reopens is 13 hours, but a response will be reinforced only for the 11 hours the store is open. A subway operates on an FI 10-minute/LH 1-minute schedule, because the response of being on the platform when the subway train pulls in is reinforced but is only available for 1 minute before the subway pulls out.

Visiting hours at a correctional facility are from 1:00 p.m. to 3:00 p.m. A response of going there to visit an inmate before 1:00 p.m. or after 3:00 p.m. will not be reinforced. A response made after 1:00 p.m. and before 3:00 p.m. will be reinforced by a visit with the inmate. This is an FI 22-hour/LH 2-hour schedule.

In **variable-interval (VI) schedules,** the reinforcer is presented contingent on performance of a response after an average (mean) amount of time has passed. The interval is randomly varied around a given time value. Thus in a VI 4-minute schedule the reinforcer is made available for a response emitted after an average of 4 minutes has passed. The individual could be reinforced for making a response after 1 minute, after 10 minutes, or after 12 minutes or more, as long as the average amount of time that passed was 4 minutes. Again, remember that not only does the designated time period have to elapse but also the response must be performed for the reinforcer to be made available.

Variable-interval schedules typically generate consistent, moderate response rates with no (or minimal) postreinforcement pauses. Most waiting behavior appears similar to the response pattern generated by a VI schedule. For example, waiting for a taxi, looking out the window while waiting for the mail to arrive, checking for e-mail messages, and waiting for the transportation van to take a woman with developmental disabilities to work are governed by VI schedules because the amount of time one must wait for each reinforcement varies.

A school social worker used a VI schedule to strengthen task-oriented behavior in Carl, a second-grade student who frequently left his seat in class. Using a timer to signal the end of an interval, the practitioner varied the amount of time required for Carl to attend to a specific task, such as writing letters of the alphabet. When the timer signaled the end of the interval, Carl had to be attending to the task to receive a gold star and praise. For example, Carl was instructed to work on a puzzle. He was told that if he was working on the puzzle when the buzzer sounded, he would receive a gold star. A VI 3-minute schedule was used—that is, the practitioner varied the interval around an average of 3 minutes. Because Carl did not know exactly when the timer would signal availability of reinforcement, he worked at the task until the end of the interval. The schedule was increased to a VI 5-minute schedule and then gradually to longer intervals. The gradual, progressive shifting to larger VI schedules required Carl to work for increasingly longer periods of time and generated a stable rate of task-oriented behavior.

Duration Schedules

Duration schedules can be fixed or variable, as are ratio and interval schedules. **Fixed-duration (FD)** and **variable-duration (VD) schedules** are also referred to as fixed-time and variable-time schedules (e.g., Carr, Kellum, & Chong, 2001). In duration schedules, the individual receives reinforcement after the behavior has occurred continuously for a specified period of time. Using the previous example with Carl, a duration schedule could be implemented to address his out-of-seat behavior in the classroom. In a fixed-duration 3-minute schedule (FD 3 minutes), for example, Carl would receive a reinforcer only after he had remained seated for the entire 3 minutes. If he left his seat at any time during that 3-minute interval, reinforcement would be withheld. In a variable-duration 3-minute schedule (VD 3 minutes), Carl would receive reinforcement after remaining seated for an average (mean) of 3 minutes, although the amount of time he was required to sit on each occasion would vary.

Duration schedules, in contrast to interval schedules, develop continuous responding. In interval schedules individuals do not have to respond continuously to receive reinforcement; they only have to perform the behavior at the end of the interval. For example, Carl may be out of his seat numerous times during an FI or VI schedule, but as long as he is seated at the end of the interval, he is reinforced. In an FD or VD schedule, Carl must remain seated continuously during the time period specified in order to receive reinforcement. Use of duration schedules, however, requires the practitioner to monitor the behavior continuously. In a classroom this may not be as practical as using an interval schedule, which requires monitoring only at the end of the interval.

Katrina is physically abused by her husband and likely reinforced on a variable-duration schedule. Her behavior of staying with him over a long period of time is reinforced by his loving behaviors, such as kissing or caressing, which occur on a random schedule. Occasionally, he hits her, tells her she's fat, and threatens to kill her. The abusive behaviors are infrequent and are followed by more loving behaviors as he apologizes profusely for the abuse and brings her flowers and candy. This reinforcement schedule may explain Katrina's seemingly inexplicable behavior of staying with someone who is physically abusive. Katrina's staying with him doesn't stop the abusive behavior, but if she stays long enough the abusive behavior does stop (at least for a while). Of course, the longer she stays the more likely it is that he will hit her again, but then he will stop again, too. This is a difficult behavior pattern to analyze because the abusive behavior does not seem to be contingent on any specific behavior of Katrina's, except her staying, and the cessation of the abusive behavior also does not appear to be contingent on anything she does.

Duration schedules produce long periods of behavior, with variable-duration schedules producing higher rates of responding than fixed-duration schedules. FD schedules produce postreinforcement pauses, whereas VD schedules are not typically followed by postreinforcement pauses.

Matching Law

At any given time we can choose the behaviors we perform from a wide variety of available behaviors. For example, at work you might make fund-raising phone calls, answer e-mail messages, catch up on office news with coworkers, or begin writing a position paper, among many other options. Different reinforcement schedules, or *concurrent schedules,* operate for each behavior choice. This means that two or more reinforcement schedules operate at the same time, but independently, delivering reinforcers for different response alternatives. The behavior you choose to perform will be influenced by the reinforcement schedule in effect. This is known as the **matching law**. The matching law states that individuals will perform concurrently available responses according to the relative frequency of reinforcement for each response (Hernnstein, 1970). Other relevant factors in response choice include the immediacy of reinforcement, the magnitude of the reinforcer, and the response effort. Thus the behavior you choose to perform in the work example above will be the one that (a) generates the highest rate of reinforcement (chatting with coworkers provides the highest rate of social reinforcement), (b) is the most immediately reinforcing (answering e-mails is immediately reinforced by task completion, whereas writing a position paper may take many hours and several drafts), (c) has the highest magnitude of reinforcement (making fund-raising phone calls may have a bigger payoff than hearing about your coworker's recent vacation), or (d) requires the least response effort (it may be easier to answer an e-mail than to write a position paper).

The matching law is especially important to consider in situations where it is necessary to decrease the rate of severe behavior, such as self-injurious behavior. For example, a child with autism could engage in self-injurious behavior, watch TV, rock back and forth, or write on a worksheet. The behavior the child performs will be based on the reinforcement schedule in effect for the behavior options. The matching law indicates that the reinforcement schedule can be altered to maximize the likelihood of performance of the desired response (e.g., Borrero & Vollmer, 2002; Neef & Lutz, 2001). The desired behavior is more likely to be performed if it results in more reinforcers, delivers reinforcers more immediately, delivers the highest-quality reinforcers, and requires the behavior of least effort in order to receive the reinforcers. In a study with autistic children, Hoch, McComas, Thompson, and Paone (2002) found that problem behavior was eliminated and tasks were completed when task completion resulted in higher-quality reinforcement than did undesired behavior.

Characteristics of Various Schedules of Reinforcement

Table 4.1 lists the characteristics of the schedules of reinforcement discussed in this chapter. As we have discussed, a response established on a CRF schedule will extinguish faster than a response maintained on an intermittent reinforcement schedule. The variable types of intermittent reinforcement schedules produce behavior that is the most resistant to extinction. Table 4.2 provides examples of the intermittent reinforcement schedules discussed in this chapter.

In describing intermittent schedules of reinforcement, we have provided examples of their application to human behavior. In everyday life, many behaviors are maintained on multiple schedules. Further research is necessary to elaborate the ways in which reinforcement schedules can be applied in human service settings.

Table 4.1   Characteristics of Reinforcement Schedules

Schedule	Definition	Characteristics
Continuous reinforcement	Reinforcer is given each time a response is performed	Used to establish a response or to strengthen one that occurs with low frequency
Fixed ratio	Reinforcer is given after a specified number of responses	High response rate with minimal hesitation between responses until the ratio is completed; postreinforcement pause
Variable ratio	Reinforcer is given after a random number of responses that varies around a mean value	Highest response rate with minimal hesitation between responses; highly resistant to extinction
Fixed interval	Reinforcer is given for the first response performed after a specified amount of time has passed	Initial low rate of responding; terminal high rate of responding; postreinforcement pause; may include limited hold feature
Variable interval	Reinforcer is given for the first response performed after a random amount of time has passed that varies around a mean value	Consistent, moderate rate of responding; highly resistant to extinction
Fixed duration	Reinforcer is given for a response performed continuously for a specified amount of time	Moderate response rate; postreinforcement pause
Variable duration	Reinforcer is given for a response performed continuously for a random period of time that varies around a mean value	High response rate; highly resistant to extinction

Table 4.2   Examples of Intermittent Reinforcement Schedules

Fixed Ratio	Variable Ratio	Fixed Interval	Variable Interval	Fixed Duration	Variable Duration
Piecework	Slot machines	Studying for exams	Waiting for a taxi	Student remaining in seat for 50 minutes during class	Running a marathon
Solving 3 math problems to get a gold star	Salesperson talking to customers to sell a car	Feeding an infant every 3 hours	Checking for e-mail	Listening to a CD	Staying with an abusive spouse
Completing a 100-item exam	Asking for a date	Watching the sunset at Key West	Waiting for fish to bite	Watching a movie	Putting your foot on the brake to stop your car at a stop sign
Working a crossword puzzle	Casting for fish	Taking pills every 4 hours	Putting gas in the car	Practicing the piano for an hour	Attending a vacation time-share presentation
		Visiting hours at a hospital (LH)			Playing "Chopsticks" on the piano

Summary

1. A positive reinforcement contingency indicates that a behavior must be performed for a positive reinforcer to follow. Delivery of the positive reinforcer is made contingent on performance of the behavior.

2. Superstitious behavior is the result of an accidental reinforcement contingency. In an accidental reinforcement contingency, a positive reinforcer follows a response, but delivery of the positive reinforcer is not functionally related to performance of the response. The accidental reinforcer strengthens the response, however, and increases the likelihood that it will be performed again in similar circumstances.

3. In a self-control reinforcement contingency, the individual provides self-administered reinforcement contingent on the performance of a desired behavior. Self-control contingencies are preferable to accidental contingencies because the individual can arrange conditions so that the reinforcer

predictably follows the desired behavior. Self-reinforcement can be overt or covert.

4. The Premack Principle states that a high-probability behavior can serve as a reinforcer for a low-probability behavior. A behavior that occurs at a low rate, therefore, can be reinforced with a high-probability behavior.

5. A schedule of reinforcement is a behavioral contingency that specifies how often and under what conditions reinforcement is presented for a response.

6. The term *continuous reinforcement* refers to a schedule of reinforcement in which a positive reinforcer is delivered each time a response occurs. A continuous reinforcement (CRF) schedule is used to establish a response or to strengthen one that occurs with low frequency.

7. The term *intermittent reinforcement* refers to a schedule of reinforcement in which a positive reinforcer is delivered on a less than continuous schedule, such as for every other response. An intermittent reinforcement schedule is used to maintain a response after it has been established and is performed consistently.

8. Intermittent reinforcement has four advantages over continuous reinforcement: (a) Fewer reinforcements are required to maintain the response, so that more efficient use is made of available reinforcers; (b) the reinforcer is effective for a longer time because satiation occurs more gradually; (c) the response is more resistant to extinction; and (d) the reinforcement schedules more closely resemble those in the individual's environment.

9. There are three major types of intermittent reinforcement schedules: ratio, interval, and duration. Each type of schedule can be further segmented into fixed and variable subtypes.

10. The FR schedule requires that a certain number of responses be performed for the reinforcer to be presented. The FR schedule generates a high response rate with minimal hesitation between responses. A postreinforcement pause is characteristic of an FR schedule. The length of the postreinforcement pause varies with the size of the ratio, with higher ratios having longer pauses.

11. If an FR schedule is increased too rapidly, the response may extinguish— this is called *straining the ratio.* The more drastic the increase in ratio, the more likely it is that the response will extinguish.

12. In a VR schedule, reinforcement is presented after an average (mean) number of responses. The ratio is randomly varied around a given value. Variable-ratio schedules generate the highest response rates, with minimal hesitation between responses and no (or minimal) postreinforcement pauses.

13. An FI schedule requires that a response be performed after a specific period of time has elapsed in order for the reinforcer to be presented. Fixed-interval schedules generate a low initial rate of responding and a high terminal rate of responding. A postreinforcement pause follows delivery of the reinforcer.

14. In a VI schedule, a reinforcer is presented for the first response performed after the passage of a random amount of time that varies around a given value. Variable-interval schedules generate consistent, moderate response rates, with no (or minimal) postreinforcement pauses.

15. An additional feature of interval schedules is a limited hold (LH) option. LH indicates that the reinforcer is available for a limited amount of time after the response is performed.

16. In an FD schedule, a reinforcer is presented after a response is performed continuously for a specified period of time. FD schedules generate moderate response rates and produce postreinforcement pauses.

17. In a VD schedule, a reinforcer is presented after a response is performed continuously for a random period of time that varies around an average (mean). VD schedules generate high response rates and no (or minimal) postreinforcement pauses.

18. The variable (VR, VI, and VD) schedules are highly resistant to extinction.

19. The matching law states that individuals will perform concurrently available responses according to the relative frequency of reinforcement for each response. The reinforcement schedule can be altered to increase the likelihood of performance of a desired response over an undesired response.

Suggested Activities

1. Identify a high-probability behavior and a low-probability behavior for yourself. Design a Premack contingency in which you use the high-probability behavior as a reinforcer for the low-probability behavior. Share your observations with the class.

2. Give an example of a superstitious behavior of yours or someone you know. Explain the behavior in terms of an accidental reinforcement contingency. Identify the reinforcers that maintain the behavior.

3. Reread the example in this chapter headed "Monsters in the Closet" (p. 46). Identify the reinforcement schedules that we used to develop Jenny's sleeping through the night. What would you do if Jenny started coming to your bed again after you told her that she needed to sleep through the night for three nights in a row to get barrettes?

References and Resources

Borrero, J. C., & Vollmer, T. R. (2002). An application of the matching law to severe problem behavior. *Journal of Applied Behavior Analysis, 35,* 13–26.

Carr, J. E., Kellum, K. K., & Chong, I. M. (2001). The reductive effects of noncontingent reinforcement: Fixed-time versus variable-time schedules. *Journal of Applied Behavior Analysis, 34,* 505–509.

Evans, J. H., Ferre, L., Ford, L. A., & Green, J. L. (1995). Decreasing attention deficit hyperactivity disorder symptoms utilizing an automated classroom reinforcement device. *Psychology in the Schools, 32,* 210–219.

Ferster, C. B., & Skinner, B. F. (1957). *Schedules of reinforcement.* Englewood Cliffs, NJ: Prentice Hall.

Hall, R. V., & Hall, M. L. (1998). *How to negotiate a behavioral contract* (2nd ed.). Austin, TX: Pro-Ed.

Hayes, S. C., & Ju, W. (1998). The applied implications of rule-governed behavior. In W. O'Donohue (Ed.), *Learning and behavior therapy* (pp. 374–391). Boston: Allyn & Bacon.

Hernnstein, R. J. (1970). On the law of effect. *Journal of the Experimental Analysis of Behavior, 13,* 243–266.

Hoch, H., McComas, J. J., Thompson, A. L., & Paone, D. (2002). Concurrent reinforcement schedules: Behavior change and maintenance without extinction. *Journal of Applied Behavior Analysis, 35,* 155–169.

Homme, L. E., Csanyi, A. P., Gonzales, M. A., & Rechs, J. R. (1969). *How to use contingency contracting in the classroom.* Champaign, IL: Research Press.

Kelley, M. E., Lerman, D. C., & Van Camp, C. M. (2002). The effects of competing reinforcement schedules on the acquisition of functional communication. *Journal of Applied Behavior Analysis, 35,* 59–63.

Kohler, F. W., Strain, P. S., Hayson, M., Davis, L., Donina, W. M., & Rapp, N. (1995). Using a group-oriented contingency to increase social interaction between children with autism and their peers. *Behavior Modification, 19,* 10–32.

Neef, N. A., & Lutz, M. N. (2001). A brief computer-based assessment of reinforcer dimensions affecting choice. *Journal of Applied Behavior Analysis, 34,* 57–60.

Premack, D. (1959). Toward empirical behavioral laws: I. Positive reinforcement. *Psychological Review, 66,* 219–233.

Premack, D. (1965). Reinforcement theory. In D. Levin (Ed.), *Nebraska Symposium on Motivation: 1965* (pp. 123–180). Lincoln: University of Nebraska Press.

Semb, G., & Semb, S. (1975). A comparison of fixed-page and fixed-time reading assignments in elementary school children. In E. Ramp & G. Semb (Eds.), *Behavior analysis: Areas of research and application* (pp. 233–243). Englewood Cliffs, NJ: Prentice Hall.

Skinner, B. F. (1948). Superstition and the pigeon. *Journal of Experimental Psychology, 38,* 168–172.

Skinner, B. F. (1953). Self-control. In B. F. Skinner, *Science and human behavior* (pp. 227–241). New York: Free Press.

Skinner, B. F. (1961). *Cumulative record* (Enlarged ed.). New York: Appleton-Century-Crofts.

Skinner, B. F. (1966). Contingencies of reinforcement in the design of a culture. *Behavioral Science, 2,* 159–166.

Timberlake, W., & Allison, J. (1974). Deprivation: An empirical approach to instrumental performance. *Psychological Review, 81,* 146–164.

Van Camp, C. M., Lerman, D. C., Kelley, M. E., Contrucci, S. A., & Vorndran, C. M. (2000). Variable-time reinforcement schedules in the treatment of socially maintained aberrant behavior. *Journal of Applied Behavior Analysis, 33,* 545–556.

Watson, D. L., & Tharp, R. G. (1997). *Self-directed behavior: Self-modification for personal adjustment* (6th ed.). Pacific Grove, CA: Brooks/Cole.

CHAPTER 5

Shaping and Response Differentiation

When Joe tries to talk with his stepfather about problems at school, his stepfather turns on the television and looks away from Joe. When Joe talks about sports, however, his stepfather looks at him, nods his head, and discusses the topic with him. Joe and his stepfather often have conversations about sports but rarely discuss the problems Joe is having at school.

Objectives

After completing this chapter, you should be able to do the following:

- Define a response class and give an example.
- Give an example of response differentiation.
- Describe how the DRO procedure can be used to decrease the rate of a response.
- Identify the steps involved in the procedure of shaping a behavior with successive approximations.

Differential Reinforcement

In Chapter 2, we defined operant behavior as behavior that is controlled by its consequences. The individual *operates* or acts on the environment to produce those consequences. The positive reinforcement procedure is used to increase the strength of an operant response. The extinction procedure is used to weaken or decrease the strength of an operant response. **Differential reinforcement** involves the use of both positive reinforcement and extinction. In this procedure, one response is reinforced while reinforcement is withheld from other responses. When the reinforced response occurs frequently, to the exclusion of responses from which reinforcement is withheld, we say that the response has become *differentiated.*

For example, when Joe tries to talk to his stepfather about his problems at school or topics other than sports, his stepfather turns on the television and looks away from Joe. When Joe talks about sports, however, his stepfather looks at him, nods his head, and discusses the topic with him. Thus responses related to Joe's talking about sports are positively reinforced with attention, whereas those related to talking about problems at school are extinguished (see Figure 5.1a). It should not be surprising to learn that Joe's conversations with his stepfather are almost exclusively about sports. Responses related to talking about sports have become differentiated—that is, they occur with greater frequency than verbal responses dealing with other topics.

Differential reinforcement produces the highly skilled responses of artists, musicians, public speakers, and professional athletes. Desired responses are selectively reinforced and strengthened; reinforcement is withheld from undesired responses, and they are weakened or extinguished. For example, compare the refined forehand stroke of a table tennis champion with that of a novice or the bowing technique of a concert violinist with that of a beginner. In both cases, the skilled responses of the experts have become highly differentiated or refined through selective reinforcement of an increasingly narrow range of desired responses. Similarly, through training, supervision, and experience, the novice practitioner becomes more skillful in interviewing clients and helping them solve problems.

Response Class

Variability is a basic feature of operant behavior because a behavior is rarely repeated in exactly the same form. When a response is performed and followed by a reinforcer, it becomes more likely that the response will be performed again. The reinforcer also increases the strength or likelihood of occurrence of other responses that have the same or similar effect on the environment as the reinforced response. Thus not only is a single response reinforced but also a class or group of responses is reinforced. This group of responses—each member or response producing the same or similar effect on its environment (e.g., reinforcement)—is called a **response class** (Skinner, 1953).

One member of a response class can have a different *topography,* or form, from other members of the response class. For example, a variety of responses can be effective in getting food from your plate into your mouth. You can raise the plate to your face and let the food slide into your mouth, you can use your hands to put food in your mouth, you can throw a piece of food into the air and catch it in your mouth, or you can use a fork to put the food in your mouth. All these different responses are members of the same response class—getting food from your plate into your mouth. Although the topography of the responses differs, they are functionally equivalent because they all result in food getting from your plate into your mouth. Some of the responses, however, could be target responses in a behavior change program to teach appropriate eating skills. You would not want to reinforce all members of the response class; rather, you would want to reinforce only those with the topography of the desired responses—that is, using a fork to move food from the plate into the mouth. Thus using a fork becomes the differentiated response for eating food from a plate.

In Joe's case, the response class that his stepfather consistently reinforces is "talking about sports." The responses associated with talking about sports are more likely to be performed because whenever one member of the response class is performed and reinforced, all other members are also reinforced. For example, there are many responses Joe could make that would be members of the reinforced response class, talking about sports. He could talk about any sport, individual athletes, last night's basketball game, or a famous baseball player. Talking about any one of these subjects with his stepfather could increase the likelihood of occurrence of any of the others (see Figure 5.1b).

Differential reinforcement can be applied to narrow the range of reinforced responses within a response class. For example, if Joe's stepfather were to positively reinforce him for talking about baseball and withhold reinforcement from other sports topics, soon Joe and his stepfather would talk only about baseball, to the exclusion of other sports (see Figure 5.1c). There are many responses involved in talking about baseball, however, and when any one of these responses is reinforced, it becomes more likely that every other member of that response class will be performed. For example, when Joe talks to his stepfather about the Florida Marlins and is reinforced, all responses included as members of the "baseball talk" response class are strengthened (see Figure 5.1d).

Figure 5.1 is a set of diagrams of the differential reinforcement procedure depicting Joe's responses. From the diagrams, you can see how an increasingly narrow range of responses becomes differentiated. The diagrams also demonstrate that the words *response* and *behavior* refer to a class of responses or behaviors rather than to one discrete response or behavior. Similarly, one member of a response class represents a subclass of responses and not a single, discrete response.

The diagram in Figure 5.1a represents the differential reinforcement of talking about sports instead of school problems. When Joe talks about sports (R_1), his stepfather pays attention. When Joe talks about school problems (R_2), his talking is extinguished by his stepfather's withholding of attention. The effect of this differential reinforcement procedure—positive reinforcement for talking about sports and extinction for talking about problems—is **response differentiation,** an increased likelihood of Joe's talking about sports rather than talking about his problems.

Figure 5.1b shows that all members of the response class "talking about sports" are reinforced. Joe's talking about any sports topic is reinforced by attention from his stepfather.

Figure 5.1c shows the further differentiation of talking about baseball over all other sports topics. When Joe talks about baseball, his stepfather pays attention. When Joe talks about football, hockey, or any other sport, his stepfather withholds attention. The effect of this differential reinforcement procedure (positive reinforcement for talking about baseball and extinction for talking about any other

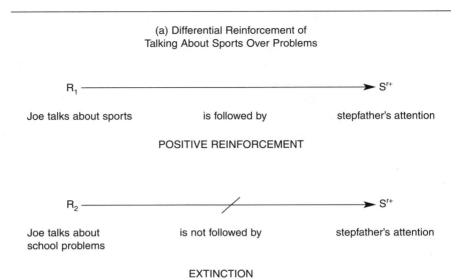

(a) Differential Reinforcement of
Talking About Sports Over Problems

R_1 —————————————————————→ S^{r+}

Joe talks about sports   is followed by   stepfather's attention

POSITIVE REINFORCEMENT

R_2 —————————————/—————————→ S^{r+}

Joe talks about   is not followed by   stepfather's attention
school problems

EXTINCTION

Effect: Joe's talking about sports with his stepfather is reinforced; Joe's talking about problems with his stepfather is extinguished. Response differentiation of sports topics.

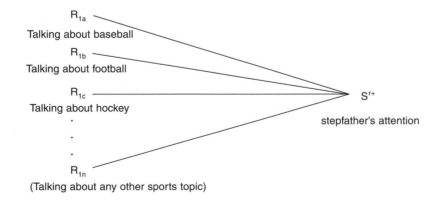

(b) Members of Response Class R_1
Talking About Sports That Produce Reinforcement

R_{1a}
Talking about baseball

R_{1b}
Talking about football

R_{1c} S^{r+}
Talking about hockey
.   stepfather's attention
.
.
R_{1n}
(Talking about any other sports topic)

(Continued)

Figure 5.1   Diagrams of Differential Reinforcement of Joe's Responses

Figure 5.1 (Continued)

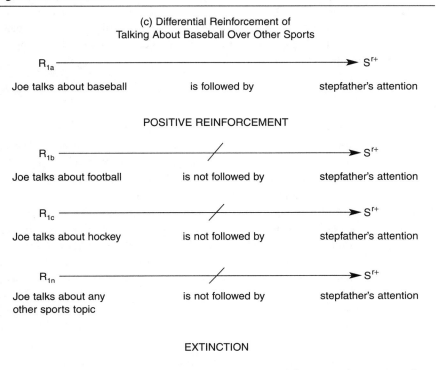

(c) Differential Reinforcement of
Talking About Baseball Over Other Sports

R_{1a} ⟶ S^{r+}

Joe talks about baseball   is followed by   stepfather's attention

POSITIVE REINFORCEMENT

R_{1b} ⟶ S^{r+}

Joe talks about football   is not followed by   stepfather's attention

R_{1c} ⟶ S^{r+}

Joe talks about hockey   is not followed by   stepfather's attention

R_{1n} ⟶ S^{r+}

Joe talks about any   is not followed by   stepfather's attention
other sports topic

EXTINCTION

Effect: Joe's talking about baseball is strengthened; talking about any other sports topic is extinguished. Response differentiation of baseball topics.

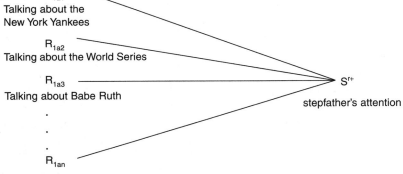
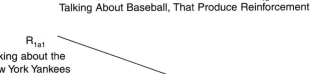

(d) Members of Response Class R_{1a},
Talking About Baseball, That Produce Reinforcement

R_{1a1}
Talking about the
New York Yankees

R_{1a2}
Talking about the World Series

R_{1a3} ⟶ S^{r+}
Talking about Babe Ruth

.
.
.

R_{1an} stepfather's attention

(Talking about any baseball topic)

Effect: All baseball topics are strengthened.

sport) is response differentiation—an increase in Joe's talking about baseball compared with talking about other sports.

Figure 5.1d shows that all members of the response class "talking about baseball" are reinforced. Joe's talking about any topic having to do with baseball is strengthened by attention from his stepfather.

The DRO Procedure

Differential reinforcement can be used to decrease the frequency of an undesired behavior by reinforcing behaviors *other than* the undesired behavior. Using the **DRO** (**d**ifferential **r**einforcement of **o**ther) procedure, the undesired behavior is extinguished and desired behaviors are positively reinforced. In Case Example 3 (p. 268), the social worker told Juanita, Carla's mother, to reinforce Carla when she put her toys away. The worker also could have instructed Juanita to reinforce *any* behavior Carla performed *other than* screaming. In applying the DRO procedure, reinforcement is withheld for undesired behaviors to decrease them. At the same time, any response other than the undesired response is reinforced and thereby strengthened.

Allen and Harris (1966) have reported on a case in which DRO was used to decrease the frequency of a child's self-injurious scratching. When the child engaged in any behavior other than scratching, her mother praised her and gave her gold stars and tangible reinforcers. In a case involving sibling conflict, the children were reinforced with pennies and parental praise after each 1-minute interval during which no conflict (e.g., hitting or name-calling) occurred (Leitenberg, Burchard, Burchard, Fuller, & Lysaght, 1977). In these cases, reinforcement was given contingent on any behavior other than the undesired behaviors of scratching or physical and verbal attacks. The DRO procedure reduced the child's scratching and the sibling conflict. Pleasant interactions also increased in both studies.

In some cases, the other behaviors that DRO might reinforce could be undesired. In the use of DRO to reduce sibling conflict, for example, any behavior other than physical and verbal attacks between siblings would be reinforced. That "other" behavior might also be undesired, however, such as throwing toys at other children, dumping clay and paint on the furniture, or lying on the floor and screaming and kicking. To avoid this, practitioners must specify the incompatible behaviors to be reinforced; this is called **DRI** (**d**ifferential **r**einforcement of **i**ncompatible) behavior. An incompatible behavior is one that cannot be performed simultaneously with the target response. For example, sitting in a chair is incompatible with standing up, putting your hands on your hips is incompatible with touching another person, talking quietly is incompatible with screaming, and playing cooperatively with a toy truck is incompatible with hitting. Other responses incompatible with hitting are working together with others on an art project or cleaning up the yard. An incompatible response interferes with the target response.

In Case Example 3 (p. 268), Juanita could have used DRI to decrease Carla's screaming. She could have positively reinforced Carla's behaviors that were incompatible with screaming, such as reading or playing quietly with her dolls, asking her mother for help, talking about where the toys should go, and quietly picking up the toys. Other reinforcement schedules involving differential reinforcement include differential reinforcement of high rates of behavior (DRH), differential reinforcement of low rates of behavior (DRL), and differential reinforcement of alternative behavior (**DRA**) (e.g., Catania, 1992; Vollmer & Iwata, 1992).

Currently, a changing philosophy about using aversive stimuli to reduce undesired behaviors focuses on reinforcement techniques to develop appropriate behaviors (e.g., Beare, Severson, & Brandt, 2004). Commonly used reinforcement techniques have included DRO and DRA. As an alternative to aversive techniques, functional analysis has also been used to identify reinforcers (e.g., attention) maintaining self-injurious or other dangerous behaviors (see Chapter 13). Reinforcement contingencies are then modified to develop alternative behaviors without using aversive stimuli (e.g., Kurtz et al., 2003).

Functional communication training (FCT) is a DRA procedure in which a client is taught to obtain a reinforcer by performing a desired behavior instead of the undesired behavior that produced that reinforcer (e.g., Wacker et al., 1998). For example, John stamps his feet on the floor to get his teacher's attention. An FCT procedure would teach John to perform an alternative behavior, such as raising his hand or holding up a picture card, to get his teacher's attention.

Shaping With Successive Approximations

Differential reinforcement, as previously discussed, is a technique for increasing the strength of selected responses that are members of a response class. To develop a response that differs significantly from members of an existing response class, we can use the procedure of **shaping with successive approximations.** The shaping procedure involves the use of differential reinforcement to strengthen members of one response class. After these responses are performed consistently, the criterion for reinforcement is shifted to another response class that more closely approximates the target response to be developed. This procedure is repeated until responses are performed and reinforced in a response class that includes the target response.

Shaping with successive approximations is a procedure used to develop a new behavior or one that rarely occurs. A shaping procedure was used as one part of a treatment program to reinstate speech in Justin, a 10-year-old boy who stopped speaking after witnessing his mother's death in a car accident. At first, Justin was reinforced with candy and praise for any speech sound he made. After he consistently made speech sounds, the criterion for reinforcement was shifted to speaking words. After Justin consistently spoke words, the criterion for reinforcement was shifted from words to phrases. In this way, Justin's speech was shaped using successive approximations until he spoke in complete sentences.

In shaping with successive approximations, a series of initial and intermediate behaviors are established in successive approximations to the desired target behavior. The initial response that is reinforced bears some resemblance to the target behavior (e.g., speech sounds and speaking in sentences) so that the intermediate responses can be progressively shaped toward the target behavior. To shape a behavior, the practitioner takes the following steps:

1. Specify the target response (desired behavior).

2. Specify the positive reinforcer(s) to be used.

3. Specify initial and intermediate responses.

4. Reinforce the initial response each time it occurs and withhold reinforcement from other responses until the initial response is performed consistently.

5. Shift the criterion for reinforcement from the initial response to an intermediate response.

6. Reinforce the intermediate response until it is performed consistently, then shift the criterion for reinforcement gradually to other intermediate responses that are increasingly similar to the target response.

7. Reinforce the target response when it is performed.

Justin's therapist used shaping with successive approximations to reinstate Justin's speech as follows:

1. The target behavior was for Justin to speak in sentences in response to questions the therapist asked.

2. The positive reinforcers given to Justin were candy and verbal praise from the therapist.

3. The initial response criterion included any speech sound. Intermediate responses included words and phrases that Justin spoke in response to questions the therapist asked.

4. Initially, any speech sound Justin made was reinforced.

5. When Justin made speech sounds consistently, the criterion for reinforcement was shifted to words. Justin was required to speak words before receiving the candy and praise.

6. When Justin was speaking words consistently, the criterion for reinforcement was shifted to another intermediate response class, phrases, which was the next approximation to the target behavior. Speaking in phrases was reinforced until Justin spoke in phrases. The criterion for reinforcement was then shifted to speaking in sentences.

7. Justin was reinforced for speaking in sentences in response to questions the therapist asked. At that point, Justin's speaking was reinforced by many people in his environment and further treatment could proceed.

A therapist employed shaping with successive approximations to teach Barbara, a teenager with muscular dystrophy, to walk with crutches instead of using a wheelchair. Although Barbara could be more independent and active on crutches, she initially refused to use them, preferring to rely on her mother or sisters to push her wheelchair. The therapist used the following steps to shape Barbara's use of crutches:

1. The target response was walking 50 steps on crutches.

2. The positive reinforcer was praise (e.g., "good," "very good," and "that's it!").

3. The initial response was movement toward the crutches, which were placed within Barbara's reach. Intermediate responses included touching the crutches with her hand, holding the crutches in her hand, using the crutches to raise herself from the wheelchair, standing up with the crutches properly positioned, and taking from 1 to 49 steps on the crutches.

4. Initially, when Barbara made any movement toward the crutches, she was reinforced with praise.

5. When Barbara reached toward the crutches each time they were placed within her reach, the criterion for reinforcement was shifted to the next intermediate response, touching the crutches.

6. Touching the crutches was reinforced until the touching responses were performed consistently. This procedure of reinforcing one response until it was performed consistently, and then shifting the criterion for reinforcement to the next intermediate response, continued until the target behavior, walking on the crutches, was performed and reinforced.

7. Barbara was reinforced for walking 50 steps on the crutches.

Shaping with successive approximations involves a gradual process in which a response must be developed at one level before reinforcement is shifted to the next level of approximation. After a desired response is performed, it is reinforced immediately to ensure that reinforcement is given only for appropriate responses. If the criterion for reinforcement is shifted too quickly to the next level, or if insufficient reinforcement is given, the response could extinguish. If a response receives too much reinforcement, however, it can become fixated at that level so that it is difficult to develop the next intermediate response. The shaping procedure relies on reinforcing responses that the individual is currently performing and gradually shifting the criterion for reinforcement to intermediate responses until the target response is performed.

Instructions and prompting are often used with shaping to facilitate the acquisition of new behaviors. Although shaping alone is useful with individuals who do not follow instructions, the shaping procedure becomes more effective when instructions or prompts are given at each step (see Chapter 6). Physical guidance can be used, where appropriate, to facilitate shaping. Demonstrations of the target behavior by a model can also be used to promote rapid development of desired behaviors (see Chapter 8).

Shaping with successive approximations can also include the use of punishers (see Chapter 9), as occurs in the children's game of "hot and cold." In this game, an object is hidden from a child who has left the room. When the child returns, he or she must find the object with the help of only two types of feedback from the rest of the group: When the child moves closer to the hidden object, the group says "hot" (positive reinforcer), and when the child moves away from the hidden object, the group says "cold" (punisher). The group uses "hot" to increase or strengthen responses toward the hidden object and "cold" to decrease or weaken responses away from the object. The child performs responses that result in the others saying "hot" and stops performing responses that are followed by their saying "cold." Thus "hot" serves as a positive reinforcer for performing responses that lead to the hidden object, whereas inappropriate responses are weakened by "cold."

Summary

1. Differential reinforcement involves the use of both positive reinforcement and extinction. One response is positively reinforced and increases in strength or likelihood of occurrence, whereas other responses are extinguished and decrease in strength or likelihood of occurrence.

2. Response differentiation is the result of differential reinforcement that involves selective positive reinforcement of certain responses and extinction of others. The reinforced responses become differentiated—that is, they are performed frequently to the exclusion of the extinguished responses.

3. The words *response* and *behavior* actually refer to a class of responses rather than a single response. When one member of a response class is reinforced, all responses in that class are also strengthened. Therefore, one member of a response class represents a subclass of responses rather than a single, discrete response.

4. The DRO procedure can be used to decrease undesired behaviors by reinforcing any behaviors other than the undesired one.

5. Differential reinforcement of incompatible behavior (DRI) is used when a behavior that interferes with the target behavior is specified to receive reinforcement, thereby reducing the likelihood that the undesired behavior will be performed.

6. Shaping with successive approximations is a procedure for establishing a new behavior or one that rarely occurs.

7. Shaping with successive approximations involves using differential reinforcement to strengthen members of one response class and then shifting the criterion for reinforcement to other response classes until the desired target behavior is performed. Intermediate behaviors are reinforced and developed as successive approximations to the desired behavior.

8. Instructions, prompting, modeling, and the use of punishers can also be used with differential reinforcement to develop new behaviors.

Suggested Activities

1. With one class member who has volunteered to be a subject out of the room, identify a behavior to shape in that person without using any verbal instructions. When the subject returns to the room, another student who has volunteered to be the shaper uses a toy clicker, a whistle, or hand clapping as a reinforcer to shape the subject's behavior. The rest of the class should remain silent and refrain from providing any cues to the subject. The only instruction the subject should receive is that whenever he or she hears the clicker, the whistle, or the clapping, he or she should imagine receiving a wonderful reinforcer.

   How long did it take to shape the correct response? Was the correct response performed and reinforced? Repeat this exercise a few more times with different shapers and subjects. Discuss your observations regarding the factors that facilitated or hampered successful shaping and the experience of being a subject or shaper.

2. Pair up with another class member and silently select a class of verbal responses (e.g., about food, clothing, cars, travel) that you will differentially reinforce in your partner using attention and conversation. Use differential reinforcement to narrow your partner's conversation so that he or she talks only about the class of responses you have identified. When both partners have had a turn at this exercise, discuss your observations regarding what seemed to work best in achieving the desired behaviors.

References and Resources

Allen, K. E., & Harris, F. R. (1966). Elimination of a child's excessive scratching by training the mother in reinforcement procedures. *Behaviour Research and Therapy, 4,* 79–84.

Ayllon, T., & Azrin, N. H. (1965). The measurement and reinforcement of behavior of psychotics. *Journal of the Experimental Analysis of Behavior, 8,* 357–383.

Beare, P. L., Severson, S., & Brandt, P. (2004). The use of a positive procedure to increase engagement on-task and decrease challenging behavior. *Behavior Modification, 28,* 28–44.

Catania, A. C. (1992). *Learning* (3rd ed.). Englewood Cliffs, NJ: Prentice Hall.

Ferster, C. B. (1953). The use of the free operant in the analysis of behavior. *Psychological Bulletin, 50,* 263–274.

Fournier, A. K., Ehrhart, I. J., Glindemann, K. E., & Geller, E. S. (2004). Intervening to decrease alcohol abuse at university parties: Differential reinforcement of intoxication level. *Behavior Modification, 28,* 167–181.

Isaacs, W., Thomas, J., & Goldiamond, I. (1960). Application of operant conditioning to reinstate verbal behavior in psychotics. *Journal of Speech and Hearing Disorders, 25,* 8–12.

Kurtz, P. F., Chin, M. D., Huete, J. M., Tarbox, S. F., O'Connor, J. T., Paclawskyj, T. R., et al. (2003). Functional analysis and treatment of self-injurious behavior in young children: A summary of 30 cases. *Journal of Applied Behavior Analysis, 36,* 205–219.

Leitenberg, H., Burchard, J. D., Burchard, S. N., Fuller, E. J., & Lysaght, T. V. (1977). Using positive reinforcement to suppress behavior: Some experimental comparisons with sibling conflict. *Behavior Therapy, 8,* 168–182.

Lennox, D. B., Miltenberger, R. G., & Donnelly, D. R. (1987). Response interruption and DRL for the reduction of rapid eating. *Journal of Applied Behavior Analysis, 20,* 279–284.

Poling, A., & Ryan, C. (1982). Differential-reinforcement-of-other-behavior schedules. *Behavior Modification, 6,* 3–21.

Rehfeldt, R. A., & Chambers, M. R. (2003). Functional analysis and treatment of verbal perseverations displayed by an adult with autism. *Journal of Applied Behavior Analysis, 36,* 259–261.

Skinner, B. F. (1953). Shaping and maintaining operant behavior. In B. F. Skinner, *Science and human behavior* (pp. 91–106). New York: Free Press.

Thompson, R. H., Iwata, B. A., Hanley, G. P., Dozier, C. L., & Samaha, A. L. (2003). The effects of extinction, noncontingent reinforcement, and differential reinforcement of other behavior as control procedures. *Journal of Applied Behavior Analysis, 36,* 221–238.

Vollmer, T. R., & Iwata, B. A. (1992). Differential reinforcement as treatment for behavior disorders: Procedural and functional variations. *Research in Developmental Disabilities, 13,* 393–417.

Wacker, D. P., Berg, W. K., Harding, J. W., Derby, M. K., Asmus, J. M., & Healy, A. (1998). Evaluation and long-term treatment of aberrant behavior displayed by young children with disabilities. *Journal of Developmental and Behavioral Pediatrics, 19,* 260–265.

Wagman, J. R., Miltenberger, R. G., & Williams, D. E. (1995). Treatment of a vocal tic by differential reinforcement. *Journal of Behavior Therapy and Experimental Psychiatry, 26,* 35–39.

CHAPTER 6

Stimulus Control

Discrimination and Generalization

The marriage counselor determined that Pat and her husband, Dick, had frequent arguments and rarely discussed topics of mutual interest. To initiate changes in the focus of their interaction from complaints and arguments to more pleasant conversation, the counselor instructed Pat to make a list of topics to discuss with her husband (List A). These topics included his work, the two children, and camping. Pat made a second list of topics that she should not discuss with her husband (List B). Topics on List B included complaints about such things as his staying out late at night, watching television at his friends' homes, not taking her shopping or to the movies, and not spending time with his family.

A role play was set up to help Pat practice talking about topics on List A and avoid talking about List B topics. When Pat talked about topics from List A, the counselor responded with attention and praise. When Pat talked about topics on List B, the counselor looked away and was silent. Pat's talking about topics on List A increased in frequency, whereas her talking about topics on List B decreased in frequency.

Objectives

After completing this chapter, you should be able to do the following:

- Describe the use of reinforcement and extinction in discrimination training.
- Describe a procedure for establishing a discrimination using two antecedent stimuli, one response, and a reinforcer.

- Specify two criteria for achievement of stimulus control.
- Give an example of stimulus generalization.

Antecedents

In the preceding chapters we have focused on relationships between operant behaviors and their consequences. We have shown that the presentation of a reinforcer after a response increases the likelihood that the response will be performed again under similar conditions. Similarly, withholding the reinforcer for a response decreases the likelihood that the response will be performed again. We have demonstrated that by changing the schedule of reinforcement, we can influence the rate and pattern of a response. We have described how a practitioner can refine a behavior by using differential reinforcement and shape a new response by shifting the criterion for reinforcement in successive approximations to the target behavior. Undesired behaviors can be weakened through the use of DRO and DRI procedures.

In summary, we have shown how consequences can be applied (a) to establish a new behavior by shaping with successive approximations; (b) to increase the strength of a behavior through positive reinforcement; (c) to decrease the strength of a behavior through extinction, DRO, and DRI; (d) to selectively increase one response class while extinguishing others through differential reinforcement; and (e) to maintain a behavior at a certain rate or pattern through the employment of a particular reinforcement schedule.

In this chapter, we focus on antecedents and their effects on behavior. **Antecedents** are stimuli that precede or accompany responses and that can influence their performance. It is necessary to consider both the antecedents and the consequences of a target behavior to determine its controlling conditions. The inclusion of antecedents allows the practitioner to consider important aspects of the client's total environment and to choose from a wider range of procedures for changing behavior than would be possible if only consequences were examined.

CASE EXAMPLE 5

Stimulus Control of Marital Interaction

Pat consulted a marriage counselor about her marital difficulties. Her husband, Dick, refused to see the counselor with her. Pat complained that Dick spent his evenings in front of the television, ignoring her and their children. They rarely went to the movies or to other entertainment, and Pat did all the food shopping by herself. She had stopped making Dick's breakfast as a result of their frequent arguments before he left for work.

Pat screamed at Dick for going out with his friends, for refusing to help around the house, and for spending little time with her and their children. Dick responded to her criticism by swearing at her and telling her to mind her own business. Pat became so upset during these arguments that she burst into tears, ran into the bedroom, and locked the door, remaining there until Dick left the house. The baseline rate of these episodes was three times per week.

In her interviews with Pat, the marriage counselor determined that Pat and Dick rarely discussed topics of mutual interest; Pat stated that pleasant conversations occurred about once per week. Their conversations revolved around Pat's complaints and Dick's responses to them. Pat said that she loved her husband and would like to have more satisfying conversations with him. She also wanted their arguments to stop and for him to participate in more activities with her and their children.

In her assessment, the marriage counselor determined that Dick refused to participate in treatment. The counselor pointed out to Pat that the goal of treatment with Pat alone participating could not directly focus on changing Dick's behaviors. Treatment could focus, however, on changing Pat's behaviors to influence Dick's undesired behaviors.

To change the focus of the couple's interactions from complaints and arguments to more pleasant conversation, the counselor instructed Pat to make a list of topics to discuss with Dick (List A). These topics included his work, their two children, and camping. Pat made a second list of topics to be avoided (List B), which included complaints about Dick's staying out late at night, watching television at his friends' homes, not taking Pat shopping or to the movies, and not spending time with his family. The counselor also instructed Pat to greet Dick with a kiss when he came home from work and to ask how his day had gone. This strategy was designed to allow Pat to take the initiative in changing her behavior, with the understanding that the intervention plan could produce the results she wanted in her marriage.

To help Pat focus on topics from List A and reduce the frequency of her talking about topics from List B, role plays were performed in the counselor's office. The counselor told Pat that this procedure would include reinforcement for talking about topics on List A and extinction for talking about topics on List B so that Pat would be more likely to talk with Dick about topics on List A.

In the role plays, when Pat talked about topics from List A, the counselor praised her and engaged in conversation with her. When Pat talked about topics from List B, the counselor looked away and was silent (withheld reinforcement). Pat began talking about topics on List A more frequently, and her talking about topics on List B decreased in frequency. Pat was then assigned to perform the desired behaviors at home with Dick.

Pat began talking about topics on List A at home with Dick and avoided talking about topics on List B. She found that their conversations were more pleasant and that Dick started paying more attention to her. Gradually, Pat suggested activities to Dick that they could do together or with the children, such as go to a movie or out to dinner, and Dick usually agreed. As their time together became more pleasant, Pat reported that their unpleasant arguments decreased, Dick was helping out with shopping and other household tasks, and he was spending more time with her and their children.

The Discrimination Training Procedure

Discriminative stimuli are antecedents that exert control over the performance of a response. There are two kinds of discriminative stimuli: the S^D (pronounced **ess-dee**) and the S^Δ (**ess-delta**). A response made in the presence of an S^D is followed by reinforcement. The S^D signals or *sets the occasion* for a response to be reinforced. If the response is performed in the presence of S^D, reinforcement will follow and increase the strength of the response to the S^D. The S^Δ signals that a response made in its presence will not be followed by reinforcement. A response performed in the presence of S^Δ is not followed by reinforcement and, therefore, the response decreases in strength.

In **discrimination training,** a response is reinforced in the presence of S^D and extinguished in the presence of S^Δ. The S^D and S^Δ are presented in alternating order until a discrimination is formed between the two stimuli. The reinforced response is referred to as a *discriminated response.* The response must initially be performed under both the reinforced S^D condition and the unreinforced S^Δ condition so that the discrimination between responding in S^D and S^Δ can be formed. In diagram form, the discrimination training procedure appears as follows:

Discrimination Training Diagram With Two Stimuli and One Response

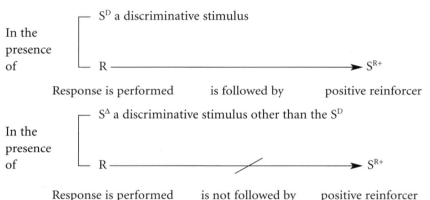

Effect: The rate of the response performed in the presence of S^D increases; the rate of the response performed in the presence of S^Δ decreases.

For example, a telephone ringing serves as the S^D for the response of answering it (picking up the receiver and saying "Hello"), which is followed by the reinforcer of a reply. If the telephone does not ring (S^Δ) and you lift the receiver and say "Hello," no reinforcer will be delivered—that is, no one will reply. Thus picking up the telephone receiver and saying "Hello" when the telephone rings occurs with high frequency, whereas picking up the receiver and saying "Hello" when it does not ring occurs with low frequency. Keys provide another example. Your door key is the S^D for unlocking the front door to your house, and your car key is the S^Δ for unlocking the front door to your house. Alternatively, your car key is the S^D for unlocking your car, and your door key is the S^Δ for unlocking your car. In both cases, reinforcement is provided for using the correct key and is withheld for using the wrong key.

In Case Example 5 (p. 76), List A was the S^D for Pat to talk about topics on that list with the marriage counselor. When Pat spoke with the counselor about the topics on List A, she received positive reinforcement in the form of attention and praise from the counselor. List B was the S^Δ. When Pat spoke about the topics on List B, the counselor looked away and withheld positive reinforcement. Pat's speaking about the topics on List B was extinguished. Her speaking about List A topics increased in frequency, whereas her speaking about List B topics decreased.

In diagram form, the marital example appears as follows:

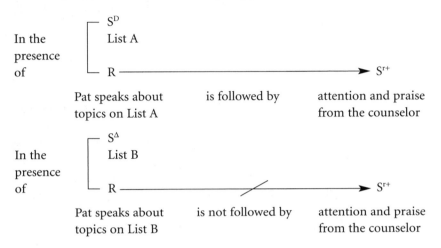

Effect: Pat's speaking about topics on List A increased; her speaking about topics on List B decreased.

In Case Example 4 (p. 269), when the green light was turned on it served as the S^D for Leon's speaking about the slides. When Leon spoke when the green light was on, he received candy and praise. When the green light was turned off, it was the S^Δ for speaking about the slides. When Leon spoke when the light was off, positive reinforcement was withheld. In diagram form, this example of discrimination training appears as follows:

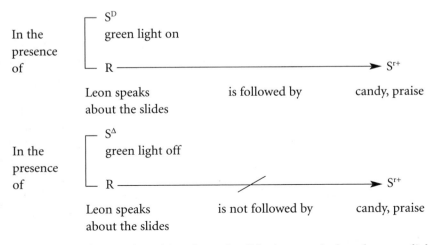

Effect: Leon's rate of speaking about the slides increased when the green light was on and decreased when the green light was off.

Both positive reinforcement and extinction are involved in the discrimination training procedure. The green light being on was the S^D for Leon to speak and be reinforced. In other words, the green light being on served as the signal or cue indicating that speaking would be reinforced. Thus responses performed when the green light was on (S^D) were reinforced and strengthened. Responses made when the green light was off (S^Δ) were not followed by positive reinforcement and, therefore, were weakened and extinguished.

Stimulus Control

When the desired response is performed in the presence of the S^D and never or rarely in the presence of the S^Δ, we say that the response is under **stimulus control.** An additional characteristic of stimulus control is that the response is performed with short latency after presentation of the S^D. **Latency** refers to the amount of time elapsing between presentation of the S^D and performance of the response. Therefore, a short latency means that the response is performed immediately or very soon after the S^D is presented. Leon's speech was under stimulus control when he spoke only when the green light was on and began to speak as soon as it went on.

Many of our behaviors are under the control of antecedents. Clocks and watches are S^Ds or cues for getting up in the morning and for arriving on time to appointments and other important events. Calendars also serve as S^Ds for responses such as giving birthday presents, sending anniversary cards, and preparing for important meetings or professional events. Other people's speech, smiles, and other nonverbal behaviors serve as S^Ds or cues for our responses to them. For example, when someone smiles at you, it usually signals that your approach response, such as saying "Hello," will be reinforced by that person. When a traffic officer says, "Right this way," this serves as an S^D for the response of driving your car through the intersection. Your waving arm is an S^D for the taxi driver to stop and pick you up. Your theater ticket is an S^D for the usher to show you to your seat.

Oral and written instructions often serve as S^Ds that exert considerable control over our behavior. **Prompts** and other cues also serve as S^Ds that signal or set the occasion for behaviors that are reinforced. For example, at a large urban university, the symbol of a pink triangle in a green circle displayed in an office served as an S^D for talking about issues related to sexual orientation (R). The symbol identified safe places for gay, lesbian, bisexual, and transgender students and others to talk about their concerns and receive assistance, counseling, and guidance (S^{r+}) from faculty and trained student volunteers.

In the example in Chapter 5, Joe learned a discrimination related to discussing his school problems at home. When he talked about school problems with his mother (S^D), she provided reinforcement in the form of attention and discussion of his concerns. His stepfather was an S^Δ for discussing school problems, however, because Joe's talking about them was extinguished in his presence. In diagram form, this example appears as follows:

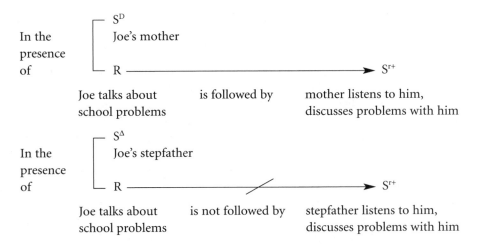

S^D
Joe's mother

In the presence of

R ———————————————————→ S^{r+}

Joe talks about   is followed by   mother listens to him,
school problems   discusses problems with him

S^Δ
Joe's stepfather

In the presence of

R ———————————————————→ S^{r+}

Joe talks about   is not followed by   stepfather listens to him,
school problems   discusses problems with him

Effect: Joe discusses his school problems with his mother; Joe does not discuss these problems with his stepfather.

Faulty Discriminations

Stimulus control is an important concept in behavior analysis and modification. Stimulus control involves considering the role of antecedents, in addition to consequences, in assessing target behaviors and in determining ways to change them. One type of problem involving antecedents is found with individuals who have acquired faulty discriminations. For example, a supervisor frequently phoned Marge, a case manager, after work on her cell phone to discuss agency matters that could have been dealt with during office hours. Marge usually accepted the calls and talked to the supervisor, thus reinforcing the calls. These inappropriate calls can be analyzed as a problem of faulty discrimination on the part of the supervisor. Discussing agency business (R), unless urgent, should occur during office hours (S^D) and should not occur outside of those hours (S^Δ). Because the supervisor was usually reinforced for calling Marge on her cell phone by Marge's taking the call (S^{r+}), the faulty discrimination was maintained.

If Marge wanted to help the supervisor make the proper discrimination, she could withhold the reinforcer of conversing with the supervisor when the supervisor called her on her cell phone regarding nonemergency matters. If Marge sometimes reinforced these calls and sometimes did not, the supervisor's response would be intermittently reinforced and strengthened. Of course, Marge could simply ask the supervisor not to call her on her cell phone to discuss routine agency matters.

Another type of problem related to antecedents involves individuals who have developed behaviors that are under the control of inappropriate antecedent stimuli. For example, people who are overweight often eat in the presence of stimuli other than hunger (food deprivation), such as shopping at the grocery store, driving in the car, and watching food commercials on TV. Although eating is an appropriate response, it can become a problem when it occurs in the presence of inappropriate S^Ds. A person who overeats can increase control over this response by removing inappropriate S^Ds in the environment, such as bowls of candy in the living room or bags of potato chips in the office.

Some people lack the skills necessary to perform appropriate responses in the presence of certain antecedent stimuli. For example, a restaurant waiter overcharged Jack on his bill. Jack did not say anything and paid the additional amount. Jack could learn to perform an assertive response to the S^D of an overcharge on his restaurant bill, such as "Excuse me. I think my bill is too high." This response would be positively reinforced by his saving the extra money. Another reinforcer for the assertive response might be Jack's telling himself, "I'm glad I told the waiter he overcharged me."

Some individuals do not provide proper antecedents for the appropriate behavior of others. For example, a child protective services worker found three children eating a diet lacking in essential nutrients because their mother did not buy the family nutritious foods such as fruits and vegetables. The mother did not provide the proper S^Ds of having nutritious foods in the house so that her children could eat appropriate and healthy foods.

Rule-Governed Behavior

Rule-governed behavior is behavior controlled by *descriptions* of the relationships between behaviors and reinforcers. This contrasts with contingency-shaped behavior, which is behavior strengthened by reinforcement without the involvement of overt or covert verbalizations (Skinner, 1969). Rule-governed behavior is under the control of antecedent stimuli in the form of instructions or self-instructions that include the antecedent, behavior, and consequences. The description of a contingency for reinforcement can serve as an S^D for an individual to perform a response that will be followed by a positive reinforcer. Rules can have an immediate effect on behavior or can control behavior more distantly removed from the reinforcer (Hayes, 1989; Hayes & Ju, 1998).

For example, when Sally giggles in class, the other students laugh. Sally continues to giggle; her giggling is shaped by the positive reinforcer of the students' laughter. If Sally's teacher tells her that she will be nominated for a student award at the end of the semester if she completes her class work without giggling, this could serve as a rule that governs Sally's desired responses of completing her class work without giggling. Although the award is far removed in time, Sally can apply the rule covertly to maintain the desired responses of doing her class work without giggling. She can say to herself, "I will complete my class work without giggling so I can get nominated for a student award at the end of the semester."

Stimulus Fading

Stimulus fading is a procedure for transferring stimulus control of a behavior from one S^D to other antecedent stimuli. The individual continues to be reinforced for responding in the presence of an S^D that is gradually faded or altered. As the S^D is altered, the individual continues to perform the correct response.

Stimulus fading techniques have been applied in situations in which verbal instructions or cues are used to teach complex verbal or mechanical skills. Initially, the individual performs appropriately only in the presence of the cues or prompts. The cues are gradually faded out in a manner that allows the individual to continue responding to changes in the S^D. For example, an actor learning his or her lines onstage may rely on prompts or cues from a prompter. These cues are gradually faded out until the actor responds to the S^Ds provided by the spoken lines of the other actors onstage. In teaching a child to ride a bicycle, a parent may initially steady the bicycle by the physical prompt of holding the back of it while the child rides. Gradually, the parent releases his or her grip on the bicycle, until the child is riding the bicycle alone.

In training a person with developmental disabilities to perform in a new job, a job coach provides prompts and cues for the individual to perform the responses needed to complete a task. The job coach begins to fade the prompts and their frequency as the individual becomes more proficient in performing the job behaviors. Initially, the job coach may work with the individual all day every day, then half a day, then three times per week, and then fade to once per week and once per month.

Similar applications of fading techniques have been used in linear-programmed instruction such as the following:

"A reinforcer is a stimulus that increases the strength of a response."

"A reinforcer is a stimulus that increases the strength of a _____ ."

"A reinforcer is a stimulus that increases the _____ of a _____ ."

"A reinforcer is a stimulus that _____ the _____ of a _____ ."

"A reinforcer is a _____ that _____ the _____ of a _____ ."

Both fading and shaping procedures are used to establish new behaviors or to increase behaviors that occur with low frequency. In shaping, the practitioner gradually changes the form of the response by shifting the criteria for reinforcement—that is, by altering the reinforcing consequences. In contrast, fading involves gradual alteration of the S^D, or antecedent stimulus. The fading procedure does not require changes in the initial response. The response remains the same throughout the procedure but is performed in the presence of gradually varied (and fading) stimulus conditions. Shaping, however, results in a target response that has become differentiated from and might bear little resemblance to the initial response (see Chapter 5).

Stimulus Generalization

Stimulus generalization is the opposite of discrimination. In discrimination training, stimulus control is achieved when the response is performed in the presence of S^D but not in the presence of S^Δ. In stimulus generalization, a response reinforced in the presence of one stimulus, S^D, will subsequently be performed in the presence of other stimuli that share some common property (Skinner, 1953). For example, a child has learned to use the word *car* when she sees a four-wheeled vehicle. The child now calls every four-wheeled vehicle she sees a car. The word *car generalized* to all such vehicles. A woman who was helped by a bearded therapist dates mostly men with beards. The association of the bearded therapist with a man who was helpful generalized to other men with beards.

Stimulus generalization is significant for human adaptation because we often perform behaviors in new situations that we learned in other contexts. Otherwise, we would have to learn how to respond to every new situation. For example, most people learn to read from books in school. Reading thereafter generalizes to (a) other reading material, such as newspapers, magazines, and cereal boxes; and (b) other places, such as libraries, doctors' offices, and buses. A person who learns to drive one standard-shift automobile can usually drive other standard-shift automobiles. Pat was reinforced for talking about List A topics in the marriage counselor's office. For counseling to be successful, however, Pat's talking about List A topics has to generalize to her talking with her husband at home. These examples involve stimulus generalization because the responses associated with reading, driving, and talking about List A topics, which were performed in the original classroom, automobile, and counselor's office, have transferred or generalized to other environments.

It is siad taht wrod oerdr is not as iprotmant as hinvag the frsit and lsat ltteer of the wrod in plcae. The preceding sentence demonstrates generalization in that most readers of English are able to read the sentence correctly even though the letters in each word are not in their proper order. We have learned to generalize whole words from their first and last letters.

In Figure 6.1, S^{D1} is the original stimulus that signals or sets the occasion for the response R_1 to be reinforced. S^{D2}, S^{D3}, and S^{D4} are stimuli that are similar along some dimension (e.g., color, size, form) to S^{D1}. Stimulus generalization takes place when R_1 is performed in the presence of S^{D2}, S^{D3}, or S^{D4} even though R_1 is not reinforced.

For example, Johnny was positively reinforced by his mother for swearing, although she intended to discourage this behavior. The mother served as the S^D for the response of swearing, and the reinforcer was the attention she paid Johnny by her facial expressions and by her saying, "Johnny, now please don't talk that way!" His mother's attention increased rather than decreased Johnny's swearing. Johnny sometimes used swear words in the presence of his aunts, female teachers, and other women but rarely in front of his male teachers or his father. Johnny's swearing was observed to occur most frequently in his mother's presence and with decreasing frequency as the stimuli became less similar to his mother in physical appearance. Figure 6.2 shows this example of stimulus generalization in diagram form.

The more similar a stimulus is to the original S^D on some property or dimension, the more likely it is that the response will be performed in the presence of the new stimulus. The probability of responding is greatest in the presence of the original S^D and decreases in frequency as the stimulus becomes less similar to the original S^D. Stimulus similarity may include properties such as size, color, form, and other physical characteristics.

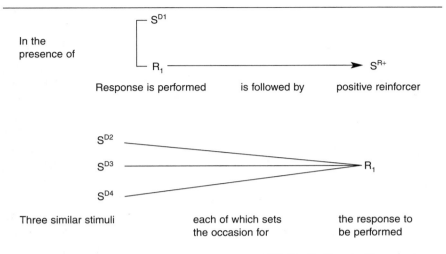

Effect: R_1 increases in frequency in the presence of S^{D1}. The likelihood of R_1 occurring in the presence of S^{D2}, S^{D3}, and S^{D4} also increases.

Figure 6.1   Stimulus Generalization Diagram

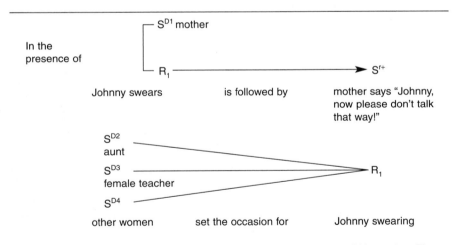

Effect: Johnny's swearing increases in frequency in the presence of his mother. The likelihood of Johnny swearing in the presence of aunts, female teachers, and other women also increases.

Figure 6.2   Stimulus Generalization Example

Sometimes, a practitioner encounters a client who is similar in some respect to a significant individual in the practitioner's life, such as a parent, friend, partner, or child. The practitioner might respond to that client in the same way he or she has behaved toward the significant individual. Stimulus generalization could be detrimental to the client in such a case if the practitioner fails to consider this factor. Similarly, a client may find a resemblance between the practitioner and a significant individual in the client's life and respond to the practitioner in the same way he or she has responded to that person. (Psychoanalytic theory uses the terms *transference* and *countertransference* to refer to similar phenomena, but with different interpretations.) If such stimulus generalization occurs and is not addressed, it could lead to the therapist's becoming overinvolved or underinvolved with the client and could interfere with the development of an appropriate intervention. A collaborative relationship between client and practitioner is important for the client's participation in a behavior change program, but it is usually not the main focus of the intervention plan. If the relationship becomes the focus, rather than the identified target behaviors, the behavior change program could be diverted from achieving the client's goals.

In Chapter 5, we explained that the term *response* actually refers to a response class rather than to a single, discrete response. Each member of a response class produces the same or similar effect on its environment. Similarly, the term *stimulus* refers to a stimulus class or group of stimuli rather than a single, discrete stimulus (Skinner, 1938). Each member of a stimulus class serves the same function for a response—for example, as an S^D signaling or setting the occasion for a response to be reinforced. For instance, chalk is an S^D for writing on the chalkboard. "Chalk" is a stimulus class, all members of which set the occasion for writing on the board. White chalk, yellow chalk, thin chalk, and thick chalk are all members of the stimulus class that serve the same function (as S^Ds) for the response of writing on the board. Similarly, "illicit drugs" is a stimulus class that may include marijuana, cocaine, hashish, and heroin as members.

A person being treated in a psychiatric hospital may be taught to perform appropriate social skills in that setting. Treatment is not complete, however, until the individual can also perform these behaviors outside the hospital. In other words, performance of appropriate social behaviors must generalize from the stimulus conditions (S^Ds) in the hospital to the individual's environment. We discuss this topic in more detail in Chapter 12.

Summary

1. Antecedents are stimulus events that precede or accompany responses and can influence their performance.

2. Discriminative stimuli are antecedents that exert control over the performance of a response. There are two kinds of discriminative stimuli: the S^D and the S^Δ.

3. The S^D signals or sets the occasion for a response made in its presence to be reinforced. The S^Δ signals that a response made in its presence will not be reinforced.

4. A response performed in the presence of an S^D is reinforced and increases in strength or likelihood of occurrence. A response performed in the presence of an S^Δ is extinguished and decreases in strength or likelihood of occurrence.

5. In the discrimination training procedure, the response is reinforced in the presence of S^D and extinguished in the presence of S^Δ. The effect of this procedure is stimulus control—the response is performed in the presence of S^D and never or rarely performed in the presence of S^Δ. An additional feature of stimulus control is short latency between presentation of the S^D and performance of the response.

6. Stimulus fading is a procedure used to transfer stimulus control from one S^D to other antecedent stimuli. As the S^D is altered, or faded, the individual continues to perform and be reinforced for the correct response.

7. In stimulus generalization, a response reinforced in the presence of one stimulus, S^D, will also be performed in the presence of other stimuli that share some common property or dimension. The more similar the stimulus is to the original S^D, the more likely it is that stimulus generalization will occur.

8. The term *stimulus* actually refers to a stimulus class in the same way that the term *response* refers to a response class. Thus each member of a stimulus class can serve the same function for a response—for example, as an S^D for a response that is reinforced.

9. Stimulus generalization can occur in situations in which a practitioner encounters a client (or a client encounters a practitioner) who is similar to a significant other. The practitioner should address this phenomenon to ensure that the focus of the intervention is not diverted from achieving the client's behavior change goals.

Suggested Activities

1. Identify a situation in your life in which an S^D exerts control over (a) a desired behavior and (b) an undesired behavior.

2. Draw a diagram of each of the two situations you have identified in activity 1.

References and Resources

Cox, B. S., Cox, A. B., & Cox, D. J. (2003). Motivating signage prompts safety-belt use among drivers exiting senior communities. *Journal of Applied Behavior Analysis, 36,* 635–638.

Engelman, K. K., Altus, D. E., Mosier, M. C., & Mathews, R. M. (2003). Brief training to promote the use of less intrusive prompts by nursing assistants in a dementia care unit. *Journal of Applied Behavior Analysis, 36,* 129–132.

Goldiamond, I. (1965). Self-control procedures in personal behavior problems. *Psychological Reports, 17,* 851–868.

Hayes, S. C. (Ed.). (1989). *Rule-governed behavior: Cognition, contingencies, and instructional control.* New York: Plenum.

Hayes, S. C., & Ju, W. (1998). The applied implications of rule-governed behavior. In W. O'Donohue (Ed.), *Learning and behavior therapy* (pp. 374–391). Boston: Allyn & Bacon.

Johnson, C. R., & Babbitt, R. L. (1993). Antecedent manipulation in the treatment of primary solid food refusal. *Behavior Modification, 17,* 510–521.

Luiselli, J. K., & Cameron, M. J. (Eds.). (1998). *Antecedent control: Innovative approaches to behavioral support.* Baltimore: Brooks.

Matson, J. L., & Francis, K. L. (1994). Generalizing spontaneous language in developmentally delayed children via a visual cue procedure using caregivers as therapists. *Behavior Modification, 18,* 186–197.

McClannahan, L. E., & Krantz, P. J. (1997). In search of solutions to prompt dependence: Teaching children with autism to use photographic activity schedules. In D. M. Baer & E. M. Pinkston (Eds.), *Environment and behavior* (pp. 271–278). Boulder, CO: Westview.

Pelaez-Nogueras, M., & Gewirtz, J. L. (1997). The context of stimulus control in behavior analysis. In D. M. Baer & E. M. Pinkston (Eds.), *Environment and behavior* (pp. 30–42). Boulder, CO: Westview.

Schnelle, J. F., Traughber, B., Sowell, V. A., Newman, D. R., Petrilli, C. O., & Ory, M. (1989). Prompted voiding treatment of urinary incontinence by nursing home staff. *Journal of the American Geriatric Society, 37,* 1051–1057.

Skinner, B. F. (1938). *The behavior of organisms.* New York: Appleton-Century-Crofts.

Skinner, B. F. (1953). *Science and human behavior.* New York: Macmillan.

Skinner, B. F. (1969). *Contingencies of reinforcement: A theoretical analysis.* New York: Appleton-Century-Crofts.

Skinner, B. F. (1983). Self-management in old age. *American Psychologist, 38,* 239–244.

Van Houten, R. (1998). *How to use prompts to initiate behavior.* Austin, TX: Pro-Ed.

CHAPTER 7

Conditioned Reinforcement and Chaining

Drew, a child in a group home for children with developmental disabilities, was given some tokens as positive reinforcers for performing household chores. Drew dropped one token on the floor and left the rest on the table. The houseparent concluded that the token did not function as a generalized conditioned reinforcer for Drew.

Objectives

After completing this chapter, you should be able to do the following:

- Describe a procedure for establishing a generalized conditioned reinforcer for a client.
- Compare the use of conditioned reinforcers and unconditioned reinforcers in maintaining behavior change in the client's environment.
- Describe a procedure to establish a neutral stimulus as a conditioned reinforcer.
- Give an example of a problem that can be analyzed as a stimulus-response chain.

Conditioned Reinforcement

The principle of conditioned reinforcement is based on the finding that a neutral or nonreinforcing stimulus can become a reinforcer for a response through association with a reinforcing stimulus. Conditioned or secondary reinforcers are stimuli that acquire reinforcing properties through pairing or association with other reinforcers. For example, money is a conditioned reinforcer for most people because it has been paired or associated with other reinforcers, such as food, drink, shelter, and entertainment. Points, coupons, tokens, movie tickets, and gift certificates can also serve as conditioned reinforcers because they can be exchanged for stimuli that are reinforcing. Similarly, social reinforcers such as approval, encouragement, and attention usually act as conditioned reinforcers because they have been associated with other reinforcers such as food and removal of physical discomfort.

Unconditioned or primary reinforcers, such as food and beverages, can be used to increase response strength. They do not require prior association with other reinforcers because of their importance for survival or biological functioning; therefore, they are considered intrinsically or naturally reinforcing. Food, sex, sleep, water, warmth, and tactile stimulation are examples of **unconditioned positive reinforcers.** Some drugs, such as cocaine or heroin, can also act as unconditioned reinforcers.

Both conditioned reinforcement and unconditioned reinforcement can be either positive or negative. This chapter focuses on conditioned positive reinforcement. We address negative reinforcement, both unconditioned and conditioned, in Chapter 10.

The diagram for conditioned positive reinforcement is similar to that for unconditioned positive reinforcement:

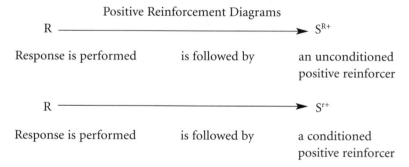

Positive Reinforcement Diagrams

R ⟶ S^{R+}

Response is performed   is followed by   an unconditioned positive reinforcer

R ⟶ S^{r+}

Response is performed   is followed by   a conditioned positive reinforcer

Effect: The response, R, increases in strength and is more likely to be performed again.

The lowercase r in S^{r+} signifies a conditioned positive reinforcer; the uppercase R in S^{R+} signifies an unconditioned positive reinforcer.

Factors that influence the effectiveness of unconditioned reinforcers also apply to conditioned reinforcers. These include the following:

- The conditioned reinforcer is most effective when it immediately follows the response.
- The effectiveness of a conditioned reinforcer is affected by conditions of deprivation and satiation.

- A response maintained on an intermittent schedule of conditioned reinforcement is more resistant to extinction than a response maintained on a continuous schedule of conditioned reinforcement.
- When a conditioned reinforcer is withheld continuously from the response it has reinforced, the response rate decreases as extinction takes place.

To remain effective, a conditioned reinforcer must be paired occasionally with another reinforcer. For example, an individual must occasionally purchase something with the money he or she accumulates for money to continue to be effective as a conditioned reinforcer for that person. That is, an individual will work for money only if money has functioned as a conditioned reinforcer for purchasing various goods and services.

Simple and Generalized Conditioned Reinforcers

Conditioned reinforcers can be of two types: simple and generalized. **Simple conditioned reinforcers** have been paired with one reinforcer and can be exchanged only for that reinforcer. For example, a new restaurant gives out coupons that can be traded only for a soft drink in that restaurant. A child with autism solves math problems and receives tokens that can be exchanged only for M&Ms.

Generalized conditioned reinforcers have been paired with a variety of reinforcers. Money is probably the most common generalized conditioned reinforcer because of the many unconditioned and conditioned reinforcers it can obtain. Additional generalized conditioned reinforcers are attention, praise, and other social reinforcers.

The effectiveness of a simple conditioned reinforcer depends on the individual's level of deprivation for that particular reinforcer. If a child can exchange a token only for bubble gum, the gum might not serve as a reinforcer if the child has been chewing gum all day and has a large supply of gum. Generalized conditioned reinforcers, however, are less dependent on deprivation levels than are simple conditioned reinforcers. For example, money and social reinforcers, such as attention, are less likely than simple conditioned reinforcers to become ineffective due to satiation because of the wide variety of reinforcers with which they are associated. If the individual is satiated on one particular reinforcer, there are others on which he or she is sufficiently deprived to ensure effectiveness of the generalized conditioned reinforcer.

For example, Carlos offered Max a token to run an errand. The token could be exchanged only for a chocolate bar. If Max had recently eaten two chocolate bars (low level of deprivation), it would be less likely that he would run the errand for the token than if he had not eaten chocolate for several days (high level of deprivation). Carlos would have been wise, therefore, to offer Max a token that could be exchanged for chocolate, gum, baseball cards, or a soft drink. By using the generalized conditioned reinforcer, Carlos would increase the likelihood that Max would run the errand regardless of whether or not he had eaten chocolate recently, because it is unlikely that Max would be satiated on all the items that he could obtain with the token.

Following are some examples of simple conditioned reinforcers, generalized conditioned reinforcers, and unconditioned reinforcers:

Simple Conditioned Reinforcers (S^{r+})	Generalized Conditioned Reinforcers (S^{r+})	Unconditioned Reinforcers (S^{R+})
Coupon for free drink	Money	Food
Subway token	Attention	Sex
Pass for a free bus ride	Coupon for money off grocery items	Water
Movie ticket	Points that can be exchanged for a variety of privileges	Warmth
Coupon for a free pizza	Gift certificate	Hugs
Coupon for a free 4-week health club membership	Airline frequent flier miles	Drugs such as cocaine

Establishing a Conditioned Reinforcer

For a **neutral stimulus** to acquire reinforcing value, the stimulus must be associated or paired with an established reinforcer. Money, tokens, and coupons typically serve as conditioned reinforcers only after the individual learns that they can be exchanged for other goods. For a neutral stimulus to become established as a conditioned reinforcer, it must be paired repeatedly with another primary or conditioned reinforcer.

For example, in a foster group home, a houseparent set up a token reinforcement program. The children living in the group home were told that they could earn tokens for performing household chores. The tokens could be exchanged for reinforcers such as television, extra spending money, and additional desserts. Drew, one of the children, was given some tokens as positive reinforcers for performing household chores. Drew dropped one token on the floor and left the rest on the table. The houseparent concluded that the token did not function as a generalized conditioned reinforcer for Drew.

To establish the tokens as conditioned reinforcers, the houseparent showed Drew a variety of items placed on a table, including chewing gum, cookies, and baseball cards. The houseparent told Drew to point to an item he would like to have. When Drew pointed to a cookie, the houseparent gave Drew a token (S^D) and then asked Drew to hand her the token. As soon as Drew gave her the token (R), she gave him the cookie (S^{R+}). The houseparent repeated this procedure with Drew and the other children until each of them had taken a token when it was offered and exchanged it for one of the established reinforcers. In this way, the tokens became conditioned reinforcers, and the houseparent then used them to reinforce the children's performance of household chores. In diagram form, this example appears as follows:

Diagram for Establishing a Token as a Conditioned Reinforcer

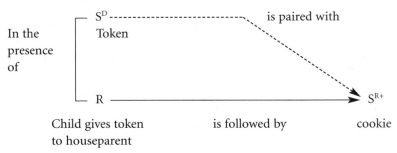

In the
presence
of

S^D -------------------------- is paired with

Token

R ———————————→ S^{R+}

Child gives token   is followed by   cookie
to houseparent

Effect: The response (giving the token to the houseparent) increases in strength; the token is paired with S^{R+}, a cookie, and becomes a conditioned positive reinforcer.

The tokens, initially neutral stimuli, became conditioned reinforcers after being paired repeatedly with the established reinforcers. The houseparent then used the tokens to reinforce the children's performance of household chores, such as clearing the table after dinner, sweeping the floor, and taking out the trash.

Positive Reinforcement Diagram With Token as Conditioned Reinforcer

R ——————————————————→ S^{r+}

Child takes out the trash   is followed by   a token

Effect: Desired response (e.g., taking out the trash) increases in strength, demonstrating that the token served as a conditioned reinforcer.

A neutral stimulus can also become a conditioned reinforcer when it is associated with the removal of a negative reinforcer (see Chapter 10).

Reinforcement History

In establishing a neutral stimulus as a conditioned reinforcer, the practitioner considers the individual's reinforcement history—that is, those stimuli that have served as reinforcers in the past and that may currently control the person's behaviors. Affection, attention, and approval are social reinforcers that are usually established during infancy and early childhood. These stimuli are called social reinforcers because they become available through interaction with other persons. Social reinforcers (e.g., smiles) are paired in childhood with the parents' ministering to the child's physical needs—for example, feeding, changing diapers, and relieving discomfort. The parents' social responses become conditioned reinforcers through association with the nurturant responses.

For example, the mother serves as an S^D in whose presence the infant eats. The mother becomes associated with food and the relief of hunger as well as with other caregiving responses, such as cuddling, smiling, and speaking. She thereby becomes a social reinforcer for the child and has tremendous influence in establishing and strengthening the child's behaviors. Usually by the time a child reaches school age, parents can use approval, recognition, and praise as reinforcers for many of the child's behaviors. The effectiveness of social reinforcers in influencing children's behaviors generalizes to other adults, such as teachers, neighbors, and relatives. During adolescence, however, social reinforcement from peers often becomes more important than social reinforcement from parents and other adults.

Some children rarely receive praise, affection, or attention contingent on appropriate behaviors. They often perform disruptive or inappropriate behaviors that produce attention from parents, teachers, or other adults. In some cases, the attention reinforces the inappropriate behaviors. Practitioners can teach adults to provide children with social reinforcement for appropriate behaviors and to withhold it for inappropriate behaviors.

For some children, however, commonly used social reinforcers, such as smiles and hugs, appear to be ineffective. These children may have been abused or neglected or may have pervasive developmental disabilities, such as autism. With such children, practitioners or other adults cannot use social reinforcers to establish or strengthen behaviors. They must first establish praise, smiling, approval, and attention as conditioned reinforcers by pairing these stimuli with unconditioned reinforcers or other known reinforcers.

Establishing Relationships With Clients

In developing an effective working relationship with a client, the practitioner serves as a conditioned positive reinforcer. Practitioners commonly establish themselves as conditioned positive reinforcers for clients by listening to their problems and personal concerns, and encouraging them to talk about themselves and their situations in a supportive, nonpunitive setting. The practitioner serves as an S^D in whose presence the client's talking about problems is followed by social reinforcers, such as the practitioner's attention, problem analysis, encouragement, or suggestions. In this way, the practitioner can become a generalized conditioned reinforcer to influence a wide range of client behaviors.

Diagram for Establishing Practitioner as a Conditioned Reinforcer

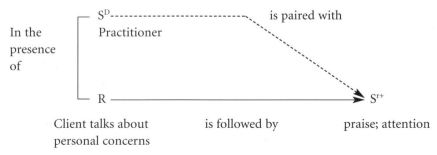

Effect: Client's talking about personal concerns increases in strength; practitioner becomes a conditioned positive reinforcer.

Socioeconomic, racial, and cultural factors can prevent clients from seeking help or receiving services. Practitioners often have to bridge such barriers to provide services to clients. In the offices of social agencies, posters of familiar scenes, signs in immigrant clients' native languages, and artworks reflecting clients' native cultures can serve as S^Ds for approach responses by minority and immigrant clients that can be reinforced by the staff's welcoming responses.

Practitioners might offer beverages, doughnuts, and other unconditioned reinforcers, coupled with friendly conversation, noncontingently to potential clients—that is, without requiring the performance of any behaviors other than taking and consuming the offered items. Practitioners can also pair themselves with reinforcers, such as playing games or sports with children or providing music, soft drinks, and food to adolescents. After the practitioner has become established as a conditioned positive reinforcer, he or she can selectively reinforce client responses by using approval, attention, and praise to develop desired client behaviors. As a conditioned positive reinforcer the practitioner can also influence a client to carry out behavioral assignments at home.

Positive Reinforcement Diagram With Practitioner as Conditioned Reinforcer

R ⟶ S^{r+}

| Client performs behavioral assignments at home | is followed by | practitioner's praise and feedback |

Effect: Client is more likely to complete behavioral assignments given by the practitioner.

In a similar way, representatives of private companies, such as home health care agencies that rely on nonprofit social service agencies (e.g., family service agencies, hospital social service departments) for referrals, may attempt to establish themselves as conditioned reinforcers for their referral sources at the nonprofit agencies. For example, representatives bring gifts to nonprofit agency staff (food is always popular) in an attempt to establish themselves and their companies as conditioned positive reinforcers. The delivery of such gifts may increase during holiday seasons. Nonprofit staff consume these delicious foods and use the pens, water bottles, portfolios, mouse pads, and other goodies. The for-profit companies become associated with the consumption of the gifts, which the representatives hope will increase the likelihood that the nonprofit staff will select their companies when making referrals.

Fading Out Unconditioned Reinforcers

Speech and other interpersonal behaviors are typically maintained with social reinforcement. For some individuals, however, common conditioned social reinforcers, such as praise and approval, may be ineffective. Unconditioned reinforcers can be used in these situations. For example, food can be used to teach social skills to a child with autism or to increase speech in an individual with a mental disorder, as in Case Example 4 (p. 269). When establishing a behavior using an unconditioned reinforcer, the practitioner pairs a conditioned reinforcer with the unconditioned reinforcer until the behavior is maintained by the conditioned reinforcer alone. For example, in Case Example 4, Leon was given candy (an unconditioned reinforcer) and praise (a conditioned reinforcer) for speaking in response to slides he was shown. When Leon's speech increased to a desired level, the candy would be faded out and his speech would be reinforced only with praise.

A social reinforcer, such as praise, can be presented along with or immediately prior to the unconditioned reinforcer to promote shifting of behavioral control from unconditioned to conditioned reinforcement. For example, in teaching arithmetic to Robbie, a child with learning disabilities, the special education teacher gives him a raisin for each problem he solves. When the teacher gives him the raisin, she says, "Very good, Robbie." The delivery of the raisin is gradually shifted from a continuous to an intermittent reinforcement schedule while the teacher continues to say "Very good, Robbie" after each correct solution. Soon the unconditioned reinforcer (the raisin) is discontinued, with only the social reinforcer ("Very good, Robbie") presented after each response. The social reinforcer is then shifted to an intermittent schedule to approximate reinforcement schedules in the child's environment. Robbie does not receive food for every math problem he solves. He can receive approval or praise from the teacher and his parents when he completes his assignments, however, and he also earns grades for his schoolwork.

Shifting from food (unconditioned reinforcers) to praise and approval (conditioned reinforcers) promotes the generalization and maintenance of the newly developed behaviors. Two advantages of using generalized conditioned reinforcers rather than unconditioned reinforcers in behavior change programs are that (a) the individual is less likely to satiate on a generalized conditioned reinforcer and (b) generalized conditioned reinforcers are more abundantly available in our society contingent on appropriate behaviors.

Token Economy

The term **token economy** refers to a planned reinforcement program in which individuals earn tokens for performing desired behaviors. They can exchange these tokens for a variety of objects or privileges that serve as *backup reinforcers* for the tokens. The tokens serve as generalized conditioned reinforcers for appropriate behaviors and are given according to values assigned to the performance of specific behaviors. For example, a teenager in a residential drug treatment program receives 1 token each time he makes his bed, 2 tokens for brushing his teeth, and 5 tokens for participating in a group meeting. He can exchange these tokens for goods or privileges, such as a candy bar (2 tokens), special time with a staff member (5 tokens), or a trip to the ice cream store (25 tokens). Similarly, teachers establish token economies when they give students gold stars or stickers for performance of various academic and classroom behaviors and the students can exchange the stars or stickers for privileges, such as extended play periods. Parents can also use conditioned reinforcers, such as points or stars, in home-based token economies to increase their children's studying, performance of household tasks, cooperative sibling behaviors, and time spent practicing musical instruments.

Token economies have been implemented in programs for juvenile offenders, individuals with developmental disabilities, children in residential care, and persons with mental disorders. Token economies tend to be most effective in institutional settings because employees there have greater control over a client's reinforcement than is possible in the client's natural environment. A token economy provides incentives for individuals to acquire and perform behaviors that are necessary for them to function in the community.

Stimulus-Response Chains

At first glance, some situations may appear too complex for behavioral analysis. In analyzing complex performances, however, we find that they often consist of **stimulus-response chains.** The practitioner uses the principle of chaining to (a) analyze behavior patterns, (b) develop sequences of behaviors to replace undesired performances, and (c) expand deficient behavior patterns. One unit of a stimulus-response chain consists of a discriminative stimulus (S^D), a response (R), and a conditioned reinforcer (S^{r+}). The entire chain is composed of a series of stimulus-response units that ends with an unconditioned or conditioned reinforcer (S^{R+} or S^{r+}). Each conditioned reinforcer in the chain also serves as the S^D for the next response, as shown in Figure 7.1. The chain is completed after the terminal response produces the desired reinforcer.

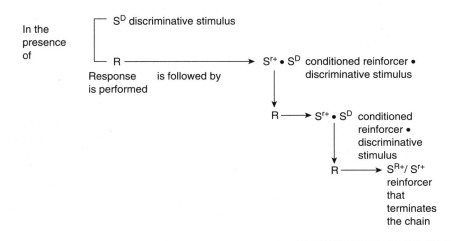

Figure 7.1   Stimulus-Response Chain

Many everyday behaviors are controlled by stimulus-response chains. For example, eating between meals often produces undesired weight gain, a pattern that can be subjected to a stimulus-response chain analysis. The inappropriate eating behavior can be broken down into a series of stimulus-response units leading to a reinforcer that supports the entire chain. Figure 7.2 provides an example of how this stimulus-response chain might appear.

Each response in the chain leads to a conditioned reinforcer that also serves as an S^D for the next response. In the example illustrated in Figure 7.2, eating was associated with watching television, and television commercials acquired a discriminative function (S^D) for food-getting responses (R) that led to the terminal response of food consumption (S^{R+}). The intermediate behaviors of going to the kitchen, opening the refrigerator, and taking the cake became conditioned as part of the total stimulus-response chain.

In analyzing a stimulus-response chain, the practitioner determines an optimal point at which the chain could be broken to prevent the undesired behaviors at the end of the chain. In the inappropriate eating example (see Figure 7.2), the stimulus-response chain could be interrupted at the final unit, when the individual sits on the couch and puts the cake into his or her mouth. It is very unlikely, however, that eating could be interrupted easily at this point, when the individual is under direct stimulus control of the cake.

The chain could be interrupted more effectively at an earlier point—for example, before the individual walks to the kitchen—so that the remaining units of the chain leading to eating can be prevented from occurring. The remaining units would not be extinguished, however, and they could be expected to recur upon reinstatement of any of the S^Ds that signal S^{r+} for their respective responses in the chain. For example, the sight of the refrigerator could be sufficient to set off the rest of the chain leading to eating of the cake. The best place to break the chain, therefore, is before it begins—in this example, before the person stands up from the couch. Interrupting the chain at this point could involve training the person to make alternative, competing responses when a commercial is shown on television, such as reading a magazine or sending an e-mail message to a friend. Similarly, early intervention in the behavior chains leading to drug abuse, stealing, and deviant sexual acts could prevent undesired terminal behaviors.

Response Priming

Sometimes the difficulty lies not in stopping a chain of undesired behaviors, but in beginning a chain of desired behaviors. **Response priming** is a technique used to help initiate early responses in a chain, when the responses have a low probability of performance. The most difficult part of writing a term paper, for example, is beginning it, in part because the reinforcer is far removed from the first response. As we have discussed, once a chain has begun, the probability is increased that it will be completed.

In nursing homes and assisted-living facilities (ALFs), residents may have a low probability of engaging in social behaviors and recreational activities, increasing their isolation. Response priming can be used to encourage residents to perform

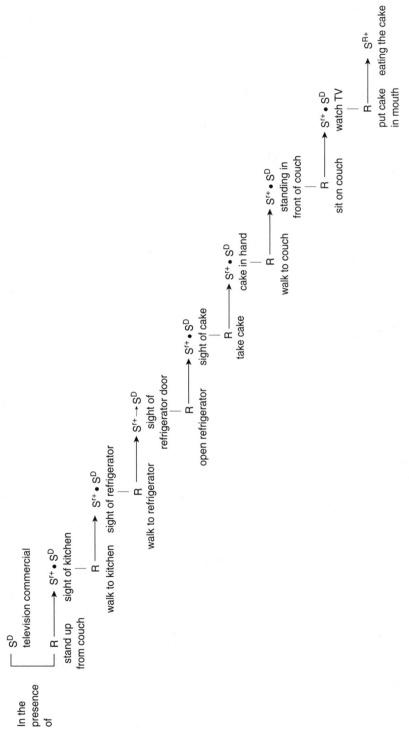

Effect: When a commercial appears on television, this individual is likely to perform the sequence of behaviors in the chain that leads to eating. Each response in the chain is strengthened. When any S^D is presented, the rest of the chain will follow.

Figure 7.2   Stimulus-Response Chain for Eating Between Meals

behaviors early in a chain or sequence leading to social interaction. For example, as we described in Chapter 2, Theresa refused to participate in the activities offered by the activities director at the ALF where she lived. The activities director could use response priming to engage Theresa in behaviors early in the sequence of recreational activity that could then be reinforced. For instance, the activities director could hand art materials (S^Ds) to Theresa as she leaves the dining room after lunch and allow her to manipulate them. As Theresa begins to perform the behaviors, the activities director would praise her and continue to provide other S^Ds (more art materials, instructions for continued involvement in the activity) to encourage Theresa to continue to engage in the behaviors. Studies have shown that response priming increases desired behaviors even after the priming is stopped (e.g., Zanolli, Daggett, & Adams, 1996).

Reinforcer sampling can be viewed as a particular type of response priming in which an individual is exposed to a small amount of a reinforcer to encourage the chain of responses leading to consumption of that reinforcer. Free samples of a product, service, or activity are examples of reinforcer sampling. The reinforcer is given noncontingently—that is, the delivery of the reinforcer is not related to performance of a specific response. If you use a particular brand of toothpaste, you are unlikely to buy a new brand; however, if you are given a free sample of a different brand, you may use it. If you try the new toothpaste and like it, you are more likely to choose it the next time you buy toothpaste. Reinforcer sampling makes the activity or item that is offered as a reinforcer more valuable to an individual, increasing the likelihood that the individual will engage in the desired behavior to earn that activity or item.

Backward Chaining

The practitioner can use a backward stimulus-response chaining procedure to develop appropriate response patterns as part of a client's behavior change program. Backward chaining does not teach the individual to perform a task backward. Rather, in **backward chaining,** the last stimulus-response unit of the chain is established first and the other units are added in reverse order until the desired chain is complete. For example, a practitioner used a backward chaining procedure to teach Molly, a child with mental retardation, to dress herself, beginning with putting on her shirt. The behaviors to be trained were taking a shirt out of a drawer, putting the shirt on her body, and buttoning it. The backward chaining procedure consisted of the following steps:

1. The practitioner put the shirt on Molly and buttoned it, except for one button that she left half buttoned. She showed Molly how to push the button through the hole (modeling the correct response) and asked her to repeat this response. The practitioner showed Molly how to grasp the button in one hand and the buttonhole in the other and push the button through the hole. When Molly grasped the buttonhole and pushed the button through the hole, the practitioner said, "Good," and gave her a piece of fruit.

2. With Molly wearing the shirt, the practitioner buttoned all but one of the buttons. When Molly pushed the button through the hole, the practitioner said, "Good job," and gave her a piece of fruit.

3. With Molly wearing the shirt, the practitioner buttoned all but two of the buttons. She then instructed Molly to button the first button and then the second button. The closed first button served as both a conditioned reinforcer (S^{r+}) for buttoning it and the S^D for buttoning the second button. After Molly closed both buttons, the practitioner said, "Good," and gave her a piece of fruit.

4. The practitioner repeated the basic steps of this procedure until Molly buttoned the entire shirt, put her arms in the sleeves, and took the shirt out of the drawer. As each new response was added, Molly performed it along with the preceding responses in the chain and received praise and fruit.

After the final response of taking the shirt out of the drawer was added, Molly took the shirt from the drawer, put each arm in the correct sleeve, and buttoned every button. At this point, the practitioner gave reinforcement only after the terminal response in the chain was performed. Each response produced a stimulus that served as (a) a conditioned reinforcer (S^{r+}) for that response and (b) an S^D for the next response in the chain. The entire chain was maintained by the positive reinforcer at the end.

Summary

1. A neutral or nonreinforcing stimulus can function as a reinforcer for a response through pairing or association with another reinforcer. A neutral stimulus that has become a reinforcer in this way is called a conditioned or secondary reinforcer. Conditioned reinforcers include social reinforcers (such as approval, praise, and attention) and tangible items (such as money, tokens, and coupons).

2. Unconditioned or primary reinforcers increase response strength and do not require prior association with other reinforcers. Unconditioned reinforcers include food, water, and sex.

3. The same factors that influence the effectiveness of unconditioned positive reinforcers influence conditioned positive reinforcers. These include deprivation, satiation, schedules, and timing of delivery.

4. To remain effective, a conditioned positive reinforcer must occasionally be paired with an established reinforcer.

5. Conditioned reinforcers can be simple or generalized. Simple conditioned reinforcers have been paired with a single reinforcer and can be exchanged only for that reinforcer. Generalized conditioned reinforcers have been paired with a variety of reinforcers. The effectiveness of a simple conditioned

reinforcer depends on the individual's level of deprivation of that particular reinforcer. Generalized conditioned reinforcers can be exchanged for a variety of reinforcers and are less dependent on deprivation levels of specific reinforcers.

6. For a neutral stimulus to become a conditioned reinforcer, the stimulus must be associated or paired with an established reinforcer. Social reinforcers such as affection, attention, and approval are conditioned reinforcers for most people because these stimuli became associated with early nurturant responses of parents and significant others.

7. Practitioners can serve as conditioned positive reinforcers through their association with stimuli that are reinforcing for their clients.

8. When unconditioned reinforcers are used to establish behaviors, conditioned reinforcers can be introduced so that the unconditioned reinforcers can be faded out. After the behaviors are performed consistently, the unconditioned reinforcers can be faded out until the behaviors are maintained by the conditioned reinforcers alone.

9. A token economy is a planned reinforcement program in which individuals earn tokens for performing desired behaviors. The tokens can be exchanged for a variety of objects or privileges that serve as backup reinforcers for the tokens.

10. The principle of chaining is used to analyze and develop sequences of behaviors. A stimulus-response chain consists of a series of stimulus-response units. Each unit consists of an S^D, a response, and a conditioned reinforcer (S^{r+}) that serves as an S^D for the next response. The chain terminates with an unconditioned or conditioned reinforcer (S^{R+} or S^{r+}). Each response produces a stimulus that serves (a) as a conditioned reinforcer for that response and (b) as an S^D for the next response in the chain.

11. Stimulus-response chains are best broken before the first response is performed because any S^D sets the occasion for the rest of the behaviors and stimuli of the chain to follow.

12. Response priming is a technique used to help initiate early responses in a chain when the responses have a low probability of performance.

13. Reinforcer sampling is a type of response priming in which an individual is exposed to a small amount of a reinforcer to encourage the chain of responses leading to consumption of that reinforcer.

14. Backward chaining can be used to help individuals develop appropriate behavioral patterns that are difficult to establish as an entire sequence of responses. In backward chaining, the last stimulus-response unit is established first, and the other units are added until the entire chain is performed and reinforced.

Suggested Activities

1. Identify a situation in your life that can be described as a stimulus-response chain.

2. Diagram the stimulus-response chain for the situation you identified in activity 1.

3. Review the diagram you made in activity 2 and describe the most effective procedure to stop the chain and how it would be implemented.

References and Resources

Ayllon, T., & Azrin, N. H. (1968). *The token economy.* Englewood Cliffs, NJ: Prentice Hall.

Foxx, R. M. (1998). A comprehensive treatment program for inpatient adolescents. *Behavioral Interventions, 13,* 67–77.

Frankel, A. J. (1975). Beyond the simple functional analysis: The chain. *Behavior Therapy, 6,* 254–260.

Glynn, S. M. (1990). Token economy approaches for psychiatric patients: Progress and pitfalls over 25 years. *Behavior Modification, 14,* 383–407.

Hupp, S. D., Reitman, D., Northup, J., O'Callahan, P., & LeBlanc, M. (2002). The effects of delayed rewards, tokens, and stimulant medication on sportsmanlike behavior with ADHD-diagnosed children. *Behavior Modification, 26,* 148–162.

Jason, L. A., & Fries, M. (2004). Helping parents reduce children's television viewing. *Research on Social Work Practice, 14,* 121–131.

Johnson, M. D., & Fawcett, S. B. (1994). Courteous service: Its assessment and modification in a human service organization. *Journal of Applied Behavior Analysis, 27,* 145–152.

Kazdin, A. E. (1982). The token economy: A decade later. *Journal of Applied Behavior Analysis, 15,* 431–445.

Krasner, L. (1962). The therapist as a social reinforcement machine. In H. H. Strupp & L. Luborsky (Eds.), *Research in psychotherapy* (pp. 61–94). Washington, DC: American Psychological Association.

Lippman, M. R., & Motta, R. W. (1993). Effects of positive and negative reinforcement on daily living skills in chronic psychiatric patients in community residences. *Journal of Clinical Psychology, 49,* 654–662.

Myles, B. S., Moran, M. R., Ormsbee, C. K., & Downing, J. A. (1992). Guidelines for establishing and maintaining token economies. *Intervention in School and Clinic, 27,* 164–169.

Phillips, E. L. (1968). Achievement Place: Token reinforcement procedures in a home-style rehabilitation setting for "pre-delinquent" boys. *Journal of Applied Behavior Analysis, 1,* 213–223.

Schoenfeld, W. N., Antonitis, J. J., & Bersch, P. J. (1950). A preliminary study of training conditions necessary for secondary reinforcement. *Journal of Experimental Psychology, 40,* 40–45.

Surezy, N. B., Matson, J. L., & Box, P. (1992). The good behavior game: A token reinforcement system for preschoolers. *Child and Family Behavior Therapy, 14,* 21–32.

Walls, R. T., Zane, T., & Ellis, W. D. (1981). Forward and backward chaining, and whole task methods. *Behavior Modification, 5,* 61–74.

Zanolli, K., Daggett, J., & Adams, T. (1996). Teaching preschool age autistic children to make spontaneous initiations to peers using priming. *Journal of Autism and Developmental Disabilities, 26,* 407–422.

CHAPTER 8

Modeling and Imitation

Neil has a hard time asking women to go out with him. He typically approaches them with statements such as "You wouldn't like to go to the movies Saturday night, would you?" and "I have two tickets to a play, if you wouldn't mind going." He speaks to them in a pleading, whining voice. The members of a therapy group in which Neil participates observed these behaviors when Neil performed a behavioral reenactment of his last attempt to ask a woman for a date. The therapist asked Nick, another group member, to model appropriate responses for Neil. Neil imitated the behaviors that Nick demonstrated and gradually learned to perform appropriate behaviors in a variety of role plays. Group members reinforced Neil with praise for appropriate imitation.

Objectives

After completing this chapter, you should be able to do the following:

- Give an example of the modeling plus reinforcement procedure to develop and strengthen a response.
- Give an example of modeling used to develop assertive behaviors in a group setting.
- Describe the use of a modeling procedure with prompts, reinforcement, and fading, given a case example.

The Role of Imitation in the Acquisition of Behaviors

Modeling and imitation play important roles in the acquisition of both desired and undesired behaviors. Children acquire many of their behavior patterns by observing and imitating their parents, teachers, friends, and others. Adults also learn many responses through observation and imitation of the behaviors exhibited by influential individuals. Television, for example, provides a variety of models for people to imitate. Cereal, toothpaste, and beer commercials make frequent use of attractive, influential, and successful individuals to promote the purchase of these products by viewers. The message is that if you buy these products, you will be as attractive, influential, successful, and popular as the models who sell them.

Maladaptive or deviant behavior can likewise be imitated. For example, Cheryl, who had never stolen anything, stole a lipstick from a drugstore after observing her friend Melanie, an admired cheerleader, take one. After seeing a movie about drag racing, Dale raced his car down the street; unfortunately, his behavior resulted in an accident in which three people were killed.

A **model** is someone whose behavior is imitated. The individual's imitation of the model's behavior is called an **imitative response.** It is not necessary for imitative responses to immediately follow the model's behavior in order for them to be performed at a future time. For example, a child watching television observes a prestigious actor throw his gum wrapper into a trash container and tell his audience to do the same. The child may *learn* this response although he or she might not perform it immediately after observing the model's behavior. Imitation of the model's behavior might occur at some later time; for example, three days later, when chewing gum with friends, the child throws the wrapper in the trash can and tells his or her friends to do the same.

Modeling can also set the occasion for performance of an already learned response. For example, Chris sees Doug light a cigarette and begin to smoke it. Chris has been trying to quit smoking, but he asks Doug for a cigarette and lights up. Seeing Doug model smoking behavior, Chris smokes too.

Symbolic modeling, in the form of filmed or videotaped models, including self-modeling (e.g., Dowrick & Raeburn, 1995), has been shown to be as effective as live modeling (Bandura, 1977) and in some cases more effective (e.g., Charlop & Milstein, 1989; Foss, Autry, & Irvin, 1989; Rapee & Hayman, 1996). Symbolic modeling has several advantages over the use of live models, including the provision of training in the client's natural environment, use of a medium designed for repeated showings, and the attention-holding property of film and television. Covert modeling is a form of symbolic modeling in which the individual imagines him- or herself or someone else performing a desired behavior.

The Use of Modeling in the Acquisition of New Behaviors

The modeling procedure facilitates the acquisition of new behaviors and sequences of behaviors. Presentation of a positive reinforcer after an imitative response strengthens the response and increases the likelihood that it will be performed again. The client observes a model—the practitioner or another group member, if the client is participating in group treatment—demonstrate appropriate behaviors in a role play of the client's problem. The client is positively reinforced for appropriate imitation.

Imitation is influenced by the prestige or attractiveness of the model and the consequences of the model's behaviors (Bandura, 1965, 1977). Individuals who are perceived as prestigious, influential, or physically attractive are often effective models—that is, their behaviors are imitated. Similarity of the model to the observer has been identified as an important factor in enhancing the effects of modeling (e.g., Bandura, 1969; Gibson, Lawrence, & Nelson, 1976). Models are also more likely to be imitated when their behaviors are followed by positive reinforcers than when they are followed by neutral or punishing consequences (e.g., Bandura, 1965, 1969). The behavioral practitioner may at times model behaviors for a client to imitate. The client is more likely to imitate such behaviors if he or she sees the practitioner as an attractive, successful person and as similar to the client, and if the modeled behaviors are reinforced.

Vicarious consequences, both reinforcing and punishing, can influence the performance of a response. Vicarious reinforcement is evident in casinos, where observing others winning money can lead to an increase in an individual's gambling behavior. As an example of vicarious punishment, if you observe another driver being pulled over by a police officer, you are likely to alter your driving behavior by taking your foot off the gas pedal.

Modeling Versus Shaping

Modeling facilitates the acquisition of behaviors or sequences of behaviors that otherwise would be more difficult and take longer to develop. For example, when a shaping procedure is used to teach a child with mental retardation to speak in sentences, the child might emit many sounds and behaviors before making an appropriate verbal response that can be reinforced. The shaping procedure consists of developing one response class at a time (for example, forming a correct vowel with the lips). The behavior modifier initially reinforces behaviors that may only faintly resemble the desired behavior, speaking in a complete sentence. The addition of prompts and instructions to shaping still might not provide enough information for the child to perform all the nuances of the desired behavior.

In contrast to shaping, modeling allows the child to observe the full range of responses involved in the behavioral sequence of speaking a complete sentence. Such complex behaviors are generally acquired more rapidly through modeling than through shaping because in modeling the entire sequence of desired behaviors is demonstrated. The modeled response may consist of a small segment of a behavioral sequence, such as saying the first letter of a word, or it may consist of a series of responses, such as speaking a complete sentence. The process of acquiring a behavior through modeling is sometimes called *observational learning* (e.g., Bandura, 1969, 1977) because the behavior is acquired through observing another individual.

Some behaviors are more effectively taught through modeling than through shaping. Just imagine trying to use shaping to teach behaviors such as tying shoelaces and driving a standard-shift car—the process would likely require many random responses before any approximation to the desired response would be made. Modeling would be a more direct and efficient method of teaching such behaviors. Adding instructions to the modeling procedure can facilitate imitation of the modeled behavior.

The Modeling Plus Positive Reinforcement Procedure

The **modeling procedure** consists of presenting a modeled stimulus (S^m) to one or more individuals. The individual's imitation of the modeled stimulus is the imitative response. The term **modeled stimulus** refers to the model's performance of the response to be imitated. The imitative response is physically similar to the modeled stimulus with regard to observable properties, such as form, position, and movement. Although the imitative response is not an exact reproduction of the modeled stimulus, it shares at least one common property with the modeled stimulus. If a more precise reproduction is desired, however, the imitative response can be further refined through the use of differential reinforcement, prompting, physical guidance, and instructions in conjunction with modeling.

Positive reinforcement can be used to increase the strength of an imitative response. The *modeling plus positive reinforcement procedure* consists of presenting a modeled stimulus (S^m) that sets the occasion for an imitative response (R) to be followed by a positive reinforcer. The modeling plus reinforcement diagram is as follows:

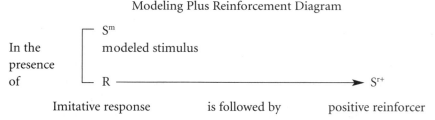

Modeling Plus Reinforcement Diagram

Effect: Increased likelihood that the imitative response, R, will be performed again.

In Case Example 1 (p. 267), Robert can complete more school assignments by saying "No" when his friends invite him to their homes before he has finished his homework. The social worker can use a modeling plus reinforcement procedure to teach Robert how to refuse his friends' invitations. Using this procedure, the social worker models an appropriate way of saying "No, I can't come over until I finish my assignments" with appropriate tone of voice, gestures, and facial expressions. Robert performs an imitative response that is similar to the modeled stimulus. In diagram form, Robert's imitation appears as follows:

Modeling Plus Reinforcement Diagram for Robert

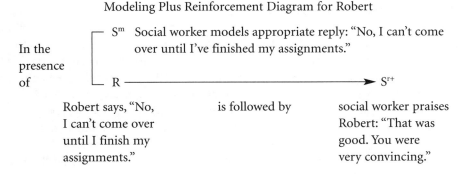

In the
presence
of

S^m Social worker models appropriate reply: "No, I can't come
over until I've finished my assignments."

R ⟶ S^{r+}

Robert says, "No,
I can't come over
until I finish my
assignments."

is followed by

social worker praises
Robert: "That was
good. You were
very convincing."

Effect: Robert is more likely to perform the imitative response (R) again.

A modeling plus reinforcement procedure was also used in Neil's behavior change program for asking women for a date. Nick, a group member, modeled appropriate responses for Neil to imitate. When Neil imitated Nick's responses, the rest of the group members praised him. In diagram form, this example appears as follows:

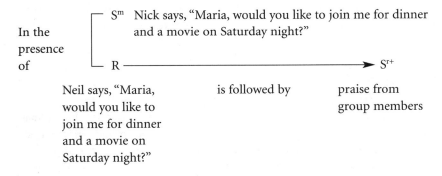

In the
presence
of

S^m Nick says, "Maria, would you like to join me for dinner
and a movie on Saturday night?"

R ⟶ S^{r+}

Neil says, "Maria,
would you like to
join me for dinner
and a movie on
Saturday night?"

is followed by

praise from
group members

Effect: Neil is more likely to perform the imitative response (R) again.

In the modeling plus reinforcement procedure, the model's performance serves as a modeled stimulus, S^m. The client observes the model and then imitates the S^m and receives a positive reinforcer for appropriate imitation. The use of prompts such as "Now you do what I do," "Follow me," or "Do this" can facilitate imitation of the modeled stimulus. If the individual does not imitate the modeled stimulus after additional instructions or prompts, it may be necessary to physically guide the behavior. For instance, in teaching Veronica to tie her shoelaces, the occupational therapist moved Veronica's hands in the same manner as the model demonstrating the responses. The therapist paired this physical guidance, or manipulation, of Veronica's hands with the verbal prompt, "Do this, Veronica." The therapist gradually withdrew the physical guidance. She then faded out the verbal prompt by gradually reducing the volume of the prompt until Veronica imitated tying her shoelaces after presentation of the modeled stimulus alone.

Application of Modeling in Practice

Verbal behaviors as well as nonverbal behaviors can be developed with modeling, reinforcement, and prompting techniques. For example, in teaching Leon (see Case Example 4, p. 269) to speak about slides he was shown, the psychologist used both visual and auditory stimuli. He showed Leon the slide of a boy and girl and asked him, "What do you see in this slide?" Leon did not answer the question. The psychologist then modeled the appropriate response by saying, "It's a boy and girl." When Leon imitated the correct response, the psychologist gave him candy and praise ("Good"). The psychologist faded out the modeled stimulus of saying "It's a boy and girl" by saying it in a gradually softer voice until it was inaudible. The psychologist also faded out the modeled stimulus by omitting one word from the prompt each time he gave it, beginning with the last word. If Leon answered before the modeled stimulus was given, he was reinforced immediately.

In Case Example 6 (p. 271), modeling was used as part of Bill's group treatment program. One of Bill's treatment goals was to learn to respond appropriately to criticism. Group members modeled appropriate behaviors for Bill, and he imitated them. When he had difficulty, the therapist provided verbal prompts until Bill performed the modeled behaviors appropriately. Bill received positive reinforcement in the form of praise from the therapist and group members for performing appropriate imitative responses.

Social Skills Training

Social skills training (SST) is a behavioral procedure for teaching individuals effective ways of interacting in social situations. SST involves model presentation, behavioral rehearsal, coaching and prompting, behavioral assignments, and positive reinforcement. The procedure targets both verbal and nonverbal behaviors (see Case Example 8, p. 272). SST has become a treatment of choice for individuals with schizophrenia (e.g., Kopelowicz, Liberman, & Zarate, 2002), and it has also been used to treat individuals with alcohol use disorders (e.g., Finney & Moos, 2002), children with attention-deficit/hyperactivity disorder (ADHD) (e.g., Hinshaw, Klein, & Abikoff, 2002), and sexual offenders (e.g., Maletzky, 2002).

Assertiveness Training

Assertiveness training is a behavioral procedure for teaching individuals how to state and express their opinions and rights without abusing the rights of others. Assertiveness training uses modeling to improve deficient social or interpersonal skills. Such behavioral deficits are commonly referred to as *nonassertive* or *unassertive* behaviors. Nonassertive behaviors can be characterized as underassertive or overassertive. Individuals with underassertive behaviors may avoid eye contact with others, look at the floor or ceiling when conversing, mumble or speak in very soft voices, and agree with others rather than state divergent views or opinions. Instead of stating positive or negative sentiments, such as pleasure or anger, these individuals typically remain silent. There are many occasions, however, when it would be both appropriate and desirable for them to state their rights and opinions. Failure to express themselves in such circumstances is detrimental to these individuals when followed by negative physical or social consequences.

Assertiveness training can help to reduce the anxiety associated with deficient performances in interpersonal situations. Relaxation training can also be used in conjunction with assertiveness training to reduce such anxiety, as in the treatment plan for Bill in Case Example 6 (p. 271). Anxiety plays an important role in conditioning maladaptive behaviors, as we will discuss in Chapter 11.

Overassertive or aggressive behaviors can also lead to negative consequences because these behaviors exceed appropriate expression of an individual's rights. Overassertive verbal and nonverbal responses often demean, humiliate, or physically harm others. Individuals with overassertive behaviors often have difficulty making the discriminations necessary to express their rights appropriately. For example, someone breaking into a line at a bank or movie theater might serve as an S^D for a person to shout an obscenity instead of making an assertive response such as stating that the line forms at the rear. Individuals who perform overassertive behaviors frequently lack appropriate interpersonal skills. Furthermore, because their overassertive or aggressive behaviors are often reinforced, they lack the incentive to act differently.

In attempting to perform assertive behaviors, some individuals may perform overassertive behaviors, such as interrupting someone who is speaking, shouting to get attention, glaring, or sneering. For example, while stating his right to go out with Tara, Tom pointed his finger at his father, who had forbidden him to see her. In this kind of situation, the practitioner can help the individual discriminate between appropriate and inappropriate attempts at assertiveness. Tom's finger pointing was offensive to his father and detracted from Tom's otherwise assertive responses. Assertiveness training can help an individual develop both verbal and nonverbal responses that are congruent with appropriate expressions of assertiveness in specific situations.

Some people are underassertive in almost every kind of social situation, whereas others behave overassertively in social encounters. Many people, however, have difficulties behaving assertively only with certain people or in certain situations (e.g., Sundel & Sundel, 1980). For example, Jerome is assertive at home but is overassertive with his coworkers. Mary Ann is assertive with her friends but underassertive with her mother-in-law. Samantha is assertive at work but has difficulty returning unwanted merchandise to stores. Drug companies aggressively advertise prescription medications to treat social anxiety. These medications may relieve some anxiety, but they do not teach the social skills that individuals need to act appropriately in social situations.

Assertiveness includes both verbal and nonverbal behaviors that state legitimate rights of the individual. The following are examples of expressions of these rights: "Excuse me, the line ends over there"; "Mother, I prefer this dress"; "Waiter, this fish is fried and I ordered it broiled"; and "Excuse me, but you charged me for two drinks and I only had one." We can all think of situations in which it is more appropriate to state one's rights and opinions than to remain silent.

Assertiveness and Human Service Workers

Human service practitioners frequently encounter situations that call for assertive responses in their relationships with clients, superiors, colleagues, subordinates, and professionals from other disciplines. Practitioners can respond assertively by (a) advocating for clients with community agencies; (b) communicating opinions and recommendations regarding clients to supervisors, supervisees, colleagues, and other professionals; and (c) identifying and correcting deficiencies in agency or institutional policies that adversely affect clients (Sundel & Sundel, 1980).

Practitioners can also act assertively to influence news media, program sponsors, legislators, government officials, and others. Examples include writing letters, sending e-mail messages, stating opinions on controversial issues, and organizing others to protest unjust policies. Assertive responses in these areas can communicate relevant knowledge and expertise necessary to combat cultural insensitivity, racism, prejudice, and discrimination.

Following are some examples of terms used to describe underassertive, assertive, and overassertive behaviors:

Underassertive	Assertive	Overassertive
Passive	Active	Aggressive
Submissive	Direct	Hostile
Meek	Self-confident	Arrogant
Weak	Goal-oriented	Insensitive
Self-deprecating	Good communicator	Offensive
Apologetic	Poised	Overbearing

Gretchen Learns Assertive Behaviors

Modeling, prompting, and reinforcement techniques are often used in assertiveness training. For example, every time Gretchen went shopping with her mother, she bought the clothes her mother selected. Gretchen, who was 22 years old, had purchased five dresses this way with her own money, but she rarely wore them. Although she sometimes told her mother which dresses she liked and wanted to buy, she always wound up buying the dresses her mother selected. Gretchen sometimes shopped alone secretly to return the clothes her mother had picked out and to buy the clothes she really wanted. Gretchen was dissatisfied with most of her wardrobe and with her failure to purchase the clothes she selected when shopping with her mother. She told the therapist, "I am a weak person because I can't even do a simple thing like tell my mother what I want to buy and buy it in front of her."

The therapist arranged role plays with Gretchen that involved behavioral reenactment of typical situations; the therapist played the part of Gretchen's mother. **Behavioral reenactment** (e.g., Sundel & Sundel, 1985) is a role-play technique that the practitioner uses to obtain information regarding the client's behaviors in the problematic situation by observing the client role-play an incident that simulates the target behaviors. By using this technique, the therapist determined that Gretchen's underassertive behaviors consisted of turning her head away from her "mother," shuffling her feet, and mumbling, "Do you mind if I try this dress on?" When her "mother" criticized the clothes she selected, Gretchen usually said, "Whatever you say, Mother."

Gretchen's underassertive behaviors led to negative consequences for Gretchen: She purchased clothes that she did not like and rarely wore, and she also had very little money left over to buy clothes that she liked. Gretchen was angry with herself for not standing up to her mother, and this prevented Gretchen from discussing more pleasant topics with her.

The therapist constructed a hierarchy of assertive behaviors (e.g., Wolpe, 1990) for Gretchen and asked her to rank the behaviors from 1 to 10, according to her difficulty in performing them. For example, Gretchen had the most difficulty buying clothes she selected in her mother's presence, so she ranked this behavior highest on her hierarchy. The item lowest on the hierarchy was stating her preference of a store in which to shop. A middle-range item was telling her mother what color dress she wanted.

The therapist and Gretchen role-played situations related to each behavior on the hierarchy, from least to most difficult, until Gretchen was able to perform appropriate assertive behaviors. For example, the therapist instructed Gretchen to tell her "mother" that because Gretchen was paying for her own wardrobe, she would buy the clothes she wanted. When Gretchen had difficulty behaving assertively in the role plays, the therapist modeled appropriate behaviors and then prompted Gretchen to imitate her. Gretchen imitated assertive statements such as "Mother, I earn the money for my clothes and I'd like to buy this dress." The therapist gave Gretchen feedback on the appropriateness of her tone of voice, eye contact, posture, facial expressions, and the verbal content of her statements. Instructions, prompting, and reinforcement were included in Gretchen's assertiveness training program.

Gretchen practiced assertive statements in the therapist's office, correcting deficiencies in her speech and nonverbal behaviors. The therapist also gave Gretchen behavioral assignments, such as looking at her mother and speaking in a calm tone of voice while stating her opinions. **Behavioral assignments** are specific tasks involving behaviors to be performed by the client outside the practice setting between sessions. Gretchen reported her experiences in carrying out these assignments to the therapist. The therapist reinforced successful performances and provided additional instructions and training to help Gretchen improve her relationship with her mother by increasing positive interactions between them.

Assertiveness Training in Groups

Assertiveness training can also be used in groups (e.g., Sundel & Sundel, 1986). Group members take part in observing and identifying underassertive and overassertive behaviors, in modeling assertive behaviors, in prompting and giving feedback on each other's performances, and in providing positive reinforcement for assertive behaviors. Group members participate in the assessment of each other's nonassertive behaviors, in the development of goals and intervention plans, and in the evaluation of their behavior change programs.

The practitioner's role as leader of an assertiveness training group centers on the following activities: assessing nonassertive behaviors, establishing goals, planning and implementing behavior change programs, and evaluating progress. We discuss each of these areas briefly below.

Assessment

During assessment, the practitioner's tasks are to (a) help group members identify underassertive and overassertive behaviors, (b) establish priorities for behavior change, and (c) teach group members how to specify target behaviors and their controlling conditions. The practitioner might use assessment checklists and questionnaires to accomplish these tasks (e.g., Gambrill & Richey, 1975; Sundel & Lobb, 1982; Sundel & Sundel, 1980). Role plays, including behavioral reenactments, are also useful for identifying and clarifying problem situations and target behaviors.

Neil has a hard time asking women to go out with him. He is participating in an assertiveness training group to improve his social interactions with women. To clarify Neil's target behaviors, the practitioner suggested a behavioral reenactment. Group members observed the following behaviors during the behavioral reenactment: In approaching a woman, Neil said, "You wouldn't like to go to the movies Saturday night, would you?" He spoke in a whining, pleading voice.

Goal Formulation

During goal formulation, the tasks of the practitioner are to help each member (a) specify desired assertive responses, (b) identify the positive consequences for performing assertive behaviors, and (c) evaluate the risks of performing assertive behaviors. The practitioner encourages group members to ask each other questions and to give each other feedback that will help in the development of appropriate goals. Such feedback typically focuses on (a) identifying behaviors that the individual performed assertively in role plays and (b) giving suggestions on how to perform assertive behaviors; for example, "Your voice came through loud and clear. Next time stand up straighter and try to look at him when you speak."

The practitioner assumes an active role in establishing and guiding group activities related to each member's goals (Sundel & Lawrence, 1977; Sundel & Sundel, 1986). The practitioner models behaviors that are unfamiliar or difficult for group members to perform, including praising members for recording assessment data and completing behavioral assignments, asking each other relevant questions, and discussing their problems in the group.

Planning and Implementing an Assertiveness Training Program

When planning an assertiveness training program, the practitioner specifies the behavioral techniques to be used and the procedures for implementing them, the individuals to be involved, the plan for optimizing performance of assertive behaviors in the individual's natural environment, and a target date for achievement of each goal.

In implementing an assertiveness training program, the practitioner sets up role plays, coaches individuals during the role plays, and models assertive responses. The practitioner also demonstrates how group members can model behaviors and coach each other with prompts, cues, and instructions. Group members are actively involved in planning and implementing each other's assertiveness training programs by serving as (a) models; (b) significant others in role plays, such as coworkers or family members; (c) social reinforcers; (d) feedback givers; and (e) evaluators.

Behavioral rehearsal is an important part of an assertiveness training program. Behavioral rehearsal is a role-play technique in which the client practices desired behaviors, often those that have been modeled by the practitioner or other group members. Behavioral rehearsal gives the client opportunities to practice assertive behaviors in a supportive environment, with corrective feedback, before attempting to perform them in actual problematic situations.

Behavioral rehearsal was included in Neil's assertiveness training group. Neil imitated the behaviors that Nick and other group members modeled in role plays. He practiced these behaviors in the group and received positive reinforcement, prompts, and other feedback on his performance from the practitioner and group members.

Group members also help each other develop behavioral assignments, or "homework," specifying behaviors to be performed between group sessions. Initially, the practitioner assumes major responsibility for giving behavioral assignments. As members develop the necessary skills, they take a more active role in structuring their own assignments and giving suggestions to others. To increase the likelihood that they can perform their assignments, members rehearse or practice the assertive responses in the group, receiving feedback and suggestions for improvement.

Evaluation

The practitioner helps group members evaluate progress toward their goals. Members use data recorded from their behavioral assignments to evaluate goal progress and also help each other evaluate changes in assertive behaviors they have observed in role plays and interactions in the group. The practitioner also may recommend additional training or booster sessions for particular members.

Summary

1. Many behaviors are learned through observation. An individual observes someone demonstrate or model a behavior or sequence of behaviors. It is not necessary for imitative behavior to immediately follow the model's behavior in order for it to be performed at a future time.

2. The modeling procedure consists of presenting a modeled stimulus (S^m) to one or more individuals. The imitation of the S^m is an imitative response. Modeling facilitates the acquisition of behaviors or behavior patterns that otherwise would be more difficult or take longer to develop.

3. Filmed or videotaped models can be as effective as live models.

4. Positive reinforcement can be used to increase the strength of an imitative response. Verbal prompts, instructions, and physical guidance can also be used with modeling to facilitate imitation.

5. Behavioral reenactment is a role-play technique that the practitioner uses to obtain information regarding the client's behaviors in the problematic situation by observing the client in a simulation of a problematic incident.

6. Behavioral rehearsal is a role-play technique in which the client practices desired behaviors in the treatment setting, often behaviors that have been modeled by the practitioner or other group members.

7. Behavioral assignments are specific tasks involving behaviors to be performed by the client outside the practice setting between sessions.

8. Assertive responses consist of speech, body gestures, and facial movements that express the rights or opinions of an individual in a nonabusive manner.

9. Assertiveness training is a behavior change procedure for changing nonassertive or unassertive behaviors. Modeling, instructions, prompts, reinforcement, shaping, relaxation training, and the use of assertive response hierarchies are techniques used in assertiveness training. Deficits in assertive behavior are called underassertive behaviors. Excesses in assertiveness are called overassertive or aggressive behaviors.

10. Assertiveness training can be applied in groups. A major advantage of groups is the variety of models available to demonstrate assertive behaviors. Group members give each other feedback on the adequacy of assertive performances and offer suggestions for improvement.

Suggested Activities

1. With one class member who has volunteered to be a subject out of the room, identify a target behavior to shape in the subject without using any verbal instructions. When the subject returns to the room, another student who has volunteered to be the shaper uses a toy clicker, a whistle, or hand clapping as a reinforcer to shape the subject's behavior. The rest of the class should remain silent and refrain from providing any cues to the subject. The only instruction the subject should receive is that whenever he or she hears the clicker, the whistle, or the clapping, he or she should imagine receiving a wonderful reinforcer. How long did it take to shape the correct response?

2. Repeat activity 1, except this time select a class member to model the desired behavior. How long did it take for the subject to learn the correct response?

3. Repeat activity 1 again, this time using both modeling and instructions. How long did it take for the subject to learn the target response? Which of the three methods—shaping, modeling, or modeling and instructions—produced the response that was closest to the target behavior identified by the class?

4. Discuss the pros and cons of shaping, modeling, and modeling with instructions as methods for developing novel behaviors.

References and Resources

Alberti, R. E., & Emmons, M. L. (2001). *Your perfect right: Assertiveness and equality in your life and relationships* (8th ed.). Atascadero, CA: Impact.

Azrin, N. H., Flores, T., & Kaplan, S. (1975). Job Finding Club: A group assisted program for obtaining employment. *Behaviour Research and Therapy, 13,* 17–22.

Bandura, A. (1965). Influence of models' reinforcement contingencies on the acquisition of imitative responses. *Journal of Personality and Social Psychology, 1,* 589–595.

Bandura, A. (1969). *Principles of behavior modification.* New York: Holt, Rinehart & Winston.

Bandura, A. (1977). *Social learning theory.* Englewood Cliffs, NJ: Prentice Hall.

Bandura, A., & Walters, R. H. (1963). *Social learning and personality development.* New York: Holt, Rinehart & Winston.

Bellack, A. S., Mueser, K. T., Gingerich, S., & Agresta, J. (1997). *Social skills training for schizophrenia: A step-by-step guide.* New York: Guilford.

Charlop, M. H., & Milstein, J. P. (1989). Teaching autistic children conversational speech using video modeling. *Journal of Applied Behavior Analysis, 22,* 275–285.

Dowrick, P. W., & Raeburn, J. M. (1995). Self-modeling: Rapid skill training for children with physical disabilities. *Journal of Developmental and Physical Disabilities, 7,* 25–37.

Finney, J. W., & Moos, R. H. (2002). Psychosocial treatments for alcohol use disorders. In P. E. Nathan & J. M. Gorman (Eds.), *A guide to treatments that work* (2nd ed., pp. 157–168). New York: Oxford University Press.

Foss, G., Autry, W., & Irvin, L. (1989). A comparative evaluation of modeling, problem-solving, and behavior rehearsal for teaching employment-related interpersonal skills to secondary students with mental retardation. *Education and Training of the Mentally Retarded, 24,* 17–27.

Gambrill, E. D. (1995). Helping shy, socially anxious, and lonely adults: A skill-based contextual approach. In W. O'Donohue & L. Krasner (Eds.), *Handbook of psychological skills training: Clinical techniques and application* (pp. 247–286). Boston: Allyn & Bacon.

Gambrill, E. D., & Richey, C. A. (1975). An assertion inventory for use in assessment and research. *Behavior Therapy, 6,* 547–549.

Gambrill, E. D., & Richey, C. A. (1985). *Taking charge of your social life.* Belmont, CA: Wadsworth.

Gibson, F., Lawrence, P. S., & Nelson, R. O. (1976). Comparison of three training procedures for teaching social responses to developmentally disabled adults. *American Journal of Mental Deficiency, 8,* 379–387.

Glueckauf, R. L., & Quittner, A. L. (1992). Assertiveness training for disabled adults in wheelchairs: Self-report, role-play, and activity pattern outcomes. *Journal of Consulting and Clinical Psychology, 60,* 419–425.

Heinssen, R. K., Liberman, R. P., & Kopelowicz, A. (2000). Psychosocial skills training for schizophrenia: Lessons from the laboratory. *Schizophrenia Bulletin, 26,* 21–46.

Hinshaw, S. P., Klein, R. G., & Abikoff, H. B. (2002). Childhood attention-deficit hyperactivity disorder: Nonpharmacological treatments and their combination with medication. In P. E. Nathan & J. M. Gorman (Eds.), *A guide to treatments that work* (2nd ed., pp. 3–24). New York: Oxford University Press.

Holt, J. A., Schlesinger, D. J., & Dineen, J. P. (1997). Social skills training in groups with developmentally disabled adults. *Research in Social Work Practice, 7,* 187–201.

Kopelowicz, A. (1998). Adapting social skills for Latinos with schizophrenia. *International Review of Psychiatry, 10,* 47–50.

Kopelowicz, A., Liberman, R. P., & Zarate, R. (2002). Psychosocial treatments for schizophrenia. In P. E. Nathan & J. M. Gorman (Eds.), *A guide to treatments that work* (2nd ed., pp. 201–228). New York: Oxford University Press.

Liberman, R. P., DeRisi, W. J., & Mueser, K. T. (1989). *Social skills training for psychiatric patients.* New York: Pergamon.

Maletzky, B. M. (2002). The paraphilias: Research and treatment. In P. E. Nathan & J. M. Gorman (Eds.), *A guide to treatments that work* (2nd ed., pp. 525–558). New York: Oxford University Press.

Nelson, R. O., Gibson, F., & Cutting, D. S. (1973). Videotaped modeling: The development of three appropriate social responses in a mildly retarded child. *Mental Retardation, 11,* 24–28.

Pierce, K., & Schreibman, L. (1995). Increasing complex social behaviors in children with autism: Effects of peer-implemented pivotal response training. *Journal of Applied Behavior Analysis, 28,* 285–295.

Rapee, R. M., & Hayman, K. (1996). The effects of video feedback on the self-evaluation of performance in socially anxious subjects. *Behaviour Research and Therapy, 34,* 315–322.

Richey, C. A., Lovell, M., & Reid, K. (1991). Interpersonal skill training to enhance social support among women at risk for child maltreatment. *Children and Youth Services Review, 13,* 41–59.

Striefel, S. (1998). *How to teach through modeling and imitation* (2nd ed.). Austin, TX: Pro-Ed.

Sundel, M., & Lawrence, H. (1977). A systematic approach to treatment planning in time-limited behavioral groups. *Journal of Behavior Therapy and Experimental Psychiatry, 8,* 395–399.

Sundel, M., & Lobb, M. L. (1982). Reinforcement contingencies and role relationships in assertiveness within a general population. *Psychological Reports, 51,* 1007–1015.

Sundel, M., & Sundel, S. S. (1985). Behavior modification with time-limited groups. In M. Sundel, P. Glasser, R. Sarri, & R. Vinter (Eds.), *Individual change through small groups* (2nd ed., pp. 440–460). New York: Free Press.

Sundel, S. S., & Sundel, M. (1980). *Be assertive: A practical guide for human service workers.* Beverly Hills, CA: Sage.

Sundel, S. S., & Sundel, M. (1986). A group work framework for teaching assertive skills to the general public. In P. Glasser & N. Mayadas (Eds.), *Group workers at work: Theory and practice in the 80's* (pp. 166–175). Totowa, NJ: Rowman & Allanheld.

Van Houten, R. (1998). *How to use prompts to initiate behavior.* Austin, TX: Pro-Ed.

Wolpe, J. (1990). *The practice of behavior therapy* (4th ed.). Elmsford, NY: Pergamon.

CHAPTER 9

Punishment

Edward, a single father, complained to a therapist at a counseling center that he found it impossible to discipline Stephen, his 10-year-old son. Stephen frequently hit his younger sister, Dianne, making her cry. Stephen broke Dianne's toys during two recent incidents. On several occasions when Edward intervened to stop Stephen from hitting Dianne, Stephen cursed and kicked him. Verbal reprimands, threats, and lecturing failed to stop Stephen's undesired behaviors.

Objectives

After completing this chapter, you should be able to do the following:

- Give an example of the two types of punishment procedures, including the criterion for evaluating their effectiveness.
- Given a case example, identify the punishment procedure and label its relevant components.
- Give an example that compares extinction with negative punishment.
- Given a case example, describe how the effectiveness of punishment can be maximized.
- Give an example of punishment applied in a self-control contingency.

Punishment Defined

In the preceding chapters, we have discussed several procedures and techniques for increasing or maintaining the strength of behaviors. We have also presented three techniques for weakening or reducing the strength of a behavior—extinction, DRO, and DRI. In this chapter we address the concepts and procedures of **punishment,** a topic that attracts controversy but is often misunderstood.

In common usage, the term *punishment* is associated with vengeance or retribution. In behavioral terms, however, *punishment* refers to procedures applied to suppress behaviors or decrease their strength and not to acts intended to inflict harm or injury on an individual. The punished behavior is not necessarily eliminated because it could be performed again when the individual who administered the punishment is not present. Thus the term *suppress* is used to indicate that the punished response is not performed in the situation in which punishment was administered. In this chapter, we discuss two punishment techniques: (a) *positive punishment,* which is response-contingent presentation of a punisher; and (b) *negative punishment,* which is response-contingent removal of a positive reinforcer.

Aversive Stimuli and Punishers

An **aversive stimulus** is an event typically described by an individual as unpleasant, annoying, or painful. Intense noise or light, physical aggression (e.g., hitting, pinching, and kicking), traffic tickets, fines, and threats are common examples of aversive stimuli. Aversive stimuli often serve as punishers and negative reinforcers. (We discuss the use of aversive stimuli as negative reinforcers in Chapter 10.)

A **punisher,** or **punishing stimulus,** is a stimulus that suppresses or weakens a response it follows. Aversive stimuli have been used as intended punishers; however, they do not always act to suppress behaviors. By definition, a punisher acts to suppress a response or decrease its strength, whether or not the punisher is an aversive stimulus. For example, someone lights up a cigarette near you while you are eating a piece of apple pie. Although smoking is pleasant and not aversive to the individual who is smoking, it is unpleasant or aversive to you, and the smoke acts as a punisher to suppress your pie eating. Another person at your table says that the smoke is aversive but continues to eat; the smoke is not a punisher for that person's eating.

The distinction we are drawing between an aversive stimulus and a punisher is analogous to the comparison we made earlier between a reward and a positive reinforcer. Recall that a reward is a reinforcer only if it acts to increase the strength of a response. Similarly, an aversive stimulus is a punisher only if it decreases the strength of a behavior.

Punishers, like reinforcers, can be unconditioned (primary) or conditioned stimuli. An **unconditioned punisher,** or **primary punisher,** is intrinsically or naturally punishing; it does not require pairing or association with another punisher to suppress behavior. Intense light or noise and physical attacks, such as punching and slapping, are common examples of unconditioned punishers. A **conditioned punisher,** or **secondary punisher,** must first be paired or associated with an established punisher before it can act to suppress a behavior. Threats, fines, failing grades, and removal of privileges are common examples of conditioned punishers.

The symbol for an unconditioned punisher is S^{R-} (note the uppercase R). The symbol for a conditioned punisher is S^{r-} (note the lowercase r). In the discussion that follows, when the punisher is known, the appropriate notation will be used:

uppercase for an unconditioned punisher and lowercase for a conditioned punisher. If the punisher is not known, the notation S^{R-} will be used.

Positive Punishment

The procedure for positive punishment consists of presentation of a stimulus immediately after a response that decreases the strength of that response. The punishment effect is suppression of the target response and a decreased likelihood that the response will be performed again under similar conditions.

Baseline measures of the target response are taken prior to the initiation of punishment. Measures of the target response are recorded again after the stimulus intended to serve as a punisher has been applied. If the stimulus acts as a punisher, response strength will decrease in relation to the baseline measures. A stimulus is not a punisher unless it suppresses or decreases the strength of a response. For example, loud rock music might serve as a punisher for Maria's dancing but as a positive reinforcer for Jan's dancing.

Positive punishment can be depicted as follows: A response (R) is performed and followed by ($\rightarrow$) presentation of a stimulus (S) that decreases (–) the strength of the response.

Diagram for Positive Punishment

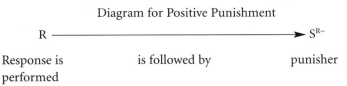

R		S^{R-}
Response is performed	is followed by	punisher

Effect: Suppression of the response, R, and decreased likelihood of its performance.

Positive punishment occurs in a wide range of situations. For example, George tracked mud into the house and his mother shouted at him (S^{r-}); Terry chewed her fingernails and her father put hot pepper sauce on them (S^{R-}); Martha volunteered to present extra cases at staff meetings and was called an apple-polisher by her coworkers (S^{r-}); and Bridget, a child with autism, bit her arm and received a slight electric shock (S^{R-}). These examples appear in diagram form as follows:

Diagrams of Positive Punishment

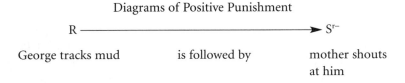

R		S^{r-}
George tracks mud	is followed by	mother shouts at him

Effect: George stops tracking mud into the house.

Terry chews   is followed by   hot pepper sauce
her fingernails

Effect: Terry stops chewing her fingernails.

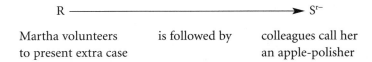

Martha volunteers   is followed by   colleagues call her
to present extra case   an apple-polisher

Effect: Martha stops volunteering to present extra cases.

Bridget bites her arm   is followed by   slight electric shock

Effect: Bridget stops biting her arm.

The decision to use positive punishment, particularly with an **unconditioned aversive stimulus** such as electric shock, has been based on the following ethical considerations:

1. The necessity for immediate effect because of serious danger or injury to the individual or others if the behavior is not suppressed

2. The relative effectiveness of other techniques that are available, considering their advantages and disadvantages

3. The ineffectiveness of previously attempted nonaversive procedures

4. The immediate and long-term negative consequences for the individual or significant others if the behavior is not suppressed or weakened

Currently, a changing philosophy about positive punishment emphasizes the use of reinforcement techniques to reduce undesired behaviors through the development of appropriate behaviors, rather than the use of aversive procedures to suppress undesired behaviors (e.g., Beare, Severson, & Brandt, 2004). Commonly used reinforcement techniques have included differential reinforcement of other (DRO) and differential reinforcement of alternative behaviors (DRA). As an alternative to aversive techniques, functional analysis has also been used to identify reinforcers (e.g., attention) that maintain self-injurious or other dangerous behaviors. Reinforcement contingencies are then modified to develop alternative behaviors without the use of aversive stimuli (e.g., Kurtz et al., 2003). In some cases, however, positive reinforcement techniques may be ineffective in developing desired behaviors, extinction or negative punishment techniques may prove to be ineffective in reducing undesired behaviors, and the undesired behavior is dangerous to the individual or others. In such situations, practitioners can consider punishment using aversive stimuli.

Mild electric shock, lasting only 1 or 2 seconds, can be effective in suppressing self-injurious behavior (Bucher & Lovaas, 1968; Prochaska, Smith, Marzilli, Colby, & Donovan, 1974). This kind of mild shock, usually applied to the hand, arm, or leg, produces a stinging sensation that lasts a few minutes. It is painful, but there is no permanent tissue damage from such a stimulus.

For example, Bridget, a child with severe autism, bit and scratched herself until her body was covered with sores. Bridget's caregivers had to tie her hands and feet to her bed to prevent her self-mutilation. Application of a mild, nonharmful electric shock to Bridget's hand immediately after she bit or scratched herself suppressed her self-destructive behaviors. After Bridget stopped self-mutilating, she was no longer confined to her bed and could begin to learn appropriate behaviors that were positively reinforced. In similar cases, positive reinforcement of incompatible responses, social isolation, and extinction techniques have proved to be less successful than electric shocks used as punishers (e.g., Linscheid, Iwata, Ricketts, & Griffin, 1990; Lovaas & Simmons, 1969). (This type of mild shock is in no way related to electroconvulsive therapy, sometimes called shock treatment, which is a treatment for severe depression.)

Other unconditioned aversive stimuli that have been used in positive punishment procedures include an ice cube held to the jaw to decrease bruxism (e.g., Blount, Drabman, Wilson, & Stewart, 1982), the smell of ammonia to decrease aggressive behavior (e.g., Doke, Wolery, & Sumberg, 1983), and the sound of an alarm to reduce severe hair pulling and finger sucking (e.g., Rapp, Miltenberger, & Long, 1998; Stricker, Miltenberger, Garlinghouse, & Tulloch, 2003).

Negative Punishment

The second type of punishment technique is called negative punishment or **response cost.** This procedure consists of removing or withdrawing a positive reinforcer contingent on performance of the target response. The punishment effect is suppression of the target response and decreased likelihood that the response will be performed again under similar conditions.

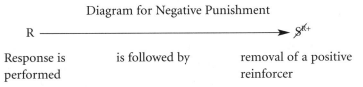

Diagram for Negative Punishment

R ⟶ S^{R+}

Response is   is followed by   removal of a positive
performed   reinforcer

Effect: Suppression of the response, R, and decreased likelihood of its performance.

The slash through the S^{R+} in the above diagram indicates a stimulus (S) whose removal ($\cancel{}$) decreases the strength of the target response (R). For example, when Sam was caught driving while intoxicated for the third time, his driver's license was revoked. In diagram form, Sam's situation appears as follows:

Diagram of Negative Punishment

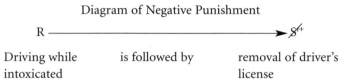

Driving while intoxicated	is followed by	removal of driver's license

Effect: Sam stopped driving while intoxicated.

In using negative punishment, the practitioner attempts to discover which items and events are reinforcers for the client. If the stimulus is a positive reinforcer, its removal will decrease the strength of the response. When punishing undesired behaviors, the practitioner should also arrange for positive reinforcement to strengthen desired behaviors.

Extinction and Negative Punishment

Extinction is different from negative punishment. In the extinction procedure, the reinforcer maintaining the response is withheld each time the response occurs until the response decreases to zero or to a desired level. The response no longer produces the positive reinforcer. In negative punishment, the response is followed by removal of a reinforcer *other than* the one maintaining the response. The response is suppressed and typically decreases immediately. The reinforcer removed for performance of the response acts to suppress the response and negate the effect of the reinforcer that has maintained the response.

For example, when Billy made farting noises in class, the other kids laughed at him. Billy continued to make farting noises in class; the children's laughter was the positive reinforcer for his making the noises. Using an extinction procedure, the teacher told the other kids to ignore Billy's noises. Billy's noisemaking gradually decreased as the reinforcer of the children's laughter was continuously withheld.

Using a negative punishment procedure, the teacher told Billy that if he continued to make farting noises he would have to stay in school instead of going on a field trip with the rest of his class. Billy stopped making farting noises in class. Removing the privilege of going on the field trip was negative punishment. The following diagrams compare the procedures for extinction and negative punishment:

Extinction Diagram			*Extinction Example*		
R ———/———▶ S^{R+}			R ———/———▶ S^{r+}		
Response is performed	is not followed by	positive reinforcer	Billy makes noises	is not followed by	kids laugh
Effect: Response decreases in strength and likelihood of occurrence.			*Effect:* Decrease in the rate of Billy's making noises in class.		

Negative Punishment Diagram			Negative Punishment Example		
R ⟶ $\not\!S^{R+}$			R ⟶ $\not\!S^{r+}$		
Response is performed	is followed by	removal of positive reinforcer	Billy makes noises	is followed by	Billy loses field trip privileges

Effect: Suppression of the response and decreased likelihood of its occurrence.   *Effect:* Billy stops making noises in class or makes them less frequently.

In extinction, the response tends to decrease in strength gradually; with punishment, suppression or decrease of the response is usually more immediate. For punishment to be effective, the positive reinforcer removed must exert greater control in decreasing the response than does the reinforcer maintaining the response. The removal of field trip privileges from Billy must, therefore, exert greater control in decreasing his noisemaking in class than the social reinforcement of laughter he receives from his classmates for engaging in that behavior.

The punishment effect can be maximized through the introduction of an extinction procedure during punishment. Billy's noisemaking might be most effectively reduced if both the extinction (termination of classmates' laughter) and the punishment (removal of field trip privileges) procedures are implemented.

In another example, Fred criticizes Marge's cooking before dinner. She ignores Fred's criticism, using an extinction procedure to decrease his criticism. If extinction is effective, Fred's criticism decreases. To use a punishment procedure, Marge cooks dinner only for herself that evening. In diagram form, this example appears as follows:

Extinction Diagram			Extinction Example		
R ⟶̸ S^{R+}			R ⟶̸ S^{r+}		
Response is performed	is not followed by	positive reinforcer	Fred criticizes Marge	is not followed by	Marge's attention

Effect: Response decreases in strength and likelihood of occurrence.   *Effect:* Decrease in the rate of Fred's criticizing Marge.

Punishment Diagram			Punishment Example		
R ⟶ $\not\!S^{R+}$			R ⟶ $\not\!S^{r+}$		
Response is performed	is followed by	removal of positive reinforcer	Fred criticizes Marge	is followed by	Fred loses a dinner cooked by Marge

Effect: Suppression of the response and decreased likelihood of its occurrence.   *Effect:* Fred stops criticizing Marge.

Time-Out

Time-out is a form of negative punishment. In time-out, the individual is removed from the problematic situation immediately after the target behavior is performed and placed for a brief period in an environment with no or minimal availability of reinforcement. The time-out procedure involves removal of S^Ds for the target response and removal of reinforcers. Case Example 7 (below) provides an example of this procedure. Edward took Stephen to the laundry room when he hit his sister. Taking Stephen to the laundry room prevented Stephen from responding to S^Ds in the problematic situation (Dianne's teasing and making faces) and removed the positive reinforcement (Dianne's crying and father's attention) for his inappropriate behaviors. The time-out room was arranged so that positive reinforcers were not available for Stephen during time-out.

When the time-out procedure is used, specific behavioral contingencies are established. For example, time-out is set for a specified, brief period of time, usually from 5 to 20 minutes. For young children, approximately 1 minute of time-out is used for each year of age. If the individual resists time-out by kicking, screaming, or cursing, a punishment contingency can be established in which such behaviors extend the time-out period—for example, by 2 to 5 minutes per incident. Release from time-out is made contingent on passage of the designated time and performance of appropriate behaviors in the time-out room. This time-out procedure, therefore, is markedly different from procedures used in some settings in which an individual is isolated for extended periods of time.

CASE EXAMPLE 7

The Parent as a Behavior Modifier

Edward, a single father, complained to a therapist at a counseling center that he found it impossible to discipline Stephen, his 10-year-old son. Stephen frequently hit his younger sister, Dianne, making her cry and inflicting bruises. He sometimes broke her toys during these incidents. When Edward intervened to stop Stephen from hitting Dianne, Stephen cursed and kicked him. Verbal reprimands, threats, and lectures failed to stop Stephen's undesired behaviors.

The therapist instructed Edward to obtain a baseline of Stephen's hitting and to identify situations in which the hitting occurred. Edward observed his children's behavior for a week and reported to the therapist that Stephen's hitting occurred 12 times during the week and that Dianne teased or made faces at Stephen on 9 of those occasions prior to his hitting her. Edward also indicated that he spent much of his time in the evenings trying to discipline Stephen.

The therapist instructed Edward to tell Dianne to stop teasing and making faces at Stephen, with the contingency that if she teased or made faces she would lose privileges, such as watching television or having a bedtime snack. On two subsequent occasions, Dianne lost television privileges and a bedtime snack. After these two experiences, Dianne stopped teasing and making faces at Stephen.

The therapist also instructed Edward to tell Stephen to go to the laundry room whenever he hit Dianne. If he refused to obey, Edward would physically carry or move Stephen to the laundry room, where he was required to remain by himself for 10 minutes. If he kicked or cursed Edward, the time-out was extended 5 minutes. If he screamed or made loud noises while in the room, the time-out was also extended 5 minutes.

The first time Edward took Stephen to the laundry room, he kicked and cursed. He also screamed while in the room. Stephen remained in the laundry room for a total of 20 minutes—the 10-minute time-out period plus two 5-minute extensions. This also happened the second time. The third time Edward instituted the treatment procedure, Stephen walked with Edward to the laundry room without cursing or kicking. The fourth time the procedure was applied, Stephen went to the laundry room by himself and quietly remained there until his time was up. After the fifth time the procedure was employed, Stephen stopped hitting his sister.

The therapist also instructed Edward to spend leisure time with Stephen in the evenings. Because Stephen liked to play cards with his father, the therapist told Edward to play cards with Stephen each evening after he finished his homework.

Maximizing the Effectiveness of Punishment

Researchers have investigated a number of variables influencing the effectiveness of punishment (e.g., Dinsmoor, 1998). The following conditions have been observed to maximize the effectiveness of the punishment procedure (Azrin & Holz, 1966):

1. The punisher immediately follows the target response.

2. The punisher is administered each time the response is performed.

3. The punisher is of sufficient intensity to suppress the target response.

4. The punishment contingency is arranged so that the individual cannot escape the punisher.

5. Alternate appropriate behaviors are specified.

6. Appropriate behaviors are positively reinforced.

7. Reinforcement for inappropriate behaviors is removed or reduced.

In both positive and negative punishment, the punisher is most effective when presented *immediately after* the response. If punishment of the target response is delayed, appropriate behaviors could be inadvertently suppressed. For example, a child disobeys his babysitter, who says, "Wait until your father gets home; then you'll get it!" Six hours later, the child is reprimanded by his father. Although the father's punishment might be associated verbally with the undesired behavior, any appropriate behaviors performed by the child are also punished, such as greeting his father at the door and talking about school.

Other factors influencing the effectiveness of punishment are the *intensity* and *frequency* of the punisher. The punishing stimulus must be sufficiently intense to suppress the target response. Similarly, when negative punishment is used, the reinforcer that is removed should exert more control over the individual's behavior than the reinforcer maintaining it. For optimal effect, the punisher is delivered on a continuous schedule—that is, each time the response is performed.

Four-year-old Jenny climbed trees after her mother told her to play on the ground. Her mother found her climbing a large tree, with other children urging her to climb higher. To maximize the effects of punishment, Jenny's mother sent the other children away (removal of positive reinforcement); yelled, "Jenny, stop! Get down from there!" (presentation of an intense punishing stimulus); specified another activity that Jenny could engage in ("Jenny, ride your tricycle"); and reinforced Jenny for playing at the appropriate activity ("You ride your tricycle so nicely").

Disadvantages of Punishment

Several side effects or disadvantages of punishment limit the effectiveness of punishment as a behavioral control technique (Azrin & Holz, 1966), including the following:

1. The punished response could reappear when the person administering the punisher is not present. For example, when Jenny's mother yelled at her for climbing a tree, she stopped climbing the tree, but Jenny might climb trees at her friend's house or at school when her mother is not present.

2. Aggression may occur in the form of physical or verbal attacks against the individual administering the punishment. For example, when the teacher gave Tanya a detention for passing notes in class, she cursed at him.

3. Aggression could be directed toward someone or something that was not responsible for delivery of the punisher. For example, the boss criticized Harry for handing his report in late. When Harry arrived home, he criticized his son for the way he wore his hair.

4. Through association with the punisher, the person who administers the punisher can become a conditioned punisher; the punished individual might then avoid that person. For example, Stan now avoids the teacher who punished him. Grandparents often reward their grandchildren and refrain from punishing them to help ensure that they will be associated only with positive reinforcement.

5. A punisher could suppress appropriate behaviors performed just before the punisher is delivered. This is especially likely if the punisher is not delivered immediately after the inappropriate response, as shown in the example of the babysitter who delayed the child's punishment until the father came home. In another example, a supervisor criticized a social worker for turning in an incomplete case report. At the time she was criticized, the social worker was reviewing case records to determine client progress. The supervisor's delayed criticism could act as a punisher to weaken the social worker's appropriate behavior of reviewing case records.

6. The person administering the punisher might be imitated by observers. For example, Adam's father screamed at him to clean up his room. Later, Adam's sister screamed at him to clean up his room in the same tone of voice her father used.

7. The intended punisher might be ineffective. It could serve instead as an S^D for an inappropriate response that is reinforced. The intended punisher could also act as a conditioned positive reinforcer that increases, rather than decreases, the strength of the target behavior. For example, when Fran was busy cooking dinner, her 3-year-old son, Tony, started playing with the telephone receiver. Although she told Tony several times to leave it alone, he persisted until she finally screamed at him. He began to cry, and she immediately ran over to him, talked to him soothingly, and played with him until he stopped crying. Tony might have learned from this experience that one way to get his mother's attention is to play with the telephone receiver. Mother will yell, but if he cries, she will talk to him and play with him. In diagram form, this example appears as follows:

Stimulus-Response Chain of Intended Punisher Serving as a Reinforcer

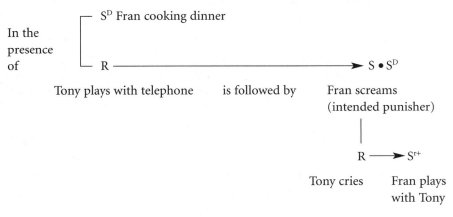

In the
presence
of

S^D Fran cooking dinner

R ⟶ S • S^D

Tony plays with telephone   is followed by   Fran screams
                                                        (intended punisher)

R ⟶ S^{r+}

Tony cries   Fran plays
                  with Tony

Effect: Tony's playing with the telephone when his mother is cooking dinner increases in strength and likelihood of occurrence.

The effect of this stimulus-response chain was that Fran's screams (S) became a conditioned positive reinforcer (S^{r+}) through association with the reinforcers of playing with and talking to Tony. Fran's screaming, therefore, unintentionally increased the likelihood of Tony's playing with the telephone; her screaming also served as an S^D for Tony's crying. Furthermore, Fran's screaming can reinforce Tony's other inappropriate behaviors, such as watching TV at bedtime or running away from her at the shopping center.

Another example of an intended punisher serving as a conditioned positive reinforcer is a marital argument. Norman came home 2 hours later than usual and missed dinner. When Rita accused Norman of having an affair, he swore at her until she began to cry. After Norman apologized and comforted her, she accepted the apology, and they had sexual intercourse. An abbreviated stimulus-response chain in diagram form for this example appears as follows:

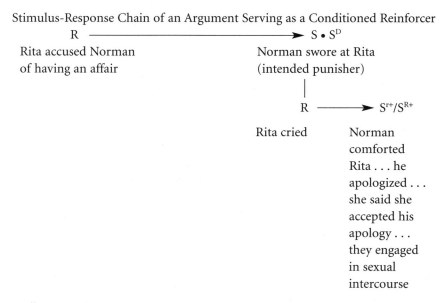

Stimulus-Response Chain of an Argument Serving as a Conditioned Reinforcer

R ⟶ S • S^D

Rita accused Norman
of having an affair

Norman swore at Rita
(intended punisher)

R ⟶ S^{r+}/S^{R+}

Rita cried

Norman
comforted
Rita . . . he
apologized . . .
she said she
accepted his
apology . . .
they engaged
in sexual
intercourse

Effect: Rita's accusations increase in strength and likelihood of occurrence.

Norman swore (S) at Rita, hoping to punish or decrease her accusations. Instead, his swearing served as the S^D for her crying (R), which was followed by sex (S^{R+}). The swearing thus became a conditioned positive reinforcer (S^{r+}) for Rita's accusations.

Argumentative behaviors can become conditioned reinforcers if they have served as S^{D}s for responses that led to reinforcers. In this case, the marriage counselor's assessment revealed the following pattern: When Rita cried, Norman comforted her and apologized and they usually had sexual intercourse. Although the S^{D}s for Rita's crying varied (Norman swore at her or spoke harshly to her), the reinforcers remained the same (he comforted her, apologized to her, and they had sex). In this way, Rita's crying came under the stimulus control of many S^{D}s, most of which were related to Norman's swearing or speaking to her in a loud voice. Thus any behavior of Rita's that resulted in Norman's swearing or shouting could set off the stimulus-response chain. Because of their association with positive reinforcers, Rita's accusations and Norman's swearing acquired the ability to function as conditioned positive reinforcers and could therefore strengthen other argumentative behaviors.

Alternatives to Punishment

Legal and professional guidelines address the appropriate use of positive punishment (e.g., Kazdin, 2001; *Wyatt v. Stickney,* 1972). As a general rule, positive punishment should be used only after alternative methods have been unsuccessful or in extreme instances in which a behavior has such damaging consequences that it must be stopped immediately. Before using a punishment procedure, the practitioner should consider other approaches to decrease the undesired behaviors. One alternative way to decrease inappropriate behaviors and increase appropriate behaviors is to specify and positively reinforce desired behaviors that are incompatible with the undesired behaviors (DRI). For example, instead of screaming at Stephen when he hits Dianne, Edward could reinforce Stephen with a cookie or praise when he plays cooperatively with her.

When accompanied by positive reinforcement for appropriate behavior, a punisher does not have to be intense to be effective in suppressing inappropriate behavior. Even a mild punisher can suppress undesired behavior. For example, a form of mild punishment was used to focus the speech of a client on discussion of his problem. The client frequently spoke about topics unrelated to his problem situation. Each time the client began to speak about a different topic when asked a question, the practitioner immediately said, "Can we please get back to the subject?" The client stopped speaking about the irrelevant topic and answered the practitioner's question. After the client answered the question, the practitioner said, "That's getting at the problem, please continue," thus reinforcing the client for staying on the topic. This procedure decreased the frequency of the client's speaking about irrelevant topics and increased the frequency of his talking about relevant topics.

Although punishment suppresses a behavior, it does not ensure performance of an appropriate response in place of that behavior. Providing S^Ds for performance of appropriate behaviors can increase the likelihood that they will be performed. For example, 7-year-old Mark tracked mud into the house. His mother spanked him and he cried. She also sent him to his room and did not give him dessert after dinner. Her punishment procedure did not specify the desired behaviors for Mark to perform to avoid tracking mud into the house. An alternate preventive intervention would be to provide an S^D to signal an appropriate behavior that could be reinforced, such as placing a mat at the front door so Mark could clean his shoes before entering the house.

We do not recommend physical punishment such as spanking or shaking children. Preferable to physical punishment are behavior change procedures providing antecedents that serve as cues or prompts for desired behaviors to be followed by positive reinforcers. Physical punishment by a parent, for example, provides a model of behavior that the child may imitate in the future. It can also limit the parent's selection of alternative techniques that could be more effective and less detrimental to the parent-child relationship. When punishment is selected as the desired procedure, negative punishment, or removal of positive reinforcers, is preferable to positive punishment, or presentation of a punisher, except in extreme circumstances as indicated in this chapter.

Overcorrection

Overcorrection is a procedure used to decrease an individual's inappropriate behaviors while at the same time providing S^Ds and reinforcers for the performance of appropriate behaviors (Azrin & Wesolowski, 1974; MacKenzie-Keating & McDonald, 1990). There are two types of overcorrection: restitutional overcorrection and positive practice overcorrection (Azrin & Bezalel-Azrin, 1999; Ollendick & Matson, 1978).

Restitutional overcorrection involves restoring the environment to the condition it was in before the inappropriate act was committed and then improving it even further. In one reported case, the restitutional overcorrection procedure for stealing food required the individual to return the stolen item to the victim (restitution) and, in addition, buy an identical item and give it to her (overcorrection) (Azrin & Wesolowski, 1974). In another example, when Stan threw his candy wrapper on the gym floor, a coach told him to pick up the wrapper and throw it in the trash (restitution). The coach also instructed Stan to pick up all the litter from the entire gymnasium and throw it in the trash (overcorrection). Overcorrection requires the individual to perform and repeat desired behaviors beyond correction of the original undesired behavior.

In *positive practice overcorrection,* the individual performs desired behaviors that are incompatible with his or her previous inappropriate behaviors and practices the desired behaviors repeatedly. Positive reinforcement is given for the positive practice to strengthen alternatives to the inappropriate behaviors. For example, when students spoke out of turn or left their seats in class without permission, they were required to state the rule they had broken, state the correct procedure, raise their hands and wait to be called on by the teacher, and ask the teacher for permission to speak (Azrin & Powers, 1975). The teacher reinforced correct practice with verbal praise. This procedure was repeated for 5 to 10 minutes during recess. Another example of positive practice overcorrection is a court program in which individuals convicted of driving under the influence of alcohol are ordered to attend 26 weeks of a psychoeducational program in order to regain their driving privileges. Participants in the program practice appropriate responses to situations that provide S^Ds to alcohol-drinking behaviors.

Stan's coach also used the positive practice overcorrection procedure when he saw Stan littering in the gym. The coach instructed Stan to throw 10 candy wrappers on the gym floor and pick them all up. This procedure was repeated every time Stan threw a candy wrapper on the gym floor. Stan received praise from the coach after he picked up each candy wrapper and threw it in the trash during the positive practice procedure. Positive practice can be used alone or in conjunction with restitutional overcorrection.

Overcorrection involves the following behavioral principles:

1. Reinforcement for the inappropriate behavior is removed (for example, a stolen food item is returned).

2. Time-out is implemented for the inappropriate behavior. When the individual is engaged in overcorrection, he or she is removed from the reinforcing environment.

3. The individual practices appropriate behaviors in the presence of appropriate S^Ds.

4. Positive reinforcement is given for correct practice.

Punishment and Self-Control

Punishment can be self-administered to control behavior. An individual can establish a punishment contingency to decrease undesired behavior. For example, a social worker who is a Democrat might establish the following contingency:

"If I complete fewer than two case reports each day this week, I will send $10 for each incomplete report to the Republican National Committee." An individual who wants to lose weight might establish this contingency: "Every time I eat between meals, I will give away one ticket to the basketball game."

To maximize the effectiveness of punishment, self-administered positive reinforcement contingencies can be added: "For every report I complete this week, I will spend 10 minutes at the beach on the weekend" or "For each day I eat only during meal times, I will put $1 away to buy a new DVD." Although self-contingency management programs lack the control provided by external behavior modifiers, these self-control procedures have been used successfully to modify undesired behaviors (e.g., Ivanoff & Stern, 1992; Watson & Tharp, 1997).

The Future of Punishment

Despite the disadvantages of punishment and the stringent requirements for ensuring its effectiveness, punishment is still commonly used as a behavioral control technique. One reason for this is that punishment usually works immediately to suppress undesired behaviors. Therefore, the short-term consequences are reinforcing for the individual who administers the punishment. For example, Mel spanked his daughter Terri when she hit her brother. Terri stopped hitting her brother; thus Mel was reinforced for spanking Terri. Because an individual's behavior is frequently governed by short-term consequences, punishment will probably continue to be commonly used for decreasing undesired behaviors. Only a radical shift toward the design of more preventive environments that focus on positive reinforcement might alter the use of punishment.

The public can become better educated in the effective use of reinforcement techniques to replace common positive punishment practices, especially the use of physical violence. Punishment with intense aversive stimuli should be used rarely, if at all, and only when (a) alternative, nonaversive techniques have not been effective, and (b) the undesired behavior is so detrimental or dangerous that its immediate cessation is necessary. It is important to recognize, however, that many of our behaviors are influenced by punishment contingencies. By analyzing problematic situations, practitioners can identify punishment contingencies used by individuals to control the behavior of others or that prevent an individual from performing desired behaviors. Wherever possible, the emphasis should be on developing and increasing desired behaviors that are incompatible with the undesired behavior.

Summary

1. Punishment is a behavior change technique that suppresses a response or decreases its strength. A response weakened by punishment is less likely to be performed again under similar conditions.

2. There are two types of punishment techniques: positive punishment, which is response-contingent presentation of a punisher; and negative

punishment, which is response-contingent removal of a positive reinforcer (also called response cost).

3. A punisher is a stimulus that suppresses a response or decreases its strength. Although a punisher suppresses a response, the punisher might not eliminate it because the response could be performed again when the punisher is not present.

4. An aversive stimulus is an unpleasant, annoying, or painful event. An aversive stimulus acts as a punisher, however, only if it suppresses a response or decreases its strength.

5. Unconditioned (or primary) punishers include electric shock, intense light or noise, and physical attacks, such as hitting and kicking. Examples of conditioned punishers are fines, failing grades, frowns, and removal of privileges.

6. Positive punishment consists of presenting a punishing stimulus immediately after the target response. The punishment effect is to suppress the response and decrease the likelihood that the response will be performed again.

7. Practitioners should take the following factors into account when deciding to use positive punishment: (a) the necessity for immediate effect, (b) the relative effectiveness of other techniques available, (c) the ineffectiveness of previously attempted nonaversive procedures, and (d) the negative consequences for the individual or significant others if the behavior is not decreased.

8. Negative punishment, or response cost, involves removing or withdrawing a positive reinforcer contingent on performance of the target response. The punishment effect is to suppress the target response or decrease its strength.

9. Extinction and negative punishment are not the same. Extinction involves withholding the positive reinforcer that maintains the response. The response is weakened and tends to decrease gradually. In negative punishment, the response is followed by removal of a reinforcer other than the one maintaining the response. The response is suppressed and typically decreases immediately.

10. Time-out involves removing the individual from the problematic situation to a place with no or minimal availability of reinforcement contingent on performance of the undesired response. The time-out period is brief.

11. The following seven conditions maximize the effectiveness of punishment: (a) The punisher is presented immediately after the target response, (b) the punisher is of sufficient intensity to suppress the undesired response, (c) the punisher follows the target response each time it is performed (that is, on a continuous schedule), (d) alternate appropriate behaviors are specified, (e) appropriate behaviors are positively reinforced, (f) reinforcement for inappropriate behaviors is removed, and (g) arrangements are made to prevent the individual's escape from the punisher.

12. The following are seven disadvantages of punishment: (a) The punished response could reappear in the absence of the punisher or the individual who administered it, (b) aggression in the form of physical or verbal attacks

could be directed against the individual administering punishment, (c) aggression might be directed toward someone or something that is not responsible for delivery of the punisher, (d) the person who administers a punisher can become a conditioned punisher through association with the punisher administered, (e) a punisher could suppress appropriate behaviors performed just before the punisher is delivered, (f) the person administering the punishment could be imitated by observers, and (g) an intended punisher can serve as an S^D for an undesired response that is reinforced.

13. Punishers can be used in self-control contingencies to decrease the strength of undesired behaviors in conjunction with the use of positive reinforcers to increase desired behaviors.

14. The public can become better educated in the use of positive reinforcement to replace punishment practices, especially the use of physical violence.

Suggested Activities

1. Give an example of a behavior of your own or someone else that you would like to decrease. How often does it occur? What are the situations (e.g., S^Ds) in which the behavior occurs? What are the reinforcers that maintain it?

2. Design a punishment procedure you could use to decrease the target behavior you identified in activity 1. Identify the procedure, the punisher, and the alternate behavior to be reinforced. Implement the punishment procedure and record the results, beginning with the baseline. Was the procedure effective? What is the basis for your conclusion?

3. Bring your results from activity 2 to class and discuss the procedure and its effects.

References and Resources

Adams, C. D., & Kelly, M. L. (1992). Managing sibling aggression: Overcorrection as an alternative to time-out. *Behavior Therapy, 23,* 707–717.

Alberto, B., Heflin, L. J., & Andrews, D. (2002). Use of the timeout ribbon procedure during community-based instruction. *Behavior Modification, 26,* 297–311.

Azrin, N. H., & Bezalel-Azrin, V. A. (1999*). How to use positive practice, self-correction, and overcorrection* (2nd ed.). Austin, TX: Pro-Ed.

Azrin, N. H., & Holz, W. C. (1966). Punishment. In W. K. Honig (Ed.), *Operant behavior: Areas of research and application* (pp. 380–447). Englewood Cliffs, NJ: Prentice Hall.

Azrin, N. H., & Powers, M. A. (1975). Eliminating classroom disturbances of emotionally disturbed children by positive practice procedures. *Behavior Therapy, 6,* 525–534.

Azrin, N. H., & Wesolowski, M. D. (1974). Theft reversal: An overcorrection procedure for eliminating stealing by retarded persons. *Journal of Applied Behavior Analysis, 7,* 577–581.

Beare, P. L., Severson, S., & Brandt, P. (2004). The use of a positive procedure to increase engagement on-task and decrease challenging behavior. *Behavior Modification, 28,* 28–44.

Blount, R. L., Drabman, R. S., Wilson, N., & Stewart, D. (1982). Reducing severe diurnal bruxism in two profoundly retarded females. *Journal of Applied Behavior Analysis, 15,* 565–571.

Bucher, B., & Lovaas, O. I. (1968). Use of aversive stimulation in behavior modification. In M. R. Jones (Ed.), *Miami Symposium on the Prediction of Behavior 1967: Aversive stimulation* (pp. 77–145). Coral Gables, FL: University of Miami Press.

Dinsmoor, J. A. (1998). Punishment. In W. O'Donohue (Ed.), *Learning and behavior therapy* (pp. 188–204). Boston: Allyn & Bacon.

Doke, L. S., Wolery, M., & Sumberg, C. (1983). Treating chronic aggression: Effects and side effects of response-contingent ammonia spirits. *Behavior Modification, 7,* 531–556.

Ivanoff, A., & Stern, S. B. (1992). Self-management interventions in health and mental health settings: Evidence of maintenance and generalization. *Social Work Research and Abstracts, 28,* 32–38.

Kazdin, A. E. (2001). Social, ethical and legal contexts. In A. E. Kazdin, *Behavior modification in applied settings* (6th ed., pp. 395–427). Homewood, IL: Dorsey.

Kurtz, P. F., Chin, M. D., Huete, J. M., Tarbox, S. F., O'Connor, J. T., Paclawskyj, T. R., et al. (2003). Functional analysis and treatment of self-injurious behavior in young children: A summary of 30 cases. *Journal of Applied Behavior Analysis, 36,* 205–219.

Lerman, D. C., & Vorndran, C. M. (2002). On the status of knowledge for using punishment: Implications for treating behavior disorders. *Journal of Applied Behavior Analysis, 35,* 431–464.

Linscheid, T. R., Iwata, B. A., Ricketts, R. W., & Griffin, J. C. (1990). Clinical evaluation of the self-injurious behavior inhibiting system (SIBIS). *Journal of Applied Behavior Analysis, 23,* 53–78.

Little, L. M., & Kelley, M. L. (1989). The efficacy of response cost procedures for reducing children's noncompliance to parental instructions. *Behavior Therapy, 20,* 525–534.

Lovaas, O. I., & Simmons, J. Q. (1969). Manipulation of self-destruction in three retarded children. *Journal of Applied Behavior Analysis, 2,* 143–157.

MacKenzie-Keating, S. E., & McDonald, L. (1990). Overcorrection: Reviewed, revisited, and revised. *The Behavior Analyst, 13,* 39–48.

Ollendick, T. H., & Matson, J. L. (1978). Overcorrection: An overview. *Behavior Therapy, 9,* 830–842.

Prochaska, J., Smith, N., Marzilli, R., Colby, J., & Donovan, W. (1974). Remote-control aversive stimulation in the treatment of head-banging in a retarded child. *Journal of Behavior Therapy and Experimental Psychiatry, 5,* 285–289.

Rapp, J., Miltenberger, R., & Long, E. (1998). Augmenting simplified habit reversal for hair pulling in three adolescents: A clinical replication with direct observation. *Journal of Applied Behavior Analysis, 31,* 299–302.

Roberts, M. W., & Powers, S. W. (1990). Adjusting chair timeout enforcement procedures for oppositional children. *Behavior Therapy, 21,* 257–271.

Stricker, J., Miltenberger, R., Garlinghouse, M., & Tulloch, H. (2003). Augmenting stimulus intensity with an awareness enhancement device in the treatment of finger sucking. *Education and Treatment of Children, 26,* 22–29.

Watson, D. L., & Tharp, R. G. (1997). *Self-directed behavior: Self-modification for personal adjustment* (6th ed.). Monterey, CA: Brooks/Cole.

Wyatt v. Stickney, 344 F. Supp. 373, 344 F. Supp. 387 (M.D., Ala. 1972); *aff'd* sub nom. Wyatt v. Aderholt, 503 F.2d 1305 (5th Cir. 1974).

CHAPTER 10

Negative Reinforcement

Pat screamed at her husband, Dick, for going out with his friends, refusing to help around the house, and spending little time with her and their children. When she criticized him, Dick swore at her and told her to mind her own business. Pat became so upset during these arguments that she burst into tears, ran into the bedroom, and locked the door, remaining there until Dick left the house.

Objectives

After completing this chapter, you should be able to do the following:

- Compare the effects of punishment and negative reinforcement.
- Give an example of escape behavior developed by negative reinforcement.
- Describe social interactions in terms of positive and negative reinforcement, given a case example.
- Describe avoidance behavior, given a case example.

Negative Reinforcers, Punishers, and Aversive Stimuli

In the example that opens this chapter, one way Pat could *escape* her husband's swearing and insults was to lock herself in the bedroom. The behavior change technique that produces escape behavior is called **negative reinforcement.** The negative reinforcement procedure consists of presenting an aversive stimulus until a response is performed that removes or reduces the effect of the stimulus. The removal of this stimulus, the **negative reinforcer,** *increases* the likelihood that the response will be performed again under similar conditions.

Aversive stimuli act as negative reinforcers when their removal *increases* response strength or as punishers when their presentation *decreases* response strength. Aversive stimuli, like rewards, are influenced by individual, social, and cultural factors. A stimulus that is unpleasant, annoying, or painful to one individual may not be aversive to another. Although a stimulus may be aversive to an individual, he or she may not always make a response to remove it. A stimulus is a negative reinforcer only when its removal increases the strength of the response that removes it.

For example, Jill says that cigarette smoke is aversive to her, but she continues to converse with Al while he is smoking. Jill does not make a response that could remove her from the smoke. In this case, the aversive stimulus (cigarette smoke) does not act as a negative reinforcer because Jill does not make an escape response. In contrast, Gloria finds cigarette smoke so aversive that she walks away from anyone who is smoking. For Gloria, smoke is a negative reinforcer, and her escape response (walking away) is reinforced and more likely to occur again. Cigarette smoke can function as a punisher, as in the example in Chapter 9, in which a person's pie eating decreased in the presence of cigarette smoke. Cigarette smoke can also function as a positive reinforcer for an individual's smoking behavior. These examples illustrate how one stimulus (cigarette smoke) can function as a positive reinforcer for the smoking response, as a punisher for the pie-eating response, and as a negative reinforcer for the escape response of walking away from someone who is smoking.

Negative reinforcers can be unconditioned or conditioned stimuli, as is the case with positive reinforcers and punishers. Examples of **unconditioned negative reinforcers** include shock, intense light, noise, foul odors, and physical attacks, such as punching or slapping. **Conditioned negative reinforcers** include threats, fines, bad grades, frowns, and insults. Recall from Chapter 9 that these same stimuli are called punishers when their presentation after a response suppresses or decreases that response. In this chapter, we examine how these stimuli function as negative reinforcers. As with positive reinforcers, the uppercase R$^-$ (S^{R-}) indicates an unconditioned negative reinforcer, and the lowercase r$-$ (S^{r-}) indicates a conditioned negative reinforcer. The uppercase R$^-$ (S^{R-}) is used here when the specific negative reinforcer is unknown.

It is important to remember that a punisher is not the same as a negative reinforcer, even though the same stimulus may be used for both. A punisher is a stimulus whose *presentation* _decreases_ response strength; a negative reinforcer is a stimulus whose *removal* _increases_ response strength.

Escape Behavior

The term *negative reinforcement* is used because the reinforcement function is to increase response strength. The word *negative* indicates the removal or reduction of the effect of the aversive stimulus. An **escape behavior,** or escape response, removes or reduces the effects of a negative reinforcer; the response allows the individual to escape from the negative reinforcer. A *negative reinforcer* is a stimulus that signals or sets the occasion for an escape response. A stimulus is defined as a negative reinforcer if its removal or reduction increases the strength of the escape response.

Following are some examples of negative reinforcers and the escape responses that can be made to remove or reduce their effects:

Negative Reinforcer	Escape Response
Pebble in shoe	Remove shoe
Mosquito bite itches	Apply ice to bite
Belt pressure on abdomen	Loosen belt
Bright sun in eyes	Put on sunglasses
Parents complain about Robert's grades	Robert goes to friend's house
Dick yells at Pat	Pat runs into the bedroom and locks the door
Todd demands sex after Sharon has said, "No"	Sharon has sex with Todd
Todd demands sex after Sharon has said, "No"	Sharon tells Todd she doesn't want to see him anymore and walks away
You receive a warning notice of eviction	You pay the rent that is past due
Baby cries	Mother shakes him

In the negative reinforcement procedure, a negative reinforcer (S^{R-}) is presented until an escape response is performed (R) that removes or reduces the effect of the negative reinforcer ($\cancel{S}^{R-}$). The S^{R-} acts as a discriminative stimulus that signals or sets the occasion for the escape response to be negatively reinforced. The following is the negative reinforcement diagram:

Negative Reinforcement Diagram

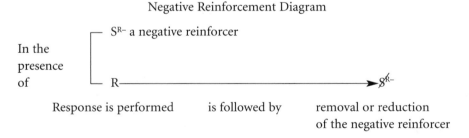

Response is performed   is followed by   removal or reduction of the negative reinforcer

Effect: The escape response (R) increases in strength and likelihood of occurrence.

The S^{R-} in this diagram indicates a negative reinforcer whose removal or reduction increases response strength.

Escape behavior occurs in a wide variety of situations. When your belt feels too tight around your waist (S^{R-}), you loosen it a notch (R). This response removes the pressure around your waist ($\cancel{S}^{R-}$). The likelihood is increased that you will perform this response on future occasions when your belt is tight. When you walk out into bright sunlight (S^{R-}), you put on your sunglasses (R) or cover your eyes with your hand (R). Either of these responses reduces the glare of the bright sun ($\cancel{S}^{R-}$).

After his sales manager criticized Ted for losing a customer (S^{r-}), Ted left work and went to a bar. Leaving work was the escape response (R) that removed him from the negative reinforcer of his boss's criticism ($\cancel{S}^{r-}$). At the bar, Ted kept saying to himself, "I hate this job. I'm never going to make it work out" (S^{r-}). As he drank more beers (R), the aversive thoughts (covert behaviors) decreased ($\cancel{S}^{r-}$). In the future, when criticized by his boss, Ted is more likely to leave work and drink at a bar.

Robert's parents complained about his poor grades (S^{r-}). Robert went to a friend's house (R) to get away from his parents' complaints ($\cancel{S}^{r-}$). The likelihood is increased that on future occasions when his parents complain, Robert will go to his friend's house. In diagram form, this example appears as follows:

Negative Reinforcement Diagram of Robert's Escape Behavior

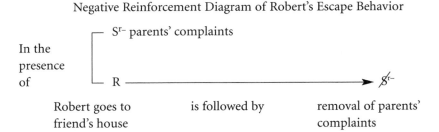

In the
presence
of

| S^{r-} parents' complaints |
| R ——————————————→ $\cancel{S}^{r-}$ |

Robert goes to   is followed by   removal of parents'
friend's house   complaints

Effect: Robert goes to his friend's house more frequently when his parents complain.

In the preceding example, Robert's response of going to his friend's house was negatively reinforced by removal of his parents' complaints about his grades. Removal of the conditioned negative reinforcer ($\cancel{S}^{r-}$) (parents' complaints) also strengthens other responses that have the same or similar effect (removing the complaints) as the reinforced response (going to his friend's house). Thus not only is a single response (going to his friend's house) reinforced but also a class of responses, each member of which could remove his parents' complaining, is strengthened. For example, bicycling to the video arcade and walking around the block are members of the response class that could remove his parents' complaints. Recall from Chapter 5 that when a response is positively reinforced, in fact, each member of the response class is also strengthened.

Escape behavior can occur when an individual feels pressured by a request or demand. For example, Sharon's boyfriend, Todd, had been asking Sharon to have sex with him for several months. Sharon always told him she was not ready, and he said he understood. Suddenly, however, his pleas became demands, and Sharon finally "gave in" because nothing she said stopped his demands. Todd's persistent and escalating demands for sex were positively reinforced by Sharon's having sex with him. Sharon's having sex with Todd was negatively reinforced by the termination of his demands—but only temporarily. After Sharon agreed to have sex, Todd began demanding it more frequently because his behavior was positively reinforced. A therapist role-played this situation with Sharon and taught her assertive ways to refuse Todd's demands for sex when she didn't want it.

Escape and Punishment

When a punisher is applied, it is important that the individual remains in the punishing situation and does not perform an escape response. An escape response made during punishment will reduce the effect of the punisher on the target response and increase the likelihood that the escape response will be performed again in a similar situation. For example, Fred was denied use of his father's car because he came home an hour past his curfew. Fred's late arrival was punished by removal of his driving privileges. Shortly afterward, Fred stole a neighbor's car and drove it. The escape responses of stealing the car and driving it were negatively reinforced by removal of the aversive condition of being without a car. Thus the escape responses were strengthened and would be more likely to be performed again in similar situations.

Although punishment and negative reinforcement techniques may involve similar stimuli, they have opposite effects on a behavior. Aversive stimuli act as punishers when their presentation decreases response strength, but they act as negative reinforcers when their removal increases response strength. For example, Jim, the quality assurance coordinator at an adult protective services agency, requested data on client outcomes from three of the agency's treatment staff members. The staff told Jim that they were too busy to supply the data, and Jim stopped asking them for the data. His response of requesting data was punished. The diagram depicting this example appears as follows:

Punishment Diagram of Jim's Request for Data

$$R \xrightarrow{\hspace{5cm}} S^{r-}$$

Jim requested data   is followed by   staff said they were too busy

Effect: Jim stopped asking for data; his response of requesting data was punished.

Rae, another quality assurance coordinator, requested similar data from the same staff members in memos she sent them every day. After Rae had sent six memos, the staff provided her with the data to satisfy her requests, thus terminating her memos. The likelihood increased that the staff would comply with Rae's future requests because providing the data was negatively reinforced by termination of her memos. In diagram form, this example appears as follows:

Negative Reinforcement Diagram of Rae's Request for Data

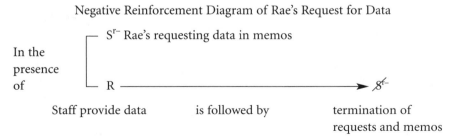

In the presence of

S^{r-} Rae's requesting data in memos

$R \xrightarrow{\hspace{5cm}} S^{r-}$

Staff provide data   is followed by   termination of requests and memos

Effect: Staff members are more likely to comply with Rae's future requests. Their responses of providing requested data were negatively reinforced.

The reinforcement and punishment diagrams are shown in Figure 10.1.

Reinforcement		*Punishment*	
R ⟶ S^{R+}		R ⟶ S^{R-}	
Positive reinforcement		Positive punishment	
Operation:	Positive reinforcer is presented	*Operation:*	Punisher is presented
Effect:	Increases response strength	*Effect:*	Suppresses R; decreases response strength
⎡ S^{R-} ⎣ R ⟶ $\cancel{S}^{R-}$		R ⟶ $\cancel{S}^{R+}$	
Negative reinforcement		Negative punishment	
Operation:	Negative reinforcer is removed	*Operation:*	Positive reinforcer is removed
Effect:	Increases response strength	*Effect:*	Suppresses R; decreases response strength

Figure 10.1   Reinforcement and Punishment Diagrams

Avoidance Behavior

One type of behavior established by negative reinforcement is escape behavior. A second type is **avoidance behavior**. An avoidance response is made in the presence of a conditioned negative reinforcer and prevents the occurrence of an established negative reinforcer. The avoidance diagram includes two conditions: the escape condition and the avoidance condition. In the escape condition, a neutral stimulus (S) is paired with an established negative reinforcer and acquires the ability to function as a conditioned negative reinforcer (S^{r-}). The conditioned negative reinforcer (formerly the neutral stimulus) signals that an escape response will be negatively reinforced. In the avoidance condition, the conditioned negative reinforcer is presented and serves as a discriminative stimulus or cue signaling that a second established negative reinforcer (S^{R-}) will follow unless an avoidance response (R) is made.

The avoidance response is negatively reinforced by removal or reduction of the conditioned negative reinforcer ($\cancel{S}^{r-}$) and prevention of the established negative reinforcer ($\nrightarrow S^{R-}$). The response is the same in both the escape condition and the avoidance condition. When the response removes the conditioned negative reinforcer and also prevents the occurrence of a second negative reinforcer, it is called an *avoidance response*.

As described above, the avoidance diagram consists of two steps: (a) the *escape condition,* in which a neutral stimulus paired with an established negative reinforcer signals that an escape response will be negatively reinforced; and (b) the *avoidance condition,* in which the conditioned negative reinforcer (formerly the neutral stimulus) signals that an avoidance response removing the conditioned negative reinforcer will prevent the onset of a second established negative reinforcer. The avoidance response is negatively reinforced by removal of the conditioned negative reinforcer and avoidance of the second established negative reinforcer. The avoidance diagram appears as follows:

Avoidance Diagram

Step 1: Escape Condition

is paired with

S --------------------- S^{R-} established negative reinforcer

Neutral stimulus

    R ————————————————▶ $\cancel{S}^{R-}$

     Response is performed   is followed by   removal of the
                         negative reinforcer

Effect: The neutral stimulus (S) becomes a conditioned negative reinforcer.

Step 2: Avoidance Condition

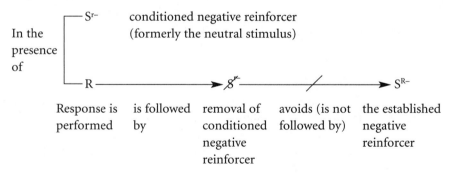

     S^{r-} conditioned negative reinforcer

In the   (formerly the neutral stimulus)

presence

of

     R ——————▶ $\cancel{S}$ ——————/——————▶ S^{R-}

    Response is is followed removal of avoids (is not the established
    performed   by   conditioned followed by) negative
               negative   reinforcer
               reinforcer

Effect: The avoidance response increases in strength and likelihood of occurrence; S^{R-} is prevented or avoided.

For example, Jerry said to his father, "Buy me that toy or I'll scream right here in the store." Jerry's father, preoccupied with his shopping, ignored him. Jerry started screaming until his father attended to him and bought him the toy. The father's response of buying Jerry a toy is strengthened and is more likely to be performed in the future when Jerry threatens to scream. In diagram form, this example appears as follows:

Avoidance Diagram of Jerry's Demand for Toy

Step 1: Escape Condition

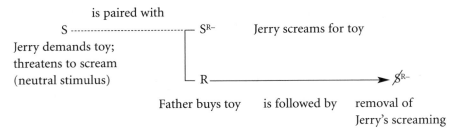

Effect: Jerry's demand for a toy and threat to scream become conditioned negative reinforcers.

Step 2: Avoidance Condition

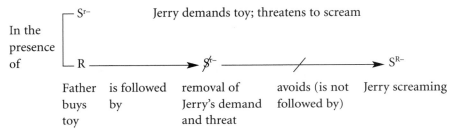

Effect: The father's avoidance response of buying Jerry a toy in the presence of Jerry's demands and threats increases in strength and likelihood of occurrence. Jerry's screaming is prevented or avoided.

Avoidance behavior is evident in many situations. When out for a walk, Raul heard a dog bark nearby (S^{r-}); he crossed the street (R) to reduce the effect of the barking and to avoid the possibility of a dog bite ($\not\to S^{r-}$). When we see steam coming out of a pot of soup on the stove (S^{r-}), we turn down the heat (R) to reduce the steam and prevent the soup from boiling over ($\not\to S^{r-}$). When parents threatened a college student who was failing math with the loss of financial support (S^{r-}), he studied math with a tutor (R) to remove the threat and to avoid losing his parents' financial support ($\not\to S^{r-}$).

In another example, Frida was packing her clothes to leave Dara, her partner. Dara screamed that if Frida left her, she would kill herself. Dara had attempted suicide on two previous occasions. Frida put her clothes away and said she would not leave. Dara's suicide threat was a conditioned negative reinforcer. Frida's avoidance response of saying that she would not leave was negatively reinforced by the removal of Dara's threats and the prevention of Dara's attempting suicide. Thus Frida's avoidance response was strengthened.

Extinction of Avoidance Behaviors

To maintain an avoidance behavior, occasional presentation of the second, established negative reinforcer is usually required. For example, if Jerry's father fails to perform the avoidance response of buying Jerry a toy, and if the negative reinforcer (screaming) does not occasionally follow, the avoidance response may extinguish—that is, Jerry's father may stop buying toys in response to Jerry's demands. If Jerry's father fails to perform the avoidance response and Jerry screams, however, this single episode could reinstate and strengthen the father's avoidance response. An avoidance response that is intermittently reinforced is highly resistant to extinction and usually requires only occasional presentation of the negative reinforcer.

An exception to this could be the threat of suicide or homicide. Because suicide is an extreme and final act, Dara's threats might be sufficient to maintain Frida's avoidance behavior. Dara's previous suicide attempts, and Frida's knowledge of them, could function as a cognitive, or covert, presentation of the established negative reinforcer for Frida, so that an actual suicide attempt would not be required to maintain Frida's avoidance responses.

Phobias and Negative Reinforcement

Certain problem behaviors, such as those related to irrational fears or phobias, are avoidance responses that were established with intense aversive stimuli (e.g., Ayres, 1998; Levis, 1989; Solomon & Wynne, 1954). In the development of a phobia, a neutral stimulus is paired with an intense aversive stimulus. This pairing increases the likelihood that the individual with the phobia will make a response in the presence of the conditioned negative reinforcer (formerly the neutral stimulus) to avoid the feared aversive stimulus. For example, Brad was terrified of going to the dentist. He never made an appointment unless he was in unbearable pain. When he approached the dentist's office, he usually turned around, drove home, and canceled his appointment. These avoidance behaviors were probably associated with a previously experienced intense aversive stimulus. Perhaps in the past Brad experienced great pain while a dentist was drilling one of his teeth, so that the sight of the dentist's office, or even the thought of making an appointment with the dentist, acquired the ability to function as a conditioned negative reinforcer (S^{r-}). Any avoidance response (R) that removed the sight of the dentist's office ($\cancel{S}^{r-}$) would also prevent the onset of a painful stimulus ($\cancel{\rightarrow} S^{R-}$) and would therefore be negatively reinforced.

Avoidance behaviors conditioned with intense traumatic stimuli are highly resistant to extinction, even on the basis of a single pairing of the dentist's office with an aversive (pain-inducing) stimulus. Brad is likely to avoid all contact with the dentist, even routine, nonpainful care. Brad might even avoid all buildings with dentists' offices in them. Brad's fear has other components, such as sweaty palms, irregular heartbeat, panting, and elevated blood pressure. These are respondent or classically conditioned behaviors, which we discuss in Chapter 11.

Stimulus generalization can occur with a negatively reinforced response as well as with a positively reinforced response. Through stimulus generalization, a response that was negatively reinforced in the presence of one stimulus can be performed in the presence of other stimuli. For example, Brad might turn away from all dentists' offices and not just the one in which he was negatively reinforced.

Ted's excessive beer drinking was negatively reinforced by escape from his boss's demands. His escape response (drinking) generalized to other situations in which demands were made of him by other individuals, including his girlfriend and his father. The more similar a situation or person is to the original stimulus that signaled the escape response, the more likely it is that stimulus generalization will occur and the escape or avoidance response will be performed.

In assessing phobic situations, the practitioner attempts to determine whether the client's target behavior is negatively reinforced by avoidance behaviors. Fear of elevators, doctors, or dentists, for example, can prevent an individual from carrying out customary activities, such as taking elevators at work or receiving medical or dental care. When an individual spends considerable time in avoidance responding, he or she has less opportunity to perform behaviors that can be positively reinforced.

Superstitious Behavior and Negative Reinforcement

In Chapter 4, we described how superstitious behavior can be established by accidental positive reinforcement contingencies. Escape behavior can also be involved in an accidental or superstitious contingency when a response is followed by removal or reduction of a negative reinforcer. The response, however, is only accidentally or coincidentally associated with removal of the stimulus, and its removal is not contingent on performance of the escape response.

For example, Mike was driving his car and suddenly the horn began to honk loudly (S^{R-}). He pushed and pulled various knobs on the dashboard and steering wheel, but the noise persisted. Finally, he shouted, "Stop!" (R), and the horn stopped honking ($\cancel{S}^{R-}$). Termination of the honking was not contingent on Mike's shouting "Stop!" Some other event, such as accidental shifting of contact wires, terminated the honking. Because Mike was negatively reinforced for shouting, however, it is likely that he will perform this behavior on similar occasions in the future. In diagram form, this example appears as follows:

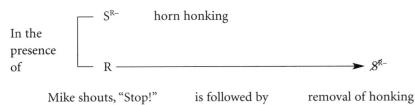

In the presence of

S^{R-} horn honking

R $\cancel{S}^{R-}$

Mike shouts, "Stop!"   is followed by   removal of honking

Effect: Mike's escape response of shouting "Stop!" is negatively reinforced; Mike is more likely to shout "Stop!" on future occasions when his horn is honking.

Some people avoid walking under ladders, crossing in front of black cats, or stepping on sidewalk cracks. These behaviors are negatively reinforced because they are not followed by anticipated aversive events. Similarly, some individuals believe that carrying good luck charms prevents the occurrence of unpleasant events. For these people, the charms also reduce the fear and anxiety associated with a potential calamity.

Some people believe that worrying (a covert behavior) can prevent bad events from taking place. Kyle said, "I worry all the time because worrying keeps bad things from happening." Kyle was certain that thinking or worrying about having a panic attack prevented his having such an attack. "When I think about having a panic attack, I don't have one," he said. "When I don't think about it, it can happen at any time." The following exchange illustrates this kind of reasoning:

Adam: Why are you carrying that plant around?

Daniel: To keep the monsters away.

Adam: There aren't any monsters here.

Daniel: See? It works!

Negative Reinforcement and Interpersonal Relationships

Negative reinforcement can be observed in interpersonal relationships. One partner's behavior may be positively reinforced while the other partner's behavior is negatively reinforced, as in the relationship between Carla and her mother in Case Example 3 (p. 268). Carla's screaming was *positively reinforced* by her mother's putting the toys away and buying Carla clothes. Juanita's behavior of putting the toys away and promising to buy Carla clothes was *negatively reinforced* by a reduction in Carla's screaming. In the example of Jerry and his father, Jerry's demand for a toy and threats that he would scream were *positively reinforced* by his father's buying him the toy. His father's response of buying the toy was *negatively reinforced* by the removal of Jerry's demand and threats.

In some relationships, one individual's behavior is punished and the other's is negatively reinforced. When Jim, the program evaluator, asked the staff for data, they said they were too busy. Their noncompliant response was *negatively reinforced* by termination of Jim's requests. Jim's response of asking for the data was *punished* by the staff members' saying that they were too busy to provide the data requested. A baby cries and his mother shakes him in an effort to stop the crying. The mother's shaking is negatively reinforced by the cessation of the crying; the baby is severely punished (and probably injured). Child abuse, such as shaking or hitting a child, is frequently negatively reinforcing to the abuser by the reduction or removal of the effects of the child's annoying or aversive behavior, such as crying or whining.

In other relationships, both individuals give and receive negative reinforcement. In Case Example 5 (p. 269), both Pat's and Dick's behaviors were *negatively reinforced*. Pat locked herself in the bedroom, which removed Dick's insults, and Dick left the house, which removed Pat's complaining.

Although negative reinforcement can be detrimental in social relationships, escape or avoidance behaviors that are negatively reinforced can also be constructive. A successful escape or avoidance response made in a dangerous situation will strengthen that response and enable the individual to respond appropriately to cues or warnings (S^{r-}), such as sirens, honking horns, and hurricane warnings, to avoid serious injury or disaster.

The Chinese government uses negative reinforcement to influence birth control practices. Couples who give birth to more than one child face fines, severe penalties, and social stigma. The couple's response of practicing birth control is negatively reinforced by removal of the threat ($\cancel{S}^{r-}$) and avoidance of the imposition of the severe penalties ($\cancel{\rightarrow}S^{r-}$).

The behavioral practitioner observes and analyzes interpersonal behavior patterns and identifies relevant positive reinforcers, negative reinforcers, and punishers. In friendships and intimate relationships, the practitioner often finds that the individuals provide insufficient positive reinforcers for each other. In counseling couples and families, the practitioner's goal is to help individuals improve their relationships by increasing their exchange of positive reinforcers and decreasing their use of punishers and negative reinforcers.

Summary

1. Negative reinforcement is a procedure to increase the strength of a response by removing or reducing the effect of a stimulus called a negative reinforcer. A negative reinforcer is an aversive stimulus that signals or sets the occasion for an escape response.

2. Escape behavior removes or reduces the effect of the negative reinforcer. The negative reinforcement procedure consists of presenting a negative reinforcer (S^{R-}) that remains in effect until an escape response (R) is made that removes or reduces the effect of the stimulus ($\cancel{\rightarrow}S^{R-}$). The removal of the negative reinforcer increases the likelihood that the response will be performed again under similar conditions.

3. Aversive stimuli can act as punishers when their presentation decreases response strength or as negative reinforcers when their removal increases response strength. Negative reinforcers can be unconditioned or conditioned.

4. Negative reinforcement is also involved in avoidance behavior. A conditioned negative reinforcer is presented that serves as a cue signaling that a second established negative reinforcer will follow unless an avoidance response is made. The avoidance response is negatively reinforced by removal or reduction of the conditioned negative reinforcer. The avoidance response also prevents the onset of the established negative reinforcer.

5. The avoidance diagram consists of two steps: (a) the escape condition, in which a neutral stimulus is paired with an established negative reinforcer; and (b) the avoidance condition, in which the conditioned negative reinforcer (formerly the neutral stimulus) is presented to signal an avoidance response that removes the conditioned negative reinforcer and prevents the onset of the established negative reinforcer.

6. Avoidance behaviors may extinguish unless the established negative reinforcer is occasionally presented. An avoidance response that is intermittently reinforced is highly resistant to extinction and usually requires only occasional presentation of the negative reinforcer.

7. Phobic reactions are related to avoidance behaviors that were established with intense aversive stimuli. In conditioning the fear, a neutral stimulus was paired with an intense negative reinforcer. This pairing increased the likelihood that the individual with the phobia will make a response in the presence of the conditioned negative reinforcer to avoid the feared stimulus (established negative reinforcer).

8. Practitioners can identify positive reinforcers, negative reinforcers, and punishers in analyzing interpersonal relationships. Although negative reinforcement can be detrimental to social relationships, escape and avoidance behaviors produced by negative reinforcement can be constructive in helping individuals respond appropriately to warnings and other stimuli signaling danger.

Suggested Activities

1. Identify three behaviors of yours or of someone you know that have been established through an escape procedure. For each behavior, (a) specify the responses and the stimuli and (b) draw a diagram showing the procedure.

2. Describe a situation that you avoid and identify the responses and stimuli involved. Draw a diagram showing the procedure.

3. Give an example of an interpersonal situation involving positive and negative reinforcement in which (a) one person receives positive reinforcement and the other receives negative reinforcement, (b) both persons receive negative reinforcement, and (c) both persons receive positive reinforcement.

References and Resources

Ayres, J. J. B. (1998). Avoidance and fear conditioning. In W. O'Donohue (Ed.), *Learning and behavior therapy* (pp. 117–136). Boston: Allyn & Bacon.

Azrin, N. H., Besalel, V. B., Bechtel, R., Michalicek, A., Mancera, M., Carroll, D., et al. (1980). Comparison of reciprocity and discussion-type counseling for marital problems. *American Journal of Family Therapy, 8,* 21–28.

Bourn, D. F. (1993). Over-chastisement, child non-compliance and parenting skills: A behavioural intervention by a family centre social worker. *British Journal of Social Work, 23,* 481–499.

Cipani, E., & Spooner, F. (1997). Treating problem behaviors maintained by negative reinforcement. *Research in Developmental Disabilities, 18,* 329–342.

Coleman, K. J., Paluch, R. A., & Epstein, L. H. (1997). A method for the delivery of reinforcement during exercise. *Behavior Research Methods, Instruments & Computers, 29,* 286–290.

Crosbie, J. (1998). Negative reinforcement and punishment. In K. A. Lattal & M. Perone (Eds.), *Handbook of research methods in human operant behavior* (pp. 163–189). New York: Plenum.

DeLeon, I. G., Neidert, P. L., Anders, B. M., & Rodriguez-Catter, V. (2001). Choices between positive and negative reinforcement during treatment for escape-maintained behavior. *Journal of Applied Behavior Analysis, 34,* 521–525.

Iwata, B. A. (1987). Negative reinforcement in applied behavior analysis: An emerging technology. *Journal of Applied Behavior Analysis, 20,* 361–378.

Kelley, M. E., Piazza, C. C., Fisher, W. W., & Oberdorff, A. J. (2003). Acquisition of cup drinking using previously refused foods as positive and negative reinforcement. *Journal of Applied Behavior Analysis, 36,* 89–93.

Levis, D. J. (1989). The case for a return to a two-factor theory of avoidance. The failure of non-fear interpretation. In S. B. Klein & R. R. Mowrer (Eds.), *Contemporary learning theories* (pp. 227–277). Hillsdale, NJ: Lawrence Erlbaum.

Lovaas, O. I., Schaeffer, B., & Simmons, J. Q. (1965). Experimental studies in childhood schizophrenia: Building social behavior in autistic children by use of electric shock. *Journal of Experimental Research and Personality, 1,* 99–109.

Malloy, P., & Levis, D. J. (1988). A laboratory demonstration of persistent human avoidance. *Behavior Therapy, 19,* 229–241.

Solomon, R. L., & Wynne, L. C. (1954). Traumatic avoidance learning: The principles of anxiety conservation and partial irreversibility. *Psychological Review, 61,* 353–385.

Zarcone, J. R., Fisher, W. W., & Piazza, C. C. (1996). Analysis of free-time contingencies as positive versus negative reinforcement. *Journal of Applied Behavior Analysis, 29,* 247–250.

CHAPTER 11

Respondent Conditioning

Alice knew it was the Rabbit coming to look for her, and she trembled till she shook the house, quite forgetting that she was now about a thousand times as large as the Rabbit and had no reason to be afraid of it.

—Lewis Carroll, *Alice's Adventures in Wonderland*, 1865

Bill felt anxious when he was criticized by his employer. He said he often became depressed after these encounters. In a role play of such situations, Bill perspired heavily, his face turned red, his breathing became rapid, and he rapped his knuckles against each other. His hands trembled, and he made excuses in replying to the criticism.

Objectives

After completing this chapter, you should be able to do the following:

- Give an example of a behavior established by respondent conditioning.
- Draw a diagram showing respondent conditioning of a phobia.
- Identify operant and respondent behaviors, given case material.
- Describe the procedure for extinguishing a classically conditioned response.

Respondent Behavior

There are two broad classes of behavior: operant and respondent. In the preceding chapters, we have focused on operant behavior. Operant behaviors are emitted or performed and are controlled by their consequences. **Respondent** or **classically**

conditioned behavior constitutes the second class of behavior. Respondent behaviors are *elicited* by antecedent stimuli.

Respondent behaviors include physiological reflexes (e.g., a knee jerk or eye blink) and other responses mediated by smooth muscles, glands, or cardiac muscle of the autonomic nervous system. Tears caused by dirt in the eye, sweating palms during a difficult exam, rapid breathing or gasping during a roller-coaster ride, and pupillary constriction on emerging into bright sunlight are all examples of respondent behaviors. Alice's trembling when the Rabbit was coming after her was a respondent behavior. Each of these responses is elicited or triggered by a preceding or antecedent stimulus.

Respondent Conditioning

The term **respondent conditioning**, or classical conditioning, refers to the development, learning, or establishment of a response based on the methods described by Ivan Pavlov (1927) and his followers. In respondent conditioning, a neutral stimulus (S) acquires the ability to elicit a **conditioned response** (CR) through pairing with an unconditioned stimulus (US). The US elicits an **unconditioned response** (UR) without requiring prior association of the US with another stimulus. The US automatically elicits the UR, with no prior conditioning required. For example, a freshly peeled onion elicits tears, food in the mouth elicits salivation, and a sudden loud noise elicits a startle reaction or crying. Through repeated pairings with the US, a neutral stimulus becomes capable of eliciting a CR that is similar, but not identical, to the UR. The neutral stimulus is then called a conditioned stimulus (CS). A CS associated with an intense aversive US can produce CRs highly resistant to extinction, sometimes on the basis of even a single pairing.

In an example of respondent conditioning, Kerri went to visit her grandmother, and as soon as she walked in the front door of her grandmother's home the aroma of fresh-baked chocolate chip cookies greeted her. Kerri was soon sitting down to a plate of the delicious cookies and a glass of milk. The cookies in her mouth (US) elicited salivation (UR). After several pairings of visiting Grandma and eating chocolate chip cookies, Kerri began salivating at the sight of Grandma's house. Grandma's house initially was a neutral stimulus that did not elicit salivation. Through respondent conditioning, however, the sight of Grandma's house acquired the ability to elicit salivation in Kerri. In diagram form, this appears as follows:

Respondent Conditioning Diagram of
Kerri's Salivation at the Sight of Grandma's House

I. Before conditioning

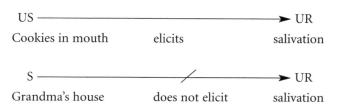

US ⟶ UR
Cookies in mouth　　　elicits　　　salivation

S ⟶ UR
Grandma's house　　　does not elicit　　　salivation

II. During conditioning

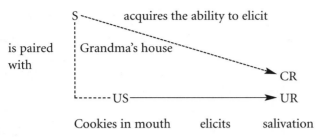

acquires the ability to elicit

III. After conditioning

S = CS ─────────────────────────────► CR

Grandma's house   elicits   salivation

Effect: The neutral stimulus (Grandma's house) becomes a conditioned stimulus capable of eliciting a conditioned response (salivation).

In an early example of respondent conditioning, Watson and Rayner (1920) demonstrated how a neutral stimulus (a small white rat) became a CS capable of eliciting crying in Albert, an 11-month-old child. The rat was initially a neutral stimulus that did not elicit the UR (crying). Albert was given a white rat, and he played with it. The researchers then produced a loud noise behind Albert by striking a steel bar with a hammer. The noise elicited a crying response (UR) from the child. The white rat and the loud noise were paired repeatedly. Then Albert was given the rat alone. On this occasion, the white rat elicited crying. It had become a CS through repeated pairing with the US. In diagram form, this example appears as follows:

Respondent Conditioning Diagram of Albert's Fear of White Rats

I. Before conditioning

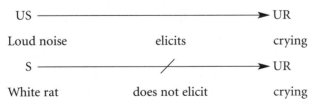

II. During conditioning

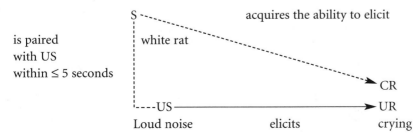

III. After conditioning

$$S = CS \longrightarrow CR$$

White rat   elicits   crying

Effect: The neutral stimulus (white rat) becomes a conditioned stimulus capable of eliciting a conditioned response (crying).

During conditioning, the neutral stimulus (S) is presented immediately prior to the US, optimally within 5 seconds, and overlapping it (Geis, Stebbins, & Lundin, 1965). In the previous example, the white rat was presented and within 5 seconds the loud noise was produced in the presence of the white rat. The neutral stimulus (white rat) was presented immediately prior to and within 5 seconds of the unconditioned stimulus (loud noise). The neutral stimulus and the unconditioned stimulus were overlapping—that is, the rat was present at the time the loud noise was introduced.

The Watson and Rayner study demonstrated that emotional responses can be conditioned. Today, it would be considered unethical to conduct a study that creates distress in a healthy individual, especially a child. To their credit, Watson and Rayner had planned to remove Albert's fear through exposure techniques that recently have been demonstrated to be effective. Unfortunately, little Albert moved away from the city before they could treat his fear. Several years later, Mary Cover Jones (1924) successfully treated Peter, a boy who had a fear of rabbits, by gradually exposing him to a rabbit while he was eating—one of the techniques Watson and Rayner had proposed to use with Albert.

In another example of respondent conditioning, Mowrer and Mowrer (1938) designed a urine alarm involving a pad and bell apparatus to reduce enuresis in children ages 3 to 13. The intervention was based on associating a full bladder with waking up, so that the child could go to the bathroom rather than wet the bed. When the pad on the bed was dry, it did not conduct electricity. When the pad became wet, however, it closed a circuit that rang a bell. The ringing of the bell coincided with the beginning of bed-wetting and, presumably, with a full bladder. The ringing of the bell was the US that elicited the UR of waking up from a sound sleep. Initially, the full bladder was a neutral stimulus that did not elicit the CR of waking up. Through repeated pairings, the full bladder, which occurred at the same time as the ringing bell, became the CS for waking up. After the child awakened, he or she could go to the bathroom rather than wet the bed. In diagram form, this example appears as follows:

Respondent Conditioning Diagram for the Treatment of Enuresis

I. Before conditioning

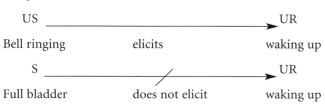

$$US \longrightarrow UR$$

Bell ringing   elicits   waking up

$$S \longrightarrow UR$$

Full bladder   does not elicit   waking up

II. During conditioning

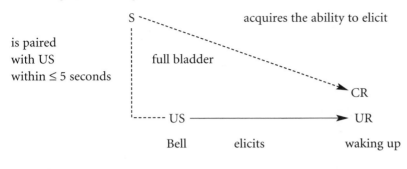

is paired
with US
within ≤ 5 seconds

III. After conditioning

Effect: The neutral stimulus (full bladder) becomes a conditioned stimulus capable of eliciting a conditioned response (waking up).

The urine alarm is the treatment of choice for nocturnal enuresis when used with relapse prevention techniques (Butler & Campise, 1998). Inexpensive commercial alarms are available for purchase from the Sears and J. C. Penney catalogs as well as from other vendors (Butler & Campise, 1998, p. 145).

Drug use can also be associated with environmental stimuli that elicit conditioned responses. For example, smoking crack cocaine (US) causes a marked decrease in skin temperature (UR). One team of researchers found that when individuals are in the process of getting high on crack, drug-related paraphernalia, such as crack pipes, are associated with the cocaine and become conditioned stimuli (CS) capable of eliciting the conditioned response of lower skin temperature (CR). Seeing a crack pipe resulted in lower skin temperature for cocaine users, and the physiological response of lowered skin temperature was associated with drug-seeking behaviors (Kirby, Lamb, & Iguchi, 1997).

Response Strength

The strength of a CR is measured by (a) the magnitude of the CR and (b) the latency or interval between presentation of the CS and elicitation of the CR. The magnitude of a CR is measured by contraction of a muscle or blood vessel or secretion of a gland. For example, heart rate is measured by pulse rate, muscle contraction is measured by the amount of electrical activity of the muscle, and salivation is measured by drops of saliva. Latency is measured by the amount of time that passes between presentation of the CS and elicitation of the CR. The shorter the latency, the stronger the response. The greater the magnitude, the stronger the response. The magnitude of the CR has been shown to be directly influenced by the number of pairings of the CS and US. Other variables affecting response magnitude and latency include the intensity of the US and the type or size of the US (Hollis, 1997; Pavlov, 1927; Turkkan, 1989).

Extinction of Respondent Behaviors

Classically conditioned responses, like operant responses, can be weakened by extinction (Falls, 1998). The CS must be paired occasionally with the US or the CR will extinguish. The extinction procedure consists of presenting the CS alone repeatedly until it fails to elicit the CR. Because the US no longer follows the CS, the CR is weakened. For example, extinction of Kerri's salivating (CR) at the sight of Grandma's house (CS) would occur if Kerri went to Grandma's house repeatedly and found no cookies available there.

Generalization in Respondent Conditioning

The CR is likely to be elicited by other stimuli similar to the CS along some dimension or characteristic. Stimuli most similar to the CS elicit the strongest CRs. As stimuli become less similar to the CS, they elicit weaker CRs. In the case of Albert described previously, a rabbit, a seal coat, and a ball of cotton also elicited crying (CR). Other items that were not similar to the white rat, such as wooden blocks, did not elicit crying. Thus stimulus generalization occurs with respondent as well as operant behaviors.

On a winter evening, a man was crossing the street in Philadelphia near train tracks when he broke into a sweat and began trembling. The tracks (CS) elicited an emotional response (CR) and a flashback to the train the man and his family were forced to board in Warsaw en route to the Auschwitz concentration camp in the winter of 1940. In another example, the sound of a car backfiring (CS) elicited the CRs of shaking and perspiring in a veteran of the Vietnam War. The CS of the car backfiring sounded like the US of gunfire on the battlefield and thus elicited similar CRs.

In Chapter 10, we discussed Brad's fear of the dentist's office. During conditioning of this fear, the dentist's office, originally a neutral stimulus (S), became capable of eliciting sweaty palms, irregular heartbeat, panting, and elevated blood pressure (anxiety CRs) in Brad. The dentist's office was paired with the painful previous drilling (US) of Brad's tooth, which elicited the anxiety responses (URs). In this way, the sight of a dentist's office became a CS that elicited the CR (anxiety).

As another example of stimulus generalization, if a boy was bitten by a dog, other dogs and other furry animals with four legs might elicit anxiety CRs in the boy. Stimuli most similar to the CS will elicit the strongest CRs. As stimuli appear less similar to the biting dog (CS), they will elicit weaker anxiety CRs. Various stimuli in the conditioning environment can also become associated with anxiety, such as the place where the incident occurred, other individuals who were present, memories of the incident, and the dog's bark. These stimuli can become CSs that elicit anxiety CRs.

Emotional Behavior

Respondent or classical conditioning is involved in the acquisition or conditioning of emotional behaviors. An emotional response is usually accompanied by physiological changes in heart rate, blood pressure, perspiration, stomach and bowel activities, and muscle tension. People learn to identify their own feeling states early in life when their parents or other significant persons in their lives associate verbal labels with certain physiological changes.

For example, 5-year-old Kevin is shaking, breathing rapidly, and crying, with tears streaming down his flushed face. His mother asks him, "What's wrong? What are you afraid of?" Kevin replies that he was playing on the swing in the park when an older boy pushed him to the ground. His mother asks, "Were you afraid of that boy?" The operant and respondent behaviors involved in Kevin's encounter with the older boy become associated with the word *afraid*. When experiencing similar physiological changes on future occasions, Kevin is likely to label them as "being afraid" or "fear." The anxiety-eliciting CS can also serve as a conditioned negative reinforcer (S^{r-}) to signal operant escape and avoidance behaviors that are negatively reinforced, such as hiding behind a rock when the older boy approaches. Many problems for which people seek treatment involve anxiety as a central component, such as conditions diagnosed as panic disorder, phobias, posttraumatic stress disorder, and obsessive-compulsive disorder. Emotional behaviors can distort reality, such as Alice's extreme reaction to the Rabbit when, in fact, she was "about a thousand times as large as the Rabbit and had no reason to be afraid of it."

Emotional behavior also includes pleasant feelings or affective states associated with particular situations. Feelings labeled as joy, elation, relaxation, sexual arousal, and happiness may involve CRs associated with pleasant persons, events, or places (CSs). For example, a photograph of yourself lying on a beach on vacation (CS) elicits the calm, relaxed emotional state (CR) associated with the vacation. Eating home-baked cookies at Grandma's house (CS) elicits pleasant feelings toward Grandma (CR). The sight of similar cookies in a bakery (CS) might elicit similar feelings (pleasant CRs). The CSs in both these examples can also serve as S^Ds— for calling the travel agent to make reservations for a vacation at the beach and for buying cookies, respectively.

Respondent Conditioning of Phobias

When maladaptive **anxiety** or fear is attached to a specific object, it is called a **phobia**. In other words, the individual is afraid of something that objectively does not warrant anxiety. For example, it is not adaptive to avoid all buildings with elevators if you once got stuck in an elevator. Phobias are acquired through a respondent conditioning process in which a neutral stimulus acquires the ability to elicit anxiety through pairing with an aversive US. For example, a painful US, such as a dog bite, elicits anxiety URs associated with the pain, such as increased heart rate and blood pressure, trembling, and shortness of breath. The US (painful bite) is paired with the sight of the dog that administered the bite. The sight of the dog is initially a neutral stimulus (S) but acquires the ability to elicit anxiety (CS). During conditioning, the neutral stimulus (S) is presented immediately prior to the US. In diagram form, this example appears as follows:

Respondent Conditioning Diagram of a Dog Phobia

I. Before conditioning

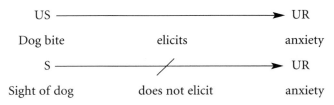

$$US \longrightarrow UR$$

Dog bite   elicits   anxiety

$$S \longrightarrow UR$$

Sight of dog   does not elicit   anxiety

II. During conditioning

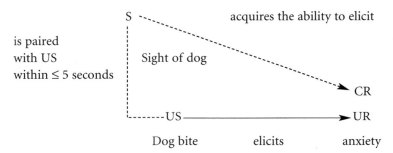

is paired
with US
within ≤ 5 seconds

S ⋯⋯   acquires the ability to elicit

Sight of dog

CR

US ———— UR

Dog bite   elicits   anxiety

III. After conditioning

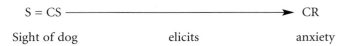

$$S = CS \longrightarrow CR$$

Sight of dog   elicits   anxiety

Effect: The sight of the dog, formerly a neutral stimulus, elicits anxiety.

Some researchers have used cognitive factors to explain clinical phenomena such as fears. For example, Rescorla (1988) considered the information that stimuli provide to the organism to be more essential to classical conditioning than the simple pairing or association between the US and the CS. Rescorla proposed that conditioning involves the learning of relationships among the stimuli that allows the organism to represent its environment. Wolpe (1990, p. 22), however, has argued against Rescorla's explanation of the role of information in classical conditioning because it leads to the conclusion that such learning occurs in the mind of an organism rather than in the nervous system at the synaptic level.

An alternate explanation for the conditioning of phobic behaviors focuses on cognitive factors leading to fear and avoidance behavior. Bandura (1977), for example, indicated that the expectation of danger or pain associated with a stimulus accounts for both the fear (cognitive element) and the avoidance (operant behaviors). This formulation, however, does not take into account the considerable evidence demonstrating the classical conditioning of fears (Ayres, 1998; Wolpe, 1990).

Escape, Avoidance, and Respondent Conditioning

Operant components of anxiety include escape and avoidance behaviors, such as making excuses, lying, and rapid pacing; and repetitive responses, such as hand washing and agitated speech patterns. These behaviors make it more difficult to extinguish the anxiety CRs. A phobic response will extinguish if the individual remains in the presence of the CS for a sufficient period of time without making an avoidance response. Phobias that are difficult to extinguish, however, usually have two major characteristics: (a) They were conditioned with an intense US and (b) they involve avoidance responses that are negatively reinforced. In this situation, the CS elicits the CR and also functions as an S^{r-}. The avoidance response removes the S^{r-} and prevents the individual from finding out that the established S^{R-} will not follow. The person is negatively reinforced by removal of the S^{r-}, with an escape response, and thereby fails to remain in its presence to test whether the S^{R-} will be presented.

For example, Margaret was bitten by a dog 10 years ago and makes an avoidance response of running away as soon as she sees a dog. She does not wait for the dog to come close so that she can determine whether it will bite her. The sight of the dog (CS) serves as a conditioned negative reinforcer (S^{r-}) that signals an avoidance response (R) that is negatively reinforced by removal of the S^{r-} with an escape response. At the same time, the CS elicits anxiety responses (CRs). The avoidance response also prevents Margaret from finding out whether the S^{R-} (dog bite) will follow. In diagram form, this example appears as follows:

Respondent Conditioning and Avoidance Diagram of Fear of Dogs

1. Respondent conditioning

CS ⟶ CR

Sight of dog   elicits   anxiety

2. Avoidance conditioning

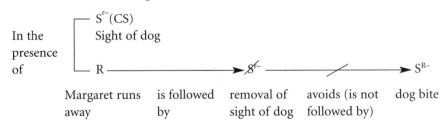

In the presence of

S^{r-}(CS)
Sight of dog

R

Margaret runs away   is followed by   removal of sight of dog   avoids (is not followed by)   dog bite

Effect: The avoidance response (running away) is negatively reinforced; it increases in strength and likelihood of occurrence. The dog bite is avoided.

Operant and Respondent Control of Behaviors

In some situations, the same stimulus serves as both a CS and an S^D. For example, when we eat in a restaurant, the presence of food on the tongue (US) elicits salivation

(UR). Through previous conditioning, the sight of the waiter approaching (CS) or a picture of pasta on the menu (CS) elicits salivation (CR). These CSs can also serve as S^Ds for the operant responses of picking up a fork or ordering the pasta from the menu. A dog's bark can serve as a CS for Victor's anxiety CRs. It can also serve as a conditioned negative reinforcer (S^{r-}) for his avoidance response of running into the house.

It is sometimes difficult to determine whether a behavior is under operant or respondent control. To do so, it is necessary to determine whether the response is elicited by a CS or US (antecedent) or controlled by a reinforcer or punisher (consequence). For example, crying can be operant or respondent. If Betsy's crying is elicited by an injection or the pain of a sprained ankle, it is respondent crying. If, however, Betsy's crying is observed to increase as a result of reinforcing consequences (e.g., Betsy's parents comply with her demands), her crying is under operant control.

Many situations involve both operant and respondent behaviors (Allan, 1998). For example, in Case Example 6 (p. 271), Bill emitted the operant responses of rapping his knuckles together and making excuses when he was criticized by his boss. Being criticized also elicited the following respondent behaviors: Bill perspired heavily, his hands trembled, his face turned red, and his breathing became rapid. In assessing problematic situations, practitioners identify respondent and operant behaviors so that they can formulate intervention plans that include relevant techniques for modifying each type of behavior.

Until the late 1960s, operant and respondent behaviors were typically regarded as constituting two separate and distinct classes of behavior. Behavioral principles applicable to one class of behavior were not considered applicable to the other. Operant behaviors were restricted to the so-called voluntary or striated, skeletal muscles. Respondent behaviors were restricted to elicited, "automatic," or "involuntary" autonomic responses involving smooth muscles, glands, and reflexes. Subsequent research made such rigid distinctions between operant and respondent behaviors more difficult to uphold (Allan, 1998; Miller, 1985), especially with the increased use of biofeedback (see, e.g., Schwartz & Andrasik, 2003).

Biofeedback and Behavioral Medicine

Biofeedback is a method in which auditory, visual, and other sensory information is used to assess and modify physiological responses, such as heart rate, blood pressure, muscle tension, brain waves, and skin temperature (e.g., Schwartz & Andrasik, 2003). The practitioner and client can observe and monitor changes in the client's physiological responses, which are measured electronically and displayed on a monitor. Biofeedback has been used with behavior change techniques to facilitate relaxation training and control of physiological responses. Behaviors categorized as respondent, previously thought to be exclusively under autonomic or involuntary control (e.g., brain waves, blood pressure, and heart rate), have been operantly strengthened and weakened with biofeedback.

Practitioners in the fields of **behavioral medicine** and health psychology use behavior change principles and techniques, including biofeedback, to treat various health problems (Graves & Miller, 2003; Rimer, 1997). Biofeedback has been applied to the treatment of a wide range of physiological dysfunctions, including insomnia, headache, hypertension, chronic pain, urinary incontinence, irritable bowel syndrome, and psychosomatic complaints (e.g., McGrady, Olson, & Kroon, 1995; Meissner, Blanchard, & Malamood, 1997; Schwartz & Andrasik, 2003).

Biofeedback technology also has significant implications for the treatment of cardiac, visceral, and psychosomatic disorders previously considered outside the individual's control. For example, a device called RESPeRATE provides biofeedback coaching that interactively guides the user through exercises that lower blood pressure (Gilbert, 2003; Viskoper et al., 2003). The device analyzes breathing rate and pattern, and emits an auditory tone to guide the user to decrease his or her breathing rate systematically by prolonging exhalation to fewer than 10 breaths per minute. Research has shown that individuals who use this device regularly can achieve notable decreases in systolic and diastolic measures of blood pressure (e.g., Viskoper et al., 2003).

Other devices take advantage of new technologies to remind people to take their pills. One of these sounds an alarm if a pill isn't taken on time and then notifies a designated third party if there is no response to the alarm. Handheld computers can provide elaborate prompts for carrying out medical regimens. Behavioral interventions have been applied widely in medical settings for purposes such as encouraging patients to keep their medical appointments (e.g., Rice & Lutzker, 1984), helping patients to cope with medical crises (e.g., DiTomasso, Martin, & Kovnat, 2000), monitoring medical procedures (e.g., Wong, Seroka, & Ogisi, 2000), and training parents to help their children comply with medical procedures (e.g., McComas, Wacker, & Cooper, 1998).

Behavioral treatment and management of pain involve interventions that reduce the individual's discomfort and increase the individual's ability to tolerate and cope with discomfort. From a behavioral perspective, pain is viewed as a behavior indicated by crying, complaining, limiting one's activities, facial contortions, and verbal behaviors identifying intense discomfort. Individuals exhibit different behaviors when they are well and healthy than they do when they are sick or in pain.

Pain, like other behaviors, is influenced by controlling antecedents and consequences. We only have to observe a college football game to see how cheering fans can reinforce an injured football player's staying in the game and continuing to play in spite of great physical discomfort. That same football player might crawl into bed complaining of severe pain and remain there for a week when he gets home.

Eliciting antecedents (USs) to pain (UR) include physical sensations of discomfort related to stimulation of the nervous system's pain receptors. Other antecedents are cognitive behaviors (e.g., self-statements) that may increase the intensity of pain sensations when the individual "can't think about anything else." Perseverating on the pain can increase the discomfort and disability. Some antecedents can be manipulated through cognitive interventions, such as self-instruction training and stress inoculation training (e.g., Meichenbaum, 1985), as well as through deep muscle relaxation and biofeedback (e.g., Andrasik, Larsson, & Grazzi, 2002; Blanchard, 1992).

Controlling the consequences of pain also plays a role in maintaining pain behaviors. Consequences can include positive reinforcement, such as attention, sympathy, and financial compensation from insurance settlements or disability payments. Negative reinforcers can also maintain pain behaviors, such as when exhibiting pain allows the individual to avoid work or other responsibilities. Receiving pain medication can maintain pain behaviors through the positive reinforcement of attention from medical personnel administering the medication and the negative reinforcement of pain relief.

Summary

1. Respondent behavior is elicited by an antecedent stimulus and involves physiological reflexes and other responses mediated by smooth muscles, glands, or cardiac muscle of the autonomic nervous system.

2. In respondent conditioning, a neutral stimulus (S) acquires the ability to elicit a CR through pairing with a US. The US elicits a UR without requiring prior association of the US with another stimulus. To establish a conditioned response, the neutral stimulus is optimally presented immediately prior to the US and overlapping it.

3. The strength of a CR is measured by its (a) magnitude and (b) latency, the interval between presentation of the CS and elicitation of the CR.

4. The CS must be paired occasionally with the US or the CR will extinguish.

5. Anxiety is a central component of many problem behaviors. Anxiety includes respondent behaviors such as changes in heart rate, blood pressure, glandular secretions, perspiration, muscle tension, and temperature.

6. A phobia involves maladaptive anxiety or fear attached to a specific object (e.g., snakes, elevators).

7. A phobia is acquired through respondent conditioning in which a neutral stimulus acquires the ability to elicit anxiety through pairing with an intense aversive US that elicits the UR.

8. Operant components of anxiety include escape or avoidance behaviors that are negatively reinforced by removal of the S^{r-} or reduction of its effects.

9. A stimulus can act both as a CS, eliciting a CR, and as an S^D, signaling an operant behavior that will be reinforced. The practitioner considers both the operant and the respondent features of a problem situation.

10. Behaviors categorized as respondent, previously thought to be exclusively under involuntary control, have been operantly strengthened and weakened (e.g., heart rate and skin temperature) with biofeedback. Biofeedback techniques involve the use of auditory, visual, and other sensory information in the assessment and modification of physiological or respondent behaviors, such as heart rate, muscle tension, and blood pressure.

Suggested Activities

1. Watch one of your favorite television shows and identify the respondent and operant behaviors you observe.

2. Identify a situation from your own life in which a behavior could be described as operant or respondent. State whether the behavior is operant or respondent and the basis for your decision.

3. Describe a fear of yours or of someone you know. Identify the CS, US, S^{r-}, and S^{R-} involved. Draw a diagram to depict the phobic situation.

References and Resources

Allan, R. W. (1998). Operant-respondent interactions. In W. O'Donohue (Ed.), *Learning and behavior therapy* (pp. 146–168). Boston: Allyn & Bacon.

Andrasik, F., Larsson, B., & Grazzi, L. (2002). Biofeedback treatment of recurrent headaches in children and adolescents. In V. Guidetti, G. Russell, M. Sillanpaa, & P. Winner (Eds.), *Headache and migraine in childhood and adolescence* (pp. 317–322). London: Martin Dunitz.

Ayres, R. (1998). Avoidance and fear conditioning. In W. O'Donohue (Ed.), *Learning and behavior therapy* (pp. 117–136). Boston: Allyn & Bacon.

Bandura, A. (1977). *Social learning theory.* Englewood Cliffs, NJ: Prentice Hall.

Barlow, D. H. (Ed.). (2002). *Anxiety and its disorders: The nature and treatment of anxiety and panic* (2nd ed.). New York: Guilford.

Blanchard, E. B. (1992). Psychological treatment of benign headache disorders. *Journal of Consulting and Clinical Psychology, 60,* 537–551.

Blechman, E., & Brownell, K. D. (Eds.). (1997). *Behavioral medicine and women: A comprehensive handbook.* New York: Guilford.

Bowbjerg, D. J., Redd, W. H., Jacobsen, P. B., Manne, S. L., Taylor, K. L., Surbone, A., et al. (1992). An experimental analysis of classically conditioned nausea during cancer chemotherapy. *Psychosomatic Medicine, 54,* 623–637.

Butler, J. G., & Campise, R. L. (1998). Enuresis and encopresis. In B. A. Thyer & J. S. Wodarski (Eds.), *Handbook of empirical social work practice* (Vol. 1, pp. 137–155). New York: John Wiley.

DiTomasso, R. A., Martin, D. M., & Kovnat, K. D. (2000). In F. M. Datillio & A. Freeman (Eds.), *Cognitive-behavioral strategies for crisis intervention* (2nd ed., pp. 409–428). New York: Guilford.

Falls, W. A. (1998). Extinction: A review of theory and the evidence suggesting that memories are not erased with nonreinforcement. In W. O'Donohue (Ed.), *Learning and behavior therapy* (pp. 205–229). Boston: Allyn & Bacon.

Geis, G. L., Stebbins, W. C., & Lundin, R. W. (1965). *Reflex and operant conditioning.* New York: Appleton-Century-Crofts.

Gilbert, C. (2003). Clinical applications of breathing regulation: Beyond anxiety management. *Behavior Modification, 27,* 692–709.

Graves, K. D., & Miller, P. M. (2003). Behavioral medicine in the prevention and treatment of cardiovascular disease. *Behavior Modification, 27,* 3–25.

Hollis, K. L. (1997). Contemporary research on Pavlovian conditioning: A "new" functional analysis. *American Psychologist, 52,* 956–965.

Jones, M. C. (1924). The elimination of children's fears. *Journal of Experimental Psychology, 7*, 383–390.

Kehoe, E. J., & Macrae, M. (1998). Classical conditioning. In W. O'Donohue (Ed.), *Learning and behavior therapy* (pp. 36–58). Boston: Allyn & Bacon.

Kirby, K. C., Lamb, R. J., & Iguchi, M. Y. (1997). Stimulus control of drug abuse. In D. M. Baer & E. M. Pinkston (Eds.), *Environment and behavior* (pp. 173–184). Boulder, CO: Westview.

McComas, J. J., Wacker, D. P., & Cooper, L. J. (1998). Increasing compliance with medical procedures: Application of the high-probability request procedure for a toddler. *Journal of Applied Behavior Analysis, 31*, 287–290.

McGrady, A., Olson, R. P., & Kroon, J. S. (1995). Biobehavioral treatment of essential hypertension. In M. S. Schwartz (Ed.), *Biofeedback: A practitioner's guide* (pp. 445–467). New York: Guilford.

McGrady, A., Wauquier, A., McNeil, A., & Gerard, G. (1994). Effects of biofeedback-assisted relaxation on migraine headache and changes in cerebral blood flow velocity in the middle cerebral artery. *Headache, 34*, 424–428.

Meichenbaum, D. H. (1985). *Stress inoculation training.* Elmsford, NY: Pergamon.

Meissner, J. S., Blanchard, E. B., & Malamood, H. S. (1997). Comparison of treatment outcome measures for irritable bowel syndrome. *Applied Psychophysiology and Biofeedback, 22*, 55–62.

Miller, N. E. (1985). Some professional and scientific problems and opportunities for biofeedback. *Biofeedback and Self-Regulation, 10*, 3–24.

Mowrer, O. J., & Mowrer, W. M. (1938). Enuresis: A method for its study and treatment. *American Journal of Orthopsychiatry, 8*, 436–447.

Pavlov, I. P. (1927). *Conditioned reflexes: An investigation of the physiological activity of the cerebral cortex* (G. V. Anrep, Trans.). London: Oxford University Press.

Pinkston, E. M., Howe, M. W., & Blackman, D. K. (1987). Medical social work management of urinary incontinence in the elderly: A behavioral approach. *Journal of Social Service Research, 10*, 179–194.

Rescorla, R. A. (1988). Pavlovian conditioning: It's not what you think it is. *American Psychologist, 43*, 151–160.

Rescorla, R. A., & Solomon, R. L. (1967). Two-process learning theories: Relationship between Pavlovian conditioning and instrumental learning. *Psychological Review, 74*, 151–182.

Rice, J. M., & Lutzker, J. R. (1984). Reducing noncompliance to follow-up appointment keeping at a family practice center. *Journal of Applied Behavior Analysis, 17*, 303–311.

Rimer, B. (1997). Toward an improved behavioral medicine. *Annals of Behavioral Medicine, 19*, 6–10.

Schloss, P. J., Smith, M., Santora, C., & Bryant, R. (1989). A respondent conditioning approach to reducing anger responses of a dually diagnosed man with mild mental retardation. *Behavior Therapy, 20*, 459–464.

Schwartz, M. S., & Andrasik, F. C. (Eds.). (2003). *Biofeedback: A practitioner's guide* (3rd ed.). New York: Guilford.

Sirois, B. C., & Berg, M. M. (2003). Negative emotions and coronary heart disease: A review. *Behavior Modification, 27*, 83–102.

Turkkan, J. S. (1989). Classical conditioning: The new hegemony. *Behavioral and Brain Sciences, 12*, 121–179.

Viskoper, R., Shapira, I., Priluck, R., Mindline, R., Chornia, L., Laszt, A., et al. (2003). Non-pharmacological treatment of resistant hypertensives by device-guided slow breathing exercises. *American Journal of Hypertension, 16,* 484–487.

Watson, J. B., & Rayner, R. (1920). Conditioned emotional reactions. *Journal of Experimental Psychology, 3,* 1–14.

Wolpe, J. (1958). *Psychology by reciprocal inhibition.* Stanford, CA: Stanford University Press.

Wolpe, J. (1990). *The practice of behavior therapy* (4th ed.). Elmsford, NY: Pergamon.

Wolpe, J., & Lang, B. J. (1964). A fear survey schedule for use in behavior modification. *Behavior Research and Therapy, 2,* 27–30.

Wolpe, J., & Plaud, J. L. (1997). Pavlov's contribution to behavior therapy: The obvious and the not so obvious. *American Psychologist, 52,* 966–972.

Wong, S. E., Seroka, P. L., & Ogisi, J. (2000). Effects of a checklist on self-assessment of blood glucose level by a memory-impaired woman with diabetes mellitus. *Journal of Applied Behavior Analysis, 33,* 251–254.

CHAPTER 12

Generalization and Maintenance of Behavior Change

A counselor has been treating Mario for alcohol abuse. As part of the intervention plan to decrease Mario's drinking, the counselor suggested several nondrinking behaviors that would be appropriate in the social situation in which Mario usually drinks. These behaviors were new to Mario, but he agreed to try them. What can the counselor do to promote the generalization and maintenance of the nondrinking behaviors?

Objectives

After completing this chapter, you should be able to do the following:

- Identify four obstacles to the generalization and maintenance of desired responses from the practice setting to the client's environment.
- State four ways to maximize the generalization of desired responses from the practice setting to the client's environment.
- Describe how behavioral rehearsal can be used to develop desired behaviors, given a case example.
- Describe the use of behavioral assignments in a practice setting, given a case example.

Generalization and Maintenance of Behavior Change

Clients seek treatment for problems they are having in their natural environments. The individual's **natural environment** consists of the physical and social surroundings in which the target behaviors were developed and in which behavior changes are designed to be performed and maintained. Intervention usually takes place in a different environment, however, such as a social agency, a private-practice office, or an institution. Although the client may learn to perform the desired behaviors in the practice setting, the practitioner cannot assume that he or she will also perform these behaviors in the natural environment. Even if the individual initially performs the behaviors in the natural environment, they may not be lasting or durable—that is, the individual may not continue to perform them over time. It is important that the practitioner and client consider the generalization and maintenance of behavior change from the practice setting to the client's natural environment when they are developing the intervention plan. They attempt to identify possible obstacles to the generalization and maintenance of change and create a plan for overcoming them. *Generalization* refers to **transfer of behavior change** from the practice setting to the client's natural environment. *Maintenance* refers to the durability of behavior change over time.

Obstacles to the Generalization and Maintenance of Behavior Change

There are four main obstacles to the generalization and maintenance of behavior change: (a) insufficient reinforcement for desired responses in the client's natural environment; (b) reinforcement of the client's undesired, maladaptive responses in the natural environment; (c) lack of similarity between the practice environment and the client's natural environment; and (d) insufficient development of desired behaviors in the practice setting. We discuss each of these obstacles briefly in turn below.

Insufficient reinforcement for desired responses in the client's natural environment. If desired behaviors are not reinforced, they will undergo extinction. For example, in the treatment setting, Walter, a cocaine user, learned alternative responses he could make in typical drug-taking situations. When Walter performed the alternative responses in those situations, however, he was not reinforced. His friends and significant others did not support his non-drug-taking behaviors; consequently, those behaviors extinguished rapidly.

Reinforcement of the client's undesired, maladaptive responses in the natural environment. In some situations, the client is reinforced for performing undesired behaviors and not reinforced for performing desired behaviors. For example, the practitioner extinguished Debbie's tantrum behaviors (kicking, whining, and banging her head on the floor) and established quiet, solitary play behaviors in his office. At home, however, Debbie's mother often worked at her computer and did not pay attention to Debbie when she played quietly. When Debbie started whining and tugging at her mother's pants, her mother scolded her or pleaded with her to stop. This attention reinforced Debbie's tugging and whining. Debbie's tantrum behaviors were more likely to be reinstated because the mother's attention, or social reinforcement, was given only after undesired, disruptive behaviors.

Lack of similarity between the practice environment and the client's natural environment. Antecedent stimuli in the client's environment must be similar enough to those in the practice environment to serve as cues for the performance of desired behaviors. The practitioner develops desired client responses in the presence of antecedent stimuli (S^Ds, USs, and CSs) in the practice setting, such as an office, group meeting room, or other agency or institutional environment. The practitioner also attempts to identify stimuli in the client's environment that (a) signal undesired operant responses to be reinforced and (b) elicit maladaptive respondent behaviors. For example, the sight of a neon sign saying "BAR" served as an S^D for Mario to enter the bar and order a drink. The neon sign might also have acted as a CS that elicited the CRs of salivation or pleasant emotional responses associated with drinking alcoholic beverages.

A therapist working with Neil to develop his social skills with women, such as eye contact and conversational behaviors, must determine whether appropriate women are available in Neil's environment to set the occasion for these desired behaviors. If Neil does not have opportunities to meet women during his normal activities, his progress toward behavior change is jeopardized unless he moves to an environment in which he can perform the desired behaviors and have them reinforced. Similarly, Walter may practice alternative behaviors to drug taking and procuring in a residential treatment facility. The situation on the street could be so different from the treatment setting, however, that it fails to provide S^Ds that would set the occasion for Walter's performance of the newly developed behaviors. The desired behaviors, therefore, would have a low probability of being performed and reinforced in Walter's natural environment.

Insufficient development of desired behaviors in the practice setting. Although appropriate stimuli (S^Ds, USs, and CSs) are present, the desired responses may not be performed in the natural environment because those responses have not been practiced sufficiently in the treatment setting. For example, a client was instructed by his social worker to state his opinions to a colleague instead of remaining silent when he disagreed with the colleague on an issue. Although the client said that he understood and agreed with the social worker's instructions, the client did not rehearse appropriate opinion-giving behaviors adequately in the practice setting. As a result, when an issue arose the next day on which he disagreed with his colleague, he did not perform the appropriate behaviors.

Strategies for Promoting the Generalization and Maintenance of Behavior Change

The practitioner can promote the generalization and maintenance of desired behaviors by identifying likely obstacles and designing an intervention plan with the client that takes these obstacles into consideration. The following are some of the strategies that a practitioner might use to promote the generalization and maintenance of behavior change in a client:

1. Involve significant individuals in the client's life, such as family members and friends, in the behavior change program.

2. Shift from continuous to intermittent reinforcement of desired behaviors established in the practice setting.

3. Develop and reinforce desired behaviors in the client's natural environment instead of, or in addition to, the practice setting.

4. Use behavioral rehearsal to give the client opportunities to practice appropriate behaviors until the desired performance level is achieved.

5. Give the client behavioral assignments to perform in the natural environment that include behaviors rehearsed in the practice setting.

6. Assess potential obstacles to client compliance with the intervention plan and involve the client in removing those obstacles.

7. Educate the client in relapse prevention techniques.

8. Collaborate with other professionals, agencies, and community groups to develop opportunities for the client to perform and be reinforced for desired behaviors.

9. Include self-management or self-control contingencies as part of the behavior change program.

10. Using behavioral traps, design intervention plans to take advantage of naturally occurring reinforcers in the client's environment (Baer & Wolf, 1970; Kohler & Greenwood, 1986).

We address each of these strategies in more detail below.

Involving Significant Individuals

Significant individuals in the client's life, such as family members and friends, can be involved in carrying out the client's behavior change program. These individuals can provide S^Ds and reinforcers for desired behaviors. To increase the likelihood that desired behaviors will generalize to the natural environment, the practitioner can instruct the client's significant others to (a) establish and carry out reinforcement contingencies involving the client and (b) act consistently in reinforcing desired behaviors and withholding reinforcement from undesired behaviors. Often the newly performed appropriate behaviors of the client will serve as reinforcers for the participation of significant others in promoting the generalization and maintenance of behavior change.

Shifting From Continuous to Intermittent Reinforcement

To strengthen desired behaviors, the practitioner can shift from continuous to intermittent reinforcement in the practice setting after the responses are developed. As we described in Chapter 4, compared with continuous reinforcement, intermittent reinforcement generates response rates that are more resistant to extinction. Usually, intermittent reinforcement more closely approximates the availability of reinforcers in an individual's natural environment. The practitioner can give significant others in the client's environment instructions on how to fade out reinforcers for desired behaviors from a continuous to an intermittent schedule. The practitioner can also fade out the frequency of treatment sessions as the client's goals are met. For example, sessions can be faded from once per week to every other week, once per month, and then once every other month.

Strengthening Desired Behaviors in the Client's Natural Environment

Behaviors learned in the practice setting are not presumed to transfer automatically to the client's natural environment. In some cases it may be more effective to develop new behaviors in the client's natural environment instead of, or in addition to, the practice setting. The behavior therapist may observe the client in his or her natural environment and intervene there to develop and reinforce desired behaviors. When desired behaviors are developed in the client's natural environment, the problem of generalization to the natural environment is removed, but the practitioner must still pay attention to maintaining the behaviors.

It may be necessary at times for the practitioner to remove the client from the natural environment so that appropriate behaviors can be established in a controlled setting. People who exhibit certain extreme kinds of behaviors are often presumed to be better treated in institutions or in settings other than their natural environments. For example, individuals who attempt suicide, talk about hearing strange voices that tell them what to do, refuse to eat or talk to anyone, or claim to be someone they are not have been removed from their homes and placed in residential treatment settings such as psychiatric hospitals. In these cases, the individuals' natural environments provide reinforcement for the maladaptive behaviors and do not provide S^Ds or reinforcers for desired behaviors.

It is important that the practitioner work with significant individuals in the client's natural environment so that positive behavior changes can be maintained. The use of more than one therapist can also help maintain behavior changes by allowing the client to practice behaviors and perform them appropriately in the presence of more than one individual (Stokes & Osnes, 1989).

In treatment programs using the assertive community treatment (ACT) model (Stein & Test, 1980), a full range of services is provided to individuals with chronic mental disorders in their homes and communities. ACT team members are available to clients as needed to help them with activities of daily living, such as shopping, getting to work, medication management, and managing finances. Studies have shown that ACT programs can reduce inpatient hospitalization rates as much as 50% (Bond, McGrew, & Fekete, 1995). Desired behaviors are learned and reinforced in the client's natural environment, with ongoing corrective feedback from staff as needed. Intensive staff involvement can be gradually faded as naturally occurring reinforcers maintain desired behaviors.

Behavioral Rehearsal

Behavioral rehearsal is a technique to promote generalization of behavior change by providing a structured situation in which the client practices desired behaviors. Advice or suggestions for behaving appropriately, although well-intentioned, may be insufficient to enable a client to perform desired behaviors. For example, clients are often told by friends, relatives, or authorities to "shape up" and change their behavior; however, such exhortative methods may be ineffective in helping clients change undesired behaviors. Clients can often identify their undesired behaviors and may also be able to specify alternative desirable behaviors. They have difficulty performing desired responses, however, because of deficient behaviors or skills, anxiety, or lack of reinforcement.

In behavioral rehearsal, the client practices desired behaviors in a supportive environment, with corrective feedback, before attempting to perform the behaviors with greater risk of failure in the actual target situation. The practitioner or the client's fellow group members give the client explicit instructions on behaviors to perform in role plays that simulate the target situation. The client practices or rehearses the desired behaviors that the practitioner or group members have suggested and modeled. During the role plays, the client may require additional instructions, prompts, coaching, and reinforcement to perform the behaviors appropriately. As the client gains proficiency and self-confidence through these rehearsals, it becomes more likely that he or she will perform the desired behaviors appropriately in the natural environment.

Behavioral rehearsal continues until the client achieves the level of performance specified in the behavior change plan. Additional practice or training sessions conducted after the client has demonstrated the desired behaviors may further help to promote their generalization to the client's natural environment. In Case Example 2 (p. 268), behavioral rehearsal was used to facilitate the generalization and maintenance of appropriate speech from the group setting to Bella's and Cliff's natural environments.

Behavioral Assignments

The practitioner gives the client assignments to perform desired behaviors in the natural environment. Performance of these behavioral assignments facilitates the generalization of desired behaviors from the practice setting to the client's environment. The assignments give the client opportunities to try out behaviors that the practitioner and client have discussed and rehearsed in the practice setting. At each meeting, the practitioner gives the client a behavioral assignment that specifies a task to be performed in the natural environment. These assignments provide continuity to the behavior change program by directing the client's activities between meetings toward performance of desired behaviors.

Behavioral assignments are structured to make it likely that the client will perform them in the natural environment. They consist of behaviors that have been rehearsed in the practice setting until they are performed proficiently. If the client has difficulty carrying out an assignment, the practitioner can create a role play in which the client demonstrates the behaviors involved in performing the assignment. The practitioner (and group members, if applicable) identifies the client's desired and undesired responses demonstrated in the role play. The practitioner and client then discuss the client's difficulties in performing the desired behaviors. The desired behaviors are rehearsed, with additional instructions, prompts, and feedback provided, until the client performs them correctly. The practitioner may then give the client the same assignment or a modified one, depending on the difficulty the client experienced in performing the previous assignment and the observed level of proficiency.

Behavioral rehearsal and behavioral assignments were used in the assertiveness training program with Gretchen (see Chapter 8, pp. 112-113). Gretchen practiced desired verbal and nonverbal behaviors in the therapist's office. She was also given behavioral assignments to carry out in her natural environment, such as looking at her mother and speaking in a calm tone of voice while stating her opinions. Gretchen reported data from these assignments to the therapist. The therapist reinforced data collection and successful performances and provided additional instructions and training to help Gretchen achieve her behavior change goals. Behavioral rehearsal and behavioral assignments were also used in the group treatment program for Bill in Case Example 6 (p. 271).

Enhancing Compliance

The failure of a client to follow an intervention plan can result in the failure of the best of plans to achieve behavior change. Such noncompliance, or nonadherence, is a major problem in medical settings (e.g., Allen & Warzak, 2000; Pratt & Jones, 1995), and it can also be an issue in behavior change programs. The client and practitioner work together to identify potential obstacles to compliance with the behavior change program so that they can develop strategies for removing those obstacles. Advances in technology have produced new tools, such as handheld computers, that have been used in medical and psychological treatment settings to increase compliance by facilitating recording and programming reminders (e.g., Dixon, 2003; Newman, Kenardy, Herman, & Taylor, 1996).

Naturally occurring contingencies may discourage the client's compliance with the behavior change program. Programs that rely on self-administered reinforcement or punishment are less likely to be followed according to specified contingencies than are programs monitored closely by a practitioner. The practitioner should select the proposed reinforcers in a behavior change program carefully, with full participation of the client, to ensure their effectiveness in increasing desired behaviors.

Relapse Prevention

Relapse refers to any desired behavior change that is not maintained in the natural environment, or to the return of the undesired target behavior. In a situation in which the client is at high risk for performing the undesired behavior, he or she can either perform appropriate behaviors or lapse into performance of the undesired behavior patterns. For example, one evening Mario went to a party after a stressful day at work. At the party, Mario found it difficult to refrain from drinking because many people there were modeling that behavior. Another antecedent for drinking was Mario's telling himself that having a drink would be relaxing (covert antecedent). As part of relapse prevention, Mario identified several high-risk situations in which he was likely to abuse alcohol, including going to a party after a stressful day at work. The counselor helped him to develop behaviors that were incompatible with drinking and for approaching high-risk situations, such as telling himself that drinking ginger ale would be relaxing and then making sure he had a glass of ginger ale with him at all times during the party.

Marlatt developed a model of the relapse process and techniques for relapse prevention, or maintenance of behavior change (see, e.g., Marlatt & Gordon, 1985). This model, originally developed for use with individuals performing addictive behaviors, suggests that the practitioner and client take the following steps in developing a program to prevent relapse:

1. Identify high-risk situations.

2. Develop the client's skills for coping with high-risk situations. These behaviors may involve staying away from certain individuals or places, using relaxation techniques, or using self-talk to focus on desired behaviors to perform in difficult situations.

3. Use behavioral rehearsal to practice coping skills, either imaginally or in the actual situations.

4. Develop a plan for coping with lapses. A lapse, which is performing the undesired behavior once, does not mean that the behavior change program has failed. Provide the client with positive reinforcement to maintain desired behavior. Use the client's social support system to provide positive reinforcement for desired behaviors.

Booster sessions can also enhance the maintenance of behavior change. One or more brief sessions, spaced over a period of time after treatment ends, can provide clients with reminders (cues) and additional reinforcement for performing desired behaviors and abstaining from undesired behaviors.

Alternatively, ongoing maintenance treatment may be necessary to foster lasting behavior change; that is, the practitioner may need to have continuing contact with the client over an extended period of time. Individuals with chronic mental disorders living in the community, for example, may need someone to follow their progress and be available to them over long periods to ensure that they continue to perform adaptive behaviors in the natural environment.

In addition to receiving social reinforcement and support from significant others, the client can be encouraged to participate in community support groups or self-help organizations, such as Alcoholics Anonymous, Parents Without Partners, sports leagues, the Alliance for the Mentally Ill, and adult Sunday school classes. Participation in such groups has been shown to enhance maintenance effects (Iodice & Wodarski, 1987).

Community Involvement

The practitioner instructs the client to rehearse behaviors in the practice setting that are likely to be reinforced in the client's community, but the client may not always have the opportunity to perform newly acquired behaviors in the community. For example, in a program to teach job interview skills to clients, the practitioner or other agency staff might have to work with businesses, community groups, and other professionals to develop job opportunities so that clients can perform appropriate interview behaviors and be reinforced. Practitioners may need to be actively involved in their clients' communities to ensure that S^Ds and reinforcers are available there for behaviors developed in practice settings.

The practitioner may need to collaborate with other professionals, agencies, and citizen groups in the client's community to ensure (a) that reinforcers are available for desire behaviors and not available for undesired behaviors and (b) that proper S^Ds are in place to facilitate the performance of desired behaviors. Cooperative relationships between practitioners and others in their clients' communities are particularly important in securing assistance for low-income, multiproblem families who have concerns about food, housing, and jobs as well as behavioral difficulties. In such relationships, practitioners may work with their clients' families and peer groups as well as with other human service workers, institutions, and agencies such as schools, employment agencies, housing authorities, and employers (e.g., Henggeler, Schoenwald, & Pickrel, 1995; Kazdin, 1997; Meyers & Smith, 1995; Stein & Test, 1980).

Self-Control Contingencies

The incorporation of a self-management contingency into a behavior change program can facilitate the generalization and maintenance of behavior change by giving the individual control over the reinforcers. For example, Rafael wanted to exercise more often. The baseline rate of his walking on the treadmill was 30 minutes once per week, and his goal was four 30-minute sessions per week. He decided to reinforce his exercising by listening to a CD of his favorite music while he walked on the treadmill. Soon, Rafael was exercising four times per week, and he has maintained that rate for more than 2 years.

Behavioral Traps

The practitioner can enhance the generalization and maintenance of behavior change by identifying behaviors under the control of naturally occurring reinforcers in the client's environment. The action of these natural reinforcers is called a **behavioral trap** because the desired behavior becomes "trapped" by reinforcers that are plentiful in the client's environment and will thus be maintained (Baer & Wolf, 1970; Kohler & Greenwood, 1986). For example, Leon's speech was reestablished in a treatment setting, but his speech generalized and was maintained in his natural environment by the many reinforcers available there for speaking, such as other individuals talking to him, asking him questions, and responding to his questions or comments. As Leon's speaking increased, the naturally occurring reinforcers maintained his speech.

Summary

1. The term *generalization of behavior change* refers to the transfer of behavior change from the practice setting to the client's natural environment. The term *natural environment* refers to the physical and social surroundings in which the client's target behavior was developed and in which behavior changes are designed to be performed and maintained. *Maintenance* refers to the durability of behavior change over time.

2. Four obstacles to the generalization and maintenance of behavior change are (a) insufficient reinforcement for desired responses in the client's natural environment, (b) reinforcement of undesired responses in the client's natural environment, (c) lack of similarity between the practice setting and the client's natural environment, and (d) insufficient development of desired responses in the practice setting.

3. The practitioner can promote the generalization and maintenance of behavior change by using the following strategies: (a) Involve significant individuals in the client's life, such as family members and friends, in the client's behavior change program; (b) shift from continuous to intermittent reinforcement of desired behaviors in the practice setting; (c) work with the client in the natural environment to develop desired behaviors; (d) use behavioral rehearsal in role plays that help the client develop and practice desired behaviors; (e) give behavioral assignments to the client that specify tasks to be performed in the natural environment between meetings with the practitioner; (f) assess potential obstacles to compliance with the intervention plan, and involve the client in removing those obstacles; (g) educate

the client in relapse prevention techniques; (h) collaborate with other professionals, agencies, and citizen groups to develop opportunities for clients to perform and be reinforced for desired behaviors in the community; (i) include self-management and self-control contingencies as part of the behavior change program; and (j) design the intervention plan to take advantage of naturally occurring reinforcers in the client's natural environment.

Suggested Activities

1. Identify a behavior that you would like to perform in a new setting or situation. Design a behavioral rehearsal exercise for yourself and report your results to the class.

2. Assume that you have successfully increased your exercise from once a week to four times per week. Design a plan for maintenance of your exercise program.

3. Describe a behavioral assignment you could give to a teenager who is being pressured by peers to smoke marijuana.

References and Resources

Abramowitz, J. S., Franklin, M. E., Zoellner, L. A., & DiBernardo, C. L. (2002). Treatment compliance and outcome in obsessive-compulsive disorder. *Behavior Modification, 26,* 447–463.

Allen, K. D., & Warzak, W. J. (2000). The problem of parental nonadherence in clinical behavior analysis: Effective treatment is not enough. *Journal of Applied Behavior Analysis, 33,* 373–391.

Baer, D. M., & Wolf, M. M. (1970). The entry into natural communities of reinforcement. In R. Ulrich, T. Stachnik, & J. Mabry (Eds.), *Control of human behavior* (Vol. 2, pp. 319–324). Glenview, IL: Scott, Foresman.

Bellg, A. L. (2003). Maintenance of health behavior change in preventive cardiology: Internalization and self-regulation of new behaviors. *Behavior Modification, 27,* 103–131.

Bond, G. R., McGrew, J. H., & Fekete, D. M. (1995). Assertive outreach for frequent users of psychiatric hospitals: A meta-analysis. *Journal of Mental Health Administration, 22,* 4–16.

Dixon, M. R. (2003). Creating a portable data-collection system with Microsoft embedded visual tools for the pocket PC. *Journal of Applied Behavior Analysis, 36,* 271–284.

Griffiths, D., Feldman, M. A., & Tough, S. (1997). Programming generalization of social skills in adults with developmental disabilities: Effects on generalization and social validity. *Behavior Therapy, 28,* 253–269.

Henggeler, S. W., Schoenwald, S. K., & Pickrel, S. A. G. (1995). Multisystemic therapy: Bridging the gap between university- and community-based treatment. *Journal of Consulting and Clinical Psychology, 63,* 709–717.

Iodice, J. D., & Wodarski, J. S. (1987). Aftercare treatment for schizophrenics living at home. *Social Work, 32,* 122–127.

Jacobson, N. S. (1989). The maintenance of treatment gains following social learning-based marital therapy. *Behavior Therapy, 20,* 325–336.

Kazdin, A. E. (1997). Practitioner review: Psychosocial treatments for conduct disorder in children. *Journal of Child Psychology and Psychiatry, 38,* 161–178.

Kohler, F. W., & Greenwood, C. R. (1986). Toward a technology of generalization: The identification of natural contingencies of reinforcement. *The Behavior Analyst, 9,* 19–26.

Laws, R. (Ed.). (1989). *Relapse prevention with sex offenders.* New York: Guilford.

Marlatt, G. A., & Gordon, J. R. (Eds.). (1985). *Relapse prevention: Maintenance strategies in the treatment of addiction behaviors.* New York: Guilford.

Marlatt, G. A., Larimer, M. E., Baer, J. S., & Quigley, L. A. (1993). Harm reduction for alcohol problems: Moving beyond the controlled drinking controversy. *Behavior Therapy, 24,* 461–504.

McComas, J. J., Wacker, D. P., & Cooper, L. J. (1998). Increasing compliance with medical procedures: Application of the high-probability request procedure for a toddler. *Journal of Applied Behavior Analysis, 31,* 287–290.

McFall, R. M., & Lillesand, D. B. (1971). Behavior rehearsal with modeling and coaching in assertion training. *Journal of Abnormal Psychology, 77,* 313–323.

Meyers, R. J., & Smith, J. E. (1995). *Clinical guide to alcohol treatment: The community reinforcement approach.* New York: Guilford.

Newman, M. G., Kenardy, J., Herman, S., & Taylor, C. B. (1996). The use of hand-held computers as an adjunct to cognitive-behavior therapy. *Computers in Human Behavior, 12,* 135–143.

O'Farrell, T. J., Choquette, K. A., Cutter, H. S. G., Brown, E., Bayog, R., McCourt, W., et al. (1996). Cost-benefit and cost-effectiveness analyses of behavioral marital therapy with and without relapse prevention sessions for alcoholics and their spouses. *Behavior Therapy, 27,* 7–24.

Patterson, G. R., McNeal, S., Hawkins, N., & Phelps, R. (1967). Reprogramming the social environment. *Journal of Child Psychology and Psychiatry, 8,* 181–195.

Pratt, J., & Jones, T. (1995). Noncompliance with therapy: An ongoing problem in treating hypertension. *Primary Cardiology, 21,* 34–38.

Rose, S. D., Sundel, M., DeLange, J., Corwin, L., & Palumbo, A. (1970). The Hartwig project: A behavioral approach to the treatment of juvenile offenders. In R. Ulrich, T. Stachnik, & J. Mabry (Eds.), *Control of human behavior* (Vol. 2, pp. 220–230). Glenview, IL: Scott, Foresman.

Stein, L. I., & Test, M. A. (1980). Alternative mental hospital treatment: I. Conceptual model, treatment program, and clinical evaluation. *Archives of General Psychiatry, 37,* 392–397.

Stokes, T., & Osnes, P. (1989). An operant pursuit of generalization. *Behavior Therapy, 20,* 337–355.

Varni, J. W., La Greca, A. M., & Spirito, A. (2001). Cognitive-behavioral interventions for children with chronic health conditions. In K. S. Dobson (Ed.), *Handbook of cognitive-behavioral therapies* (2nd ed., pp. 291–333). New York: Guilford.

Wong, S. E., Martinez-Diaz, J. A., Massel, H. K., Edelstein, B. A., Wiegand, W., Bowen, L., et al. (1993). Conversational skills training with schizophrenic inpatients: A study of generalization across settings and conversants. *Behavior Therapy, 24,* 285–304.

CHAPTER 13

Behavioral Assessment

Denice, a computer programmer employed by a software firm, was referred for counseling by her supervisor because of her "moodiness" and "emotional outbursts" at work. When the therapist asked Denice for an example of the problem, she described a recent incident with a coworker. After the incident, her boss had called her into his office and asked her what was wrong. She said she was "frustrated and angry" and did not know why other people had to interfere with how she did her job. The therapist used this information in initiating a behavioral assessment.

Objectives

ing this chapter, you should be able to do the following:

amples of deficit and excess problematic behaviors.

e a target behavior in measurable terms.

antecedents of a target behavior and negative consequences of that
r, given a sample case.

a target behavior, a possible controlling antecedent, and the reinforc-
sequences, given a sample case.

one hypothesis about the conditions that exert control over a target
behavior, given a sample case.

Introduction to Behavioral Assessment

The practitioner conducts a **behavioral assessment** to analyze an individual's problems or circumstances in order to identify probable controlling antecedents and

consequences of target behaviors. Through behavioral assessment, the practitioner seeks to determine controlling or functional relationships between environmental events and the client's target behaviors. The results of this assessment provide the basis on which the practitioner and client formulate the client's behavior change goals (see Chapter 14). The client is involved as much as possible during each step of this procedure.

During the past decade, the terms **functional assessment** and **functional analysis** have appeared more frequently in regard to the assessment of target behaviors and their environmental determinants (e.g., Beare, Severson, & Brandt, 2004; Hanley, Iwata, & McCord, 2003). The terms are sometimes used interchangeably, but some behavior analysts use the term *functional analysis* only in reference to the manipulation of antecedents and consequences to determine their role in maintaining the target response (e.g., Kurtz et al., 2003; Piazza et al., 2003; Smith & Churchill, 2002). For example, the controlling conditions of Carl's self-injurious behavior, such as slapping his face, are hypothesized to be (a) positive reinforcement in the form of his mother's attention, (b) negative reinforcement (escape) from having to do a chore, or (c) self-reinforcement from the stimulating effects of the slapping. A practitioner using functional analysis would attempt to manipulate the variables to test which of these hypothesized conditions is operating to maintain the self-injurious behavior.

To obtain the necessary information from the client, it is important that the practitioner establish a collaborative, trusting relationship with him or her. The client must perceive the practitioner as someone with the capacity to provide reinforcers, such as helping to relieve the client's concerns and improving the client's situation. The practitioner also acts as a social reinforcer for the client's problem-solving behaviors.

Intake

Before the behavioral assessment is conducted, the practitioner and client determine whether the social service agency or practitioner can provide treatment or services that will address the client's problem. The initial interactions between an individual and an agency or practitioner occur during *intake,* the beginning phase of the problem-solving process, in which a potential client becomes a client. During the intake process, the practitioner begins to develop a working relationship with the client. The practitioner can become a conditioned positive reinforcer for the client by smiling, answering questions, giving information, asking questions, and providing other social reinforcers. In this way, the practitioner can increase client participation in behavioral assessment, goal setting, and problem solving.

Most social service agencies require new clients to complete intake forms that request identifying data, including name, address, phone numbers, and date of birth; information on marital status, family members, and significant others; referral source; employment information; information about insurance coverage; and other necessary data. The intake form also asks the client to state the reason for seeking service from the agency. Typically, the client completes the intake form prior to meeting with the practitioner for the first time.

During intake, the client is informed about agency policies, procedures, and conditions related to service provision. The client is also told about the practitioner's professional qualifications. Many agencies give clients a form that provides basic information about services, including fees; confidentiality; the agency's compliance with the Federal Health Insurance Portability and Accountability Act of 1996 (HIPAA), which went into effect in 2003; and client and agency responsibilities. Both the practitioner and the client sign this form to indicate the agency's commitment to provide service and the client's consent to receive service. HIPAA requires agencies to inform clients of their adherence to federal guidelines regarding confidentiality of client treatment records and client rights.

One of the practitioner's tasks during intake is to screen for the presence of a crisis condition affecting the client or significant others. Such a condition can take the form of child or elder abuse, suicide risk, domestic violence, recent trauma, or severe financial deprivation. If the practitioner determines that a crisis condition exists, he or she may initiate immediate intervention prior to conducting the behavioral assessment.

In summary, the practitioner's tasks during intake include developing a collaborative and reinforcing relationship with the client, obtaining basic identifying information from the client, informing the client about agency policies and procedures, obtaining the client's commitment and consent to service, affirming the practitioner's commitment to service, and screening for crises. If the practitioner determines that the client requires services or resources elsewhere, he or she refers the client to the appropriate agencies, organizations, or practitioners. If the practitioner and client agree to proceed with service provision, behavioral assessment can begin.

Behavioral Assessment and Diagnostic Issues

In the preceding chapters, we discussed the basic behavioral principles and illustrated their applications to a variety of settings and problems. In this chapter, we consider these principles within a behavioral assessment framework. The practitioner uses behavioral assessment to analyze the client's problems or circumstances. Behavioral assessment provides the basis for the formulation of behavior change goals and the development of an appropriate intervention plan (e.g., Antony & Barlow, 2001) (see Chapter 14). The behavioral assessment framework presented here is applicable to both community and institutional settings.

Human service practitioners frequently encounter clients who lack effective problem-solving skills or complain about unmanageable "anxiety" or "depression." Based on these presenting complaints, the client might be diagnosed as having "obsessive-compulsive disorder," "generalized anxiety disorder," or "major depression, single episode." Such diagnoses are based on specific criteria found in the fourth edition of the *Diagnostic and Statistical Manual of Mental Disorders* (*DSM-IV;* American Psychiatric Association, 1994). The practitioner can use the Structured Clinical Interview for the *DSM-IV* (SCID; First, Spitzer, Gibbon, & Williams, 1995) to determine which *DSM-IV* criteria a particular client meets. Most practitioners and insurance companies rely on the diagnostic categories of the *DSM-IV* to identify client problems. Insurance companies reimburse practitioners based on *DSM-IV* diagnoses; therefore, it is important for practitioners to be familiar with this system of classification of mental disorders.

Successive editions of the *DSM*, particularly *DSM-III, DSM-III-R,* and *DSM-IV,* have increasingly included criteria that specify symptoms and behaviors, their severity, and time parameters required for meeting a particular diagnosis (Axis I and Axis II). A complete diagnosis also includes reporting of general medical problems (Axis III); an indication of psychosocial stressors (Axis IV), such as inadequate social support or unemployment; and a rating of the individual's global functioning (Axis V) on a scale of 0 to 100.

Critics of the *DSM-IV* argue that it relies too much on the medical model of mental disorders, which presumes that a mental disorder is manifested as a disease or illness within the person and does not give adequate consideration to environmental factors. Some social workers have proposed an alternative classification system for problems in social functioning (Karls & Wandrei, 1994), but this system has not been widely adopted.

In a 1991 publication, the American Psychiatric Association (APA) Task Force on *DSM-IV* stated, "After 10 years of experience and one revision (*DSM-III-R*), there is disappointment about the relative infrequency of use of the multiaxial system in clinical and research settings" (p. W1). Even when the multiaxial system is used, reliability is modest, and the validity of Axis IV with regard to predicting outcome is questionable (Kutchins & Kirk, 1995).

Kutchins and Kirk (1995) point out that not only is it possible to help people without using mental illness labels, it is perhaps preferable. For example, clients with the same diagnosis can exhibit different maladaptive behaviors. Diagnostic labels can establish or reinforce clients' beliefs or fears that they have permanent pathological conditions that cannot be altered. Although diagnostic labels may communicate standardized information, especially to professionals from other disciplines (Williams & Spitzer, 1995), Kutchins and Kirk argue that what is communicated is not necessarily in the client's best interest, truthful, or reliable (see also Kirk & Kutchins, 1988). Psychiatric labels can have consequences that are harmful to clients, such as when a label communicates to the client and others that the client's problem is permanent and the situation is hopeless, or when a label leads to social stigmatization.

Behavioral practitioners recognize that diagnosis is not the same as behavioral assessment. Although it might be necessary for the sake of insurance reimbursement to give a client a *DSM-IV* diagnosis, it is important that the practitioner conduct the behavioral assessment to arrive at a basis for the intervention plan. Behavioral assessment is part of a problem-solving process that involves systematic data gathering to describe target behaviors and their controlling environmental conditions. Instead of resulting in diagnostic labels, behavioral assessment leads to specification of the client's target behaviors, their controlling antecedents and consequences, and formulation of behavior change goals. The behavior change goals delineate the desired behaviors and their supporting antecedents and consequences. The intervention plan is based on these goals and involves selection of intervention techniques directed toward goal achievement and specification of procedures to implement the plan. The focus on target behaviors and their controlling stimuli in the environment provides the practitioner with concrete, measurable data for analyzing the client's situation.

Elements of Behavioral Assessment

Behavioral assessment involves consideration of four elements: target response, antecedents, consequences, and response strength. RAC-S is an acronym for *response, antecedents, consequences, and response strength.* Response is identified as the first term in RAC-S to emphasize the focus on the target response in relation to controlling antecedents and consequences, even though antecedents occur first in time. The acronym ABC has also been used similarly to designate *antecedents, behaviors, and consequences,* but we prefer RAC-S because of its focus on the response and its measures.

In crisis situations, as we stated earlier, the practitioner may have to intervene prior to carrying out the behavioral assessment to provide the client with necessary resources, referrals, or direct assistance. Such emergencies include situations in which the client is suicidal or requires immediate hospitalization, or in which immediate action is required to provide food, housing, medical care, or physical protection, such as in cases of suspected child or elder abuse.

Target Response

The client may have difficulty identifying specific target responses during an initial interview. It may be helpful for the practitioner to focus on RAC-S information by first looking at a *problem area,* a broad concern or role difficulty that can then be analyzed in more specific terms.

Various problem checklists and questionnaires are available for use in conjunction with interviewing and observation to help identify an individual's problem areas. Figure 13.1 presents one such form designed to help an individual identify his or her major problem areas. The items on the Problem Inventory represent areas of functioning or lack of resources that might lead a person to seek help, such as food, housing, job, and mental health concerns. This inventory can help the practitioner identify the individual's complaints in terms of general categories. By ranking his or her problem areas, the client indicates the ones that are of most concern. The practitioner should refer to a physician any client with issues that are or might be related to physical health concerns to address or rule out physical health problems.

A problem area is often manifested in the role or position in which the individual experiences difficulty—for example, as a mother, teacher, employee, or husband. Thus a problem area for a mother might include disciplining her children; for a teacher might include classroom management; for an employee, social skills; and for a husband, marital relations. Figure 13.2 presents the Problem Checklist, which the practitioner can use to help the client specify problem roles. The checklist lists 20 roles from which the client can identify those that he or she finds difficult to perform.

If the client identifies more than one problem area, the practitioner can help the client prioritize the problems to be addressed by considering the following:

Below are some things that may be a problem for you. If you have concerns in any of these areas, please check the box next to it.

Rank order the three problems that most concern you by writing 1, 2, or 3 beside the box next to each of the three problems you select.

☐ Food   ☐ Alcohol

☐ Clothing   ☐ Trouble sleeping

☐ Housing   ☐ Nervousness, anxiety

☐ Money   ☐ Physical violence

☐ Family   ☐ Get confused about things

☐ Job   ☐ Difficulty showing emotions

☐ School   ☐ Can't make decisions

☐ Physical health   ☐ Eating

☐ Mental health   ☐ Smoking

☐ Feeling lonely   ☐ Headaches

☐ Sex   ☐ Feeling down or blue

☐ Police or courts   ☐ Fears

☐ Legal   ☐ Other (specify)

☐ Drugs

Figure 13.1   Problem Inventory

1. Which problem is of immediate concern to the client, significant others (e.g., family members, friends, teachers), or both? For example, Ralph wants to stop drinking; Sophie seeks help in managing her diabetic son's diet. Health-related problems that require physician referral are given highest priority.

2. Which problem has the most severe aversive or negative consequences for the client, significant others, or society if not handled immediately? For example, Herman will be fired from his job unless he can start working cooperatively with coworkers; Sally will be expelled from school unless she attends more frequently.

3. Which problem requires handling before other problems can be treated? For example, Mr. and Mrs. Lee decide that they must resolve their child-rearing disagreements before they can develop a program to modify their children's behavior problems.

4. Which problem can be corrected most quickly, considering resources and obstacles? For example, Bob and Jean decide to work on resolving their arguments over the household budget before dealing with their more complicated sexual problems.

In which of the following roles do you experience difficulty? Check (✓) the role(s) that you have trouble performing.

Circle the role that *most* concerns you.

_____ Mother	_____ Classmate
_____ Father	_____ Student
_____ Sister	_____ Teacher
_____ Brother	_____ Friend—same sex
_____ Son	_____ Friend—opposite sex
_____ Daughter	_____ Employee
_____ Spouse/partner	_____ Coworker
_____ Step-relative	_____ Subordinate
_____ Other relative (specify)	_____ Neighbor
_____ Employer or supervisor	_____ Myself
	_____ Other (specify)

Figure 13.2   Problem Checklist

These questions are intended as guidelines for the practitioner to use in decision making with clients. Problem selection might involve the consideration of one or more of these questions, depending on the client's situation. For example, Michael decided to focus on his poor job performance before addressing his difficulties in relating to his partner because he was afraid he might lose his job and be unable to support his family.

The client's target responses are stated in terms that clearly specify the actions. Responses are described in measurable terms, without labels or judgments such as "inadequate personality" or "passive-aggressive." Physiological measures of heart rate, temperature, muscle tension, and blood pressure can be obtained with appropriate instruments. Other unobservable responses, such as an individual's thoughts, feelings, and attitudes, although experienced subjectively, can be described in self-reports along with corresponding observations by the practitioner of the person's actions or verbal responses.

A problematic target response can be classified as either a behavioral excess or a behavioral deficit. The term **behavioral excess** refers to a high frequency of inappropriate operant or respondent behaviors. Examples of behavioral excesses include overeating, alcohol abuse, telling lies, and anxiety responses such as sweaty palms and rapid heartbeat. **Behavioral deficit** refers to an absence or low frequency of appropriate operant or respondent behaviors. Examples of behavioral deficits include remaining silent instead of speaking up for one's rights, attending work sporadically, turning in few class assignments, and lack of sexual arousal to a spouse.

Behaviors can also be considered problematic when they are under faulty stimulus control. That is, the individual makes a response that is appropriate in some situations but inappropriate in others. For example, yelling "Fire!" and breaking the fire alarm box are appropriate behaviors when there is a fire (S^D), but such responses are inappropriate and potentially dangerous when there is no fire. Masturbation may be appropriate in the privacy of one's room, but it is inappropriate in public places. Problematic target behaviors are also described as *maladaptive, deviant, inappropriate,* and *undesired.*

Controlling Conditions (Antecedents and Consequences)

In behavioral assessment, the practitioner attempts to identify the antecedents and consequences maintaining the target behavior. Antecedents are the stimuli that precede, signal, or elicit a specific behavior. For example, an antecedent condition for Roger's punching Charlotte with his fist was Charlotte's calling Roger "stupid." A second antecedent was her refusal to have sexual intercourse with him, and a third antecedent was Roger's self-statement, "I'll have to teach her to show me some respect."

It is sometimes difficult to identify the controlling antecedents that elicit or set the occasion for target behaviors. The practitioner should describe in specific terms when and where the behavior is performed, who is present, and what is said or done by whom prior to performance of the behavior. As a rule, the practitioner focuses on current stimuli that appear to be closely associated with the target behavior. In some instances, however, the practitioner might explore earlier antecedent events to determine their influence on the client's current behavior. For example, a woman experiences intense anxiety and avoids eye contact in the presence of her stepfather, who sexually abused her when she was a child.

Reinforcing consequences are events that follow a target response and strengthen it. For example, when Maria breaks into line ahead of the other children, she is positively reinforced by receiving ice cream before them, and she is more likely to perform this behavior again in similar circumstances. Reinforcing consequences can also occur when a negative reinforcer is removed (see Chapter 10). For example, when Pat criticized Dick for going out with his friends, he left the house. Dick's leaving was negatively reinforced by his escaping from Pat's criticism and is more likely to occur again in similar situations.

Aversive or negative consequences are events following a target behavior that are undesired or unpleasant to the individual or significant others. Aversive consequences can decrease the likelihood that the response will be performed again under similar conditions. Aversive consequences that decrease response strength are called punishers (see Chapter 9). For example, when Frances was caught looking at another student's exam paper, the professor tore up Frances's paper and gave her a zero on the test. Frances stopped cheating in that class.

Sometimes a single behavior has both reinforcing and aversive consequences. In the example above, Maria was positively reinforced for breaking into the line for ice cream ahead of the other children. Breaking into the line also had aversive consequences for Maria, however, when her mother scolded her and sent her home alone after she got her ice cream cone.

Immediate or short-term reinforcing consequences often have a stronger effect in maintaining a behavior than long-term negative consequences exert in suppressing or preventing that behavior. Sometimes it seems puzzling that certain behaviors continue to occur despite severe negative consequences that eventually follow them. Some examples:

- A teenager steals a pen at the grocery store, even though he was taken to the police station last month for a similar offense.
- The immediate benefits of passing a test by cheating may offset the possible negative consequences of being caught and disciplined.
- Staying in bed a few minutes longer may consistently result in an individual's arriving late to work and being reprimanded by the boss.
- The immediate pleasure of an extramarital affair may be offset later by the consequences of being discovered and the conflicts that discovery sets off among family members.
- The immediate and enormous financial gain that can come from using illegal or unethical business practices can also result in harsh legal consequences, including imprisonment. In recent years several famous names, including Martha Stewart, Enron, and Tyco, have become associated with such practices.

Individuals continue to engage in short-term pleasurable activities even though they may risk significant health impairment because of these activities in the long run. For example, considerable research evidence demonstrates the relationships between smoking and lung diseases, between obesity and cardiovascular impairment, and between alcohol drinking and liver disease. Similar relationships have been shown between certain kinds of sexual behaviors and intravenous drug use and the risk of becoming infected with the human immunodeficiency virus (HIV), which can lead to AIDS. Short-term reinforcers exert greater control over these health-risking behaviors than do the severe negative consequences that are further removed in time. The behavioral approach has been used in the development of prevention programs aimed at reducing high-risk behaviors such as those that contribute to the transmission of HIV (e.g., Roffman et al., 1997; St. Lawrence, Jefferson, Alleyne, & Brasfield, 1995).

Response Strength

The strength of an operant response is determined through the measurement of its rate (frequency per time unit), duration, or intensity. Rate is the most commonly used measure of response strength. The number of times the target behavior is performed within a given time period is counted and recorded. Recording each occurrence of the target behavior provides a continuous record. Sometimes more than one type of measure is used. For example, "Tracy cried three times this week (rate) for 10 or more minutes (duration) each time."

The strength of a respondent behavior is measured by (a) the magnitude of the conditioned response and (b) the latency or interval between presentation of the conditioned stimulus and elicitation of the conditioned response. The magnitude of a classically conditioned response is measured by the contraction of a muscle or blood vessel or the secretion of a gland. For example, heart rate is measured by pulse rate, muscle contraction is measured by the amount of electrical activity of the muscle, and salivation is measured by the amount of saliva. Latency is measured by the amount of time that passes between presentation of the CS and elicitation of the CR. The shorter the latency, the stronger the response. The greater the magnitude, the stronger the response.

Recording Response Strength

Continuous recording of response rate is particularly appropriate for self-management programs. The individual is instructed to record target behaviors, such as the number of pages read per day, number of candy bars eaten per week, or number of telephone calls made per week to clients. Other examples of target behaviors appropriate for continuous recording include the number of math problems a college student solves per day, the number of minutes a tennis player practices her serve per week, and the number of times a child says "no" per hour. Continuous recording is not always feasible or efficient for keeping track of high-frequency behaviors (such as facial tics or head banging) or monitoring several behaviors (e.g., biting fingernails and spending time in a chat room) of one or more individuals.

Interval recording and time sampling are two alternatives to continuous recording of response rate. *Interval recording* involves selecting a block of time (e.g., 30 minutes) during which the target behavior will be observed and then further dividing this block into brief intervals (e.g., 15 seconds). If the target behavior occurs during the brief interval, the observer records a check mark for that interval on a form created for that purpose. If the target behavior is not performed during the interval, the observer records zero for that interval. The behavior must be performed at least once during the interval to be recorded. Regardless of the number of times the behavior occurs during the interval, the observer records one check mark for that interval. At the end of the larger block of time selected, the observer counts the number of intervals in which the target behavior occurred.

Interval recording is appropriate for behaviors that occur with high frequency, such as facial tics, head banging and other self-injurious behaviors, and inappropriate classroom talking. The interval record can provide an accurate indicator of the rates of these behaviors without an observer's having to count each occurrence. Interval recording is most reliable when an external event, such as a tape-recorded or digital tone, is used to signal the end of each interval. For example, the observer might wear a headset through which such a tone or other signal is transmitted. Figure 13.3 shows a sample interval record of a student's out-of-seat behavior during his social studies class.

Date: <u>11/15</u>

Time: <u>10:15–10:30 (Social Studies)</u>

Subject: <u>Sam P.</u>

Target behavior: <u>out of seat</u>

          ✓ = out of seat   0 = in seat

Intervals (15 seconds)

1	✓	16	✓	31	✓	46	✓	61	✓	76	0
2	✓	17	✓	32	✓	47	0	62	✓	77	0
3	✓	18	✓	33	✓	48	0	63	0	78	0
4	✓	19	✓	34	0	49	0	64	0	79	0
5	0	20	✓	35	0	50	0	65	0	80	0
6	✓	21	✓	36	0	51	0	66	0	81	0
7	✓	22	0	37	0	52	0	67	0	82	0
8	✓	23	0	38	0	53	0	68	0	83	0
9	0	24	0	39	✓	54	0	69	0	84	0
10	✓	25	0	40	✓	55	0	70	0	85	0
11	0	26	0	41	✓	56	0	71	✓	86	✓
12	✓	27	0	42	✓	57	0	72	✓	87	✓
13	0	28	✓	43	✓	58	0	73	✓	88	✓
14	0	29	✓	44	✓	59	✓	74	✓	89	✓
15	0	30	✓	45	✓	60	✓	75	✓	90	0

Total: 42/90 = 47% out-of-seat intervals

Observer's initials: <u>SS</u>

Figure 13.3   Interval Record of Sam's Out-of-Seat Behavior

Time sampling involves recording whether or not the target behavior is performed at certain times of the day. For example, a rehabilitation counselor can record the work behavior of several adults with developmental disabilities. The counselor observes the clients at specified intervals—for example, at the end of every 30 minutes during a 6-hour workday—and records the presence or absence of the target behaviors at those times (see Figure 13.4). Like interval recording, time sampling can be used to monitor high-frequency behaviors. It is also useful for monitoring several behaviors of one or more individuals (such as working steadily and talking to coworkers). Time sampling requires less of the observer's time and involvement than does either continuous or interval recording. (For further discussion of recording procedures and related issues, see Bailey & Burch, 2002; Bellack & Hersen, 1998; Bloom, Fischer, & Orme, 2003.)

Recorder: SS

Date: T1 = 1/12, T2 = 1/19

Code: W = working steadily[a]   O = not working, but not disruptive

X = not working, disruptive

S: LT		S: NB		S: CS		S: AC	
T1	T2	T1	T2	T1	T2	T1	T2
W	W	W	W	W	W	O	O
W	W	W	O	W	W	O	W
W	W	W	O	W	W	O	O
W	W	O	W	W	W	O	O
W	W	W	W	W	W	O	O
W	W	O	W	W	W	W	O
W	W	O	O	W	W	W	W
W	W	W	O	W	W	W	W
W	W	W	O	W	W	W	W
W	W	W	W	W	W	W	W
W	W	W	W	W	W	O	W
W	W	LUNCH	LUNCH	W	W	O	O
LUNCH	LUNCH	LUNCH	LUNCH	W	W	O	O
LUNCH	LUNCH	W	W	LUNCH	LUNCH	O	O
W	W	W	O	LUNCH	LUNCH	LUNCH	LUNCH
W	W	O	O	W	W	LUNCH	LUNCH
W	W	W	O	W	W	O	O
W	W	W	W	W	W	O	O
W	W	O	O	O	W	O	O
W	W	W	W	O	O	O	W
W	W	W	W	W	O	O	W
W	W	W	W	W	O	W	W
W	W	O	W	X	W	W	O
W	W	O	W	W	O	W	W
W	W	W	W	O	W	O	W
W	W	O	O	O	O	O	W

a. Working steadily: performing job task, raising hand for more work, asking for more work from supervisor, and asking supervisor for help with work.

Figure 13.4   Time Sampling Record of the Work Behavior of Four Employees in a
Sheltered Workshop (15 minutes)

Single-Subject Designs

In Chapter 3, we discussed single-subject research designs. These types of research designs are also called single-case or single-system designs. The three terms are interchangeable, but in recent years social work scholars have shown a preference for the term *single-system design* because a client can be an individual, a family or other group, or a community. The sample size in a design of this kind is one, whether the sample is a single individual, a family or other group, or a community (e.g., Thyer, 1998).

The basic single-subject design discussed in Chapter 3 is the AB design, where A indicates the baseline phase and B indicates the intervention phase. If a shift in the target behavior is observed during the intervention phase (after a steady baseline phase in which there was no change in the target behavior), it is possible that the intervention led to change in the target behavior. It is also possible, however, that something other than the intervention was responsible for the change in the target behavior. The AB design does not provide any control to demonstrate the efficacy of an intervention. The AB design is relatively easy to incorporate in practice settings because it involves only one baseline and one intervention, and it interferes minimally with service provision. The AB design can be useful in demonstrating behavior change or improvement, but not in determining causality.

An ABAB, or reversal, design can increase one's confidence that the intervention is responsible for a change in the target behavior. If the behavior change occurs at the times of the shifts in phases from A to B and B to A, it is likely that the intervention is responsible for the behavior change. It may not be desirable or ethical, however, to use an ABAB design to decrease an appropriate response or increase an inappropriate response. It is more important to achieve behavior change than to confirm that a particular intervention was responsible for that change. For example, an individual who lost 35 pounds may not want to reverse that weight loss to demonstrate the effectiveness of the behavior change program that produced the weight loss.

Another type of single-subject design is the *multiple-baseline design,* which can demonstrate that a particular intervention is likely to be related to change in a target behavior without reversing to baseline conditions. In a multiple-baseline design, initiation of the intervention is staggered over two or more target behaviors. Baselines are measured for all target behaviors simultaneously, but the intervention is introduced at a different point for each target behavior. Technically, to be considered a multiple-baseline design, the intervention can be used for two or more target behaviors that are relatively independent of each other; the current consensus on the minimum number of target behaviors required to show strong evidence of causality, however, is three (Bloom et al., 2003).

For example, in one multiple-baseline study, Sundel (1990) used videotaped modules to teach job-related social skills to adults with mental retardation. The three target behaviors were (a) following instructions, (b) working steadily, and (c) responding to correction. Rates of all three behaviors were collected for three sessions. The intervention was then applied to the first target behavior (following instructions) while baseline rates continued to be collected for the other two behaviors. After three more sessions, intervention began for the second target behavior (working steadily) while baseline rates continued to be collected for the third behavior. After another three sessions, intervention began for the third target behavior (responding to correction). Therefore, the number of baseline points for the first target behavior was three, that for the second target behavior was six, and that for the third target behavior was nine.

In analyzing data from a multiple-baseline design, the practitioner visually inspects graphs of the target behaviors to determine whether behavior change occurred and, if so, when. Figure 13.5 shows an example of a multiple-baseline design using hypothetical data in graphs of three behaviors (following instructions, working steadily, and responding to correction). In this case it is likely that the intervention led to the behavior changes because the changes occurred at different times for each behavior. Following instructions can be seen to increase after initiation of the intervention at Session 4. Working steadily can be seen to increase only after initiation of the intervention at Session 7. Responding to correction can be seen to increase only after initiation of the intervention at Session 10.

If an event other than the intervention led to improvement in the target behavior, the behavior change would most likely occur at the same time for all three behaviors, as shown in the hypothetical data in Figure 13.6. All three behaviors increased at the same time, at Session 4, even though the intervention was applied only to the first behavior (following instructions) at that time. The results of the intervention are inconclusive regarding its effects on the second and third target behaviors, thus the behavior change cannot be attributed to the intervention. Other conditions are likely to be responsible for the behavior change.

We can analyze the data from this research by looking for visual patterns in the graphs. In Figure 13.5, the data indicate stable baseline rates and a clear trend of increases in the target behavior following the intervention. It is likely, therefore, that the intervention was responsible for the behavior changes. We could also compute the statistical probability that such behavior changes were part of the expected fluctuations in the target behavior rather than attributable to the intervention, but this is not commonly done in clinical practice (Bloom et al., 2003; Rubin & Babbie, 1997).

The Sundel (1990) study described above used a *multiple-baseline design across behaviors* or problems—that is, the three targets were different behaviors. Multiple-baseline designs can also measure different settings and different clients. For example, the target behavior "following instructions" could have been measured in three different settings, such as the group home, the sheltered workshop, and the bowling alley. This would be a *multiple-baseline design across settings*. The same target behavior, following instructions, could be measured across three or more different clients in a *multiple-baseline design across clients* or cases.

The use of single-subject designs allows the practitioner to combine clinical practice and evaluation research. The goals of these two pursuits, however, are not always compatible. Scholars have discussed the possibility of conflict between treatment goals and the goals of knowledge building related to the experimental nature of single-subject designs (e.g., Wakefield & Kirk, 1997). For example, some clients may see the collection of baseline data in an AB design as delaying treatment of their problems. If the practitioner does not collect baseline data, however, it is difficult to determine whether the intervention is effective.

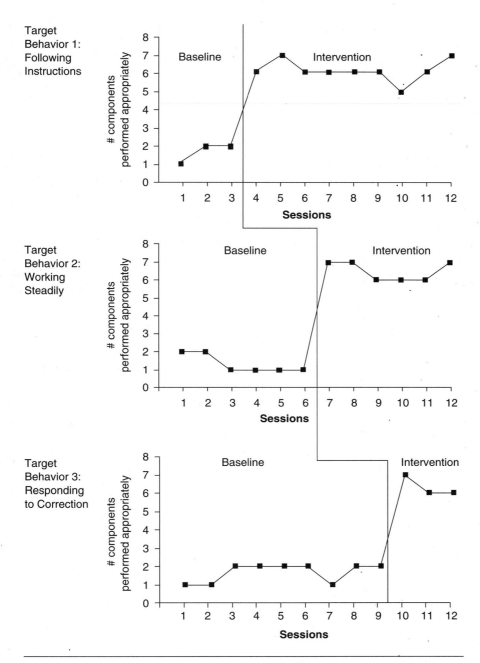

Figure 13.5 Multiple-Baseline Graphs Indicating Effective Intervention for Three Behaviors

Interobserver Agreement

Target behaviors must be clearly specified so that different observers are likely to identify the behaviors when they are performed. In Figure 13.4, for example, the

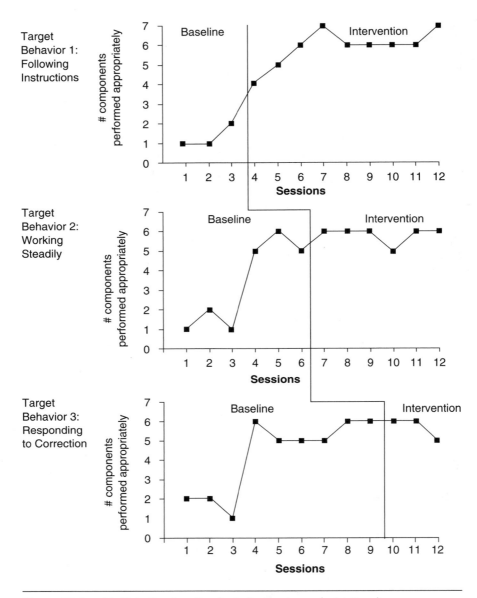

Figure 13.6　Multiple-Baseline Graphs Indicating Inconclusive Results

responses that constitute "working steadily" are noted on the bottom of the recording form as an aid to the observers who record the performance of those behaviors. Two or more observers record the data independently—that is, without consulting or signaling each other. The practitioner calculates the extent of agreement between observers to ensure that the behaviors have been adequately specified and recorded.

Interobserver agreement, or reliability, can be determined through a comparison of the numbers of observations recorded the same way by different raters. For example, one observer recorded 38 intervals as +, indicating that the subject was working steadily, and another observer recorded 40 intervals as +. These observers agreed on 38 intervals and disagreed on 2.

To compute interobserver agreement (IA), one divides the number of identical observations (IO) by the number of identical observations plus the number of different observations (DO):

$$IA = \frac{IO}{IO + DO}.$$

Interobserver agreement is expressed in terms of a percentage. In this example, it is calculated as follows:

$$IA = \frac{IO}{IO + DO} = \frac{38}{38 + 2} = 95\%.$$

According to convention, interobserver reliability should be 80% to 100% (Kazdin, 1994). Reliability lower than 80% indicates a substantial number of errors in recording. A major source of these errors could be inadequate specification of the target response.

Other Measures of Target Behaviors

Where applicable, observers record the duration of the target behavior in addition to its rate. For example, observers recorded that "Sally giggled in class three times today for 3 minutes or longer per occurrence" and that "Fred talked to Melanie on the phone five times last week, with each call lasting 30 minutes or longer."

The intensity or severity of behaviors such as hitting, teasing, crying, and anxiety is often difficult to measure. The problematic feature of these behaviors involves the aversive consequences or effects that they have for the client or significant others. Individuals differ in their tolerance for the behaviors of others and in their own reactions to physical and social stimulation. Examination of the aversive or negative consequences of the target behavior for the client and significant others provides an indicator for judging the intensity of the behavior. For example, the degree of "noisiness" of Dick's playing his stereo in the house is determined by a neighbor who complains to the police, and the intensity of Sam's "tapping" Gloria on the arm is indicated by the victim's bruises or complaints to a police officer.

The magnitude of respondent behaviors reported as anxiety can be measured by increases in blood pressure and heart rate. An individual's subjective rating of the magnitude of anxiety can also be measured on a self-report scale of subjective units of discomfort (e.g., on a scale of 1 to 100) such as that used in systematic desensitization (see Chapter 15).

Latency, an indication of the strength of a classically conditioned response, is measured by the interval between presentation of the conditioned stimulus (CS) or unconditioned stimulus (US) and the elicitation of the conditioned response (CR) or unconditioned response (UR), respectively. A short latency indicates a strong response; a long latency indicates a weak response. For example, when Mary sees Jack's photograph (CS), tears immediately come to her eyes (CR) (short latency and strong response).

Latency is also a measure of stimulus control related to performance of an operant response in the presence of an S^D. Latency is measured by the interval of time that transpires between presentation of the S^D and performance of the response. A short latency indicates strong control of the response by the stimulus; a long latency indicates weak control. For example, Pedro's father called him to the dinner table and Pedro came immediately (short latency and strong control of the response). The nurse told the patient to put on a robe and he did so 20 minutes later (long latency and weak control of the response). Measures of response latency give the practitioner and client information on the effects of various stimuli on target behaviors.

Sources of Assessment Information

Behavioral assessment requires the accurate and systematic collection of data on the target responses and their controlling antecedents and consequences. Response data are collected before intervention, during intervention, and at follow-up periods so that the practitioner can monitor and evaluate the effects of the interventions. The practitioner analyzes these data to determine whether target behaviors have increased or decreased in strength and whether problematic antecedents and consequences have been altered (see, e.g., Hanley et al., 2003).

The practitioner can validate his or her observations and analysis by interviewing individuals associated with the client's problem, such as parents, other relatives, neighbors, teachers, and peers. The practitioner obtains descriptions of the client's problem as perceived by these individuals, including information on their possible roles in supporting or discouraging the client's problematic behaviors. The practitioner can instruct these individuals to observe the client and record occurrences of the target behaviors and the conditions under which they are performed. This monitoring procedure might also reveal the monitor's role in generating or maintaining the target behavior—that is, how he or she provides problematic antecedents or consequences related to performance of the client's target behavior. For example, a mother monitoring her son's refusal to perform chores became aware that she was making excuses for him and was doing the chores herself.

The RAC-S diagram in Figure 13.7 provides a behavior analytic scheme for examining (a) the relationship between the target response and its possible controlling antecedents, (b) the relationship between the target response and its possible controlling consequences, and (c) the target response and its measures of rate, intensity, duration, magnitude, and/or latency. The practitioner analyzes these assessment data to determine functional or controlling relationships between the target behavior and its controlling antecedents and consequences.

To delineate the client's problem, the practitioner obtains examples of it through direct observation and by asking the client or significant others to describe a recent

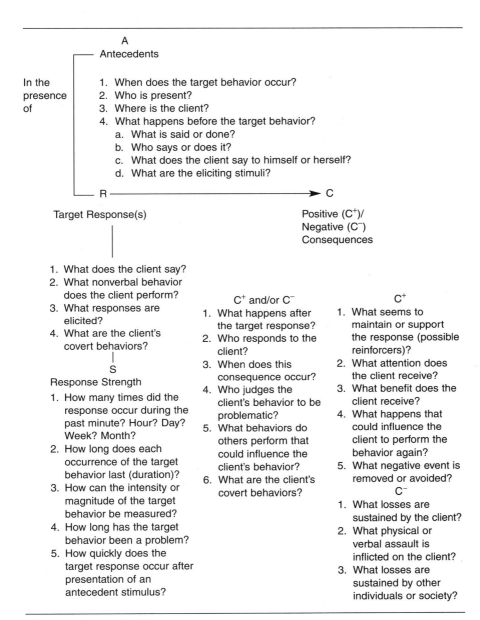

A
Antecedents

In the presence of

1. When does the target behavior occur?
2. Who is present?
3. Where is the client?
4. What happens before the target behavior?
   a. What is said or done?
   b. Who says or does it?
   c. What does the client say to himself or herself?
   d. What are the eliciting stimuli?

R ─────────────────────────────➤ C

Target Response(s)

Positive (C⁺)/
Negative (C⁻)
Consequences

1. What does the client say?
2. What nonverbal behavior does the client perform?
3. What responses are elicited?
4. What are the client's covert behaviors?

S

Response Strength

1. How many times did the response occur during the past minute? Hour? Day? Week? Month?
2. How long does each occurrence of the target behavior last (duration)?
3. How can the intensity or magnitude of the target behavior be measured?
4. How long has the target behavior been a problem?
5. How quickly does the target response occur after presentation of an antecedent stimulus?

C⁺ and/or C⁻

1. What happens after the target response?
2. Who responds to the client?
3. When does this consequence occur?
4. Who judges the client's behavior to be problematic?
5. What behaviors do others perform that could influence the client's behavior?
6. What are the client's covert behaviors?

C⁺

1. What seems to maintain or support the response (possible reinforcers)?
2. What attention does the client receive?
3. What benefit does the client receive?
4. What happens that could influence the client to perform the behavior again?
5. What negative event is removed or avoided?

C⁻

1. What losses are sustained by the client?
2. What physical or verbal assault is inflicted on the client?
3. What losses are sustained by other individuals or society?

Figure 13.7   RAC-S Diagram

example of the problem, if both methods are feasible. The practitioner asks the client or significant others to give an explicit account of the event. Using the examples observed or provided, the practitioner attempts to identify the RAC-S components, including (a) the target response(s), (b) the controlling antecedent(s), (c) the negative consequence(s), (d) the controlling consequence(s), and (e) measures of response strength, such as rate (frequency per time unit), duration, intensity, magnitude, or latency. The practitioner asks questions similar to those listed in Figure 13.7 to elicit details necessary to complete this initial assessment.

Behavioral questionnaires and checklists, such as the Problem Inventory and Problem Checklist discussed above, can provide supplemental assessment information. The Beck Depression Inventory (BDI; Beck, Steer, & Garbin, 1988; Beck, Ward, Mendelsohn, Mock, & Erlbaugh, 1961) is a 21-item self-report scale that assesses the severity of depression. The Yale-Brown Obsessive Compulsive Scale (Y-BOCS; Goodman, Price, Rasmussen, Mazure, Delgado, et al., 1989; Goodman, Price, Rasmussen, Mazure, Fleischmann, et al., 1989) is a symptom checklist and severity scale. The Fear Survey Schedule (Wolpe & Lang, 1964) and the Fear Questionnaire (Marks & Mathews, 1979) are used to identify events that are anxiety producing for an individual. The Reinforcement Survey Schedule (Cautela & Kastenbaum, 1967) identifies stimuli that can be considered potential reinforcers for specific individuals. Other assessment instruments and behavioral questionnaires include the Couples Precounseling Inventory (Stuart & Jacobson, 1987), the Sundel Assertiveness Scale (Sundel & Sundel, 1980), and the Life History Questionnaire (Wolpe & Lazarus, 1966). A manual of behavior analysis forms for clinical intervention with clients is also available (Cautela, 1977). By using such instruments, the practitioner can obtain information that otherwise might require extensive interviewing or observation.

Corcoran and Fischer (2000; Fischer & Corcoran, 2000) have published a two-volume sourcebook for human service professionals that includes a collection of more than 400 questionnaires and scales that can be used as client self-report measures for a wide range of problems. The instruments can be used to supplement and confirm the data that the practitioner acquires through observations and the reports of significant others as well as for intervention planning and evaluation. This collection of questionnaires and brief scales, or "rapid assessment instruments" (RAIs), includes materials for use in assessing clients in culturally diverse populations and in managed care settings.

Hudson (1982, 1992) developed a computerized set of standardized questionnaires for single-subject evaluation in clinical practice called the WALMYR Assessment Scales (WAS). The WAS is designed to monitor and assess the severity of a client's problem and evaluate the effectiveness of the intervention through periodic administration of one or more brief questionnaires. The 22 WAS scales include a generalized contentment scale, an index of self-esteem, scales that measure clinical stress and anxiety, scales that measure marital and sexual satisfaction, an index of family relations, and scales that measure parent-child relationship problems. The scales can be scored by computer program. Hudson (1995) also developed the Brief Adult Assessment Scale (BAAS), which has 16 subscales that assess personal and social functions, and the Multidimensional Adolescent Assessment Scale (MAAS), which has 16 subscales that assess adolescent personal and social functioning (Hudson, 1996; Mathiesen, Cash, & Hudson, 2002).

The practitioner can also use mechanical, electrical, and other devices to obtain important physiological measures related to a client's respondent behaviors. These include devices for monitoring blood sugar, heart rate, blood pressure, and other physiological responses. Human service practitioners are increasingly making use of new developments in information technology such as computerized assessment, computer-assisted therapy, and computer-aided documentation and evaluation of services (Dixon, 2003; Nurius & Hudson, 1993; Sturges, 1998). Palmtop computers have been used to collect self-report data on individuals with generalized anxiety disorder (e.g., Newman, Consoli, & Taylor, 1999) and on food consumption and exercise for obese clients (e.g., Agras, Taylor, Feldman, Losch, & Burnett, 1990). Practitioners have used computer-assisted programs in the treatment of mild to moderate depression, smoking, phobias, obesity, and other problems (e.g., Sturges, 1998).

Cultural Diversity

Behavioral practitioners attempt to identify the diversity issues that are important for behavioral assessment, including client ethnicity, race, socioeconomic status, sexual orientation, gender, and disability. Behavioral assessment requires that the practitioner consider cultural factors in determining functional relationships between stimuli and responses. Although behavioral approaches have been viewed as value-free and culture-free (Blechman, 1984; Paniagua, 1998), in reality they are subject to the same cultural biases evident in society. For example, members of certain cultural or ethnic groups, such as Asian Americans, may underuse mental health services (Sue, Nakamura, Chung, & Yee-Bradbury, 1994), and the treatment of women in society is often different from the treatment of men (e.g., Blechman, 1984). Environmental supports and stressors may be culturally determined. For example, environmental stressors for members of certain minority groups may include discrimination in housing, lack of opportunity structure in employment, and living in a community where the mainstream culture is different from theirs.

Knowledge of cultural practices is not a substitute, however, for behavioral analysis of an individual's behavior and its controlling conditions. Cultural or religious practices may dictate specific behavioral rules, but practitioners cannot assume that all members of a given group will follow a specific cultural or religious rule, or that no members of a group will follow a particular rule. For example, in one family a basket of bread on the dinner table could serve as an S^D indicating that the responses of sitting down and eating will be reinforced (by the food). In another family, a basket of bread on the table could serve as an S^D for the response of saying a prayer before eating the bread. Specific knowledge about each family could provide information useful to the practitioner in performing the behavioral analysis.

Behavioral practitioners should be familiar with the cultural norms of their clients and the functions of those norms as antecedents, reinforcers, and punishers. Knowledge of common cultural practices, however, can lead to stereotyping of individual members of a particular group, or to other forms of bias on the part of the behavioral practitioner. Used appropriately, such knowledge can provide the practitioner with important information that may not be available directly from the client. Consideration of these issues may result in relevant assessment data for an individual client or family, especially if the practitioner is from a different cultural background. For example, some cultures value respect and submissiveness over assertiveness. A Chinese American woman might be reinforced for assertive behavior by her peers, but the same behavior would likely be viewed negatively by her parents. Similarly, making eye contact might be viewed as overassertive, rather than assertive, in some cultures (e.g., Tanaka-Matsumi, Higginbotham, & Chang, 2002).

In some ethnic groups the family is more important than the individual. This can create difficulties for families in which the generations acculturate to mainstream U.S. culture at different speeds. In one study, Szapocznik and Kurtines (1993) found that Hispanic parents continued to be reinforced for behavior consistent with Hispanic culture, whereas their adolescent children were reinforced by their Anglo peers for behaviors consistent with American culture.

Behavioral Reenactment

The practitioner will sometimes find it difficult to specify RAC-S data accurately on the basis of examples provided by the client. Although clients might accurately describe the behaviors of others in problematic situations, they may lack awareness of their own behaviors influencing those situations.

Behavioral reenactment is a role-play technique that the practitioner can use to obtain RAC-S information on the client's behaviors in the problematic situation (Lawrence & Sundel, 1972; Sundel & Sundel, 1985a, 1985b). In behavioral reenactment, the client role-plays him- or herself in the problematic situation. The practitioner, the client's family members, or group members (if the assessment is occurring in a family or group setting) play the roles of significant others according to the client's descriptions. The practitioner observes the client's verbal and nonverbal behaviors during the role play and compares these observations with the client's previous descriptions. This technique can be useful for confirming the accuracy or consistency of a client's verbal report of the target behavior and its controlling conditions.

For example, Sheila, a supervisor with child protective services, complained that her department director singled her out for criticism. She insisted that nothing she did or said was responsible for the criticism. In a group session, Sheila reenacted a recent incident in which the director criticized her after a staff meeting. During the role play, Sheila spoke in short, clipped phrases, sneered, and stood defiantly with her hands on her hips when the person role-playing the director asked her about cases she was supervising. After the reenactment, the practitioner and Sheila's fellow group members pointed out discrepancies between Sheila's account of the incident and the behaviors they observed during the reenactment. The group members identified some of Sheila's nonverbal responses as inappropriate reactions to reasonable questioning by the director. Sheila had been unaware of how her nonverbal behaviors were contributing to the director's negative assessment of the situation. The behavioral reenactment provided a concrete example of Sheila's problematic responses and their possible controlling antecedents and consequences.

Collecting Assessment Information

The practitioner obtains measures of response strength (rate, intensity, duration, magnitude, latency) as baseline data prior to working with the client to formulate behavior change goals and develop the intervention plan. The practitioner instructs the client to record baseline data at home, work, school, or elsewhere in the client's environment using prepared forms such as the assessment form

1. State the problem and give an example of its occurrence.

2. Specify the target response(s) to be observed in precise terms. Be sure that a stranger reading this description would know exactly what the client is saying or doing.

   Behavioral excesses:

   Behavioral deficits:

3. Describe the antecedents related to the target response(s).

4. Describe in specific terms the negative consequences of this problem.

5. State the possible reinforcers for the target response(s).

Figure 13.8   Assessment Form

Description of Target Response:

Days	Target Response	Response Strength[a]
Monday		
Tuesday		
Wednesday		
Thursday		
Friday		
Saturday		
Sunday		
		Total:
		Average:

a. Specify measure(s) of response strength to be used (e.g., rate, intensity, duration, magnitude, latency).

Figure 13.9   Daily Behavioral Recording Chart

illustrated in Figure 13.8 and the daily behavior recording chart shown in Figure 13.9. The client might also carry a 3-by-5-inch index card or use a PDA (personal digital assistant) to record target behaviors. Wrist counters and other devices are also available for this purpose. The client then reports the data he or she has collected at each interview.

Individuals other than the client may be responsible for collecting and recording assessment data. The practitioner explains the recording assignment to each recorder and then asks the individual to repeat the instructions to be sure they are clear. The practitioner answers any questions the recorder has and clarifies any ambiguities related to the assignment. Confirming the understanding and readiness of the client or significant other to carry out the assignment can prevent inaccurate or incomplete data collection.

The practitioner instructs the client to record the target responses and one or more measures of response strength, such as rate or duration. The practitioner might also assign the client to record antecedents or consequences, or both, related to the target behaviors. The practitioner then uses these RAC-S data to determine the functional or controlling relationships between the target behaviors and environmental events, and to formulate goals with the client.

Behavioral Assessment and Application of RAC-S

In the behavioral assessment procedure, the practitioner takes the following steps to determine functional relationships between target behaviors and their controlling conditions:

1. List the client's problems.

2. Reconcile discrepancies in client problems from different sources.

3. Select one problem for immediate attention.

4. Obtain examples of the problem that specify the target response(s), possible controlling antecedents, negative consequences, possible controlling consequences, and response strength.

5. Design a measurement plan, specifying baseline measures of response strength to be recorded.

6. Collect assessment data.

7. Analyze the data to determine probable controlling antecedents and consequences.

By taking these steps, the practitioner obtains the data needed to analyze the relationships between the target response and the antecedents and consequences that control it. Many antecedents and consequences may be related to the target response, but not all will be involved in its maintenance. Analyzing the data allows the practitioner to formulate a hypothesis as to what is controlling the behavior and, therefore, what conditions need to be altered in order to produce behavior change.

For example, two couples argue frequently. One couple makes up soon after each argument and then has sex. The other couple separates after each argument, with the wife going to her mother's house and the husband going to a neighborhood bar. The behavior (frequent arguing) is the same for both couples, but the consequences are quite different. Conducting a behavioral assessment allows the practitioner to identify the consequences and formulate a hypothesis for what is controlling the arguments.

In another example, Tyler may scream every night at bedtime, refuse to eat more than a bite of dinner most evenings, and cry before being dropped off at day care three times a week. These are very different behaviors, but in looking at the antecedents the practitioner finds that Tyler engages in these behaviors when his parents begin to raise their voices to each other. When he screams, refuses food, and cries, both parents attend to him and stop raising their voices. By conducting a behavioral assessment, the practitioner identifies these factors and is thus able to formulate a hypothesis as to what controlling conditions need to be altered to produce behavior change.

Denice, a computer programmer employed by a software firm, was referred for counseling by her supervisor because of her "moodiness" and "emotional outbursts" at work. When the therapist asked her for an example of the problem, Denice described a recent incident with a coworker. The coworker gave Denice some suggestions for completing her part of the team project, and Denice became angry, lost her temper, and shouted at the coworker. Denice told her coworker that she had been in the business longer than he had and said, "You have a lot of nerve thinking that you know more about programming than I do." Denice also told her coworker that she did not ask for his opinions and would thank him to stay out of her business. After the incident, Denice's boss called her into his office and asked her what was wrong. She said she was "frustrated and angry" and did not know why other people had to interfere with how she did her job. The therapist used this information in initiating a behavioral assessment.

Denice's presenting problem (i.e., the problem that she said brought her to seek help) was a coworker's interfering with her doing her job. Information gathered through the use of the Problem Inventory and the Problem Checklist indicated that Denice also had difficulty disciplining her teenage son and getting along with her ex-husband. After further discussion with the therapist to prioritize her concerns, Denice indicated that her work situation was of most concern because the coworker complained to her boss about her and she was in danger of losing her job. Denice had worked at the company for 4 years. In discussing an example of the problem, the therapist asked Denice how often she had unpleasant conversations with coworkers. Denice said that this was not the first time she had "lost it" when talking with a coworker. Although Denice feared that she would be fired if her behavior continued, she said she did not know why other people had to interfere with how she did her job. Denice discussed this problem with her family physician, who agreed that counseling was appropriate after determining that Denice was in good physical health.

When questioned, Denice had difficulty specifying the circumstances of her last unpleasant encounter with a coworker. To obtain more specific data, the therapist arranged a behavioral reenactment to provide concrete examples of Denice's behavior in the problematic situation. The therapist role-played one of Denice's coworkers and Denice role-played herself in a simulation of a recent incident in which she lost her temper. Denice described the situation as follows: Denice was complaining to a coworker about the tight deadline for completing a project and commented that management was becoming more rigid. The coworker suggested that Denice try to change her work pattern and work more collaboratively with the rest of the team.

During the behavioral reenactment, the therapist observed that Denice shouted, clenched her fists, frowned, and moved her arms rapidly up and down. Denice told her coworker that she had been in the business longer than he had and said, "You have a lot of nerve thinking that you know more about computer programming than I do." She said that she did not ask for his opinions and would thank him to stay out of her business. When questioned after the role play, Denice reported feeling "frustrated and angry." She said that she had behaved similarly during other incidents at work.

To determine the controlling antecedents for Denice's inappropriate responses, the therapist asked Denice questions similar to those in the RAC-S diagram shown in Figure 13.7. For example, Where and when were the target behaviors performed? Who was present? What was said? What were you thinking and feeling? The therapist determined that the target behaviors occurred when Denice was in her cubicle complaining to a coworker about the project deadline. Just before Denice became angry, the coworker made a suggestion about how Denice could better meet her deadlines. Denice told herself that she did not deserve criticism from her coworker and "he thinks I can't do my job." Frequently, other coworkers were within hearing distance when the target behaviors occurred. Denice also reported that she felt very anxious when coworkers criticized her because she sometimes felt that she was "not smart enough to do this job."

Denice stated the negative consequences of her target responses: Her boss criticized her and she could lose her job if she continued to shout at her coworkers. Further interviewing or observation was necessary to discover the controlling consequences for Denice's target behaviors. The RAC-S diagram in Figure 13.7 suggests questions that the therapist could use to help identify possible reinforcers for her behaviors. For example, What maintains the responses? What attention or other benefits does the client receive? When Denice shouts at a coworker, she is negatively reinforced by the coworker's walking away from her and the other employees leaving the area. Denice also reported that her anxiety decreased after she shouted and the coworkers walked away from her, another negatively reinforcing consequence for her shouting.

Denice's assessment form is shown in Figure 13.10. After completing the assessment form, the therapist instructed Denice to record the baseline data of frequency and duration of the target behavior of shouting at coworkers on her behavior recording chart. The chart that Denice filled out is shown in Figure 13.11.

The information recorded on the daily behavioral recording chart allows the practitioner to compare the client's subjective recall of the problematic situation with a record based on the client's actual performance. The practitioner can also use a written record to correct subjective estimates of response data. Sometimes, the client's activities of observing and recording RAC-S data produce a temporary change in the frequency of a target response in the desired direction, possibly because of the client's heightened awareness of performing the target behavior.

Denice recorded the frequency and duration of her target responses for one week. She recorded shouting incidents with coworkers three times during the week and recorded one instance of speaking calmly to coworkers. She estimated the mean duration of each shouting incident to be about 2 minutes. She spoke calmly to coworkers for about 15 seconds. Table 13.1 displays RAC-S information about Denice's problem.

The RAC-S data of Denice's problem reveal multiple antecedents prior to her shouting at the coworker and several consequences following that behavior. The challenge for the practitioner in behavioral assessment is to determine which of the antecedents and consequences have a functional or controlling relationship to the target responses. When Denice complained to a coworker about the difficulty in meeting tight deadlines,

1. State the problem and give an example of its occurrence.
   Denice is afraid that she will be fired. Coworkers complain to her boss about her emotional outbursts and uncooperative behaviors. When a coworker gave her a suggestion about improving her work efficiency, she became angry, lost her temper, and shouted at the coworker.

2. Specify the target response(s) to be observed in precise terms. Be sure that a stranger reading this description would know exactly what the client is *saying* or *doing*.
   Behavioral excesses: Shouting, clenching her fists, frowning, moving her arms rapidly up and down.
   Behavioral deficits: Discussing her work performance in a calm and pleasant manner with coworkers.

3. Describe the antecedents related to the target response(s).
   a. Denice complained to a coworker about tight deadlines.
   b. Coworker made a suggestion about how Denice could improve her work performance.
   c. Denice says to herself, "I don't deserve criticism from my coworker"; "He thinks I can't do my job."
   d. Denice feels very anxious about her ability to do her job.

4. Describe in specific terms the negative consequences of this problem.
   a. Boss called Denice into his office and criticized her for shouting at a coworker.
   b. Boss warned Denice that she could lose her job.
   c. Denice became frustrated and angry.
   d. Anxiety about her ability to do her job.

5. State the possible reinforcers for the target response(s).
   a. Coworkers stay away from Denice.
   b. Decrease in suggestions from coworkers about how she does her job.

Figure 13.10   Assessment Form for Denice

the coworker gave her suggestions about how she could better meet the deadlines and Denice became very anxious (antecedents). Denice shouted, "You have a lot of nerve thinking you know more about programming than I do" (response). Denice's boss criticized her shouting and warned her that she could lose her job (negative consequences). Denice's coworkers avoided her (positive consequences).

Analyzing the data allows the practitioner to formulate a hypothesis regarding which conditions exert control over the target behaviors. In summary, Denice felt anxious in work situations involving deadlines. When she complained to a coworker about the deadlines and he criticized her performance, Denice's anxiety increased, resulting in her shouting at the coworker. Immediately after the shouting incident, Denice's anxiety decreased, the coworker stopped giving suggestions, and other coworkers left her alone, events that were positive consequences for Denice. Her anxiety increased again, however, when her boss criticized her for her uncooperative relationships with coworkers. The therapist developed the following hypothesis regarding Denice's problematic situation: Denice's shouting was reinforced and maintained by negative reinforcement (anxiety decreased, coworker stopped giving suggestions, coworkers left her alone). The therapist then used this hypothesis in determining goals and developing an intervention plan for Denice.

Description of Target Responses:
A. Shouts at coworker
B. Speaks calmly to coworker

Days	Target Response	Response Strength[a] (Frequency/Day; Duration)
Sunday	Day off	
Monday	Spoke calmly with coworkers	15 seconds, 1 occurrence
Tuesday	Sick day	
Wednesday	Did not speak to coworkers at all	0
Thursday	Shouted at coworker	2 minutes, 1 occurrence
Friday	Shouted at coworker	2 minutes, 1 occurrence
Saturday	Day off	
		Shouting: total, 2 times/ week; average, 2 minutes/incident *Spoke calmly:* 1/week; average 15 seconds

a. Specify measure of response strength to be used. In this case, specify response strength in terms of frequency per day or duration, or both.

Figure 13.11 Daily Behavioral Recording Chart for Denice

Table 13.1 RAC-S Information for Denice

Responses(s)	Antecedents	Consequences	Strength
Denice shouted; clenched her fists; frowned; moved her arms rapidly up and down; said to coworker, "You have a lot of nerve thinking you know more about programming than I do"; she thought, "I feel anxious and angry."	Coworker made a suggestion about how Denice could better meet deadlines; Denice said to herself, "I don't deserve criticism from B (coworker)"; anxiety about completing her assignment on time; feeling exhausted at the end of the day; worrying about her son's failing a class at school	*Negative:* Boss criticized Denice's shouting ("You can't shout at your coworkers like that"); Denice could lose her job *Positive:* coworkers stop making suggestions; coworkers stay away from her	Two times per week; mean duration of each incident was estimated to be about 2 minutes

Summary

1. Behavioral assessment is used to analyze a client's problem or circumstances as the basis for formulating behavior change goals and developing an intervention plan.

2. Behavioral assessment leads to specification of the client's target behaviors and their controlling antecedents and consequences, and to formulation of behavior change goals.

3. *RAC-S* is an acronym for the major elements of behavioral assessment: target response(s), antecedent(s), consequence(s), and response strength. The practitioner uses the RAC-S diagram to examine a target response in relation to its possible controlling antecedents and consequences.

4. A problem area is a broad concern that is often manifested in the role or position in which the individual experiences difficulty.

5. The practitioner considers the following in determining problem priorities for intervention: (a) the problem of most immediate concern of the client, significant others, or both; (b) the problem that will have the most severe negative consequences if not handled immediately; (c) the problem that requires handling before other problems can be treated; and (d) the problem that can be corrected most quickly.

6. The term *problematic behaviors* refers to behavioral excesses, behavioral deficits, and faulty discriminations.

7. The term *controlling conditions* refers to antecedents and consequences that maintain a target behavior. Antecedents such as a US, CS, or S^D precede, signal, or elicit a target behavior. Consequences follow a target behavior and influence the likelihood that it will be performed again. Positive and negative reinforcers increase the probability of a behavior recurring, and punishers decrease the likelihood of a behavior recurring.

8. The practitioner analyzes the RAC-S data to identify controlling antecedents and consequences and their effects on the client's behaviors. The practitioner attempts to determine functional relationships between target behaviors and their possible controlling antecedents and consequences. The results of this analysis allow the practitioner to formulate a hypothesis regarding which conditions are maintaining the behavior.

9. The strength of an operant response is measured by rate (frequency per time unit), duration, and intensity. Rate is the most commonly used measure of operant response strength. Magnitude and latency are the measures of response strength of respondent behaviors. More than one type of operant or respondent measure can be used in obtaining assessment data.

10. Continuous recording, interval recording, and time sampling are ways of recording data. If there is more than one observer recording data, the practitioner calculates interobserver reliability to determine the extent of agreement between the observers.

11. Multiple-baseline designs can be used to demonstrate that an intervention is responsible for change in a target behavior without reversing to baseline conditions (as in the ABAB design).

12. Data related to the strength and controlling conditions of a target behavior are recorded during assessment, intervention, and follow-up periods. These data can be obtained through direct observations, client reports, and the use of physiological measurement devices (e.g., to measure blood pressure and heart rate). Additional supportive data can be obtained from reports of significant others, assessment checklists, and questionnaires.

13. Behavioral reenactment is a role-play technique used to obtain assessment data regarding the client's target behaviors and their possible controlling antecedents and consequences. The practitioner compares the client's behavior during reenactments with the client's previous description of the situation.

14. In the behavioral assessment procedure the practitioner takes the following steps to determine functional relationships between target behaviors and their controlling conditions: (a) List the client's problems; (b) reconcile discrepancies in reports of client problems from different sources; (c) select one problem for immediate attention; (d) obtain examples of the problem that specify the target response(s), possible controlling antecedents, negative consequences, possible controlling consequences, and response strength; (e) design a measurement plan, specifying measures of response strength to be recorded; (f) collect assessment data; and (g) analyze the data to determine functional relationships between a target behavior and its controlling antecedents and consequences, and develop a hypothesis about the conditions that exert control over the target behavior.

Suggested Activities

1. Watch several episodes of your favorite television sitcom and identify RAC-S data for a target response of one of the program's characters. Share your data with classmates.

2. Use behavioral reenactment with a friend or family member to identify RAC-S data for a response you would like to change. What information did you obtain that you did not have prior to the reenactment?

References and Resources

Agras, W. S., Taylor, C. B., Feldman, D. E., Losch, M., & Burnett, K. F. (1990). Developing computer-assisted therapy for the treatment of obesity. *Behavior Therapy, 21,* 99–109.

American Psychiatric Association. (1991). *DSM-IV options book: Work in progress.* Washington, DC: Author.

American Psychiatric Association. (1994). *Diagnostic and statistical manual of mental disorders* (4th ed.). Washington, DC: Author.

Antony, M. M., & Barlow, D. H. (Eds.). (2001). *Handbook of assessment and treatment planning for psychological disorders*. New York: Guilford.

Bailey, J. S., & Burch, M. R. (2002). *Research methods in applied behavior analysis*. Thousand Oaks, CA: Sage.

Beare, P. L., Severson, S., & Brandt, P. (2004). The use of a positive procedure to increase engagement on-task and decrease challenging behavior. *Behavior Modification, 28,* 28–44.

Beck, A. T., Steer, R. A., & Garbin, M. G. (1988). Psychometric properties of the Beck Depression Inventory: Twenty-five years of evaluation. *Clinical Psychology Review, 8,* 77–100.

Beck, A. T., Ward, C. H., Mendelsohn, M., Mock, J., & Erlbaugh, J. (1961). An inventory for measuring depression. *Archives of General Psychiatry, 4,* 561–571.

Bellack, A. S., & Hersen, M. (1998). *Behavioral assessment: A practical handbook* (4th ed.). Boston: Allyn & Bacon.

Blechman, E. A. (1984). *Behavior modification with women*. New York: Guilford.

Blechman, E., & Brownell, K. D. (Eds.). (1997). *Behavioral medicine and women: A comprehensive handbook*. New York: Guilford.

Bloom, M., Fischer, J., & Orme, J. G. (2003). *Evaluating practice: Guidelines for the accountable professional* (4th ed.). Boston: Allyn & Bacon.

Cautela, J. R. (1977). *Behavior analysis forms for clinical intervention*. Champaign, IL: Research Press.

Cautela, J. R., & Kastenbaum, R. (1967). A reinforcement survey schedule for use in therapy, training, and research. *Psychological Reports, 20,* 1115–1130.

Corcoran, K., & Fischer, J. (2000). *Measures for clinical practice: A sourcebook: Vol. 1. Couples, families and children* (3rd ed.). New York: Free Press.

Dixon, M. R. (2003). Creating a portable data-collection system with Microsoft embedded visual tools for the pocket PC. *Journal of Applied Behavior Analysis, 36,* 271–284.

First, M. B., Spitzer, R. L., Gibbon, M., & Williams, J. B. (1995). *Structured clinical interview for the DSM-IV: Axis-I*. New York: New York State Psychiatric Institute, Biometrics Research Department.

Fischer, J., & Corcoran, K. (2000). *Measures for clinical practice: A sourcebook: Vol. 2. Adults* (3rd ed.). New York: Free Press.

Goldiamond, I. (1965). Justified and unjustified alarm over behavioral control. In O. Milton (Ed.), *Behavior disorders: Perspectives and trends*. Philadelphia: J. B. Lippincott.

Goodman, W. K., Price, L. H., Rasmussen, S. A., Mazure, C., Delgado, P., Heninger, G. R., et al. (1989). The Yale-Brown Obsessive Compulsive Scale: II. Validity. *Archives of General Psychiatry, 46,* 1012–1016.

Goodman, W. K., Price, L. H., Rasmussen, S. A., Mazure, C., Fleischmann, R. L., Hill, C. L., et al. (1989). The Yale-Brown Obsessive Compulsive Scale: I. Development, use, and reliability. *Archives of General Psychiatry, 46,* 1006–1011.

Hanley, G. P., Iwata, B. A., & McCord, P. E. (2003). Functional analysis of problem behavior: A review. *Journal of Applied Behavior Analysis, 36,* 147–185.

Hudson, W. W. (1982). *The clinical measurement package: A field manual*. Homewood, IL: Dorsey.

Hudson, W. W. (1992). *The WALMYR Assessment Scales scoring manual*. Tempe, AZ: WALMYR.

Hudson, W. W. (1995). *The Brief Adult Assessment Scale*. Tallahassee, FL: WALMYR.

Hudson, W. W. (1996). *Multidimensional Adolescent Assessment Scale (MAAS)*. Tempe, AZ: WALMYR.

Iwamasa, G. Y. (1996). Ethnic issues in behavioral psychology: A review of the literature. *Behavior Modification, 20,* 45–59.

Karls, J. M., & Wandrei, K. E. (Eds.). (1994). *Person-in-environment system: The PIE classification system for social functioning problems.* Annapolis Junction, MD: National Association of Social Workers Press.

Kazdin, A. E. (1994). *Behavior modification in applied settings* (5th ed.). Pacific Grove, CA: Brooks/Cole.

Kirk, S. A., & Kutchins, H. (1988). Deliberate misdiagnosis in mental health practice. *Social Service Review, 62,* 225–237.

Knox, L. S., Albano, A. M., & Barlow, D. H. (1996). Parental involvement in the treatment of childhood OCD: A multiple-baseline examination incorporating parents. *Behavior Therapy, 27,* 93–115.

Kurtz, P. F., Chin, M. D., Huete, J. M., Tarbox, S. F., O'Connor, J. T., Paclawskyj, T. R., et al. (2003). Functional analysis and treatment of self-injurious behavior in young children: A summary of 30 cases. *Journal of Applied Behavior Analysis, 36,* 205–219.

Kutchins, H., & Kirk, S. A. (1995). Should DSM be the basis for teaching social work practice? No! *Journal of Social Work Education, 31,* 159–168.

Lawrence, H., & Sundel, M. (1972). Behavior modification in adult groups. *Social Work, 17,* 34–43.

Marks, I., & Mathews, A. (1979). Brief standard self-rating for phobic patients. *Behaviour Research and Therapy, 17,* 263–267.

Mash, E. J., & Terdal, L. G. (Eds.). (1997). *Behavioral assessment of childhood disorders* (3rd ed.). New York: Guilford.

Mathiesen, S. G., Cash, S. J., & Hudson, W. W. (2002). The multidimensional assessment scale: A validation study. *Research on Social Work Methods, 12,* 9–28.

Newman, M. G., Consoli, A., & Taylor, C. (1999). A palm-top computer program for the treatment of generalized anxiety disorder. *Behavior Modification, 23,* 597–619.

Newman, M. G., Kenardy, J., Herman, S., & Taylor, C. B. (1997). Comparison of palmtop-computer-assisted brief cognitive-behavioral treatment to cognitive-behavioral treatment for panic disorder. *Journal of Consulting and Clinical Psychology, 65,* 178–183.

Nurius, P. S., & Hudson, W. W. (1993). *Human services practice, evaluation, and computers: A practical guide for today and beyond.* Pacific Grove, CA: Brooks/Cole.

Paniagua, F. A. (1998). *Assessing and treating culturally diverse clients: A practical guide* (2nd ed.). Thousand Oaks, CA: Sage.

Piazza, C. C., Fisher, W. W., Brown, K. A., Shore, B. A., Patel, M. R., Katz, R. M., et al. (2003). Functional analysis of inappropriate mealtime behaviors. *Journal of Applied Behavior Analysis, 36,* 187–204.

Rodgers, A. Y., & Potocky, M. (1997). Evaluating culturally sensitive practice through single subject design: Methodological issues and strategies. *Research in Social Work Practice, 7,* 391–401.

Roffman, R. A., Downey, L., Beadnell, B., Gordon, J. R., Craven, J. N., & Stephens, R. S. (1997). Cognitive-behavioral group counseling to prevent HIV transmission in gay and bisexual men: Factors contributing to successful risk reduction. *Research in Social Work Practice, 7,* 165–186.

Rogers, C. R., & Skinner, B. F. (1956). Some issues concerning the control of human behavior: A symposium. *Science, 124,* 1057–1066.

Rubin, A., & Babbie, E. (1997). *Research methods for social work* (3rd ed.). Pacific Grove, CA: Brooks/Cole.

St. Lawrence, J. S., Jefferson, K. W., Alleyne, E., & Brasfield, T. L. (1995). Comparison of education versus behavioral skills training interventions in lowering sexual HIV-risk behavior of substance-dependent adolescents. *Journal of Consulting and Clinical Psychology, 63,* 154–157.

Smith, R. G., & Churchill, R. M. (2002). Identification of environmental determinants of behavior disorders through functional analysis of precursor behaviors. *Journal of Applied Behavior Analysis, 35,* 125–136.

Stuart, R. B., & Jacobson, B. (1987). *Couples precounseling inventory.* Champaign, IL: Research Press.

Sturges, J. W. (1998). Practical use of technology in professional practice. *Professional Psychology: Research and Practice, 29,* 183–188.

Sue, S., Nakamura, C. Y., Chung, R. C., & Yee-Bradbury, C. (1994). Mental health research on Asian Americans. *Journal of Community Psychology, 22,* 61–67.

Sundel, M., Radin, N., & Churchill, S. R. (1985). Diagnosis in group work. In M. Sundel, P. Glasser, R. Sarri, & R. Vinter (Eds.), *Individual change through small groups* (2nd ed., pp. 117–139). New York: Free Press.

Sundel, M., & Sundel, S. S. (1985a). Behavior modification in groups: A time-limited model for planning, intervention and evaluation. In D. Upper & S. Ross (Eds.), *Handbook of behavioral group therapy* (pp. 3–24). New York: Plenum.

Sundel, M., & Sundel, S. S. (1985b). Behavior modification with time-limited groups. In M. Sundel, P. Glasser, R. Sarri, & R. Vinter (Eds.), *Individual change through small groups* (2nd ed., pp. 440–460). New York: Free Press.

Sundel, S. S. (1990). The effects of videotaped modeling on the acquisition, performance, and generalization of job-related social skills in adults with mental retardation living in group homes (Doctoral dissertation, University of Texas at Arlington, 1990). *Dissertation Abstracts International, 51,* 2522-A.

Sundel, S. S., & Sundel, M. (1980). *Be assertive: A practical guide for human service workers.* Beverly Hills, CA: Sage.

Szapocznik, J., & Kurtines, W. M. (1993). Family psychology and cultural diversity. *American Psychologist, 48,* 400–407.

Tanaka-Matsumi, J., Higginbotham, H. N., & Chang, R. (2002). Cognitive-behavioral approaches to counseling across cultures: A functional analytic approach for clinical applications. In P. B. Pedersen, J. G. Draguns, W. J. Lonner, & J. E. Trimble (Eds.), *Counseling across cultures* (5th ed., pp. 337–354). Thousand Oaks, CA: Sage.

Thyer, B. A. (1998). Promoting research on community practice: Using single-system designs. In R. H. MacNair (Ed.), *Research strategies for community practice* (pp. 47–61). Binghamton, NY: Haworth.

Wakefield, J. C., & Kirk, S. A. (1997). What the practitioner knows versus what the client is told: Neglected dilemmas of informed consent in an account of single-system experimental designs. *Journal of Social Work Education, 33,* 275–291.

Williams, J. B. W., & Spitzer, R. L. (1995). Should DSM be the basis for teaching social work practice in mental health? Yes! *Journal of Social Work Education, 31,* 148–158.

Wolpe, J. (1990). *The practice of behavior therapy* (4th ed.). Elmsford, NY: Pergamon.

Wolpe, J., & Lang, B. J. (1964). A fear survey schedule for use in behavior therapy. *Behavior Research and Therapy, 2,* 27–30.

Wolpe, J., & Lazarus, A. A. (1966). Life history questionnaire. In J. Wolpe & A. A. Lazarus, *Behavior therapy techniques: A guide to the treatment of neuroses* (pp. 165–169). Elmsford, NY: Pergamon.

CHAPTER 14

Goal Setting, Intervention Planning, and Evaluation

> "Would you tell me, please, which way I ought to go from here?"
>
> "That depends a good deal on where you want to get to," said the Cat.
>
> "I don't much care where—" said Alice.
>
> "Then it doesn't matter which way you go," said the Cat.
>
> "—so long as I get somewhere," Alice added as an explanation.
>
> "Oh, you're sure to do that," said the Cat, "if you only walk long enough."
>
> —Lewis Carroll, *Alice's Adventures in Wonderland*, 1865

Tim was a resident in a group home for individuals with mental retardation. He spent much of his free time sitting alone in a corner with his arms folded, unshaven and unkempt. Behavior change goals for Tim included development of self-care skills, such as washing, brushing his teeth, combing his hair, and shaving. The intervention plan for developing these self-care skills involved the following behavior change techniques: modeling, shaping, and positive reinforcement.

Baseline measures were obtained for use in evaluating the effectiveness of Tim's intervention plan. Behavioral changes on these measures were used to evaluate movement toward attainment of his goals.

Objectives

After completing this chapter, you should be able to do the following:

- Formulate a behavior change goal, including the desired client response, a relevant antecedent, and a probable positive reinforcer.

- Identify environmental and client resources supporting goal attainment and obstacles to goal attainment.
- Formulate an intervention plan, specifying the behavior change techniques and procedures for implementing them.
- State three criteria for evaluating the effectiveness of a behavior change program.
- Describe a method for evaluating the results of a behavior change program.

Formulating Behavior Change Goals

In this chapter, we show how behavioral and cognitive principles and techniques can be conceptualized within a problem-solving framework for goal setting, intervention planning, implementation, and evaluation. This framework builds on the behavioral assessment framework presented in Chapter 13.

After the practitioner has collected and analyzed baseline measures of the target response and its controlling antecedents and consequences (RAC-S), he or she can formulate behavior change goals. These goals specify the desired responses and their controlling antecedents and consequences. Whenever feasible, the practitioner also indicates measures of desired response strength. The practitioner establishes initial and intermediate objectives as approximations to the desired goals. Goals and objectives delineated in this manner provide the practitioner with explicit criteria to use in evaluating the client's behavior change program.

The practitioner encourages the client to participate actively in establishing behavior change goals. The more committed the client is to the goals, the more likely it is that he or she will perform the behaviors required to achieve them. For example, one possible goal initially stated by Denice (in Chapter 13) was to obtain a different job. The decision to leave a problematic situation rather than attempt to modify the problematic behavior or conditions of that situation is ultimately the client's choice. The practitioner, however, can point out possible alternative goals for the client. After Denice's therapist identified some goals other than leaving her job, Denice decided to work on modifying the target behaviors she had reported.

The two behavior change goals for Denice were to (a) decrease the frequency of undesired verbal and nonverbal behaviors in response to suggestions from coworkers and (b) increase the frequency of desired verbal and nonverbal behaviors in response to suggestions from coworkers.

In regard to Denice's first goal, when coworkers make suggestions about better ways to meet work deadlines (antecedent), Denice will decrease the frequency of the following undesired verbal and nonverbal responses: shouting at coworkers, clenching her fists and waving her arms, and making negative remarks about coworkers. Positive consequences for Denice could include pleasant conversations with coworkers, learning new work strategies to improve her work performance, and positive comments from her boss about her improved behavior and work performance.

In regard to Denice's second goal, when coworkers make suggestions about better ways to meet work deadlines (antecedent), Denice will increase the frequency of the following desired responses: responding to the coworkers' suggestions in a calm and pleasant tone of voice, telling coworkers in a calm and pleasant way that she does not want to discuss her work habits with them, and discussing with coworkers their suggestions and how they might help her. Positive consequences for Denice could include pleasant conversations with coworkers, learning new work strategies that could improve her work performance, and positive comments from her boss about her improved behavior and work performance.

When a goal is established to decrease problematic behaviors, such as shouting at coworkers, the practitioner also includes a goal to increase appropriate behaviors to be performed in that situation. Decreasing undesired behaviors does not necessarily result in an increase in desired behaviors. For example, Denice's first goal was to decrease inappropriate verbal and nonverbal responses when coworkers made suggestions regarding work deadlines. Denice's second goal was to increase appropriate responses to coworkers' suggestions.

Sometimes clients or significant others find it easier to specify target behaviors they want decreased than to describe appropriate behaviors to be performed in problematic situations. For example, a mother complained that her 3-year-old son started climbing on chairs whenever she talked on the phone. The mother stated the goal as "Johnny stops climbing on chairs when I am talking on the phone." The practitioner asked the mother also to specify acceptable behaviors for Johnny during that time—for example, play quietly with his toys, look at a book, or watch television.

Mary told Ed to stop interrupting her when she was talking to the neighbors. The practitioner helped Mary state what she wanted Ed to do instead during that time. For example, Mary told Ed that when she was talking to the neighbors she would appreciate it if he would either stay in the house or come over to her and put his arm around her silently.

After a behavior change goal is established, initial and intermediate objectives can be developed as successive approximations to the goal. The attainment of intermediate objectives of increasing difficulty or complexity allows the client to progress systematically through the behavior change program. The practitioner arranges for positive reinforcement for the client's performance as the client reaches each objective or approximation to the goal. In Denice's case, the therapist praised her as she achieved each objective and taught her how to provide self-reinforcement (e.g., "I handled that conversation well") for desired behaviors.

An initial objective for Denice was to respond in a soft voice to suggestions from the therapist in role plays. An intermediate objective for Denice was to respond appropriately in role plays of situations involving coworkers, such as lowering her voice when discussing work deadlines with coworkers.

Ethical Issues in Goal Setting

Goal setting involves consideration of the personal, social, legal, and cultural factors necessary to make goals attainable for the client. The most important factor, however, is that the goals and objectives are established with the collaboration and consent of the client. If the practitioner disagrees with the client's goals, he or she discusses the conflicting issues with the client. If the client has a goal that violates the practitioner's professional ethics (for instance, because it involves the exploitation of other individuals), the practitioner should try to persuade the client to modify that goal. For example, a client may wish to continue a sexual relationship with a partner without disclosing that he has tested positive for HIV. In such a case, the practitioner should discuss with the client the ethical issues and negative consequences involved in withholding information from the partner about the client's HIV status.

If the client insists on pursuing a goal that violates the practitioner's personal moral code, the practitioner could terminate the relationship and offer to assist the client in obtaining professional help elsewhere. For example, a client may seek therapy for depression related to a recent abortion. A practitioner who is uncomfortable with or opposed on moral grounds to working with clients who have had abortions should refer this client to another practitioner.

Resources and Obstacles to Goals

After measurable goals are established, the practitioner and client assess the resources available that support goal attainment as well as the obstacles to goal attainment that the client is likely to face. It is important to identify the resources that would be helpful to the client in achieving the goals so that the practitioner and client can consider them during the intervention phase. Such resources include various factors in the client's life that can provide support and positive reinforcement to the client during implementation of the behavior change program. They include the client's commitment to achieving the goals, client behaviors that demonstrate goal pursuit, personal and environmental reinforcers, and available social, legal, medical, and financial services. For example, in Case Example 8 (p. 272), resources that Bruce can use to his benefit include his stated cooperation and desire to improve his situation, his good work record, and the fact that Bruce is self-supporting and has marketable skills.

The practitioner and client also identify obstacles to goal attainment, which could interfere with successful completion of the behavior change program. Obstacles include client behaviors that detract from goal pursuit and individuals and organizations that adversely control the delivery of reinforcers and punishers to the client. In some cases, obstacles may need to be addressed directly before the client undertakes a behavior change program, especially when the obstacle is a client behavior that detracts from pursuit of the goal. In Case Example 8, obstacles to Bruce's goal of getting a raise from his boss include high anxiety in interpersonal situations and negative self-statements that were reinforced by his boss.

Intervention Planning

Behavioral assessment involves a systematic procedure for specifying and collecting data on target responses and their controlling conditions. Clients play an active role in behavioral assessment and goal setting that is compatible with their personal, social, and cultural values. A successful behavior change program relies on the adequacy of the behavioral assessment, the specificity of the behavior change goals and objectives, and the client's and practitioner's commitment to implementing the plan.

During **intervention planning** (or **treatment planning**), the practitioner develops an **intervention plan** to address the client's problems based on the behavioral assessment and behavior change goals. The intervention plan specifies the behavior change techniques and procedures to be applied in the behavior change program (e.g., Antony & Barlow, 2001). After the intervention plan is implemented, the practitioner monitors the application of the interventions and determines their effects. Evaluation of the behavior change program involves (a) comparing changes in the client's target behaviors before, during, and after implementation of the behavior change program and (b) determining the client's progress toward goal achievement and its effects on the client and significant others.

The Behavioral Approach to Problem Solving

The behavioral approach to problem solving consists of six major phases: (a) intake, (b) behavioral assessment, (c) goal setting, (d) intervention planning, (e) implementation of the behavior change program, and (f) evaluation. The topics and procedures involved in each of the phases of the problem-solving framework are outlined below.

Outline of the Problem-Solving Framework

I. Intake
  A. Develop a collaborative and reinforcing relationship with client.
  B. Obtain identifying information from client.
  C. Inform client about agency policies and procedures.
  D. Screen for crises.
  E. Determine appropriateness of agency or practitioner as service provider.
     1. If not appropriate, make referral.
     2. If appropriate, obtain client's commitment and consent to service; state the practitioner's commitment to providing service.

II. Behavioral assessment
  A. List all client problems identified through assessment sources, such as the following:
     1. Interviews
     2. Observations
     3. Checklists and questionnaires
     4. Referral sources
     5. Reports of significant others
     6. Physiological measures (e.g., heart rate and blood pressure)
  B. Record similarities or differences in descriptions of client problems identified by various sources and attempt to reconcile discrepancies.
  C. Rank order the problems according to their priorities for service. Select one problem for immediate attention.

D. Obtain concrete examples of the problem. Specify RAC-S data, including target responses, controlling antecedents, negative and positive consequences, and response strength (rate, intensity, duration, magnitude, latency). Examples can be obtained from the following sources:
1. Client self-reports
2. Behavioral reenactment
3. Observation of client in the natural environment
4. Reports from referral source
5. Reports of significant others
6. Physiological measures (e.g., heart rate and blood pressure)
E. Specify measures of RAC-S to be recorded and design a measurement plan. Indicate who will observe and record the data.
F. Obtain measures of RAC-S.
G. Analyze the RAC-S data to identify controlling stimuli and their effects on the client's behaviors and develop a hypothesis about the conditions exerting control over the target behavior.

III. Formulate behavior change goals with the client, including initial and intermediate objectives.
A. Specify desired responses, antecedents, and reinforcers.
B. Identify potential negative consequences of the desired response.
C. Identify probable reinforcers for the desired response.
D. Identify client and environmental resources and obstacles to goal attainment, including the following:
1. Client's statement of commitment to achieving behavior change goals
2. Client behaviors that support goal pursuit
3. Client behaviors that detract from goal pursuit
4. Available reinforcers
5. Individuals and organizations that control the delivery of reinforcers and punishers to clients
6. Other relevant services rendered to the client (e.g., social, legal, medical, and financial)

IV. Intervention planning
A. Develop the intervention plan, specifying the following:
1. Behavior change techniques to be used and the procedures for implementing them
2. Individuals to be involved
3. Plan for generalization and maintenance of behavior change in the client's natural environment
4. Target date for achievement of each goal and objective
B. Treatment contract: Obtain the client's verbal (and written, if indicated) commitment to the behavior change goals and the intervention plan.

V. Implementation of behavior change program
A. Apply the techniques and procedures prescribed in the intervention plan.
B. Collect RAC-S data.
C. Record progress notes in client chart.

VI. Evaluation
   A. Compare strength of target responses before, during, and after implementation of behavior change program.
   B. Evaluate goal attainment using the criteria stated in the behavior change goals and objectives.
   C. After a behavior change goal has been achieved, select the problem of next highest priority. Repeat the sequence from IID above. When all goals are achieved, make arrangements for follow-up contact.
   D. If a behavior change goal has not been achieved, reassess the target behavior to determine the accuracy of the previous assessment. If the assessment is accurate, determine whether the intervention procedures were applied correctly. If they were applied correctly, revise the intervention plan based on reassessment of the target behavior and reformulation of the behavior change goal. Select and implement alternative intervention procedures and evaluate their effects.

The flowchart in Figure 14.1 illustrates the problem-solving framework outlined above.

Treatment Contracts

When an individual seeks assistance from a social service agency or practitioner, a preliminary assessment is made of the situation to determine the practitioner's or agency's suitability for providing assistance. If the practitioner decides that appropriate service can be provided and the individual decides to accept service, this voluntary action by both parties forms the basis for an agreement that can be formalized in a treatment contract.

The **treatment contract** is an agreement between the client and the practitioner to collaborate on problem-solving activities that can improve the client's situation. The treatment contract is sometimes a verbal agreement, but in other cases it is a more formal written agreement that is signed by all parties concerned. The practitioner and client agree to work together on problem selection, behavioral assessment, goal setting, intervention planning, and evaluation. The client agrees to perform and report on all behavioral assignments given by the practitioner. The practitioner agrees to provide expertise and guidance that will help the client attain his or her goals.

Classification of Behavior Change Techniques

Behavior change techniques can be classified according to their effects in modifying a behavior in relation to four intervention outcomes or directions of change. Behavior change techniques can be applied to (a) develop a new behavior, (b) increase the strength of a behavior, (c) maintain a behavior at a particular strength or pattern of occurrence, or (d) decrease the strength of a behavior (see Table 14.1). Behavior change techniques are applied as interventions to influence the frequency, intensity,

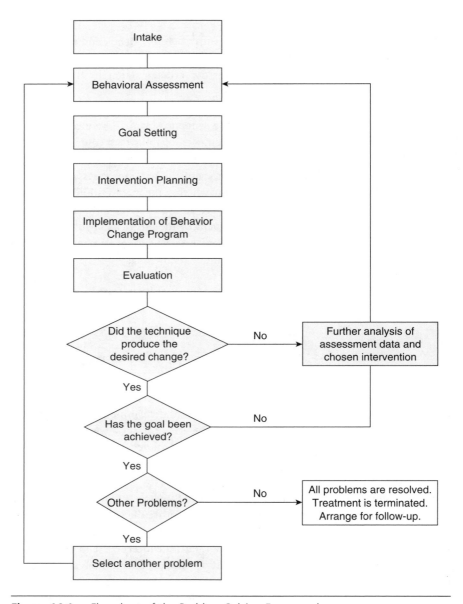

Figure 14.1   Flowchart of the Problem-Solving Framework

and duration of operant behaviors and the magnitude and latency of respondent behaviors. In selecting techniques, the practitioner considers the directional changes specified in the behavior change goals. For example, if the behavior change goal states that a behavior is to be decreased in strength, the practitioner can select relevant techniques from among those listed in Table 14.1 under the column heading "Decrease Response Strength."

In Table 14.1, behavior change techniques are classified according to their applicability in modifying response strength in a given direction. Some of these techniques

Table 14.1   Classification of Behavior Change Techniques

Develop a New Behavior	Increase Response Strength	Maintain Response Strength	Decrease Response Strength
Shaping with successive approximations (Chapter 5)	Positive reinforcement (Chapter 2)	Positive reinforcement (Chapter 2)	Satiation (Chapter 2)
Stimulus fading (Chapter 6)	Deprivation (Chapter 2)	Schedules of reinforcement (Chapter 4)	Operant extinction (Chapter 3)
Chaining (Chapter 7)	Differential reinforcement (Chapter 5)	Differential reinforcement (Chapter 5)	DRO, DRI, DRA (Chapter 5)
Backward chaining (Chapter 7)	Discrimination training (Chapter 6)	Discrimination training (Chapter 6)	Discrimination training (Chapter 6)
Model presentation (Chapter 8)	Negative reinforcement (Chapter 10)	Negative reinforcement (Chapter 10)	Punishment (Chapter 9)
Assertiveness training (Chapter 8)			Overcorrection (Chapter 9)
Social skills training (Chapter 8)			Respondent extinction (Chapter 11)
Negative reinforcement (Chapter 10)			Systematic desensitization (Chapter 15)
Respondent conditioning (Chapter 11)			In vivo desensitization (Chapter 15)
Self-instruction training (Chapter 15)			Flooding (Chapter 15)
Stress inoculation training (Chapter 15)			Rational-emotive behavior therapy (Chapter 15)
Problem-solving methods (Chapter 15)			Cognitive therapy (Chapter 15)
Aversion relief (Chapter 15)			Panic control treatment (Chapter 15)
Cognitive therapy (Chapter 15)			Aversion therapy (Chapter 15)
Rational-emotive behavior therapy (Chapter 15)			Covert sensitization (Chapter 15)
			Thought stopping (Chapter 15)
			Habit reversal (Chapter 15)
			Exposure and ritual prevention (Chapter 15)

can be combined to form *treatment packages* (also called *intervention packages*). For example, assertiveness training might include positive reinforcement, model presentation, behavioral rehearsal, and differential reinforcement. Covert sensitization includes negative reinforcement and respondent conditioning techniques.

In selecting a behavior change technique, the practitioner considers certain factors, including relative effectiveness of alternative techniques, comfort to the client, efficiency, environmental and client resources and obstacles, community norms, and ethical considerations. For example, although a punishment technique using aversive stimuli may be more immediately effective and efficient, a positive reinforcement and shaping procedure may have greater long-term effectiveness and fewer detrimental side effects. In addition, the use of positive reinforcement techniques probably will result in fewer objections from the community than will the use of techniques involving aversive stimuli.

Ethical Considerations

Behavior change techniques should be used in accordance with the ethical codes and values of the human service professions (e.g., American Psychological Association, 1992; Bernstein, Borkovec, & Hazlett-Stevens, 2000; Florida Association for Behavior Analysis, 1988; National Association of Social Workers, 1996). Like other therapeutic modalities, behavior change programs should be implemented only with the informed consent of the client. *Informed consent* means that the client understands the proposed interventions and voluntarily agrees to participate. If the client does not have the capacity to understand the proposed intervention, the practitioner should obtain informed consent from the client's legal guardian. In order to meet informed consent requirements, the practitioner must tell the client about the costs, benefits, and alternatives to all procedures, including the use of a single-subject design rather than a traditional case study, or B only, design (e.g., Wakefield & Kirk, 1997).

If the client volunteers for treatment but subsequently refuses to cooperate with the practitioner, the practitioner should reassess the treatment contract or basis for service. The practitioner can review the initial and current basis for intervention with the client and point out the negative consequences, for the client or significant others, of the client's failure to modify the target behaviors. The practitioner can also discuss the positive consequences for the client of achieving the behavior change goals.

In providing services to children and to members of institutionalized populations, such as individuals with developmental disabilities, juvenile offenders, incarcerated adults, nursing home residents, and individuals diagnosed with severe mental disorders, practitioners should exercise special care to ensure that these individuals are not subjected to cruel or harsh interventions. Some institutions appoint committees or advocates for each resident to safeguard their rights and protect them from harmful interventions.

Individuals who reside in correctional settings or in other situations in which treatment is imposed by the court enter treatment as involuntary clients. Practitioners can discuss the benefits of a cooperative therapeutic relationship with such individuals and encourage them to view the practitioner as a professional who can help them improve their situation. For example, a divorced father who was a substance abuser was told by the court that he was required to enter a treatment program and demonstrate progress on treatment goals before he would be allowed to have unsupervised visitation with his son. Although the father entered treatment involuntarily, he decided that cooperating with the treatment program could help him achieve his goal of unsupervised visitation with his son.

Developing the Intervention Plan

After the practitioner and client work together to formulate the behavior change goals, the practitioner develops an intervention plan. This plan provides a strategy for systematically carrying out the behavior change program to attain the client's goals. One or more behavior change techniques may be included in the intervention plan as part of a treatment package. Detailed manuals are also available that can facilitate the replication of empirically supported intervention procedures for specific diagnoses of behavioral problems such as panic disorder (Barlow & Cerny, 1988; Barlow & Craske, 1994), obsessive-compulsive disorder (Steketee, 1993), and depression (Muñoz & Miranda, 1986; Organista, Muñoz, & Gonzalez, 1994).

Behavior change techniques are employed within the context of an intervention plan. Without an explicit plan, application of a behavior change technique could be inappropriate or irrelevant to the client's well-being. For example, Tim, an adult with mental retardation, often sat in a chair in a corner of the group home where he lived, with his arms folded, unshaven and unkempt. Positive reinforcement could be applied to increase the frequency of a response such as arm raising. Although positive reinforcement would increase Tim's arm raising, strengthening this behavior might not be beneficial for Tim unless it is related to developing a desired behavior, such as combing his hair.

Tim's behavior change goals included development of self-care skills such as brushing his teeth, shaving, washing, and combing his hair. Toothbrushing was selected as the first self-care skill because of the potential for negative consequences if Tim did not develop this skill, such as tooth decay and gum disease, both of which were found in Tim's recent dental examination. An intervention plan for developing Tim's self-care skills might include the following behavior change techniques: modeling, shaping with instructions, and positive reinforcement. Modeling can be used to demonstrate the appropriate self-care behaviors, shaping with instructions can be used to develop successive approximations to the desired behaviors, and positive reinforcement can be used to increase and maintain Tim's performance of the behaviors.

Implementing the Behavior Change Program for Toothbrushing

Prior to implementing the behavior change program for toothbrushing, the practitioner obtained baseline measures of Tim's toothbrushing. Tim was given a toothbrush and toothpaste every morning and every night for a week. The staff observed him daily and recorded the frequency of his toothbrushing. The following data were recorded: (a) the number of times Tim brushed his teeth with and without toothpaste each day, (b) the number of times Tim attempted to brush his teeth with and without toothpaste, and (c) the amount of time Tim spent brushing on each attempt. For example, Tim might pick up the toothbrush and put it in his mouth but not actually brush his teeth with it. Tim's behavior change goal was to brush his teeth with toothpaste on the brush for 3 minutes (see Figure 14.2) two times per day, 7 days each week, without prompts, during a 3-month period.

The behavior change program for toothbrushing involved the techniques of modeling, shaping with instructions, and positive reinforcement. The staff at Tim's group home carried out the procedures for applying these techniques in accordance with the intervention plan. After baseline data were collected, a staff member brought Tim a toothbrush and toothpaste and, using another toothbrush, demonstrated the correct way to put toothpaste on the toothbrush and brush his teeth. After modeling toothbrushing for Tim, the staff member gave Tim the following instructions: "Put toothpaste on the toothbrush, put the toothbrush in your mouth, and brush your teeth the way I just did." Tim took the toothbrush and put it in his mouth. The staff member immediately reinforced Tim's response by giving him a baseball card

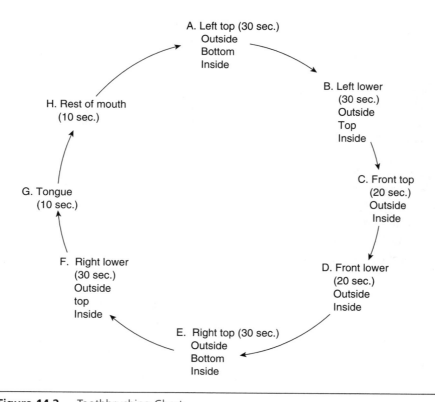

Brush for 3 minutes total

A. Left top (30 sec.)
Outside
Bottom
Inside

B. Left lower
(30 sec.)
Outside
Top
Inside

C. Front top
(20 sec.)
Outside
Inside

D. Front lower
(20 sec.)
Outside
Inside

E. Right top (30 sec.)
Outside
Bottom
Inside

F. Right lower
(30 sec.)
Outside
top
Inside

G. Tongue
(10 sec.)

H. Rest of mouth
(10 sec.)

Figure 14.2   Toothbrushing Chart

and verbal praise. The practitioner had determined prior to implementing the intervention plan that Tim was fond of baseball cards. Tim had no way of getting the cards on his own, so they were likely to serve as reinforcers in his program.

The staff continued to model each step involved in toothbrushing, and they instructed and prompted Tim to imitate the behaviors that they demonstrated. Correct imitations were immediately followed by baseball cards and praise. The staff gradually raised the requirements for reinforcement to include more tooth-brushing behaviors and brushing for a longer duration, using a timer to signal the end of toothbrushing time. In this manner, Tim learned to brush his teeth with toothpaste for 3 minutes when given a toothbrush and toothpaste.

After Tim performed the desired toothbrushing behaviors consistently, the base-ball cards were faded out and praise alone was used as the positive reinforcer. A similar procedure was used to shape other desired behaviors, such as Tim's getting the toothbrush and toothpaste from the cabinet and brushing his teeth independently, without prompting by staff. Tim received a baseball card at the end of the week if he had brushed his teeth independently for the 7 previous days.

Evaluating the Effectiveness of the Behavior Change Program

A hallmark of the behavioral approach is the emphasis on evaluation of the effectiveness of the interventions. Evaluation of a behavior change program is usually based on case analysis using single-subject designs, although more elaborate group evaluation designs and statistical data analysis have also been used (e.g., Bloom, Fischer, & Orme, 2003).

In Tim's case, the criterion for attainment of the toothbrushing goal was for Tim to brush his teeth with toothpaste independently twice a day for 7 days each week. When observed during the initial weeks of intervention, Tim partially brushed his teeth once or twice a week without staff prompts. After 4 weeks, Tim independently brushed his teeth an average of three times a week. By the end of 8 weeks, the tooth-brushing goal was achieved, so that Tim brushed his teeth with toothpaste independently twice a day for 7 days each week.

If Tim's target behavior (toothbrushing) had not changed from its baseline rate after the interventions were employed for a reasonable amount of time (e.g., 2 weeks), the intervention plan would have been reassessed and altered. Many organizations set case review dates for supervisory or team review of clients' progress toward goal achievement. It is advisable for practitioners or case managers to monitor and record their clients' goal progress regularly as well as prepare for formal case reviews.

Behaviorally Oriented Record Keeping

To determine the effectiveness of the behavior change program, the practitioner uses a systematic procedure in planning and recording the client's treatment. The practitioner establishes a record-keeping plan consistent with the problem-solving framework described above (see p. 217) that (a) delineates the client's problems,

(b) states the behavior change goals, (c) describes the interventions that have been applied, and (d) monitors the client's progress toward goal attainment. Each problem is listed separately in such a plan, with specified target responses, controlling antecedents and consequences, and a corresponding behavior change goal(s). The record-keeping plan also identifies client and environmental resources and obstacles for each goal. The intervention plan in the client's record specifies the behavior change techniques and procedures to be applied. The practitioner records notes on the client's progress toward each goal by date and documents the effects of the various interventions. When the client's goals are reached, the practitioner records follow-up contacts, including information on the client's current situation.

CASE EXAMPLE 8

Developing Social Skills

Bruce is a 30-year-old single man who complained about "stress and anxiety." He said that he was exploited at work and also was unable to establish and maintain satisfying relationships with women. He stated that women find his company unpleasant, and he never knows what to say in their presence. Of the last four women Bruce has taken out, all have refused a second date. He has one male friend with whom he plays tennis each week.

Bruce is a bookkeeper for an insurance company, where he has worked for the past 9 years. Although he was promised a promotion and raise 2 years ago, he still earns the same salary in the same position as when he started working for the company. Bruce has never discussed his feelings about being treated unfairly with his boss, although other employees in similar circumstances have benefited from doing so.

The practitioner asked Bruce to describe what happened the last time he went out with a woman. Bruce said that he and the woman were having coffee in a restaurant after seeing a movie, and he could not think of anything interesting to say to her. Bruce concluded that he just "bored her to death" talking about his work. When the therapist asked Bruce to describe the woman's part of the conversation, Bruce said that he could not remember much about what she said because he was so concerned about making a good impression. On one occasion, Bruce said, a woman he took out fell asleep while he was trying to explain a complicated bookkeeping procedure. The therapist observed that Bruce kept his head down during the interview and often held his hand in front of his mouth when speaking, so that his speech was difficult to understand. He sometimes drifted from one topic to another without waiting for the therapist to respond to what he had said, and he frequently spoke in a monotone.

The practitioner asked Bruce to describe his most recent conversation with his boss. Bruce related that he was seated in his boss's office, across the desk from his boss, and his boss asked him what he wanted. Bruce mumbled, looked down at the floor, and began to talk about his financial problems. When the boss responded by asking Bruce why he could not manage his finances properly, Bruce stammered and tried to defend his way of managing money. He reported to the practitioner that he felt very anxious. Finally, Bruce mumbled, "I'm sorry," and walked out of the boss's office without raising the issues of promotion and salary increase.

On further questioning, Bruce indicated that he often found himself being taken advantage of in situations in which he should have stated his opinions or defended his rights. Bruce said that he hoped to improve this situation through therapy and would cooperate with the therapist's recommendations. The therapist gave Bruce an assignment to record RAC-S data about the situations in which he felt exploited and to rate his anxiety on a subjective units of discomfort scale (SUDS) ranging from 0 to 100 (e.g., Wolpe, 1990).

The following excerpts are taken from a sample record based on the information in Case Example 8. Bruce's problem at work was selected as the top priority for intervention after the therapist and Bruce reviewed all of the problems Bruce identified on the Problem Inventory and the Problem Checklist.

Problem selected for immediate attention: Bruce said that he feels exploited at work. He was promised a raise and promotion 2 years ago, but he is in the same position, earning the same salary, as he has been for 9 years. Bruce has not discussed this issue with his boss.

> *Example of problem with RAC-S data:* Bruce approached his boss to request a promotion and raise. When the boss asked what he wanted, however, Bruce spoke about his financial problems. Bruce left the boss's office without discussing the promotion or raise.

> *Target responses:* Bruce looked at the floor, mumbled, and left the office without discussing the promotion or raise. His palms began to sweat, his heart rate increased, and he had trouble breathing. He reported anxiety level of 80 SUDS.

Controlling conditions:

> *Antecedents:* Bruce is in his boss's office; says to himself, "The boss will get angry and think I'm out of line if I ask for a raise"; boss asks him what he wants; Bruce feels anxious (self-rating of 80 on a 100-point scale), and his palms sweat and heart rate increases.

> *Consequences: Negative* (probable punishers)—Bruce does not get a raise or promotion; remains in same position at same salary; is dissatisfied with his behavior in this situation; says to himself, "I'm a spineless coward." *Positive* (probable positive or negative reinforcers or both)—Bruce avoids possible conflict with boss and his anxiety decreases (negative reinforcement).

> *Response strength:* Two weeks of baseline data collected by Bruce indicated that the target behaviors were performed two to four times each week, during every interaction Bruce had with his boss.

Analysis of RAC-S data (hypothesis): Bruce's target responses are negatively reinforced by his avoiding possible conflict with his boss and lowering his anxiety by leaving (escaping) the unpleasant situation (being in the boss's office and thinking about asking for a raise).

Behavior change goal: Bruce asks his boss for a raise and promotion with minimal anxiety (self-rating of 20 SUDS or less). Desired reinforcers include the boss gives him a raise and Bruce tells himself, "I finally told him exactly what I wanted. I did a great job!"

> *Initial objectives:* Bruce decreases mumbling and speaking with his hand over his mouth; increases eye contact; increases the volume of his voice and varies the pitch in conversation; reduces anxiety to a rating lower than 80 SUDS.
>
> *Intermediate objectives:* Bruce states reasons justifying a raise and promotion while maintaining eye contact and speaking clearly.
>
> *Possible negative consequences:* Boss could say no or express anger.
>
> *Possible reinforcers:* Boss acknowledges legitimacy of Bruce's request; boss agrees to the request. Bruce tells himself that he has done well in making the request, regardless of the outcome.

Resources and obstacles: Resources—Bruce's stated cooperation and desire to improve his situation; his work record is good; he earns a steady income and is self-supporting; he has marketable job skills; he has a supportive friend. *Obstacles*—Bruce's negative self-statements were previously reinforced by unpleasant encounters with his boss; he lacks the social skills to relate effectively to his boss; he reports high anxiety when meeting with his boss.

Intervention plan: Verbal instructions, modeling, positive reinforcement, behavioral rehearsal, behavioral assignments, and relaxation training will be used in the behavior change program to (a) decrease Bruce's mumbling and speaking with his hand over his mouth, (b) increase the amount of time Bruce maintains eye contact while speaking in a clear tone of voice, (c) instruct Bruce on ways to discuss a raise and promotion with his boss, and (d) decrease Bruce's anxiety in social situations. Bruce will practice desired behaviors in role plays with the practitioner until he can perform the desired behaviors with no anxiety. Bruce will identify someone in his natural environment with whom he can practice desired behaviors and get feedback on his performances. Target dates for achievement of each objective are specified. Bruce verbally commits to the behavior change goals and intervention plan.

Target date: 3 months for achievement of the behavior change goal

Case review: 8 weeks

Practitioner's signature _____ Date _____

Client's signature _____ Date _____

Implementing the intervention plan: The practitioner gave Bruce instructions on how to speak clearly and maintain eye contact. The practitioner modeled clear speech and eye contact, and provided social reinforcement for Bruce's approximations to desired speech. Behavioral rehearsal was used with Bruce in the practitioner's office. The practitioner also assigned Bruce various speaking exercises using a tape recorder at home, and Bruce brought the tapes of his practice to the practitioner for review. The practitioner specified the RAC-S data that Bruce was to collect.

The following is a sample progress note from Bruce's fifth session:

Date: 2/11, 5th session—Bruce's mumbling has decreased in role plays. He no longer places his hand in front of his mouth while speaking. Bruce reported having a pleasant conversation with his boss about a complicated accounting technique that he was able to explain. He reported initial anxiety of about 75 SUDS that decreased to about 40 during the conversation with his boss. Bruce continues to speak in a monotone, although the volume of his voice has increased when he speaks into a tape recorder. He still has difficulty maintaining eye contact for more than several seconds.

   Plan for next contact: Bruce was given an assignment to practice the speaking exercises on his tape recorder and to practice relaxation exercises. He will role-play a conversation with his boss at the next session.

The following is a sample progress note from Bruce's tenth session:

Date: 3/28, 10th session—Bruce has achieved his goal of approaching his boss and asking for a raise and promotion with a self-rating of anxiety of 20 or less. Bruce received a raise and promotion and reported anxiety in the range of 5 to 15 when interacting with his boss. Bruce said that he would now like to work on improving his relationships with women.

   The practitioner can give the client a treatment evaluation form at the final session to obtain the client's evaluation of the behavior change program. Such a form includes brief statements of the client's problems and goals filled in by the practitioner. Figure 14.3 shows Bruce's treatment evaluation form. On the form, the client rates the extent to which each problem has been solved and the extent to which each goal has been achieved. If the client lacks the skills required to fill out the form, the practitioner can ask one of the client's significant others (e.g., a parent or other relative, teacher, or guardian) to do so.

   The practitioner can send the client (or the client's significant other, with the client's consent) treatment evaluation forms at periodic intervals (e.g., 3 months, 6 months, and 1 year) following termination. The practitioner can also schedule periodic interviews with the client to evaluate the extent to which treatment gains have been maintained and provide additional treatment, if indicated. The practitioner should make arrangements for follow-up contacts prior to termination of treatment.

Client Satisfaction

The client can also rate his or her level of satisfaction with the functioning achieved in the problematic situations and with the results of treatment. The practitioner might also obtain satisfaction ratings from significant others and referral sources, if indicated, with the client's written consent. The client's satisfaction with services is expected to be consistent with the client's attainment of the behavior change goals. With client consent, or when legally permissible, the practitioner can

The following are the problems you worked on and the goals you wanted to achieve in treatment. Please make any corrections you think are necessary to make them accurate.

Problems and goals worked on:

Problems	Goals
1. I feel exploited at work. I am in the same position at the same salary as when I was first hired.	1. Decrease mumbling and talking with my hand in front of my mouth.
2. When I go in to speak with the boss about a raise and promotion, I mumble and leave without asking.	2. Increase the volume of voice when speaking with the boss.
	3. Decrease anxiety when speaking with the boss.
	4. Clearly state my request to the boss.

1. To what extent were the above-listed problems solved?

	Completely Solved	Much Better	Better	Same	Worse	Much Worse
Problem 1	✓					
Problem 2		✓				

Comments:

2. To what extent were the above-listed goals achieved?

	Completely Achieved	Mostly Achieved	Moderate Improvement	Small Improvement	Not at All Achieved/ Worse
Goal 1	✓				
Goal 2	✓				
Goal 3		✓			
Goal 4		✓			

Comments:

Figure 14.3   Treatment Evaluation Form for Bruce

ask the client and significant others to give their appraisals of treatment at various points in the behavior change program as well as at termination and follow-up contacts.

In evaluating the success of a behavior change program, the practitioner considers the client's personal evaluation of the program (see Figure 14.4). The practitioner

1. How satisfied are you with your behaviors in the problematic situation?

	Very Satisfied	Satisfied	Neutral	Dissatisfied	Very Dissatisfied
Problem 1					
Problem 2					

Comments:

2. Overall, how satisfied are you with the results of treatment?

	Very Satisfied	Satisfied	Neutral	Dissatisfied	Very Dissatisfied
Problem 1					
Problem 2					

Comments:

3. Compared with the time of your first visit, how would you rate your problem today?

	Completely Solved	Much Better	Better	Same	Worse	Much Worse
Problem 1						
Problem 2						

Comments:

Figure 14.4   Client Satisfaction Form

discusses objective measures of progress toward goal achievement with the client and relates these measures to the client's ratings of personal satisfaction with the behavior change program. If the client's goals are achieved but the client feels dissatisfied, this could indicate a failure to have established goals the client considered to be important. Such a finding might also indicate that other problem areas need to be addressed in the client's behavior change program.

A client who indicates minimal progress toward achieving behavior change goals might still report satisfaction with the behavior change program. The client could derive sufficient social reinforcement from the relationship with the practitioner to compensate for lack of goal progress. The practitioner can provide objective data on goal progress to help such a client distinguish this objective evaluation from the client's satisfaction derived from the relationship with the practitioner.

Social Validity

Social validity refers to evaluation of the social significance of behavior change programs by the program's consumers. Consumers may include the client, referral sources, significant others, and people in the community with whom the client comes in contact. Three areas considered in the assessment of social validity are training objectives, training procedures, and treatment outcomes (Kazdin, 1977; Sundel, 1994; Wolf, 1978). The problem-solving framework presented earlier in this chapter addresses the questions raised in each of these areas.

In regard to training objectives or behavior change goals, we ask the question: Are the behaviors selected for change not only important for the individual but also valued by society? In the problem-solving framework presented above, the client, practitioner, and significant others (if indicated) are involved in the formulation of behavior change goals and the criteria for evaluating their achievement. For example, Tim's toothbrushing was considered to be a socially valid goal because it could improve his dental health and prevent painful dental procedures, such as having teeth pulled.

The selection of training procedures or behavioral interventions raises a second important question: If more than one technique or procedure has been demonstrated to be effective, which one would consumers and society choose? As indicated in this chapter, the selection of behavior change techniques involves consideration of the effectiveness, cost, and acceptability to the client and significant others. For example, modeling and behavioral rehearsal were selected for Bruce's intervention plan because they were effective, convenient, and acceptable to Bruce.

In regard to treatment outcomes, we ask the question: Do clients and society judge the results of treatment to be effective and socially important? As indicated in this chapter, the practitioner discusses the outcomes of the behavior change program with the client and, where indicated, with other relevant individuals, including significant others and referral sources, to determine their importance. Personnel in residential facilities are often concerned about the high prevalence of dental problems among individuals with mental retardation who rarely or never brush their teeth without prompting, reminders, and supervision. Tim's improved dental health resulted in fewer and less painful dental procedures.

Summary

1. Behavior change goals are formulated with the active participation of the client. Initial and intermediate objectives are established as approximations to the desired goals.

2. Issues related to goal setting include consideration of legal, cultural, social, moral, and ethical factors.

3. Intake, behavioral assessment, goal setting, intervention planning, implementation, and evaluation are elements of a comprehensive problem-solving framework.

4. A treatment contract specifies the tasks to be performed by the client and the practitioner in addressing the client's difficulties.

5. Behavior change techniques can be classified according to their effects in modifying a behavior in relation to four outcomes or directions of change: (a) to develop a new response, (b) to increase the strength of a response, (c) to maintain the strength of a response, or (d) to decrease the strength of a response.

6. A behavior change program should be carried out with the informed consent of the client or the client's legal guardian.

7. The intervention plan includes specification of behavior change techniques and the procedures to be followed that can lead to attainment of the client's behavior change goals.

8. Evaluation of the effectiveness of a behavior change program involves comparing the client's target responses before, during, and after intervention. The practitioner collects and analyzes data to determine the direction and extent of desired behavioral change.

9. A client's treatment record includes information on the following components: problems, controlling conditions, goals, resources supporting goal achievement, obstacles to goal achievement, intervention plan and procedures for implementation, evaluation of progress, and follow-up.

10. Client satisfaction is measured through client ratings of the effectiveness of the behavior change program. The practitioner and client discuss objective measures of goal achievement and relate them to the client's satisfaction with behavior change.

11. *Social validity* refers to evaluation of the social significance of behavior change programs by consumers. Consumers may include the client, referral sources, significant others, and people in the community with whom the client comes in contact.

Suggested Activities

1. Describe the ethical issues involved in goal setting with clients from different cultural backgrounds. Give an example from your experience that illustrates these issues.

2. Discuss social validity as it relates to behavior change goals, selection of behavioral interventions, and treatment outcomes. Give an example that illustrates a social validity issue.

References and Resources

American Psychological Association. (1992). Ethical principles of psychologists and code of conduct. *American Psychologist, 47,* 1597–1611.

Antony, M. M., & Barlow, D. H. (Eds.). (2001). *Handbook of assessment and treatment planning for psychological disorders.* New York: Guilford.

Barlow, D. H., & Cerny, J. A. (1988). *Psychological treatment of panic.* New York: Guilford.

Barlow, D. H., & Craske, M. G. (1994). *Mastery of your anxiety and panic: II.* Albany, NY: Graywind.

Bernstein, D. A., Borkovec, T. D., & Hazlett-Stevens, H. (2000). *New directions in progressive relaxation training: A guidebook for helping professionals.* Westport, CT: Praeger.

Bloom, M., Fischer, J., & Orme, J. G. (2003). *Evaluating practice: Guidelines for the accountable professional* (4th ed.). Boston: Allyn & Bacon.

Bradshaw, W., & Roseborough, D. (2004). Evaluating the effectiveness of cognitive-behavioral treatment of residual symptoms and impairment in schizophrenia. *Research on Social Work Practice, 14,* 112–120.

Eifert, G. H., Schulte, D., Zvolensky, M. J., Lejuez, C. W., & Lau, A. W. (1997). Manualized behavior therapy: Merits and challenges. *Behavior Therapy, 28,* 499–509.

Florida Association for Behavior Analysis. (1988). *The behavior analyst's code of ethics.* Tallahassee, FL: Author.

Giles, T. R. (1990). Bias against behavior therapy in outcome reviews: Who speaks for the patient? *the Behavior Therapist, 13,* 86–90.

Kazdin, A. E. (1977). Assessing the clinical or applied importance of behavior change through social validation. *Behavior Modification, 1,* 427–451.

Kazdin, A. E. (1994). *Behavior modification in applied settings* (5th ed.). Pacific Grove, CA: Brooks/Cole.

Kennedy, C. H. (2002). The maintenance of behavior change as an indicator of social validity. *Behavior Modification, 26,* 596–604.

Mullen, E. J., & Magnabosco, J. L. (Eds.). (1997). *Outcomes measurement in the human services: Cross-cutting issues and methods.* Annapolis Junction, MD: National Association of Social Workers Press.

Muñoz, R. F., & Miranda, J. (1986). *Group therapy for cognitive-behavioral treatment of depression.* San Francisco: San Francisco General Hospital, Depression Clinic.

National Association of Social Workers. (1996). *Code of ethics.* Silver Spring, MD: Author.

Organista, K. C., Muñoz, R. F., & Gonzalez, G. (1994). Cognitive-behavioral therapy for depression in low-income and minority medical outpatients: Description of a program and exploratory analysis. *Cognitive Therapy and Research, 18,* 241–259.

Paul, G. L., & Lentz, R. J. (1977). *Psychosocial treatment of chronic mental patients: Milieu versus social learning programs.* Cambridge, MA: Harvard University Press.

Steketee, G. (1993). *Treatment of obsessive compulsive disorder.* New York: Guilford.

Sundel, M., & Lawrence, H. (1977). A systematic approach to treatment planning in time-limited behavioral groups. *Journal of Behavior Therapy and Experimental Psychiatry, 8,* 395–399.

Sundel, S. S. (1994). Videotaped training of job-related social skills using peer modeling: An evaluation of social validity. *Research on Social Work Practice, 4,* 40–52.

Sundel, S. S., & Sundel, M. (1980). *Be assertive: A practical guide for human service workers.* Beverly Hills, CA: Sage.

Thyer, B. A. (2002). Principles of evidence-based practice and treatment development. In A. R. Roberts & G. J. Greene (Eds.), *Social workers' desk reference* (pp. 739–742). New York: Oxford University Press.

Umbreit, J. (1995). Functional assessment and intervention in a regular classroom setting for the disruptive behavior of a student with attention deficit hyperactivity disorder. *Behavioral Disorders, 20,* 267–278.

Wakefield, J. C., & Kirk, S. A. (1997). What the practitioner knows versus what the client is told: Neglected dilemmas of informed consent in an account of single-system experimental designs. *Journal of Social Work Education, 33,* 275–291.

Wolf, M. M. (1978). Social validity: The case for subjective measurement or how applied behavior analysis is finding its heart. *Journal of Applied Behavior Analysis, 11,* 203–214.

Wolpe, J. (1990). *The practice of behavior therapy* (4th ed.). Elmsford, NY: Pergamon.

CHAPTER 15

Intervention Techniques

Stan, an appliance salesman, is 36 years old and lives alone. During the past 6 months, he has become increasingly anxious about driving his car from home to work and back. On the freeway, he starts to perspire heavily, gets dizzy, feels his heart beating faster, and sometimes experiences chest pain. Stan worries about having these attacks in public and has started taking longer alternate routes to work to avoid the panic attacks. Last year, he was involved in an automobile accident on the freeway in which he received minor injuries as a passenger, and he thinks this might have caused his current difficulties. At the time, he had a new supervisor and was concerned about losing his job.

Objectives

After completing this chapter, you should be able to do the following:

- Compare the use of exposure techniques, including systematic desensitization, in vivo desensitization, and flooding in the treatment of a phobia.
- Describe the use of panic control treatment to decrease panic attacks.
- Describe the use of covert sensitization to decrease an undesired behavior.
- Give an example of thought stopping to decrease unwanted cognitions.

This chapter focuses on the application of selected behavioral and cognitive-behavioral intervention techniques. The topics covered include exposure techniques and cognitive-behavioral techniques. Exposure techniques include systematic desensitization, in vivo desensitization, flooding, and exposure and ritual prevention (EX/RP). Cognitive-behavioral techniques include cognitive restructuring, self-instructional training, panic control treatment, problem-solving therapy, covert sensitization, thought stopping, and habit reversal. We evaluate all these techniques in the pages that follow. We also consider current issues and future trends in the field, including evidence-based interventions and practice guidelines.

Exposure Techniques

Various exposure techniques can be used to change behaviors related to fear and anxiety. Some interventions use imaginal exposure, and some use in vivo exposure. The common element in all of them is that the client is exposed to anxiety-evoking stimuli without negative consequences. Successful treatment involves modification of operant escape and avoidance behaviors as well as respondent behaviors (conditioned responses, or CRs) involving anxiety. Techniques include systematic desensitization, in vivo desensitization, and flooding (both imaginal and in vivo). Exposure therapies appear to be the most potent behavioral intervention techniques for treating anxiety-related disorders (Barlow, Raffa, & Cohen, 2002; Trull, Nietzel, & Main, 1988), including specific and social phobias (Antony & Barlow, 2002; Koch, Spates, & Himle, in press; Plaud & Vavrovsky, 1998).

Systematic Desensitization

Systematic desensitization is an exposure technique for decreasing phobic responses using a graduated hierarchy of anxiety-evoking stimuli that the client visualizes. It is based on the premise that an individual who is deeply relaxed in the presence of an imagined feared stimulus cannot be anxious and tense at the same time. Systematic desensitization involves pairing phobic or anxiety-eliciting stimuli with relaxation stimuli until the former no longer elicit anxiety. In this section, we will describe the basic features of systematic desensitization and its applications. The conceptual framework and desensitization procedure, which were developed by Joseph Wolpe, have been presented in detail elsewhere (e.g., Wolpe, 1958, 1990, 1995; Wolpe & Lazarus, 1966).

Systematic desensitization consists of three distinct operations: relaxation training, the construction of anxiety hierarchies, and the pairing of relaxation with anxiety-eliciting stimuli from the hierarchies. The first step in this procedure is to teach the client deep muscle relaxation, which is usually completed within six 15- to 20-minute sessions. The practitioner gives the client instructions in progressive relaxation procedures and assigns relaxation exercises for the client to practice at home (e.g., Bernstein, Borkovec, & Hazlett-Stevens, 2000; Wolpe, 1990). Relaxation instructions for desensitization are based on Jacobson's (1938) method of progressive relaxation.

During relaxation training, the client comfortably reclines in a quiet room and the practitioner teaches the client how to alternately tense and relax all the muscle groups in the body. The client learns to relax each muscle group to an increasingly greater extent until the entire body is deeply relaxed. Sometimes practitioners use imagery to enhance the relaxation effect—for example, the practitioner instructs the client to imagine him- or herself resting in a peaceful setting, such as lying on a lounge chair on a quiet beach or taking a warm bath.

The client is instructed to work on muscle groups in the following order: arms, hands, forehead, eyes, nose, mouth, tongue, jaws, neck, shoulders, back, chest, stomach, buttocks, legs, calves, and feet. The practitioner gives the client relaxation instructions several times for each muscle group. The practitioner also instructs the client to practice the relaxation exercises at home, and may provide the client with relaxation instructions on tape or CD to use until he or she has memorized them and can relax without such an aid.

The following excerpt is typical of the narrative used in relaxation training:

> Settle back as comfortably as you can. Let yourself relax to the best of your ability. . . . Now, as you relax like that, clench your right fist, just clench your fist tighter and tighter, and study the tension as you do so. Keep it clenched and feel the tension in your right fist, hand, forearm . . . and now relax. Let the fingers of your right hand become loose, and observe the contrast in your feelings. . . . Now, let yourself go and try to become more relaxed all over. . . . Once more, clench your right fist really tight . . . hold it, and notice the tension again. . . . Now let go, relax; your fingers straighten out, and you notice the difference once more. . . . Now repeat that with your left fist. (Wolpe & Lazarus, 1966, p. 177)

The second step in systematic desensitization is to construct a hierarchy of responses related to the feared stimulus. This can be done in conjunction with relaxation training. The hierarchy begins with the least anxiety-eliciting item and progresses to the most anxiety-producing event. The individual's subjective level of anxiety is measured on a subjective units of discomfort scale (SUDS) of 0 to 100, with 0 being the least amount of anxiety and 100 being the most anxiety the individual can imagine. The following is an example showing the items on a hierarchy developed with Lara, a client who complained of an airplane phobia after the terrorist attacks on the World Trade Center on September 11, 2001 (Lara's SUDS ratings appear in parentheses):

1. Going online to make plane reservations (35)

2. Driving to the airport the day of the flight (40)

3. Seeing a plane take off and land at the airport (50)

4. Standing in line to go through security check (60)

5. Waiting in the lounge before boarding the plane (70)

6. Walking down the ramp to the plane (75)

7. Sitting on the plane, waiting for takeoff (80)

8. Sitting on the runway, waiting for takeoff (90)

9. Hearing the plane build speed on the runway prior to takeoff (95)

10. Hearing the roar of the engines as the plane lifts off the ground (100)

Prior to treatment, Lara had never actually progressed past the third item on this hierarchy. She usually became so anxious that she canceled her airline reservation and took a train or drove her car to her destination.

In the desensitization procedure, Lara imagines one item or scene at a time from her hierarchy while relaxed, beginning with the least anxiety-producing item. The practitioner instructs her to imagine a particular scene—for example, calling to make airplane reservations—and to signal anxiety by raising her index finger. Lara reports her subjective level of anxiety after imagining each scene. If she indicates anxiety, the practitioner instructs her to relax again and then presents the same scene. If Lara still indicates anxiety, the practitioner presents the next lower item on the hierarchy. If Lara does not indicate anxiety while imagining the weaker scene, the practitioner again presents the next item on the hierarchy. If Lara signals anxiety, the practitioner tells her to relax and presents the same scene again. This procedure is repeated until Lara no longer signals anxiety while imagining the scene. The remaining items on the hierarchy are presented in the same manner until the entire hierarchy is completed. This part of the treatment procedure usually lasts for approximately 20 to 30 minutes of each session.

After 16 sessions, Lara made airline reservations to visit her sister. She reported slight anxiety (20 SUDS) as she boarded the plane but completed the flight with minimal discomfort. She completed her return trip several days later with almost no anxiety (5–10 SUDS) and reported enjoying the flight. At 6-month and 12-month follow-ups, Lara told the practitioner that she was flying on airplanes with little or no fear (0–10 SUDS).

In systematic desensitization, the client is not treated in the actual problematic situation. The effects of relaxation in the presence of imagined anxiety-arousing stimuli, however, have been found to transfer from the treatment setting to the real situation once the client has achieved relaxation capable of suppressing or inhibiting anxiety responses (CRs) (Wolpe, 1990). Discovering the original unconditioned stimulus (US) that elicited the unconditioned anxiety responses (URs) is not considered essential for successful treatment of the phobia because the physiological responses of anxiety continue to be elicited by the feared object (CS). The client's awareness of, or insight into, the conditions under which the phobia was first conditioned, therefore, usually is insufficient to reduce the client's anxiety or alter the client's avoidance of the feared stimulus. For example, Lara knew that she developed the airplane phobia after the terrorist attacks, but this knowledge, even coupled with assurances of greater security measures by airline personnel and the reasoning and encouragement of friends, was not sufficient to enable her to overcome her fear of flying.

In Vivo Desensitization

In vivo desensitization is a graduated exposure technique used to treat phobic responses in actual feared situations by extinction of anxiety CRs and avoidance responses. This technique is similar to systematic desensitization except that the individual progresses through the anxiety hierarchy in real-life situations rather than in imagination. The individual remains in the presence of the feared stimulus for a brief period of time, from a few seconds to a few minutes. In vivo desensitization requires the client to work through the anxiety hierarchy in the phobic environment or in a simulation of the real-life situation that the client fears. In vivo desensitization removes an obstacle to generalization of the desired behaviors because the client learns to perform these behaviors in the feared situation rather than in the practitioner's office. When using in vivo desensitization, the practitioner frequently accompanies the client through the hierarchy, although clients also have been successful in self-administering in vivo desensitization (e.g., Goldfried & Davison, 1994).

Both operant and respondent behaviors related to the phobia are treated with in vivo desensitization as the client remains in the anxiety-evoking situation without experiencing negative consequences. Anxiety CRs are extinguished by repeated presentation of the conditioned stimulus (CS) in the absence of the US. The operant avoidance response also extinguishes because of the removal of the negative reinforcement contingency established by the previously feared stimulus.

For example, Damien suffered from acrophobia—that is, he was afraid of heights. When he reached the second floor of any building more than three stories tall, he began to sweat profusely, his heart rate increased, and he had difficulty breathing. He ran down the stairs as fast as he could and exited the building.

The practitioner helped Damien construct a hierarchy of anxiety-evoking situations that began with Damien entering the lobby of a 25-story building. Using in vivo desensitization, Damien and the practitioner entered the lobby and looked outside for 2 minutes. If Damien indicated no or low anxiety (0–10 SUDS), he attempted the next item on the hierarchy, going to the second floor and looking out a window. If Damien indicated anxiety at that point, he returned to the previous item on the hierarchy (i.e., he returned to the lobby) and the practitioner prompted relaxation responses until Damien showed no anxiety. Then he again attempted the next higher item. This procedure continued until Damien was exposed to the highest item on the hierarchy. Damien remained in the presence of the CS (looking out a window on the 25th floor of the building) until his anxiety CRs extinguished. The escape and avoidance responses of turning and running away also extinguished as Damien remained in the feared situation with minimal or no anxiety and as incompatible responses, such as talking and joking with the practitioner, were positively reinforced. Six months after treatment, Damien was able to go to any floor of this building and others.

Flooding

Flooding is an intense, prolonged exposure technique for treating phobias by extinction of anxiety CRs and avoidance responses. Flooding consists of exposing the individual directly or in imagination to the full intensity of the feared stimulus (CS) for a prolonged period while preventing any escape or avoidance responses. Instead of gradually working up through a hierarchy of anxiety-eliciting stimuli, as in systematic desensitization or in vivo desensitization, the client faces the feared stimulus at full intensity for a prolonged period of time until his or her anxiety peaks and then begins to decrease. The client remains in the presence of the feared stimulus until the anxiety responses demonstrably decrease. Reports of the successful use of flooding have involved exposure durations of 100 minutes or more (e.g., Chaplin & Levine, 1981; Fiegenbaum, 1988).

In treating Damien's acrophobia with flooding, the practitioner instructs Damien to go directly to the top of the 25-story building and look out a window for a prolonged period of time (e.g., 50 minutes). Damien is likely to be very anxious in this situation, but no negative consequences will occur. Damien's anxiety will peak and then begin to decrease. The practitioner using flooding usually accompanies the client to prevent the client from performing anxiety-reducing avoidance behaviors. Any escape and avoidance responses Damien makes will interfere with extinction of his anxiety by removing him from the feared situation.

Researchers who have studied flooding have reported mostly positive results (e.g., Barlow & Brown, 1996; King & Ollendick, 1997), and some have found that flooding is superior to drug treatment and placebo (Turner, Beidel, & Jacob, 1994). Imaginal flooding has been used to treat posttraumatic stress disorder (PTSD) effectively in children and adolescents (e.g., Saigh, Yule, & Inamdar, 1996) as well as in rape victims (Foa, Rothbaum, Riggs, & Murdock, 1991)—situations that do not allow for in vivo flooding—and has been found to be at least as effective as in vivo flooding in the treatment of simple phobias (Borden, 1992). In vivo flooding appears to be effective in treating public speaking anxiety, bulimia, and agoraphobia (Craske, 1993). Successful results have also been reported in the treatment of obsessive and compulsive behavior patterns (e.g., Stanley & Turner, 1995; Steketee, 1993; Wolpe, 1990). Questions have been raised, however, regarding the possible negative effects of flooding, such as increased anxiety to the phobic stimulus when presented in full strength and psychological discomfort to the client (e.g., Barlow & Brown, 1996; Wolpe, 1990).

When considering the use of flooding, the practitioner informs the client about the procedure and the likely discomfort the client will feel when experiencing the full intensity of the phobic stimulus. Some clients cannot tolerate high levels of anxiety and will elect not to participate in flooding. Dropout rates for those who do participate in flooding can be as high as 30% to 40% if exposure procedures are too rigorous (Barlow & Brown, 1996).

Researchers have compared the efficacy of massed exposure (conducted daily) with that of spaced exposure (conducted weekly) in treating agoraphobia and simple phobia. Some studies have found no differences between the two conditions; for example, Chambless (1990) found that both were equally effective in the short term and at 6-month follow-up, with no differential dropout rate or differential relapse rate. In contrast, Fiegenbaum (1988) found intense massed exposure to be more effective than gradual exposure in treating agoraphobia: At a 5-year follow-up, 76% of group members who received intensive massed exposure were symptom-free compared with 35% of group members who received spaced exposure. Others have found gradual self-paced exposure to be as effective as, if not more effective than, intense massed exposure (e.g., Barlow, 1988; Rachman, Craske, & Tallmark, 1986). Dropout rates and relapse rates have also been shown to be lower with gradual self-paced exposure (Barlow & Brown, 1996).

Exposure and Ritual Prevention

Exposure and ritual prevention (originally referred to as *response prevention*) is a well-established intervention technique for obsessive-compulsive disorder (OCD) in adults (Franklin & Foa, 2002). Individuals with this problem have both obsessions (excessive repetitive thoughts or images) and behavioral rituals (excessive repetitive overt acts or responses) that have negative consequences for them or others. Washing and cleaning rituals are common among people with OCD. An example is the title character in the popular television comedy-drama *Monk,* who is preoccupied with cleaning and germs. For Adrian Monk, repetitive thoughts of dirt and germs function as CSs that elicit anxiety. The anxiety builds when he sees dirt or believes he has been exposed to germs, and his cleaning rituals reduce the anxiety by removing the dirt or wiping off the germs.

To stop Monk's excessive cleaning using EX/RP, a practitioner would have Monk remain in the presence of the dirt (exposure) for a specified period of time (for example, 60–90 minutes). Monk would have strong urges to clean, but the practitioner would instruct him to refrain from cleaning or, if necessary, actually prevent him from cleaning (ritual prevention). Fifteen to 20 such sessions would be conducted over a period of several weeks. For example, every time Monk shakes hands with someone he immediately uses a sanitary wipe to clean his hands. In treatment using exposure, he would be required to shake hands without cleaning them for an extended period of time. During this time the practitioner would prevent him from making any response to clean his hands. Exposure operates by extinction of anxiety responses (CRs), and ritual prevention allows extinction of the avoidance behaviors.

EX/RP that includes the essential components of (a) prolonged exposure, (b) the assistance of a therapist, and (c) strict ritual prevention is considered the treatment of choice for obsessive-compulsive disorder (Franklin & Foa, 2002), with reported success rates of 60% to 70% (Baer & Minichiello, 1998) and even up to 83% (Foa, Franklin, & Kozak, 1998). If the obsessive thoughts cannot be presented in vivo (e.g., if they are thoughts about hurricanes, diseases, or other calamities), they can be confronted with imaginal exposure (Foa & Goldstein, 1978). Further research is required to determine the role of cognitive therapy in OCD. In one study, Steketee (1993) found that adding cognitive components to exposure and response prevention did not improve the outcome in individuals with obsessive-compulsive behaviors.

Cognitive-Behavioral Techniques

Cognitions are covert behaviors that refer to private or unobservable events, including thoughts, beliefs, and attitudes. Emotions and feelings are also covert behaviors that both influence and are influenced by cognitions. For example, belief that a trip to the dentist will be painful can result in one's feeling anxious when making the appointment. Alternatively, belief that a trip to the dentist will make one's teeth clean and attractive can evoke pleasant feelings. Cognitions and emotions have become increasingly important to behavioral practitioners because, although these events cannot be observed, clients frequently seek help from behavior therapists for problems they define as primarily cognitive or emotional. Also, although covert behaviors cannot be observed, they can be measured through self-reports, self-ratings, and biofeedback instruments that record physiological responses such as muscle tension and relaxation.

Cognitive-behavioral techniques include two broad types of interventions. One of these focuses directly on changing cognitions, with the expectation that behavior change will follow. The other focuses on changing behavior, with the expectation that cognitive change will follow (e.g., Festinger, 1957). **Cognitive restructuring** techniques focus directly on changing cognitions. These techniques are used in Ellis's (1995) rational-emotive behavior therapy (REBT) and Beck's (1976) cognitive therapy. Techniques that focus on teaching clients adaptive behavioral and cognitive responses or coping skills include self-instructional training (e.g., Meichenbaum, 1977) and problem-solving therapy (D'Zurilla & Goldfried, 1971). Panic control treatment (e.g., Barlow & Cerny, 1988; Barlow & Craske, 2000) combines both types of interventions, teaching behavioral coping skills and using cognitive restructuring. Cognitive-behavioral techniques have been increasingly used to change both overt and covert target behaviors in mental health problems such as depression, anxiety and panic, obsessive-compulsive behaviors, eating disorders, and anger (e.g., Craighead, Hart, Craighead, & Ilardi, 2002; Wilson & Fairburn, 2002).

Cognitive Restructuring

Albert Ellis (1995; Ellis & Dryden, 1998) developed REBT as a cognitive restructuring technique to change what he calls *dysfunctional beliefs*. Originally called rational-emotive therapy (RET; Ellis, 1962, 1984), Ellis's approach is based on the premise that emotional distress is the result of irrational thought patterns and their illogical conclusions. REBT has been used with individuals suffering from anxiety, depression, anger, and guilt. Ellis uses cognitive restructuring to help individuals change their assumptions and interpretations about their experiences that lead to maladaptive behavior. Ellis added the word *behavior* to the name of this technique to reflect its emphasis on changing overt behavior through behavioral assignments in addition to challenging and changing irrational, covert beliefs.

REBT involves identifying irrational beliefs, challenging the irrational beliefs, and substituting thoughts based on rational beliefs. In Ellis's (e.g., 1991) ABC model of human disturbance, A is the activating event, B is the client's belief about the event, and C represents the emotional and behavioral consequences derived from B. REBT is used to restructure the irrational thought patterns (B) through disputation or rational argument to promote the client's emotional well-being.

Aaron Beck (1976) developed a cognitive therapy approach similar to Ellis's based on the premise that emotional disorders result from what Beck calls *automatic thoughts* or *cognitive distortions*. The goal of therapy, therefore, is to change the irrational cognitions. Beck developed his cognitive therapy as an intervention for depression, but it has also been used to treat anxiety disorders, obesity, substance abuse, marital distress, eating disorders, and psychosomatic disorders, among other problems (e.g., Beck & Emery, 1985; Beck, Sokol, & Clark, 1992; Beck, Wright, Newman, & Liese, 1993; Nauta, Hospers, Kok, & Jansen, 2000). Beck's cognitive therapy uses both cognitive and behavioral interventions (e.g., homework assignments to gather data) in treating target behaviors. Cognitive interventions challenge the client's dysfunctional beliefs by searching for empirical evidence that the beliefs are true or untrue (in contrast to Ellis's use of rational argument), generating alternative interpretations to the beliefs, and identifying realistic outcomes.

Negative cognitions are reported as the most frequent symptom of depression (e.g., Beck, Rush, Shaw, & Emery, 1979; Burns, 1980). Individuals who complain of depression, however, have both overt and covert behaviors that are problematic. The overt behaviors include difficulty completing daily tasks, reduced interest in sex and other formerly pleasurable activities, and changes in sleeping and eating patterns. Depression is also linked to suicide and is comorbid with many other mental and physical disorders.

According to Beck and his colleagues, the depressed individual can be taught to substitute positive thoughts for negative thoughts in response to cues that trigger symptoms of depression. Depression is manifested in distressed affect (feelings of sadness), negative cognitions (hopelessness about the future, negative beliefs about oneself, and suicidal ideation), and marked reduction in pleasurable and productive activity (especially eating, sleeping, and sex), although some avoidance behaviors may increase (e.g., sleeping and binge eating). Some negative cognitions result from cognitive distortions and faulty assumptions that depressed individuals make about their behavior and the behavior of others. Individuals can be taught to alter their cognitions and attribute more positive motives to replace their negative assumptions.

In Case Example 6, Bill complained of feeling depressed after he was criticized by his employer. When the therapist questioned him further in individual sessions, Bill reported that his feeling depressed was accompanied by thoughts of worthlessness and hopelessness. He frequently had the following thoughts: "My situation is hopeless. I will never be able to do this job right and I'll never be able to get another job. I'm a failure." As he persisted in having these thoughts, he also began to worry that his wife, Alice, would leave him for someone else. He then felt even more depressed.

Using cognitive behavior therapy, the therapist worked with Bill to (a) identify faulty cognitions and challenge them, (b) generate alternative beliefs, and (c) explore realistic outcomes. Bill's cognitive distortions included overgeneralization (e.g., the belief that he would never succeed in anything) and all-or-nothing thinking (e.g., the belief that because he was having trouble in his job he was a total failure). Like many clients, Bill was not aware of the faulty beliefs related to his depression. The therapist gave Bill a form like the one below and instructed him to record his automatic thoughts (cognitive distortions) as they occurred each day. This type of recording form can help clients to identify dysfunctional thoughts and challenge them by generating alternative beliefs. Bill completed the form as a homework assignment, recording each situation, his emotion and automatic thoughts at the time, and alternative interpretations of problematic situations.

Situation	Emotion	Automatic Thought	Alternative Interpretation
Boss criticized my work.	Anxious; depressed	I'll never get this right; I'm a failure.	I can do the work; I just need to pay more attention to how I do it.
Alice went shopping with a friend.	Sad; lonely	Why would Alice want to stay with me? I'm a failure.	I'm going through a bad time right now, but I'll get another job and we'll be all right.

Bill's worst-case scenario could turn out to be true—that is, his wife could leave him for another man. In that case, cognitive therapy would focus on helping Bill recognize that although the situation is painful, he wouldn't want to be married to someone who doesn't want to be with him, and that he can use the opportunity to learn new ways to improve himself. Cognitive therapy would help Bill change his automatic thoughts from "My life is over; I'll never find anyone else who will marry me" to "This is really painful, but I will find someone else I can be happy with and who will be happy with me."

Bill's treatment also involved increasing his activity level. His therapist encouraged him to pursue an outside interest or hobby, which he did with his wife. They joined a bowling league. It is likely that at least part of Bill's "boredom" was related to his lack of engagement in any activity. Exercise has been shown to have significant positive effects in the treatment of depression (e.g., Tkachuk & Martin, 1999).

Behavior marital therapy has also been effective in treating depression among individuals with both depression and marital discord (e.g., Craighead et al., 2002). Behavior marital therapy has been found to be as effective as individual cognitive behavior therapy for depression and superior to individual cognitive behavior therapy in the reduction of marital discord (e.g., Jacobson, Dobson, Fruzetti, Schmaling, & Salusky, 1991; O'Leary & Beach, 1990).

Self-Instruction Training

Self-instruction training (e.g., Meichenbaum, 1977, 1985) is a form of cognitive behavior modification that focuses on helping individuals develop coping skills. Through such training, the practitioner teaches individuals how to give themselves instructions that help them to cope effectively with difficult situations. Self-instruction training has been used to address problems such as childhood anxiety (e.g., Kendall, 1994), poor academic skills (Guevremont, Osnes, & Stokes, 1988), impulsive behaviors (Guevremont, Tishelman, & Hull, 1985), and nonassertive behaviors

(Kazdin & Mascitelli, 1982). The major components of self-instruction training are cognitive modeling and cognitive behavior rehearsal. The practitioner models appropriate self-instructions (verbally) while performing a task. The practitioner then has the client perform the task while the practitioner provides verbal guidance. The client then says the instructions aloud while performing the task. The client repeats the task, gradually fading the volume of the spoken instructions until he or she is performing the task while saying the instructions covertly.

For example, Brett, a violinist, reported a high level of anxiety before performing with the orchestra. Using self-instruction training, the practitioner told Brett to imagine performing a concert and then modeled verbalizations of appropriate self-instructions for Brett to tell himself as the first step in the procedure. The cognitive modeling that the practitioner performed included the following components:

- *Problem definition* (What am I trying to do?): "I am getting ready to play a concert."
- *Response guidance* (specific instructions to myself): "Relax. I am playing a piece I have practiced hundreds of times. I am going to focus on the notes that I know so well."
- *Coping self-statements and evaluative error correction:* "Even if I am anxious about making a mistake, I can still go on. It's okay to be a little nervous."
- *Self-reinforcement:* "I'm doing fine." "I can do it!" "I did it!"

Cognitive behavior rehearsal is used to facilitate the transfer of instructional control from overt external instructions (the practitioner saying them aloud) to covert self-instructions (the client saying them to him- or herself). Brett prepared to play his violin in the practitioner's office with the practitioner verbalizing the instructions. Brett then began to play while repeating the instructions aloud. He continued to play while gradually fading the volume of the instructions to a whisper. Finally, Brett began to play while saying the instructions to himself (covertly).

Stress Inoculation Training

Stress inoculation training (e.g., Meichenbaum, 1977, 1985) can be included in a treatment package with self-instruction training. Stress inoculation training is a technique for teaching physical and cognitive coping skills in response to stressful situations by having the client rehearse the skills in the presence of stressors. The stressors may be physical (e.g., putting your arm in freezing water), visual (e.g., seeing a graphic or gruesome film), or imaginal (e.g., imagining a dentist drilling one of your teeth). Stress inoculation training has been used in managing anxiety reactions, chronic headaches, asthma, physiological pain, and dental anxiety (e.g., Maag & Kotlash, 1994; Ross & Berger, 1996; Timmons, Oehlert, Sumerall, & Timmons, 1997). Anger control (e.g., Novaco, 1975) is an application of stress inoculation training that teaches individuals coping techniques to provide alternate responses to anger-eliciting stimuli.

Panic Control Treatment

Panic control treatment (PCT) was developed to treat symptoms of anxiety and panic directly (e.g., Barlow, Craske, Cerny, & Klosko, 1989; Barlow & Craske, 2000). In treating panic disorder without agoraphobia, PCT is used alone. In treating panic disorder with agoraphobia, in vivo desensitization is added to PCT. In vivo desensitization reduces the escape and avoidance responses of anxiety; PCT reduces the cognitive and somatic components of anxiety. PCT focuses on the following components:

- Breathing retraining to induce calming and decrease hyperventilation if present. Some therapists substitute relaxation training or use both techniques.
- Cognitive therapy (Beck & Emery, 1985) focusing on two cognitive errors: (a) overestimating the likelihood of danger as a result of panic attacks (e.g., having a heart attack and dying despite the lack of any evidence for such an outcome based on the client's physical condition and previous panic attacks) and (b) the tendency to catastrophize the consequences of having a panic attack (e.g., perceiving one's fainting in a concert hall as a calamity).
- Interoceptive exposure: The client is systematically exposed to the physical sensations (e.g., dizziness and heart racing) that elicit or trigger the attacks and remains in the situation until the panic symptoms extinguish.

In using PCT, the practitioner conducts an assessment to ascertain the specific mix of physical sensations that are involved for the client. Specially designed exercises are then used to re-create the client's symptoms in the therapist's office. For example, the client is spun around in an office chair to produce audiovestibular symptoms such as dizziness. After the client reports that he or she can tolerate the various physical sensations at full intensity in the therapist's office, the therapist assigns the client a series of in vivo exercises that provide interoceptive exposure in the natural environment and also instructs the client in coping techniques. For example, the client might exercise vigorously or drink a cup of coffee to induce panic symptoms and then practice breathing exercises to reduce those symptoms. The usual duration of panic control treatment is approximately 10 to 12 sessions. Self-help manuals are available to help clients during treatment and follow-up (Barlow & Craske, 2000).

Stan, an appliance salesman, is 36 years old and lives alone. During the past 6 months, he has become increasingly anxious about driving his car from home to work and back. On the freeway, he starts to perspire heavily, gets dizzy, feels his heart beating faster, and sometimes experiences chest pain. Stan worries about having these panic attacks in public and has started taking longer alternate routes to work to avoid the freeway and the possibility of having a panic attack. Last year, Stan was involved as a passenger in an automobile accident on the freeway and received minor injuries; he thinks this accident could have caused his current difficulties. At the time, he had a new supervisor and was concerned about losing his job.

After the practitioner conducted an assessment of Stan's situation and a physician had ruled out any physical health problems, the practitioner taught Stan how to breathe more slowly and comfortably. Cognitive interventions focused on correcting Stan's unrealistic concerns about having a heart attack while driving and about how news of his critical condition or death would cause his mother to die. The practitioner gave Stan exercises, both in the office and as home assignments, to simulate the physical sensations of panic, such as running in place to experience an increase in heart rate. The practitioner also taught Stan breathing retraining as a method for decreasing the symptoms when they occurred. During the next 3 weeks, Stan began to feel less anxious driving his car and drove part of the way to work on the freeway. After 10 sessions, Stan was able to drive to work on the freeway without panic symptoms. A 2-year follow-up contact by the therapist indicated that Stan was panic-free.

Evaluation of Cognitive-Behavioral Techniques

Rational-emotive behavior therapy. Gossette and O'Brien (1992) reviewed studies using RET and found that this type of therapy had no effect on behavioral measures such as the approach to phobic stimuli. Similar findings have been obtained for individuals with obsessive-compulsive disorders. Behavioral components of REBT, such as homework assignments, appeared to be the basis for effectiveness of the interventions. A major methodological weakness of outcome studies of REBT is the failure to establish an operational definition of the intervention (e.g., Kendall et al., 1995) or to differentiate the components necessary for its effectiveness (e.g., Franklin & Foa, 2002; Haaga & Davison, 1993).

Cognitive behavior therapy. Studies have shown that clients receiving cognitive therapy for panic disorder improved significantly on panic measures compared with clients receiving brief supportive therapy (Beck et al., 1992) and compared with those receiving applied relaxation, imipramine, or wait-list control (Clark et al., 1994). These gains were maintained at 1-year follow-up.

A meta-analysis of cognitive therapy studies (Dobson, 1989) concluded that Beck's cognitive therapy (Beck et al., 1979) was the treatment of choice for depression. Beck's cognitive therapy (CT), also referred to as cognitive behavior therapy (CBT), has been the most extensively evaluated psychosocial treatment for depression (Craighead et al., 2002). Cognitive therapy has been shown to be at least as effective as medication for acute episodes of depression (Antonuccio, Danton, & DeNelsky, 1995) but less effective for chronic depression (Thase et al., 1994). In another study, CBT was found to be more effective than a pill-placebo control in treating atypical depression (Jarrett et al., 1999) and equally effective as antidepressant medication (Blackburn & Moore, 1997). Studies have shown that relapse rates have been lower and maintenance of treatment gains have been better for individuals treated with CBT than for individuals treated with medication (e.g., Evans et al., 1992; Hirschfeld et al., 1997; Paykel et al., 1999).

A major review of the literature on cognitive therapy for the treatment of depression concluded that cognitive behavior therapy may be no more effective than a placebo (American Psychiatric Association, 1993). Hollon and Shelton (2001), however, questioned that conclusion. They evaluated the guidelines for major depressive disorder, based on a review of the literature, including new guidelines from the American Psychiatric Association (2000a, 2000b). The guidelines identified interventions that were evidence based and those that were not. The American Psychiatric Association (2001) guidelines recommend that CBT can be considered as the sole treatment for individuals with mild to moderate depression, but drugs or electroconvulsive therapy (ECT) should be provided for individuals with moderate to severe disorders. The guidelines recommend combined treatment for individuals with other psychosocial or interpersonal issues, or personality disorders (*DSM-IV,* Axis II).

Evaluation of self-instruction training. Although Bornstein and Quevillon (1976) found that self-instruction training was effective in reducing disruptive classroom behaviors, their results have not been replicated in other research (e.g., Billings & Wasik, 1985; Bryant & Budd, 1982; Cormier & Cormier, 1991). Results of studies investigating the conditions under which self-instruction training is effective have been unclear regarding the benefit of self-instruction compared with instruction provided by another individual (therapist, parent, or teacher) (Roberts, Nelson, & Olson, 1987).

Evaluation of panic control treatment. In a comparison of four conditions for treating individuals with panic disorder, Barlow et al. (1989) found that 87% of clients receiving PCT or PCT plus relaxation were panic-free after treatment compared with approximately 60% of clients receiving applied progressive muscle relaxation and 30% in a wait-list control group. In a 2-year follow-up, 81% of the PCT group members were panic-free compared with 43% for the PCT plus relaxation group and 36% for the relaxation-only group (Craske, Brown, & Barlow, 1991). PCT alone appeared to have a long-term effect not found in the combined treatment, in which clients learned both PCT and relaxation simultaneously (Barlow & Brown, 1996). In a subsequent study, Barlow, Gorman, Shear, and Woods (2000) found that PCT alone was as effective as PCT plus antianxiety medication (imipramine). In addition, individuals who received medication, either with PCT or alone, were more likely to relapse than were those receiving PCT without medication.

Aversion Therapy

The treatment of behavioral excesses using aversive stimuli is complex and requires not only knowledge of behavioral principles and procedures but also supervised training and experience in a treatment setting. Aversive conditioning techniques are usually chosen as a last resort or for specific problems that are otherwise difficult to treat. During the past two decades, practitioners have used aversive techniques, or **aversion therapy,** less frequently because of the disadvantages of these techniques, which include high dropout rates and the unpleasantness of the procedures for clients and their families (e.g., Beare, Severson, & Brandt, 2004; Maletzky, 2002).

Respondent conditioning techniques include the use of aversive stimuli such as electric shock, noxious odors, or nausea-inducing drugs (emetics) to treat behavioral excesses, such as drug addiction, alcoholism, smoking, and sexual deviations (e.g., Earls & Castonguay, 1989; Maletzky, 2002; Rimmele, Howard, & Hilfrink, 1995; Smith & Frawley, 1993; Wolpe, 1990). In many situations, it is inappropriate or inconvenient for practitioners to use actual aversive stimuli such as shock. Several covert conditioning techniques, such as covert sensitization and thought stopping, have been developed to treat behavioral excesses based on research findings indicating that imagined aversive events can be effective in suppressing inappropriate behaviors (e.g., Cautela & Kearney, 1993; Maletzky, 2002).

In using aversion therapy to treat an individual who has molested children, the picture of a naked child (CS) elicits sexual arousal (UR). Treatment consists of pairing the picture with an aversive stimulus such as a noxious odor (US) until the picture elicits nausea (CR) instead of sexual arousal. The client removes the noxious odor by performing an escape response (S^{R-}), such as turning away from the picture of the child (CS/S^D). The client could also perform an avoidance response that prevents the onset of the aversive stimulus (US). The therapist specifies an appropriate avoidance response the client can make, such as turning from the picture of the child to a picture of an adult female. The CS of the naked child also functions as the S^D (S^{r-}) for the avoidance response (turning to the woman's picture), which is negatively reinforced by the prevention of the onset of a foul odor (US/S^{R-}). In this way, the client learns to increase the performance of appropriate responses that are incompatible with the undesired behavior (e.g., Maletzky, 2002).

Covert Sensitization

Covert sensitization is an anxiety-eliciting technique in which imaginal stimuli are used to decrease an undesired behavior. This technique avoids the ethical and practical problems involved with USs such as electric shock or chemical aversion. Instead of pairing anxiety-evoking stimuli with relaxation as in systematic desensitization, covert sensitization employs stimuli that elicit anxiety in clients with maladaptive behavioral excesses. This technique has been used in the treatment of stealing, overeating, sexual deviations, smoking, drug addiction, and alcoholism (e.g., Cautela, 1966; Cautela & Kearney, 1993).

In covert sensitization, the maladaptive behavior is described in great detail and paired in the client's imagination with highly aversive stimuli. A typical aversive scene used in covert sensitization includes a vivid description of nausea and vomiting induced by the individual's approach toward the attractive but inappropriate stimulus (e.g., an alcoholic beverage). The pleasant respondent behaviors associated with the maladaptive operant behavior (e.g., taking a drink) are suppressed by the anxiety or nausea responses elicited by the imagined aversive stimuli (e.g., insects crawling in the drink).

When implementing covert sensitization, the therapist instructs the client to imagine making appropriate escape and avoidance responses (e.g., refusing or turning away from the alcoholic beverage or walking past the bar instead of going inside), which are negatively reinforced by removal of the imagined aversive stimuli. Practicing appropriate covert responses in the treatment setting is intended to increase the likelihood that the client will perform appropriate overt responses in the actual problematic situation.

In using covert sensitization to decrease alcohol abuse, the therapist instructs the client to imagine taking a drink at work, at home, and in other places where the client usually drinks. These drinking stimuli are then paired, also in the client's imagination, with highly aversive stimuli (e.g., vivid descriptions of insects crawling all over the alcohol and glass) that elicit the CRs of anxiety and nausea. These two scenes—the pleasant drinking situations and the highly aversive crawling insects—are paired repeatedly until the alcohol-drinking scenes alone elicit the nausea CRs previously associated with the insects.

There is some empirical support for the effectiveness of covert sensitization in treating alcoholism (e.g., Miller et al., 1995; Rimmele et al., 1995). Although the research on covert sensitization has primarily taken the form of case studies (e.g., Cautela & Kearney, 1993), most cognitive-behavioral programs for the treatment of sexual paraphilias (e.g., pedophilia, exhibitionism, fetishism) incorporate this technique (e.g., Alexander, 1999; Maletzky, 2002).

Other covert techniques have been applied in the treatment of client behaviors, including covert positive reinforcement, covert negative reinforcement, covert extinction, and covert modeling (Cautela & Kearney, 1993). The primary advantage of the covert procedures is that the individual does not have to perform the undesired behaviors; instead, he or she simply imagines them. In addition, a physically aversive or painful stimulus is not administered.

Thought Stopping

Thought stopping is a covert technique used to decrease the frequency of recurring negative or self-defeating thoughts. Thoughts of death, losing control, low self-worth, overeating, and unrequited love are among the problems that have been treated using this technique (e.g., Cautela & Kearney, 1993; Wolpe, 1990). Thought stopping typically progresses from overt to covert control. For example, the procedure begins with the client describing the obsessive or negative thoughts. When the client starts to verbalize the negative or obsessive thoughts (e.g., "Frank broke up with me; I'll never find another man; I'll be alone for the rest of my life."), the therapist shouts "Stop!" The purpose of this intervention is to block the undesired thoughts and redirect the client's attention. The therapist then instructs the client to concentrate on the unwanted thoughts and signal the therapist by raising a finger when the thoughts begin. The therapist shouts "Stop!" to disrupt the thoughts and then discusses with the client the effect of the shout in disrupting the thoughts. This procedure is repeated, with the shouting of the therapist gradually fading out and the client taking over saying "Stop!"—first aloud and then silently to him- or herself. The procedure continues until the client reports that all problematic thoughts have been blocked.

Thought stopping is most effective when followed by redirection of thoughts to positive, assertive, or self-reinforcing statements that are incompatible with the unwanted thoughts (Wolpe, 1990). The client says these positive self-statements covertly. In the previous example, the client's positive self-statement might be something like "I'm an attractive, intelligent woman, and I will meet another man who will care about me." The positive self-statement, however, does not have to be related to the problematic situation. Another positive self-statement this client might make could be about recent successes at work, such as "It felt great when the boss complimented me on my high sales figures for this month." Covert techniques such as thought stopping are convenient to use in the practice setting because they do not require special equipment or materials.

Thought stopping is frequently used in practice as part of a treatment package to decrease persistent, intrusive thoughts (e.g., Broder, 2000; Lerner, Franklin, Meadows, Hembree, & Foa, 1998). The technique is easy for clients to use and gives them self-control. Case reports indicate that thought stopping has been used successfully to treat a variety of problems (e.g., Cautela & Kearney, 1993), although when the technique is used as part of a treatment package it is difficult to isolate its effects.

Habit Reversal

More than three decades ago, Azrin and Nunn (1973) developed the technique of habit reversal as a method for treating various nervous habits and tics, currently referred to as repetitive behavior problems (e.g., Woods, 2002; Woods & Miltenberger, 2001). Habit reversal is still a basic feature of many interventions for repetitive behavior problems such as hair pulling, skin picking, and thumb or finger sucking. Repetitive behavior problems can have adverse physical, psychological, and social consequences. For example, trichotillomania (hair pulling) can lead to extreme hair loss. Thumb or finger sucking may result in digital or dental deformities. Chronic skin picking can produce sores, scars, and infections. These behavior problems can also result in irritability and feelings of depression, avoidance of pleasurable activities, and nonaccepting reactions from peers (Woods & Miltenberger, 2001).

In habit reversal, the practitioner instructs the client to use self-monitoring to obtain a baseline of the undesired behavior. The practitioner then shows the client how to perform competing responses that are incompatible with the undesired response. For example, the therapist teaches an individual with excessive skin picking how to make a fist instead of picking the skin and how to engage in other activities incompatible with skin picking.

Intervention Packages

The effective treatment of some problem behaviors may include the use of intervention packages, or treatment packages, that involve a combination of covert and overt intervention components. For example, in treating pedophilia and exhibitionism, Maletzky (1980) found a combination of techniques to be effective, including covert sensitization, exposure to foul odors, masturbatory reconditioning, and cognitive therapy. An effective treatment for generalized anxiety disorder includes relaxation training to decrease physiological arousal, cognitive techniques to modify excessive worry, and graduated exposure to reduce avoidance behaviors (Stanley, Diefenbach, & Hopko, 2004). One of the most effective treatments for social phobia is an intervention package called cognitive-behavioral group treatment (CBGT), which includes exposure, cognitive restructuring, and homework exercises (Heimberg, Salzman, Halt, & Blendell, 1993).

The use of covert or cognitive techniques raises questions about the practicality of measuring and controlling unobservable events and scientifically evaluating their effects. Many intervention packages, however, include at least one covert component (e.g., Broder, 2000; Lerner et al., 1998). The frequent inclusion of covert techniques in intervention packages may be related to several factors, including their ease of use, their acceptability to clients and the community, and the belief that even in the absence of evidence on their effectiveness, such techniques will do no harm.

Evidence-Based Interventions

Increased emphasis on the measurement of treatment outcomes, and the use of psychosocial interventions based on demonstrated research efficacy and clinical effectiveness, has resulted in a movement among mental health professionals toward embracing empirically validated treatments and scientific or **evidence-based practice** (EBP; e.g., Corcoran, 2003; Gambrill, 1999; Kazdin & Weisz, 2003; Thyer, 2003). Many examples of evidenced-based treatments are available (e.g., Nathan & Gorman, 2002b). Current evaluation standards stress that treatment efficacy must be demonstrated by at least two different research teams (Chambless & Ollendick, 2001).

The credibility of research evidence on treatment outcomes relies on a study's adherence to the randomized controlled trial (RCT), with random assignment of participants to treatment and control groups, and without the evaluators' knowledge of who is assigned to what group. Single-case research designs can also provide empirical justification of treatments if a large ($N = 10$ or more) series of well-designed individual case studies have been conducted that compare intervention effects with at least one other treatment (Task Force on Promotion and Dissemination of Psychological Procedures, 1995).

Efficacy of an intervention technique is different from clinical effectiveness. The term *efficacy* refers to treatment effects obtained in RCTs, whereas *effectiveness* refers to treatment impact in clinical practice settings. Efficacy trials typically involve a clearly defined treatment, usually operationalized in a written manual and delivered by trained therapists whose adherence to the treatment protocol is monitored. Efficacy studies alone are insufficient to guide effective clinical practice; more studies are needed that evaluate efficacious interventions under clinical conditions (Nathan & Gorman, 2002a).

Practice Guidelines

As evidence-based practice has evolved, managed care organizations and others in the health care system have shown increasing interest in the development and application of practice guidelines for psychological and physical problems (e.g., McCrady, 2001; Rosen & Proctor, 2003; Thyer, 2003). Of these, practice guidelines produced by the American Psychiatric Association (e.g., 1995, 1997, 2000a, 2000b) have been the most prominent and widely disseminated. In 2001, the journal *Behavior Therapy* devoted a special issue to an examination of the APA guidelines (e.g., Hayes & Gregg, 2001; Hollon & Shelton, 2001; McCrady, 2001; McCrady & Ziedonis, 2001). The authors of the articles, who included established clinical researchers, reviewed the scientific evidence supporting the treatment of eating disorders, panic disorder, schizophrenia, major depressive disorders, and substance use disorders. They evaluated the strengths and limitations of the scientific bases for the APA guidelines, the applicability of the guidelines to the practice of behavior therapy and the training of behavior therapists, and the extent to which the guidelines addressed issues of population diversity.

These authors concluded that the APA guidelines are based on scientific evidence as well as on attempts to integrate the scientific findings with clinical experience. They criticized the guidelines, however, for relying too heavily on practice experience in the absence of empirical data. Behavioral and cognitive-behavioral interventions, which have a strong research base, are prominent among the treatment alternatives for the specific disorders discussed. The authors expressed concerns about the difficulty of training practitioners to provide competent treatment for the many disorders included in the guidelines, considering that practitioners are often expected to serve a wide range of clients. The authors also noted that more science-based knowledge is needed to fill the gaps in interventions to treat diverse populations.

The development of evidence-based practice appears to be an evolutionary process that requires establishment of a more comprehensive body of scientific research to fulfill the promise of EBP guidelines. An interdisciplinary approach to developing practice guidelines could have the advantage of minimizing the biases and limitations of particular disciplines or organizations (e.g., Hayes & Gregg, 2001; Thyer, 2003). Several interdisciplinary efforts, involving professional associations of social workers, psychologists, psychiatrists, and other payers and providers, are currently under way to develop and evaluate practice guidelines (McCrady, 2001; Thyer, 2003).

A practitioner's acceptance of evidence-based research dictates that empiricism will determine which intervention techniques are viable and which should be dismissed. This raises the question of whether certain interventions that have been popular should continue to be used. Lilienfeld, Lynn, and Lohr (2003) recently concluded that a number of controversial procedures (e.g., eye movement desensitization reprocessing, or EMDR; Shapiro, 1989) lack sufficient evidence supporting their use and may even exacerbate client problems. These authors suggest several ethical guidelines, including the following: (a) Practitioners should select empirically valid interventions over those that lack such support, and (b) training institutions and licensing boards should help practitioners identify and differentiate empirically valid treatments from those that lack such support.

The question arises whether practitioners should abandon interventions that may appear to be promising but have not been empirically validated or use them because alternative efficacious techniques are not available. Examples include acceptance and commitment therapy (Hayes, Strosahl, & Wilson, 1999), dialectical behavior therapy (Linehan, 1993), and neurotherapy (also called EEG biofeedback and neurofeedback; Evans & Abarbanel, 1999). Because evidence-based practice is an evolving process based on scientific research, we rely on findings that corroborate or question the efficacy of particular interventions. In the continuing search for the most effective and efficacious treatments for human problems, empirically validated intervention techniques, other than those based on behavior change principles (e.g., interpersonal psychotherapy for depression; Klerman, Weissman, Rounsaville, & Chevron, 1984), can also demonstrate their value.

Conclusion

A science-based approach to behavior change in the human services has evolved largely over the past 40 years. Research progressed from laboratory studies with animals to single-case studies with humans to large-scale RCTs aimed at empirically testing and validating interventions for specific psychosocial problems. The challenge for the future is to continue developing, testing, and refining intervention techniques that can improve the quality of individual and community life.

Future trends in behavior change will likely build on the tremendous growth of evidence-based practice and promising new developments. We discuss some possible future developments briefly below.

Inside the "black box." Technology has made it possible to examine areas of the brain related to target behaviors and problems such as depression, anxiety, and schizophrenia. The roles of emotions and thoughts (cognitive phenomena) are also being examined in this way. Mental health professionals have a long history of focusing on individuals' feelings, and new technologies will provide additional tools for practice.

A recent study using PET (positron emission tomography) imaging showed that antidepressant medication reduced activity in the brain's limbic system (emotion center, origin of stress and negative emotions), whereas cognitive behavior therapy decreased activity in the cerebral cortex (the brain's rational center for planning, conceptual thought, analysis and logic) (Goldapple et al., 2004). The study's hypothesis that the brain would have changed in the same way regardless of the treatment was rejected. These findings suggest new choices for clients and therapists in selecting treatments.

Human-machine interfaces. Technology has provided ways to treat phobias and panic disorder in the form of computer-based interventions (e.g., Bobicz & Richard, 2003; Calbring, Westling, Ljungstrand, Ekselius, & Andersson, 2001; Gilroy, Kirkby, Daniels, Menzies, & Montgomery, 2003; Gruber, Moran, Roth, & Taylor, 2001). Virtual technology has created new ways of serving clients. The first controlled study on the efficacy of a self-help treatment program on the Internet for panic disorder found that the program produced positive outcomes for clients (Calbring et al., 2001).

New ethical issues. Ethical issues will arise in relation to such new developments as Internet-based therapies, virtual technology, and the use of new and unproven intervention techniques (e.g., Manhal-Baugus, 2001). Questions regarding confidentiality, privacy, and liability will have to be addressed.

Increased emphasis on prevention of psychosocial and health problems, and innovative ways of applying behavior change approaches to larger systems such as organizations, communities, and societies (e.g., Bellg, 2003; Gardenswartz & Craske, 2001; Graves & Miller, 2003; Thyer, 1998). The adoption of evidence-based practice shows promise for the development of interventions that are effective in preventing and alleviating public health and social problems (e.g., Elder, 2001; Thyer, 2003) as well as problems of individuals.

Increased empirical research on interventions with diverse populations. Researchers have begun to examine the effectiveness of treatment interventions with people of diverse ethnic and minority backgrounds (e.g., Hays, 1995; Iwamasa & Smith, 1996; McCrady, 2001) and sexual orientations (e.g., Purcell, Campos, & Perilla, 1996), as well as individuals at different developmental periods of the life course (e.g., midlife women; Hunter, Sundel, & Sundel, 2002). As the U.S. population ages, new or adapted intervention techniques for the care of older adults need to be addressed. Innovations include the adaptation of existing interventions to better suit the elderly, such as relaxation training employing imagery rather than tensing of muscles, which may be painful to individuals with arthritis and joint disease (e.g., Dick-Siskin, 2002). Other interventions for older adults include a cognitive-behavioral treatment for generalized anxiety disorder that can be used in primary care settings (e.g., Stanley et al., 2004). Preventive interventions that make use of new technologies, such as sensors on floor mats near exits, can address problems of adults with Alzheimer's disease and other impairments who pose dangers to themselves.

Innovative approaches to severe and chronic problems. Researchers are increasingly applying innovative approaches to problems such as schizophrenia (e.g., Kavanagh & Mueser, 2001; Kopelowicz, Liberman, & Zarate, 2002), substance use disorders (e.g., McCrady & Ziedonis, 2001), and developmental disabilities (e.g., Kearney, 2001).

Training and dissemination of user-friendly, evidence-based practice guidelines to ensure their correct use to reach the greatest number of people (e.g., Barlow et al., 2002). This training should address generalization issues regarding effectiveness across populations, settings, and practitioners.

Behavior change principles provide a solid foundation for new practice developments in the 21st century. Concepts such as reinforcement, punishment, and generalization and maintenance of behavior change will continue to be part of the evolving knowledge base from which efficacious intervention techniques will be developed. The knowledge gained from intervention research, which is essential to ethical practice, can only be transferred to practice in "leaky buckets." The transfer of knowledge from research to practice does not result in a perfect fit; more effective interaction between researchers and practitioners might help to reduce this gap. As Nathan and Gorman (2002a) have noted, efficacy studies alone are insufficient to guide effective clinical practice. New generations of researchers and practitioners will continue the process of innovation, testing, and refinement of interventions to benefit individuals and society.

Summary

1. Exposure techniques are used to modify behaviors related to anxiety. Techniques include systematic desensitization, in vivo desensitization, and flooding.

2. Systematic desensitization is an exposure technique for modifying phobic responses using a graduated hierarchy of anxiety-evoking stimuli that the client visualizes. The procedure involves relaxation training, construction of anxiety hierarchies, and pairing relaxation with anxiety-eliciting stimuli from the hierarchies.

3. In vivo desensitization is a graduated exposure technique to treat phobic responses. It is similar to systematic desensitization except that treatment occurs in the actual feared situation rather than in the imagination. In vivo desensitization requires the client to work through the anxiety hierarchy in the phobic situation or in a simulation of it.

4. Flooding is an intense, prolonged exposure technique for treating phobias. The individual is exposed to the phobic stimulus directly or in the imagination. Flooding differs from systematic desensitization and in vivo desensitization in that exposure to the phobic stimulus is intense and prolonged rather than graduated.

5. Cognitive restructuring interventions focus directly on changing cognitions or covert behaviors. These interventions include rational-emotive behavior therapy (REBT) and Beck's cognitive therapy.

6. Self-instruction training focuses on helping individuals develop coping skills. It includes cognitive modeling and cognitive behavior rehearsal.

7. Stress inoculation training is a technique for teaching physical and cognitive coping skills in stressful situations through rehearsal of the skills in the presence of stressors.

8. Panic control treatment uses cognitive restructuring and teaches behavioral coping skills in treating panic attacks. Panic control treatment includes breathing retraining, cognitive therapy, and interoceptive exposure.

9. Aversion therapy techniques have been used to treat behavioral excesses, such as drug addiction, alcoholism, and sexual deviations. An aversive stimulus is presented that competes with the undesired stimulus to inhibit

the undesired response. The client is also instructed to perform an appropriate avoidance response that is negatively reinforced by removal or prevention of the onset of the aversive stimulus.

10. Covert sensitization is an anxiety-eliciting technique employing imaginal stimuli to decrease an undesired behavior. This technique is used to reduce behavioral excesses, such as stealing, overeating, and sexual deviations. Appropriate escape and avoidance responses are negatively reinforced.

11. Thought stopping is a cognitive intervention used to treat recurring negative or self-defeating thoughts. It is most effective when followed by redirection of thoughts to positive, assertive, or self-reinforcing statements.

12. The effective treatment of some problem behaviors may include the use of treatment packages that involve a combination of behavioral and cognitive intervention techniques.

13. Increased emphasis on the measurement of treatment outcomes has led to the development of empirically validated treatments and practice guidelines.

14. Future developments in behavior change will likely involve consideration of the use of technology, human-machine interface, ethics related to new technology, innovative application of interventions to solve individual and social problems, new or adapted techniques for the care of older adults, and training and dissemination practices.

Suggested Activities

1. Discuss with your classmates the importance of using an evidence-based intervention technique with a client. Does your opinion change if the technique is potentially harmful as opposed to innocuous? What about if the technique gives the client self-control?

2. How important do you think it is to focus on outcomes of intervention programs?

3. What do you envision as a behavioral intervention for addressing an important social problem? How would you implement it and evaluate its effectiveness?

References and Resources

Alexander, M. A. (1999). Sexual offender treatment efficacy revisited. *Sexual Abuse, 11,* 101–116.

American Psychiatric Association. (1993). Practice guidelines for the treatment of major depressive disorder in adults. *American Journal of Psychiatry, 150*(Suppl. 4), 1–26.

American Psychiatric Association. (1995). Practice guidelines for the treatment of patients with substance abuse disorders. *American Journal of Psychiatry, 152,* 1–26.

American Psychiatric Association. (1997). Practice guidelines for the treatment of patients with schizophrenia. *American Journal of Psychiatry, 154*(Suppl. 4), 1–63.

American Psychiatric Association. (2000a). Practice guidelines for the treatment of patients with eating disorders (revision). *American Journal of Psychiatry, 157*(Suppl. 1), 1–39.

American Psychiatric Association. (2000b). Practice guidelines for the treatment of patients with major depressive disorder (revision). *American Journal of Psychiatry, 157*(Suppl. 4), 1–45.

American Psychological Association. (2001). *Guidelines for multicultural counseling proficiency for psychologists: Implications for education and training, research and clinical practice.* Washington, DC: Author.

Antonuccio, D. O., Danton, W. G., & DeNelsky, G. Y. (1995). Psychotherapy versus medication for depression: Challenging the conventional wisdom with data. *Professional Psychology: Research and Practice, 26,* 574–585.

Antony, M. M., & Barlow, D. H. (2002). Specific phobias. In D. H. Barlow (Ed.), *Anxiety and its disorders: The nature and treatment of anxiety and panic* (2nd ed., pp. 380–417). New York: Guilford.

Azrin, N. H., & Nunn, R. G. (1973). Habit reversal: A method of eliminating nervous habits and tics. *Behaviour Research and Therapy, 34,* 269–272.

Baer, L., & Minichiello, W. E. (1998). Behavior therapy for obsessive-compulsive disorders. In M. A. Jenike, L. Baer, & W. E. Minichiello (Eds.), *Obsessive-compulsive disorders: Practical management* (3rd ed., pp. 337–367). Boston: Mosby.

Barlow, D. H. (Ed.). (1988). *Anxiety and its disorders: The nature and treatment of anxiety and panic.* New York: Guilford.

Barlow, D. H. (Ed.). (2001). *Clinical handbook of psychological disorders* (3rd ed.). New York: Guilford.

Barlow, D. H., & Brown, T. A. (1996). Psychological treatments for panic disorder and panic disorder with agoraphobia. In M. R. Mavissakalian & R. F. Prien (Eds.), *Long-term treatments of anxiety disorders* (pp. 221–240). Washington, DC: American Psychiatric Press.

Barlow, D. H., & Cerny, J. A. (1988). *Psychological treatment of panic.* New York: Guilford.

Barlow, D. H., & Craske, M. G. (2000). *Mastery of your anxiety and panic: Client workbook for anxiety and panic.* San Antonio, TX: Graywind Psychological Corporation.

Barlow, D. H., Craske, M. G., Cerny, J. A., & Klosko, J. S. (1989). Behavioral treatment of panic disorder. *Behavior Therapy, 20,* 261–282.

Barlow, D. H., Gorman, J. M., Shear, M. K., & Woods, S. W. (2000). Cognitive-behavioral therapy, imipramine, or their combination for panic disorder: A randomized control trial. *Journal of the American Medical Association, 283,* 2529–2536.

Barlow, D. H., Raffa, S. D., & Cohen, E. M. (2002). Psychosocial treatments for panic disorders, phobias, and generalized anxiety disorder. In P. E. Nathan & J. M. Gorman (Eds.), *A guide to treatments that work* (2nd ed., pp. 301–335). New York: Oxford University Press.

Beare, P. L., Severson, S., & Brandt, P. (2004). The use of a positive procedure to increase engagement on-task and decrease challenging behavior. *Behavior Modification, 28,* 28–44.

Beck, A. T. (1976). *Cognitive therapy and the emotional disorders.* New York: International Universities Press.

Beck, A. T., & Emery, G. (1985). *Anxiety disorders and phobias: A cognitive perspective.* New York: Basic Books.

Beck, A. T., Rush, A. J., Shaw, F. B., & Emery, G. (1979). *The cognitive therapy of depression.* New York: Guilford.

Beck, A. T., Sokol, L., & Clark, D. A. (1992). A crossover study of focused cognitive therapy of panic disorder. *American Journal of Psychiatry, 147,* 778–783.

Beck, A. T., Wright, F. D., Newman, C. F., & Liese, B. S. (1993). *Cognitive therapy of substance abuse.* New York: Guilford.

Bellg, A. L. (2003). Maintenance of health behavior change in preventive cardiology: Internalization and self-regulation of new behaviors. *Behavior Modification, 27,* 103–131.

Bernstein, D. A., Borkovec, T. D., & Hazlett-Stevens, H. (2000). *New directions in progressive relaxation training: A guidebook for helping professionals.* Westport, CT: Praeger.

Billings, D. C., & Wasik, B. H. (1985). Self-instructional training with preschoolers: An attempt to replicate. *Journal of Applied Behavior Analysis, 18,* 61–67.

Blackburn, I. M., & Moore, R. G. (1997). Controlled acute and follow-up trial of cognitive therapy and pharmacotherapy in out-patients with recurrent depression. *British Journal of Psychiatry, 171,* 328–334.

Bobicz, K. P., & Richard, D. C. S. (2003). The virtual therapist: Behavior therapy in a digital age. *the Behavior Therapist, 26,* 265–270.

Borden, J. W. (1992). Behavioral treatment of simple phobia. In S. M. Turner, K. S. Calhoun, & H. E. Adams (Eds.), *Handbook of clinical behavior therapy* (pp. 77–94). New York: John Wiley.

Bornstein, P. H., & Quevillon, R. P. (1976). The effects of a self-instructional package on overactive preschool boys. *Journal of Applied Behavior Analysis, 9,* 179–188.

Broder, M. S. (2000). Making optimal use of homework to enhance your therapeutic effectiveness. *Journal of Rational-Emotive & Cognitive-Behavior Therapy, 18,* 3–18.

Bryant, L. E., & Budd, K. S. (1982). Self-instructional training to increase independent work performance in preschoolers. *Journal of Applied Behavior Analysis, 15,* 259–271.

Burns, D. (1980). *Feeling good.* New York: William Morris.

Calbring, P., Westling, B. E. Ljungstrand, P., Ekselius, L., & Andersson, G. (2001). Treatment of panic disorder via the Internet: A randomized trial of a self-help program. *Behavior Therapy, 32,* 751–764.

Cautela, J. R. (1966). Treatment of compulsive behavior by covert sensitization. *Psychological Record, 16,* 33–41.

Cautela, J. R., & Kearney, A. J. (Eds.). (1993). *Covert conditioning casebook.* Pacific Grove, CA: Brooks/Cole.

Chambless, D. L. (1990). Spacing of exposure sessions in treatment of agoraphobia and simple phobia. *Behavior Therapy, 21,* 217–229.

Chambless, D. L., & Ollendick, T. H. (2001). Empirically supported psychological interventions: Controversies and evidence. *Annual Review of Psychology, 52,* 685–716.

Chaplin, E. W., & Levine, B. A. (1981). The effects of total exposure duration and interrupted versus continuous exposure in flooding therapy. *Behavior Therapy, 12,* 360–368.

Clark, D. M., Salkovskis, P. M., Hackman, A., Middleton, H., Anastasiades, P., & Gelder, M. (1994). A comparison of cognitive therapy, applied relaxation, and imipramine in the treatment of panic disorder. *British Journal of Psychiatry, 164,* 759–769.

Corcoran, J. (2003). *Clinical applications of evidence-based family interventions.* New York: Oxford University Press.

Cormier, W. H., & Cormier, L. S. (1991). *Interviewing strategies for helpers: Fundamental skills and cognitive behavioral interventions* (3rd ed.). Monterey, CA: Brooks/Cole.

Craighead, W. E., Hart, A. B., Craighead, L. W., & Ilardi, S. S. (2002). Psychosocial treatments for major depressive disorder. In P. E. Nathan & J. M. Gorman (Eds.), *A guide to treatments that work* (2nd ed., pp. 245–261). New York: Oxford University Press.

Craske, M. G. (1993). Assessment and treatment of panic disorder and agoraphobia. In A. S. Bellack & M. Hersen (Eds.), *Handbook of behavior therapy in the psychiatric setting* (pp. 229–250). New York: Plenum.

Craske, M. G., Brown, T. A., & Barlow, D. H. (1991). Behavioral treatment of panic disorder: A two-year follow-up. *Behavior Therapy, 22,* 289–304.

Dick-Siskin, L. P. (2002). Cognitive-behavioral therapy with older adults. *the Behavior Therapist, 25,* 3–6.

Dixon, M. R. (2003). Creating a portable data-collection system with Microsoft embedded visual tools for the pocket PC. *Journal of Applied Behavior Analysis, 36,* 271–284.

Dobson, K. S. (1989). Meta-analysis of the efficacy of cognitive therapy for depression. *Journal of Consulting and Clinical Psychology, 57,* 414–419.

D'Zurilla, T. J., & Goldfried, M. R. (1971). Problem solving and behavior modification. *Journal of Abnormal Psychology, 78,* 107–126.

Earls, C. M., & Castonguay, L. G. (1989). The evaluation of olfactory aversion for a bisexual pedophile with a single-case multiple baseline design. *Behavior Therapy, 20,* 137–146.

Elder, J. P. (2001). *Behavior change and public health in the developing world.* Thousand Oaks, CA: Sage.

Ellis, A. (1962). *Reason and emotion in psychotherapy.* New York: Lyle Stuart.

Ellis, A. (1984). *Rational-emotive therapy and cognitive behavior therapy.* New York: Springer.

Ellis, A. (1991). The revised ABC's of rational-emotive therapy (RET). *Journal of Rational-Emotive & Cognitive-Behavior Therapy, 9,* 139–172.

Ellis, A. (1995). Changing rational-emotive therapy (RET) to rational-emotive behavior therapy (REBT). *Journal of Rational-Emotive & Cognitive-Behavior Therapy, 13,* 85–89.

Ellis, A., & Dryden, W. (1998). *The practice of rational emotive behavior therapy* (2nd ed.). New York: Free Association.

Evans, J. R., & Abarbanel, A. (Eds.). (1999). *Introduction to quantitative EEG and neurofeed-back.* New York: Academic Press.

Evans, M. D., Hollon, S. D., DeRubeis, R. J., Piasecki, J., Grove, W. M., Garvey, M. J., et al. (1992). Differential relapse following cognitive therapy and pharmacotherapy for depression. *Archives of General Psychiatry, 49,* 802–808.

Festinger, L. (1957). *A theory of cognitive dissonance.* Evanston, IL: Row, Peterson.

Fiegenbaum, W. (1988). Long-term efficacy of ungraded versus graded massed exposure in agoraphobics. In I. Hand & H. U. Wittchen (Eds.), *Panic and phobias 2: Treatments and variables affecting the course and outcome* (pp. 83–88). Berlin: Springer-Verlag.

Foa, E. B., Franklin, M. E., & Kozak, M. J. (1998). Psychosocial treatments of obsessive compulsive disorder. In R. Swinson, M. M. Antony, S. Rachman, & M. Richter (Eds.), *Obsessive-compulsive disorder: Theory, research, and treatment* (pp. 258–276). New York: Guilford.

Foa, E. B., & Goldstein, A. (1978). Continuous exposure and complete response prevention in the treatment of obsessive-compulsive neurosis. *Behavior Therapy, 9,* 821–829.

Foa, E. B., Rothbaum, B. O., Riggs, D. S., & Murdock, T. B. (1991). Treatment of posttraumatic stress disorder in rape victims: A comparison between cognitive-behavioral procedures and counseling. *Journal of Consulting and Clinical Psychology, 59,* 715–723.

Franklin, M. E., & Foa, E. B. (2002). Cognitive behavioral treatments for obsessive compulsive disorder. In P. E. Nathan & J. M. Gorman (Eds.), *A guide to treatments that work* (2nd ed., pp. 367–386). New York: Oxford University Press.

Gambrill, E. D. (1999). Evidence-based practice: An alternative to authority-based practice. *Families in Society, 80,* 341–350.

Gardenswartz, C. A., & Craske, M. G. (2001). Prevention of panic disorder. *Behavior Therapy, 32,* 725–737.

Gilroy, L. J., Kirkby, K. C., Daniels, B. A., Menzies, R. G., & Montgomery, I. M. (2003). Long-term follow-up of computer-aided vicarious exposure versus live graded exposure in the treatment of spider phobia. *Behavior Therapy, 34,* 65–76.

Goldapple, K., Segal, Z., Garson, C., Lau, M., Bieling, P., Kennedy, S., et al. (2004). Modulation of cortical-limbic pathways in major depression: Treatment-specific effects of cognitive behavior therapy. *Archives of General Psychiatry, 61,* 34–41.

Goldfried, M. R., & Davison, G. C. (1994). *Clinical behavior therapy* (Expanded ed.). New York: John Wiley.

Gossette, R. L., & O'Brien, R. M. (1992). The efficacy of rational-emotive therapy in adults: Clinical fact or psychometric artifact? *Journal of Behavior Therapy and Experimental Psychiatry, 23,* 9–24.

Graves, K. D., & Miller, P. M. (2003). Behavioral medicine in the prevention and treatment of cardiovascular disease. *Behavior Modification, 27,* 3–25.

Gruber, K., Moran, P. J., Roth, W. T., & Taylor, C. B. (2001). Computer-assisted cognitive behavioral therapy for social phobia. *Behavior Therapy, 32,* 155–165.

Guevremont, D. C., Osnes, P. G., & Stokes, T. F. (1988). The functional role of preschoolers' verbalizations in the generalization of self-instructional training. *Journal of Applied Behavior Analysis, 21,* 45–55.

Guevremont, D. C., Tishelman, A. C., & Hull, D. B. (1985). Teaching generalized self-control to attention-deficit boys with mothers as adjunct therapists. *Child and Family Behavior Therapy, 7,* 23–36.

Haaga, D. A. F., & Davison, G. C. (1993). An appraisal of rational-emotive therapy. *Journal of Consulting and Clinical Psychology, 61,* 215–220.

Hayes, S. C., & Gregg, J. (2001). Factors promoting and inhibiting the development and use of clinical practice guidelines. *Behavior Therapy, 32,* 211–217.

Hayes, S. C., Strosahl, K. D., & Wilson, K. G. (1999). *Acceptance and commitment therapy: An experiential approach to behavior change.* New York: Guilford.

Hays, P. A. (1995). Multicultural applications of cognitive-behavioral therapy. *Professional Psychology: Research and Practice, 26,* 309–315.

Heimberg, R. G., Salzman, D. G., Halt, C. S., & Blendell, K. A. (1993). Cognitive-behavioral group treatment for social phobia: Effectiveness at five-year followup. *Cognitive Therapy and Research, 17,* 325–339.

Himle, J. A., & Fischer, D. J. (1998). Panic disorder and agoraphobia. In B. A. Thyer & J. S. Wodarski (Eds.), *Handbook of empirical social work practice: Vol. 1. Mental disorders* (pp. 311–326). New York: John Wiley.

Hirschfeld, R. M., Keller, M. B., Panico, S., Arons, B. S., Barlow, D. H., Davidoff, F., et al., (1997). The National Depressive and Manic-Depressive Association consensus statement on the undertreatment of depression. *Journal of the American Medical Association, 277,* 333–340.

Hollon, S. D., & Shelton, R. C. (2001). Treatment guidelines for major depressive disorder. *Behavior Therapy, 32,* 235–258.

Hunter, S., Sundel, S. S., & Sundel, M. (2002). *Women at midlife: Life experiences and implications for the helping professions.* Washington, DC: National Association of Social Workers Press.

Iwamasa, G. Y., & Smith, S. K. (1996). Ethnic diversity in behavioral psychology: A review of the literature. *Behavior Modification, 20,* 45–59.

Jacobson, E. (1938). *Progressive relaxation.* Chicago: University of Chicago Press.

Jacobson, N. S., Dobson, K. S., Fruzetti, A. E., Schmaling, K. B., & Salusky, S. (1991). Marital therapy as a treatment for depression. *Journal of Consulting and Clinical Psychology, 59,* 547–557.

Jarrett, R. B., Schaffer, M., McIntire, D., Witt-Browden, A., Kraft, D., & Risser, R. C. (1999). Treatment of atypical depression with cognitive therapy or phemelzine: A double-blind placebo-controlled trial. *Archives of General Psychiatry, 56,* 431–437.

Kavanagh, D. J., & Mueser, K. T. (2001). The future of cognitive and behavioral therapies in the prevention and early management of psychosis: Opportunities and risks. *Behavior Therapy, 32,* 693–724.

Kazdin, A. E., & Mascitelli, S. (1982). The opportunity to earn oneself off a token system as a reinforcer for attentive behavior. *Behavior Therapy, 11,* 68–78.

Kazdin, A. E., & Weisz, J. R. (Eds.). (2003). *Evidence-based psychotherapies for children and adolescents.* New York: Guilford.

Kearney, C. A. (2001). Introduction [Special series: A futuristic look at behavior therapy for persons with developmental disabilities]. *Behavior Therapy, 32,* 617–618.

Keefe, F. J., Dunsmore, J., & Burnett, R. (1992). Behavioral and cognitive-behavioral approaches to chronic pain: Recent advances and future directions. *Journal of Consulting and Clinical Psychology, 60,* 528–536.

Kendall, P. C. (1994). Treating anxiety disorders in children: Results of a randomized clinical trial. *Journal of Consulting and Clinical Psychology, 62,* 100–110.

Kendall, P. C., Haaga, D. A. F., Ellis, A., Bernard, M., DiGiuseppe, R., & Kassinove, H. (1995). Rational-emotive therapy in the 1990s and beyond: Current status, recent revisions, and research questions. *Clinical Psychology Review, 15,* 169–185.

King, N. J., & Ollendick, T. H. (1997). Treatment of childhood phobias. *Journal of Child Psychology and Psychiatry and Allied Disciplines, 38,* 389–400.

Klerman, G. L., Weissman, M. M., Rounsaville, J. J., & Chevron, E. S. (1984). *Interpersonal psychotherapy of depression.* New York: Basic Books.

Koch, E. I., Spates, R., & Himle, J. A. (in press). Comparison of behavioral and cognitive-behavioral one-session exposure treatments for small animal phobias. *Behaviour Research and Therapy.*

Kopelowicz, A., Liberman, R. P., & Zarate, R. (2002). Psychosocial treatments for schizophrenia. In P. E. Nathan & J. M. Gorman (Eds.), *A guide to treatments that work* (2nd ed., pp. 201–228). New York: Oxford University Press.

Lerner, J., Franklin, M. E., Meadows, E. A., Hembree, E., & Foa, E. B. (1998). Effectiveness of a cognitive-behavioral treatment program for trichotillomania: An uncontrolled evaluation. *Behavior Therapy, 29,* 57–171.

Lilienfeld, S. O., Lynn, S. J., & Lohr, J. M. (Eds.). (2003). *Science and pseudoscience in clinical psychology.* New York: Guilford.

Linehan, M. M. (1993). *Cognitive-behavioral treatment of borderline personality disorder.* New York: Guilford.

Lohr, J. M., Meuier, S. A., & Parker, L. M. (2001). Neurotherapy does not qualify as an empirically supported behavioral treatment for psychological disorders. *the Behavior Therapist, 24,* 97–104.

Maag, J. W., & Kotlash, J. (1994). Review of stress inoculation training with children and adolescents: Issues and recommendations. *Behavior Modification, 18,* 443–469.

Maletzky, B. M. (1980). Self-referred versus court-referred sexually deviant patients: Success with assisted covert sensitization. *Behavior Therapy, 11,* 302–314.

Maletzky, B. M. (2002). The paraphilias: Research and treatment. In P. E. Nathan & J. M. Gorman (Eds.), *A guide to treatments that work* (2nd ed., pp. 525–558). New York: Oxford University Press.

Manhal-Baugus, M. (2001). E-therapy: Practical, ethical, and legal issues. *CyberPsychology and Behavior, 4,* 551–563.

McCrady, B. S. (2001). Introduction [Special series: Behavior therapy perspectives on the American Psychiatric Association practice guidelines]. *Behavior Therapy, 32,* 209–210.

McCrady, B. S., & Ziedonis, D. (2001). American Psychiatric Association practice guidelines for substance use disorders. *Behavior Therapy, 32,* 309–336.

McGlynn, F. D., Smitherman, T. A., & Gothard, K. D. (2004). Comment on the status of systematic desensitization. *Behavior Modification, 28,* 194–205.

Meichenbaum, D. H. (1977). *Cognitive behavior modification: An integrative approach.* New York: Plenum.

Meichenbaum, D. H. (1985). *Stress inoculation training.* New York: Pergamon.

Miller, W. R., Brown, J. M., Simpson, T. L., Handmaker, N. S., Bien, T. H., Luckie, L. F., et al. (1995). What works? A methodological analysis of the alcohol treatment outcome literature. In R. K. Hester & W. R. Miller (Eds.), *Handbook of alcoholism treatment approaches* (2nd ed., pp. 12–44). Boston: Allyn & Bacon.

Nathan, P. E., & Gorman, J. M. (2002a). Efficacy, effectiveness, and the clinical utility of psychotherapy research. In P. E. Nathan & J. M. Gorman (Eds.), *A guide to treatments that work* (2nd ed., pp. 643–654). New York: Oxford University Press.

Nathan, P. E., & Gorman, J. M. (Eds.). (2002b). *A guide to treatments that work* (2nd ed.). New York: Oxford University Press.

Nauta, H., Hospers, H., Kok, G., & Jansen, A. (2000). A comparison between a cognitive and a behavioral treatment for obese binge eaters and obese non–binge eaters. *Behavior Therapy, 31,* 441–462.

Novaco, R. W. (1975). *Anger control: The development and evaluation of an experimental treatment.* Lexington, MA: D. C. Heath.

O'Leary, K. D., & Beach, S. R. H. (1990). Marital therapy: A viable treatment for depression and marital discord. *American Journal of Psychiatry, 147,* 183–186.

Paykel, E. S., Scott, J., Teasdale, J. D., Johnson, A. L., Garland, A., Moore, R., et al. (1999). Prevention of relapse in residual depression by cognitive therapy. *Archives of General Psychiatry, 56,* 829–835.

Plaud, J. L., & Vavrovsky, K. G. (1998). Specific and social phobias. In B. A. Thyer & J. S. Wodarski (Eds.), *Handbook of empirical social work practice: Vol. 1. Mental disorders* (pp. 327–341). New York: John Wiley.

Purcell, D. W., Campos, P. E., & Perilla, J. L. (1996). Therapy with lesbians and gay men: A cognitive behavioral perspective. *Cognitive and Behavioral Practice, 3,* 391–415.

Rachman, S. J., Craske, M. G., & Tallmark, K. (1986). Does escape behavior strengthen agoraphobic avoidance? A replication. *Behavior Therapy, 17,* 366–384.

Rimmele, C. T., Howard, M. O., & Hilfrink, M. L. (1995). Aversion therapies. In R. K. Hester & W. R. Miller (Eds.), *Handbook of alcoholism treatment approaches* (2nd ed., pp. 134–147). Boston: Allyn & Bacon.

Roberts, R. M., Nelson, R. O., & Olson, T. W. (1987). Self-instruction: An analysis of the differential effects of instruction and reinforcement. *Journal of Applied Behavior Analysis, 20,* 235–242.

Rosen, A., & Proctor, E. (Eds.). (2003). *Developing practice guidelines for social work interventions: Issues, methods, and research agenda.* New York: Columbia University Press.

Ross, M. J., & Berger, R. S. (1996). Effects of stress inoculation training on athletes' postsurgical pain and rehabilitation after orthopedic injury. *Journal of Consulting and Clinical Psychology, 64,* 406–410.

Saigh, P. A., Yule, W., & Inamdar, S. C. (1996). Imaginal flooding of traumatized children and adolescents. *Journal of School Psychology, 34,* 163–183.

Shapiro, F. (1989). Efficacy of the eye movement desensitization procedure in the treatment of traumatic memories. *Journal of Traumatic Stress, 2,* 199–223.

Shapiro, F. (2001). *Eye movement desensitization and reprocessing EMDR: Basic principles, protocols, and procedures* (2nd ed.). New York: Guilford.

Smith, J. W., & Frawley, P. J. (1993). Treatment outcome of 600 chemically dependent patients treated in a multimodal inpatient program including aversion therapy and Pentothal interviews. *Journal of Substance Abuse Treatment, 10,* 359–369.

Stanley, M. A., Diefenbach, G. J., & Hopko, D. R. (2004). Cognitive behavioral treatment for older adults with generalized anxiety disorders: A therapist manual for primary care settings. *Behavior Modification, 28,* 73–117.

Stanley, M. A., & Turner, S. M. (1995). Current status of pharmacological and behavioral treatment of obsessive-compulsive disorder. *Behavior Therapy, 26,* 163–186.

Steketee, G. (1993). *Treatment of obsessive compulsive disorder.* New York: Guilford.

Sweet, A. A., & Loizeaux, A. L. (1991). Behavioral and cognitive treatment methods: A critical comparative review. *Journal of Behavior Therapy and Experimental Psychiatry, 22,* 159–185.

Task Force on Promotion and Dissemination of Psychological Procedures. (1995). Training in and dissemination of empirically validated psychological treatments: Report and recommendations. *The Clinical Psychologist, 48,* 3–23.

Thase, M. E., Reynolds, C. F., Frank, E., Simons, A. D., Garamoni, G. D., McGeary, J., et al. (1994). Response to cognitive-behavioral therapy in chronic depression. *Journal of Psychotherapy Practice and Research, 3,* 204–214.

Thyer, B. A. (1998). Promoting research on community practice: Using single system designs. In R. H. MacNair (Ed.), *Research strategies for community practice* (pp. 47–61). Binghamton, NY: Haworth.

Thyer, B. A. (2001). Evidence-based approaches to community practice. In H. E. Briggs & K. Corcoran (Eds.), *Social work practice: Treating common client problems* (pp. 54–65). Chicago: Lyceum.

Thyer, B. A. (2003). Empirically based interventions. In R. English (Ed.), *Encyclopedia of social work* (19th ed., suppl., pp. 21–29). Washington, DC: National Association of Social Workers Press.

Timmons, P. L., Oehlert, M. E., Sumerall, S. W., & Timmons, C. W. (1997). Stress inoculation training for maladaptive anger: Comparison of group counseling versus computer guidance. *Computers in Human Behavior, 13,* 51–64.

Tkachuk, G. A., & Martin, G. L. (1999). Exercise therapy for psychiatric disorders: Research and clinical implications. *Professional Psychology: Research and Practice, 30,* 275–282.

Trull, T. J., Nietzel, M. T., & Main, A. (1988). The use of meta-analysis to assess the clinical significance of behavior therapy for agoraphobia. *Behavior Therapy, 19,* 527–538.

Turner, S. M., Beidel, D. C., & Jacob, R. G. (1994). Social phobia: A comparison of behavior therapy and atenolol. *Journal of Consulting and Clinical Psychology, 62,* 350–358.

Wilson, G. T., & Fairburn, C. G. (2002). Treatments for eating disorders. In P. E. Nathan & J. M. Gorman (Eds.), *A guide to treatments that work* (2nd ed., pp. 559–592). New York: Oxford University Press.

Wolpe, J. (1958). *Psychotherapy by reciprocal inhibition.* Stanford, CA: Stanford University Press.

Wolpe, J. (1990). *The practice of behavior therapy* (4th ed.). Elmsford, NY: Pergamon.

Wolpe, J. (1995). Reciprocal inhibition: Major agent of behavior change. In W. O'Donohue & L. Krasner (Eds.), *Theories of behavior therapy: Exploring behavior change* (pp. 23–58). Washington, DC: American Psychological Association.

Wolpe, J., & Lazarus, A. A. (1966). *Behavior therapy techniques: A guide to the treatment of neuroses.* Elmsford, NY: Pergamon.

Woods, D. W. (2002). Introduction to the special issue on repetitive behavior problems. *Behavior Modification, 26,* 315–319.

Woods, D. W., & Miltenberger, R. G. (Eds.). (2001). *Tic disorders, trichotillomania, and other repetitive behavior disorders: Behavioral approaches to analysis and treatment.* Boston: Kluwer Academic.

Appendix 1

Case Examples

Robert is a 13-year-old junior high school student who started drinking beer 6 months ago at a party given by one of his friends. He liked the feeling of acceptance from the older kids at the party and continued his experimentation with other drugs, including crack cocaine. During the past 2 months, Robert has turned in incomplete class assignments, sometimes handing in blank sheets of paper. His midterm report card showed four Fs and one C in an art course. Robert's parents were concerned that he would drop out of school or not pass to the next level. Last week, his mother found crack and some of her diet pills in Robert's desk drawer. When confronted with this evidence, Robert admitted to taking drugs but argued that his drug use did not interfere with his functioning in school or at home.

Shortly after the midterm grades came out, a teacher referred Robert to the school social worker, describing him as "inattentive in the classroom, poorly motivated, and having low self-esteem." He was failing most of his classes.

Robert complained to the school social worker that his parents frequently grounded him, nagged him, withheld his allowance, and denied him privileges such as watching television and going out with his friends. Upon further questioning, Robert said that his parents disciplined him because of his poor grades. Robert admitted that he might flunk out of school but denied that his drug taking was interfering with his studying. When the social worker asked him to describe his use of drugs and alcohol, Robert stated that he drank beer every weekend with his friends and smoked crack once a month. Robert said that when he started studying, his friends often invited him over to listen to music and drink beer and that this happened about three times a week. He also spent an average of three evenings per week at his girlfriend's home, and they usually began these evenings by drinking beer or wine. When he was home alone, Robert typically looked in his notebook for class assignments, took a drink or two before beginning them, and completed only parts of his assignments or none of them at all. The baseline rate of Robert's drug use, including alcohol, was 7 days per week. The baseline rate of Robert's drinking before beginning homework assignments was 4 days per week.

Case Example 2:
Developing Appropriate Conversation

Bella and Cliff were older adults with memory impairment in a group conducted at a senior center. In social situations, they often asked questions and made comments that were unrelated to the topic being discussed. For example, when several group members were discussing a recent film, Cliff asked the person speaking if he was going grocery shopping that afternoon. The baseline rate of Bella's speaking on topic was zero. In addition, Bella and Cliff were frequently observed talking continuously for 5 minutes or more without pausing for responses from others. These speech patterns resulted in their being ridiculed and excluded from conversations held by other group members.

The social worker devised a conversational exercise for the six members of a group in which Bella and Cliff participated. The social worker began the exercise by making a statement and then asking each of the group members to add a statement to her introduction. Each new statement was required to bear logical connection to the preceding statement. For example, the social worker began speaking about how to cook dinner for oneself. At first, Bella and Cliff both added inappropriate statements, such as "You should see my grandson. He is so smart," or "You know, when I was selling cars in New York I always was the top salesman of the month." On these occasions, they were stopped by the social worker or group members, who asked them to make appropriate statements and complimented or praised them for doing so. Group members prompted Bella and Cliff, offering hints and suggestions for correct statements.

As they practiced this exercise on subsequent occasions, both Bella and Cliff made fewer inappropriate remarks and increasingly more appropriate ones. The rate of Bella's speaking on topic increased to five times per group meeting after six group sessions. The frequency of Bella's and Cliff's appropriate remarks during conversations outside the group was also observed to increase. Staff members and relatives reinforced Bella's and Cliff's appropriate speech.

Case Example 3: Decreasing Tantrum Behaviors

In a parent training group, Carla's mother, Juanita, told the social worker that almost every time she told 5-year-old Carla to put her toys away, Carla screamed. The baseline duration of Carla's screaming averaged 5.5 minutes per episode. Juanita would attempt to placate Carla by promising to buy her new clothes and by putting the toys away herself.

The social worker suspected that Juanita was positively reinforcing Carla's screaming by putting the toys away and promising to buy Carla new clothes. She showed Juanita how to use extinction to decrease Carla's screaming. The procedure involved withholding the positive reinforcers for Carla's screaming.

The social worker instructed Juanita to stop making promises, stop putting away the toys, and walk away from Carla when she screamed about putting away her toys. She told Juanita that Carla's screaming might get worse before it got better but that if she held firm, Carla's screaming would gradually decrease. Juanita carried out these instructions and the duration of Carla's screaming gradually decreased, after an increase on the second day of extinction. By the sixth day of the extinction intervention, Carla no longer screamed when told to put her toys away.

The social worker also instructed Juanita to praise Carla and give her tangible reinforcers, such as gum or cookies, when she put her toys away. Juanita followed these instructions, and Carla began putting her toys away more frequently.

Case Example 4: Conditioning Verbal Behavior

Leon is a 59-year-old man who has been a patient in a state psychiatric hospital for 21 years. Hospital staff describe him as mute and withdrawn. Leon spends much of the day sitting in a chair looking at the floor or pacing up and down the halls of the unit. He remains silent when spoken to and does not initiate conversation with other patients or with staff.

In Leon's treatment, he was placed in a room and a slide projector was used to show him images of animals, people, and landscapes. The psychologist asked Leon to talk about the pictures each time a green light appeared on a panel. When the green light was off, the psychologist spoke about the pictures and Leon was instructed to look at them silently. When the green light was turned on, Leon was instructed to speak. When Leon made any speech sound, he was given a piece of candy. In addition, the psychologist said "Good" immediately after each sound Leon made. An automatic recorder counted each second of speech as one response.

Leon made no speech sounds during the initial treatment session, 5 responses in the second session, and 48 responses in the fifth session. During the tenth treatment session, Leon said 76 words, including "boy and girl," "cat," and "house and yard." During the next five sessions, the psychologist asked Leon specific questions about the content of the pictures and gave him cues and prompts that facilitated correct responding. In the fifteenth session, Leon appropriately described a slide as follows: "A boy and girl are playing on the swing." After 15 sessions, unit staff reported that for the first time in many years Leon had spoken to several persons and had made short replies to comments directed to him by staff.

Case Example 5: Stimulus Control of Marital Interaction

Pat consulted a marriage counselor about her marital difficulties. Her husband, Dick, refused to see the counselor with her. Pat complained that Dick spent his evenings in front of the television, ignoring her and their children. They rarely went to the movies or to other entertainment, and Pat did all the food shopping by herself. She had stopped making Dick's breakfast as a result of their frequent arguments before he left for work.

Pat screamed at Dick for going out with his friends, for refusing to help around the house, and for spending little time with her and their children. Dick responded to her criticism by swearing at her and telling her to mind her own business. Pat became so upset during these arguments that she burst into tears, ran into the bedroom, and locked the door, remaining there until Dick left the house. The baseline rate of these episodes was three times per week.

In her interviews with Pat, the marriage counselor determined that Pat and Dick rarely discussed topics of mutual interest; Pat stated that pleasant conversations occurred about once per week. Their conversations revolved around Pat's complaints and Dick's responses to them. Pat said that she loved her husband and would like to have more satisfying conversations with him. She also wanted their arguments to stop and for him to participate in more activities with her and their children.

In her assessment, the marriage counselor determined that Dick refused to participate in treatment. The counselor pointed out to Pat that the goal of treatment with Pat alone participating could not directly focus on changing Dick's behaviors. Treatment could focus, however, on changing Pat's behaviors to influence Dick's undesired behaviors.

To change the focus of the couple's interactions from complaints and arguments to more pleasant conversation, the counselor instructed Pat to make a list of topics to discuss with Dick (List A). These topics included his work, their two children, and camping. Pat made a second list of topics to be avoided (List B), which included complaints about Dick's staying out late at night, watching television at his friends' homes, not taking Pat shopping or to the movies, and not spending time with his family. The counselor also instructed Pat to greet Dick with a kiss when he came home from work and to ask how his day had gone. This strategy was designed to allow Pat to take the initiative in changing her behavior, with the understanding that the intervention plan could produce the results she wanted in her marriage.

To help Pat focus on topics from List A and reduce the frequency of her talking about topics from List B, role plays were performed in the counselor's office. The counselor told Pat that this procedure would include reinforcement for talking about topics on List A and extinction for talking about topics on List B so that Pat would be more likely to talk with Dick about topics on List A.

In the role plays, when Pat talked about topics from List A, the counselor praised her and engaged in conversation with her. When Pat talked about topics from List B, the counselor looked away and was silent (withheld reinforcement). Pat began talking about topics on List A more frequently, and her talking about topics on List B decreased in frequency. Pat was then assigned to perform the desired behaviors at home with Dick.

Pat began talking about topics on List A at home with Dick and avoided talking about topics on List B. She found that their conversations were more pleasant and that Dick started paying more attention to her. Gradually, Pat suggested activities to Dick that they could do together or with the children, such as go to a movie or out to dinner, and Dick usually agreed. As their time together became more pleasant, Pat reported that their unpleasant arguments decreased, Dick was helping out with shopping and other household tasks, and he was spending more time with her and their children.

Case Example 6: Treating Depression and Anxiety in a Group

At a group therapy meeting, Bill complained of frequent "anxiety and depression." He had recently been laid off from his job, was bored, and had no outside interests. He spent most of his time sleeping, eating, or watching television.

When the therapist asked Bill to specify the behavioral components of his anxiety and depression, he replied that he felt "anxious" in situations in which he was criticized by his employer. He often felt "depressed" after these encounters. In role plays of these situations, Bill perspired heavily, his face turned red, his breathing became rapid, and he rapped his knuckles against each other. His hands trembled, and he made excuses as he replied to the criticism.

To assess Bill's behavior patterns, other members of the group role-played situations in which Bill's employer criticized him. They also conducted role plays to allow Bill to observe someone else demonstrating his problematic behaviors and their effects on others.

To model appropriate responses to correction, several group members played the part of Bill in role plays and responded appropriately to criticism. Afterward, Bill played himself in role plays of the situations in which he was criticized. When Bill had difficulty imitating the modeled behaviors, the therapist prompted him until he performed the behaviors appropriately. Bill practiced responding appropriately in role plays and received praise from the therapist and group members as soon as he demonstrated appropriate behaviors. He was then given assignments to perform the practiced behaviors at home. He also learned relaxation exercises to practice at home.

Similar procedures were used to help Bill prepare for an interview for a new job. Shortly afterward, he completed a successful job interview and was hired as a bus driver.

To deal with Bill's boredom, the group assigned him to pursue an outside interest or hobby. Bill decided to reestablish his interest in bowling, an activity he had enjoyed in previous years. The therapist instructed Bill to go to a bowling alley, to observe people bowling, and to discuss his experience with two persons. Shortly after Bill had completed this assignment, he and his wife joined a bowling league.

Case Example 7: The Parent as a Behavior Modifier

Edward, a single father, complained to a therapist at a counseling center that he found it impossible to discipline Stephen, his 10-year-old son. Stephen frequently hit his younger sister, Dianne, making her cry and inflicting bruises. He sometimes broke her toys during these incidents. When Edward intervened to stop Stephen from hitting Dianne, Stephen cursed and kicked him. Verbal reprimands, threats, and lectures failed to stop Stephen's undesired behaviors.

The therapist instructed Edward to obtain a baseline of Stephen's hitting and to identify situations in which the hitting occurred. Edward observed his children's behavior for a week and reported to the therapist that Stephen's hitting occurred 12 times during the week and that Dianne teased or made faces at Stephen on 9 of those occasions prior to his hitting her. Edward also indicated that he spent much of his time in the evenings trying to discipline Stephen.

The therapist instructed Edward to tell Dianne to stop teasing and making faces at Stephen, with the contingency that if she teased or made faces she would lose privileges, such as watching television or having a bedtime snack. On two subsequent occasions, Dianne lost television privileges and a bedtime snack. After these two experiences, Dianne stopped teasing and making faces at Stephen.

The therapist also instructed Edward to tell Stephen to go to the laundry room whenever he hit Dianne. If he refused to obey, Edward would physically carry or move Stephen to the laundry room, where he was required to remain by himself for 10 minutes. If he kicked or cursed Edward, the time-out was extended 5 minutes. If he screamed or made loud noises while in the room, the time-out was also extended 5 minutes.

The first time Edward took Stephen to the laundry room, he kicked and cursed. He also screamed while in the room. Stephen remained in the laundry room for a total of 20 minutes—the 10-minute time-out period plus two 5-minute extensions. This also happened the second time. The third time Edward instituted the treatment procedure, Stephen walked with Edward to the laundry room without cursing or kicking. The fourth time the procedure was applied, Stephen went to the laundry room by himself and quietly remained there until his time was up. After the fifth time the procedure was employed, Stephen stopped hitting his sister.

The therapist also instructed Edward to spend leisure time with Stephen in the evenings. Because Stephen liked to play cards with his father, the therapist told Edward to play cards with Stephen each evening after he finished his homework.

Case Example 8: Developing Social Skills

Bruce is a 30-year-old single man who complained about "stress and anxiety." He said that he was exploited at work and also was unable to establish and maintain satisfying relationships with women. He stated that women find his company unpleasant, and he never knows what to say in their presence. Of the last four women Bruce has taken out, all have refused a second date. He has one male friend with whom he plays tennis each week.

Bruce is a bookkeeper for an insurance company, where he has worked for the past 9 years. Although he was promised a promotion and raise 2 years ago, he still earns the same salary in the same position as when he started working for the company.

Bruce has never discussed his feelings about being treated unfairly with his boss, although other employees in similar circumstances have benefited from doing so.

The practitioner asked Bruce to describe what happened the last time he went out with a woman. Bruce said that he and the woman were having coffee in a restaurant after seeing a movie, and he could not think of anything interesting to say to her. Bruce concluded that he just "bored her to death" talking about his work. When the therapist asked Bruce to describe the woman's part of the conversation, Bruce said that he could not remember much about what she said because he was so concerned about making a good impression. On one occasion, Bruce said a woman he took out fell asleep while he was trying to explain a complicated book-keeping procedure. The therapist observed that Bruce kept his head down during the interview and often held his hand in front of his mouth when speaking so that his speech was difficult to understand. He sometimes drifted from one topic to another without waiting for the therapist to respond to what he had said, and he frequently spoke in a monotone.

The practitioner asked Bruce to describe his most recent conversation with his boss. Bruce related that he was seated in his boss's office, across the desk from his boss, and his boss asked him what he wanted. Bruce mumbled, looked down at the floor, and began to talk about his financial problems. When the boss responded by asking Bruce why he could not manage his finances properly, Bruce stammered and tried to defend his way of managing money. He reported to the practitioner that he felt very anxious. Finally, Bruce mumbled, "I'm sorry," and walked out of the boss's office without raising the issues of promotion and salary increase.

On further questioning, Bruce indicated that he often found himself being taken advantage of in situations in which he should have stated his opinions or defended his rights. Bruce said that he hoped to improve this situation through therapy and would cooperate with the therapist's recommendations. The therapist gave Bruce an assignment to record RAC-S data about the situations in which he felt exploited and to rate his anxiety on a subjective units of discomfort scale (SUDS) ranging from 0 to 100.

Appendix 2

Chapter Pretest Questions

Chapter 1: Specifying Behavior

(2) 1. State two essential criteria for specifying a response.

(6) 2. A. Indicate with a plus sign (+) which of the following statements are written in behaviorally specific terms, and indicate with a minus sign (−) the statements that are vague and require further specification.
   B. After completing question 2A, rewrite in specific terms only those statements in which the responses are not described behaviorally.
   a. Ted saw three clients today and made four phone calls.
   b. Bob is becoming a drug addict.
   c. Bruce kissed Sally on the cheek.
   d. She acted out her anger toward him.

(1) 3. Name the most commonly used measure of response strength.

Chapter 2: Positive Reinforcement

(1) 1. To maximize the effectiveness of a positive reinforcer for a response, when should the positive reinforcer be delivered?

(3) 2. Give one example of a conditioned positive reinforcer and one example of an unconditioned positive reinforcer. How do you know that each is a positive reinforcer and not a reward?

(1) 3. It has been demonstrated that presentation of a certain event following a behavior can increase the likelihood that the behavior will recur. What is the name of the behavioral principle to which this statement refers?

(3) 4. In the example that begins this chapter, what behavior does the social worker positively reinforce? What are the reinforcers?

Chapter 3: Extinction

(4) 1. Renumber the following steps to show the correct order for determining whether a specific stimulus served as a positive reinforcer for a target behavior:

_____ 1. Withhold the stimulus each time the target response occurs.

_____ 2. Determine the strength of the target behavior.

_____ 3. Observe a decrease in strength of the target behavior.

_____ 4. Present stimulus after the target behavior occurs and observe an increase in its strength.

(2) 2. What are two practical difficulties that you might encounter in applying an extinction procedure to decrease the strength of an undesired response?

(1) 3. What is spontaneous recovery?

(2) 4. Describe the extinction procedure and its effect.

Chapter 4: Positive Reinforcement Contingencies

(4) 1. Which of the following are statements of positive reinforcement contingencies? (Circle the correct ones.)

A. Finish your math assignment, and you may play outside.

B. If you wash the dishes, I'll give you an ice cream cone.

C. If you fight with your brother, you will get a spanking.

D. He completed his chores in 3 hours.

(1) 2. Briefly describe how superstitious behavior is acquired.

(1) 3. Intermittent reinforcement makes a well-learned response more resistant to extinction. (Circle one.)

A. True

B. False

(1) 4. When is it more appropriate to use continuous reinforcement than to use intermittent reinforcement?

(6) 5. Match the following schedules in Column A with their examples in Column B.

A		B
1. Fixed ratio _____		A. Deadlines
2. Variable ratio _____		B. Braking at a stop sign
3. Fixed interval _____		C. Slot machines
4. Variable interval _____		D. Piecework
5. Fixed duration _____		E. Watching a movie
6. Variable duration _____		F. Waiting for a taxi

Chapter 5: Shaping and Response Differentiation

(1) 1. In Case Example 4 (p. 269), the psychologist could help develop Leon's speech by using which of the following techniques? (Circle one.)
   A. Extinction
   B. Intermittent reinforcement
   C. Shaping with successive approximations
   D. Differential reinforcement of approximation of incompatible responses

(1) 2. To shape a new behavior, you would not use differential reinforcement. (Circle one.)
   A. True
   B. False

(2) 3. For the response class "talking about sports," name two responses.

(2) 4. How are positive reinforcement and extinction involved in differential reinforcement?

(2) 5. Give an example of a DRO procedure that could be used to decrease Carla's screaming in Case Example 3 (p. 268).

Chapter 6: Stimulus Control

(2) 1. What is an S^D for a response? What is an S^Δ?

(1) 2. What is the effect of a discrimination training procedure involving two discriminative stimuli (S^D and S^Δ) and one response?

(1) 3. In Case Example 4 (p. 269), what function did the green light serve?

(6) 4. In the following examples, identify the discriminative stimulus, the response, and the reinforcer by labeling the S^D, R, and S^{r+} in the diagrams.
   A. Bob sees Joe walking down the street. Bob says, "Hello," and Joe says, "Good morning."

   S^D
   R —————————————————————————→ S^{r+}

   B. Shirley hears the ice cream truck and asks her aunt for a dollar; her aunt gives her the dollar.

   S^D
   R —————————————————————————→ S^{r+}

(1) 5. When a response is reinforced in the presence of one S^D, it will not occur in the presence of other similar stimuli. (Circle one.)
   A. True
   B. False

Chapter 7: Conditioned Reinforcement and Chaining

(2) 1. Which is usually more effective, a simple conditioned reinforcer or a generalized conditioned reinforcer? Support your answer.

(1) 2. What is the difference between an unconditioned reinforcer and a conditioned reinforcer?

(4) 3. Give two examples of generalized conditioned reinforcers and two examples of unconditioned reinforcers.

(1) 4. For a neutral stimulus to function as a conditioned reinforcer, a minimum of 100 pairings is necessary. (Circle one.)
   A. True
   B. False

(3) 5. Identify the components of one unit of a stimulus-response chain.

Chapter 8: Modeling and Imitation

(3) 1. Describe how a modeling plus reinforcement procedure can be used to develop a child's imitation of an adult using a fork correctly.

(3) 2. For each of the following statements, indicate true (T) or false (F):
   A. _____ If an individual does not perform a response after observing someone perform it, the individual has not learned it.
   B. _____ Filmed models are less effective than live models.
   C. _____ Imitative behavior cannot be conditioned through reinforcement.

(3) 3. Using the information in Case Example 6 (p. 271), how could modeling and reinforcement be used to help Bill obtain a new job?

Chapter 9: Punishment

(2) 1. Name the two types of punishment procedures that can be used to suppress a response.

(1) 2. Briefly describe a time-out procedure.

(2) 3. Briefly describe two disadvantages of punishment procedures.

(4) 4. As Mrs. Kelly went out, she asked her daughter Sharon to fold the laundry after it had been washed and dried. When Mrs. Kelly returned, Sharon was talking to a friend on the phone and the laundry had not been folded. What should Mrs. Kelly do in regard to Sharon's behavior to demonstrate her

knowledge of the necessary conditions to maximize the effectiveness of punishment?

Chapter 10: Negative Reinforcement

(1) 1. What is a major advantage of avoidance conditioning in maintaining a response?

(3) 2. Give an example of the behavioral procedure that produces escape behavior and draw a behavioral diagram to illustrate your example.

(4) 3. Give an example of the behavioral procedure that results in avoidance behavior and draw a behavioral diagram to illustrate your example.

(2) 4. Give an example of (a) an unconditioned aversive stimulus that could be used as a negative reinforcer and (b) a conditioned aversive stimulus that could be used as a negative reinforcer.

Chapter 11: Respondent Conditioning

(1) 1. Describe a procedure for extinguishing a classically conditioned response.

(8) 2. Given the following information, specify operant and respondent behaviors: A man gets in his car and drives home. As he walks through his front door, the aroma of dinner cooking makes his mouth water. He runs to the kitchen, and when he arrives there, panting, he kisses his wife and sits down at the table.

(1) 3. Explain the persistence of emotional respondent behavior in the absence of identifiable reinforcing consequences for the individual.

(2) 4. What are the two measures of response strength for a classically conditioned response?

Chapter 12: Generalization and Maintenance of Behavior Change

(2) 1. You are treating an alcohol-abusing client. As part of the treatment program to decrease his drinking, you suggest several nondrinking behaviors that would be appropriate in the social situations in which he usually drinks. These behaviors are new to him, but he agrees to try them.
A. What is the most likely obstacle to success for this part of therapy?
B. What can you do to counteract this effect or to plan for this problem?

(1) 2. Using the information in Case Example 6 (p. 271), describe how Bill's therapist and group used behavioral rehearsal with Bill to facilitate generalization of appropriate responses to correction.

(1) 3. Behavioral assignments are given for which of the following reasons? (Circle the correct answer[s].)
  A. To structure the client's activities between therapy sessions
  B. To help the client apply in his or her natural environment what he or she has learned in treatment
  C. To provide feedback to the client from the therapist based on a specific behavior the client has attempted to perform
  D. All of the above

(1) 4. It is usually more difficult for a desired behavior to generalize beyond the practice setting when more than one therapist is involved in developing the behavior. (Circle one.)
  A. True
  B. False

(3) 5. Turn to Case Example 4 (p. 269). State three ways in which you could maximize successful generalization of Leon's speech.

Chapter 13: Behavioral Assessment

(2) 1. Rewrite the following sentences so that the strength of the response is stated in measurable terms.
  A. Hortense has repeatedly phoned the adoption agency.
  B. Roger rarely kisses his wife.

(2) 2. In Case Example 2 (p. 268), what were the behavioral excesses shown by Bella and Cliff?

(2) 3. What were the negative consequences of Bella and Cliff's behavioral excesses?

(3) 4. From the information given in the following paragraph, identify Henry's target responses, the antecedent, and the negative consequences.

> When someone comes over to talk to Henry or ask him a question, he mutters and speaks in a low voice so that the person has difficulty hearing what he is saying. Typically, individuals who approach Henry stop talking and walk away from him soon after he begins to mutter.

(2) 5. What are two questions that a practitioner should ask about a client's problems in establishing priorities for treatment?

(2) 6. How is behavioral reenactment used in behavioral assessment?

Chapter 14: Goal Setting, Intervention Planning, and Evaluation

(1) 1. What does the term *informed consent* refer to in the context of a behavioral change program?

(1) 2. An intervention plan for teaching an individual with mental retardation self-care skills could include which of the following? (Circle one.)
   A. Covert sensitization and modeling
   B. Positive reinforcement and systematic desensitization
   C. Positive reinforcement, shaping, and chaining
   D. None of the above

(3) 3. State three ways of evaluating a client's progress.

(2) 4. What is the purpose of a treatment contract?

Chapter 15: Intervention Techniques

(1) 1. Which of the following intervention techniques is *not* used to decrease anxiety? (Circle one.)
   A. Systematic desensitization
   B. Flooding
   C. Covert sensitization
   D. In vivo desensitization

(1) 2. Covert sensitization is most appropriate for which of the following purposes? (Circle one.)
   A. To decrease anxiety to a feared stimulus
   B. To treat adolescent panic disorder
   C. To develop alternative behaviors to overeating
   D. To treat the negative effects of depression

(1) 3. Cognitive restructuring is used for which of the following purposes? (Circle one.)
   A. To extinguish delinquent behavior among high school dropouts
   B. To substitute effective covert behaviors for self-defeating cognitions
   C. To shape successive approximations to nondrinking behaviors
   D. To reinforce the performance of desired overt behaviors

(1) 4. Give two examples of problem behaviors that can be treated with thought stopping.

(1) 5. Panic control treatment includes breathing retraining, cognitive therapy, and exposure to physiological components of panic. (Circle one.)
   A. True
   B. False

Appendix 3

Chapter Pretest Answers

Chapter 1: Specifying Behavior

(2) 1. State two essential criteria for specifying a response.

Answers:

A. The response is stated in positive terms.
B. The response is specified in terms of observable or measurable actions.

(6) 2. A. Indicate with a plus sign (+) which of the following statements are written in behaviorally specific terms, and indicate with a minus sign (−) statements that are vague and require further specification.

B. After completing question 2A, rewrite in specific terms only those statements in which the responses are not described behaviorally.

+ a. Ted saw three clients today and made four phone calls.
− b. Bob is becoming a drug addict.

Sample answer: Bob takes sleeping pills at night and amphetamines in the morning.

+ c. Bruce kissed Sally on the cheek.
− d. She acted out her anger toward him.

Sample answer: She threw his new fishing rod in the garbage.

(1) 3. Name the most commonly used measure of response strength.

Answer: Frequency per time unit or rate

Scoring: The total point value of this test is 9 (each question's point value appears in parentheses before the question number). Score 1 point for each of the two parts of question 1, score 1 point for each correctly identified statement in question 2A and 1 point for each correctly rewritten statement in question 2B, and score 1 point for a correct answer to Question 3. (For guidelines on scoring your answers, see pp. xix-xx.)

Criterion score for this test is 8. If your score is at least 8, you may take the posttest for this chapter now. If your score is less than 8, read the chapter before you take the posttest.

Chapter 2: Positive Reinforcement

(1) 1. To maximize the effectiveness of a positive reinforcer for a response, when should the positive reinforcer be delivered?

Answer: The reinforcer should be delivered immediately after the response is performed.

(3) 2. Give one example of a conditioned positive reinforcer and one example of an unconditioned positive reinforcer. How do you know that each is a positive reinforcer and not a reward?

Criteria for correct examples: Conditioned positive reinforcers increase the strength of a behavior through association with other stimuli; unconditioned positive reinforcers are intrinsically reinforcing.

Sample answers: Conditioned positive reinforcers include money, points, stars, and attention. Unconditioned positive reinforcers include food, sex, sleep, water, and tactile stimulation.

A positive reinforcer increases the strength of a response it follows; a reward is a pleasant or desirable event that might or might not act as a reinforcer to increase the strength of a response it follows.

(1) 3. It has been demonstrated that presentation of a certain event following a behavior can increase the likelihood that the behavior will recur. What is the name of the behavioral principle to which this statement refers?

Answer: Positive reinforcement

(3) 4. In the example that begins this chapter, what behavior does the social worker positively reinforce? What are the reinforcers?

Answers: The social worker reinforces the client's arriving late to his appointments. The reinforcers are (a) the social worker's telling the client how glad he is to see him and (b) extra time at the end of the session.

Criterion score: 7

Chapter 3: Extinction

(4) 1. Renumber the following steps to show the correct order for determining whether a specific stimulus served as a positive reinforcer for a target behavior:

___2___ 1. Withhold the stimulus each time the target response occurs.
___1___ 2. Determine the strength of the target behavior.
___3___ 3. Observe a decrease in strength of the target behavior.
___4___ 4. Present stimulus after the target behavior occurs and observe an increase in its strength.

(2) 2. What are two practical difficulties that you might encounter in applying an extinction procedure to decrease the strength of an undesired response?

Answers:

A. Difficulty in withholding the reinforcer each time the response occurs
B. Difficulty in making sure that the client is not reinforced for the behavior by someone else

(1) 3. What is spontaneous recovery?

Answer: Spontaneous recovery is the recurrence of an extinguished response at a future time in a situation similar to the one in which the behavior was reinforced.

(2) 4. Describe the extinction procedure and its effect.

Answer: The extinction procedure consists of withholding the positive reinforcer each time the target response is performed. The effect is a decrease in frequency of the target response to zero or to a prespecified rate.

Criterion score: 8

Chapter 4: Positive Reinforcement Contingencies

(4) 1. Which of the following are statements of positive reinforcement contingencies? (Circle the correct ones.)
    Ⓐ Finish your math assignment, and you may play outside.
    Ⓑ If you wash the dishes, I'll give you an ice cream cone.
    C. If you fight with your brother, you will get a spanking.
    D. He completed his chores in 3 hours.

(1) 2. Briefly describe how superstitious behavior is acquired.

Answer: Superstitious behavior is the result of an accidental relationship between a behavior and a reinforcer. An individual makes a response that is followed by an unplanned reinforcer that coincidentally strengthens the response.

(1) 3. Intermittent reinforcement makes a well-learned response more resistant to extinction. (Circle one.)
    Ⓐ True
    B. False

(1) 4. When is it more appropriate to use continuous reinforcement than to use intermittent reinforcement?

Answer: It is more appropriate to use continuous reinforcement when the purpose is to establish a response or to strengthen a response that occurs with low frequency.

(6) 5. Match the following schedules in Column A with their examples in Column B.

A		B
1. Fixed ratio	D	A. Deadlines
2. Variable ratio	C	B. Braking at a stop sign
3. Fixed interval	A	C. Slot machines
4. Variable interval	F	D. Piecework
5. Fixed duration	E	E. Watching a movie
6. Variable duration	B	F. Waiting for a taxi

Criterion score: 12

Chapter 5: Shaping and Response Differentiation

(1) 1. In Case Example 4 (p. 269), the psychologist could help develop Leon's speech by using which of the following techniques? (Circle one.)
   A. Extinction
   B. Intermittent reinforcement
   C. Shaping with successive approximations
   D. Differential reinforcement of approximation of incompatible responses

(1) 2. To shape a new behavior, you would not use differential reinforcement. (Circle one.)
   A. True
   B. False

(2) 3. For the response class "talking about sports," name two responses.

Criterion for correct answers: Each member of the response class has the same effect on the environment—for example, reinforcement by conversation.

Sample answers:

Discussing players' batting averages
Talking about the upcoming hockey game
Discussing football strategy

(2) 4. How are positive reinforcement and extinction involved in differential reinforcement?

Answer: Responses that meet specific criteria are positively reinforced, whereas reinforcement is withheld from other responses—that is, they are extinguished.

(2) 5. Give an example of a DRO procedure that could be used to decrease Carla's screaming in Case Example 3 (p. 268).

Answer: Carla's mother could reinforce any behaviors other than Carla's screaming, such as helping her mother put groceries away, fixing a broken toy, or playing quietly by herself. Reinforcement is thus withheld to extinguish the undesired screaming, and other behaviors are strengthened.

Criterion score: 7

Chapter 6: Stimulus Control

(2) 1. What is an S^D for a response? What is an S^Δ?

Answers: An S^D is a discriminative stimulus that signals or sets the occasion for a response made in its presence to be reinforced. An S^Δ is a discriminative stimulus that signals or sets the occasion for a response made in its presence not to be followed by a reinforcer.

(1) 2. What is the effect of a discrimination training procedure involving two discriminative stimuli (S^D and S^Δ) and one response?

Answer: Stimulus control. The response rate in the presence of S^D increases, and the response rate in the presence of S^Δ decreases.

(1) 3. In Case Example 4 (p. 269), what function did the green light serve?

Answer: When the green light was on, Leon's speech was reinforced; when the green light was off, his speech was not reinforced. The green light's being on thus served as an S^D for Leon's speech.

(6) 4. In the following examples, identify the discriminative stimulus, the response, and the reinforcer by labeling the S^D, R, and S^{r+} in the diagrams.
   A. Bob sees Joe walking down the street. Bob says, "Hello," and Joe says, "Good morning."

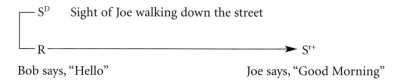

B. Shirley hears the ice cream truck and asks her aunt for a dollar; her aunt gives her the dollar.

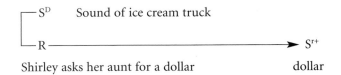

S^D Sound of ice cream truck

R S^{r+}

Shirley asks her aunt for a dollar   dollar

(1) 5. When a response is reinforced in the presence of one S^D, it will not occur in the presence of other similar stimuli. (Circle one.)
A. True
B. False

Criterion score: 10

Chapter 7: Conditioned Reinforcement and Chaining

(2) 1. Which is usually more effective, a simple conditioned reinforcer or a generalized conditioned reinforcer? Support your answer.

Answer: A generalized conditioned reinforcer is more effective than a simple conditioned reinforcer because it is associated with a wide variety of reinforcers, whereas a simple conditioned reinforcer is associated with just one reinforcer. A generalized conditioned reinforcer is therefore less susceptible to the effects of satiation. If an individual is satiated with regard to one reinforcer, there are usually other reinforcers of which he or she is sufficiently deprived to ensure the effectiveness of the generalized conditioned reinforcer.

(1) 2. What is the difference between an unconditioned reinforcer and a conditioned reinforcer?

Answer: An unconditioned reinforcer increases response strength without requiring prior association with other reinforcers. A conditioned reinforcer is a neutral or nonreinforcing stimulus that becomes a reinforcer through association with a reinforcing stimulus.

(4) 3. Give two examples of generalized conditioned reinforcers and two examples of unconditioned reinforcers.

Criteria for correct answers: Generalized conditioned reinforcers are stimuli or items that can be exchanged for a variety of unconditioned and conditioned reinforcers. Unconditioned reinforcers increase the strength of a response without requiring prior association with other reinforcers.

Sample answers: Examples of generalized conditioned reinforcers include attention, money, coupons, and tokens. Examples of unconditioned reinforcers include food, water, sex, warmth, and tactile stimulation.

(1) 4. For a neutral stimulus to function as a conditioned reinforcer, a minimum of 100 pairings is necessary. (Circle one.)
   A. True
   B. False

(3) 5. Identify the components of one unit of a stimulus-response chain.

   Answer: The components of one unit of a stimulus-response chain consist of a discriminative stimulus (S^D), a response (R), and a conditioned reinforcer (S^{r+}) that also serves as the S^D for the following response in the chain.

Criterion score: 10

Chapter 8: Modeling and Imitation

(3) 1. Describe how a modeling plus reinforcement procedure can be used to develop a child's imitation of an adult using a fork correctly.

   Answer: The adult models or demonstrates the proper use of a fork. The adult's behaviors serve as the modeled stimulus. When the child imitates the modeled stimulus, the adult provides a positive reinforcer, such as praise.

(3) 2. For each of the following statements, indicate true (T) or false (F):
   A. __F__ If an individual does not perform a response after observing someone perform it, the individual has not learned it.
   B. __F__ Filmed models are less effective than live models.
   C. __F__ Imitative behavior cannot be conditioned through reinforcement.

(3) 3. Using the information in Case Example 6 (p. 271), how could modeling and reinforcement be used to help Bill obtain a new job?

   Answer: Bill's fellow group members could model appropriate job interview behaviors—for example, speaking clearly and making eye contact—in role plays, which Bill observes. Bill then imitates the modeled behaviors, and the therapist and group members praise Bill for successfully doing so.

Criterion score: 8

Chapter 9: Punishment

(2) 1. Name the two types of punishment procedures that can be used to suppress a response.

Answers:

A. Positive punishment
B. Negative punishment

(1) 2. Briefly describe a time-out procedure.

Answer: Time-out consists of removing an individual from a reinforcing situation immediately after performance of an inappropriate behavior and placing him or her in an environment with minimal availability of reinforcement for a fixed, brief period of time.

(2) 3. Briefly describe two disadvantages of punishment procedures.

Answers: Any two of the following are acceptable:

A. The punished response could reappear when the individual administering punishment is not present.
B. Aggression may be directed toward someone or something that is unrelated to delivery of the punisher.
C. Aggression may be directed against the individual administering the punishment.
D. Appropriate behaviors occurring immediately prior to delivery of the punisher may be suppressed.
E. The person administering the punisher may become a conditioned punisher through association with the punisher.
F. The person administering the punisher may be imitated by observers.
G. The intended punisher might in fact serve as an S^D for responses that are positively reinforced.

(4) 4. As Mrs. Kelly went out, she asked her daughter Sharon to fold the laundry after it had been washed and dried. When Mrs. Kelly returned, Sharon was talking to a friend on the phone and the laundry had not been folded. What should Mrs. Kelly do in regard to Sharon's behavior to demonstrate her knowledge of the necessary conditions to maximize the effectiveness of punishment?

Criteria for correct answer: A correct answer should include the following points: (a) delivery of a punisher immediately after performance of the target response, (b) use of a punisher that has sufficient intensity to suppress the target response, (c) specification of an appropriate response, and (d) positive reinforcement for performance of the appropriate response.

Sample answer: Mrs. Kelly tells Sharon to get off the phone, and immediately after Sharon complies, Mrs. Kelly informs her that she cannot visit her friends that afternoon as she had planned. Mrs. Kelly then tells Sharon to fold the laundry. After Sharon does so, Mrs. Kelly says, "Thank you. You did a really nice job."

Criterion score: 8

Chapter 10: Negative Reinforcement

(1) 1. What is a major advantage of avoidance conditioning in maintaining a response?

Answer: A response that is conditioned through an avoidance procedure is highly resistant to extinction.

(3) 2. Give an example of the behavioral procedure that produces escape behavior and draw a behavioral diagram to illustrate your example.

Criteria for correct answer: A correct answer specifies (a) a negative reinforcer that remains in effect until (b) a response is made that (c) removes or reduces the effect of that stimulus (negative reinforcer).

Sample answer: Chuck comes home drunk and repeatedly demands that his wife, Brenda, have sex with him. Brenda has sex with him, which removes Chuck's demands.

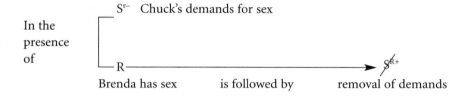

(4) 3. Give an example of the behavioral procedure that results in avoidance behavior and draw a behavior diagram to illustrate your example.

Criteria for correct answer: A correct answer specifies (a) a conditioned negative reinforcer that is presented as a cue for (b) a response that (c) removes the conditioned negative reinforcer and (d) avoids or prevents the onset of another negative reinforcer.

Sample answer: Jimmy tells Billy that he will have Billy investigated unless Billy tells Jimmy where he got $10,000. Billy then tells Jimmy that Libby gave him the money.

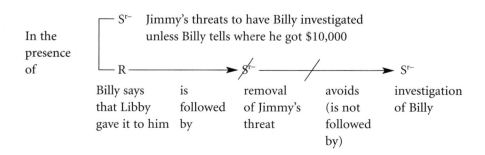

(2) 4. Give an example of (a) an unconditioned aversive stimulus that could be used as a negative reinforcer and (b) a conditioned aversive stimulus that could be used as a negative reinforcer.

Answers:

A. Examples of unconditioned negative reinforcers include shock, physical attack (e.g., hitting and pinching), and intense light, noise, odor, or temperature. The stimulus does not require prior pairing or association with another stimulus.

B. Examples of conditioned negative reinforcers include threats, fines, demerits, failing grades, and harsh or demeaning words (such as calling someone "stupid"). The stimulus requires pairing or association with another stimulus before it can act as a negative reinforcer.

Criterion score: 9

Chapter 11: Respondent Conditioning

(1) 1. Describe a procedure for extinguishing a classically conditioned response.

Answer: Present the conditioned stimulus repeatedly without presenting the unconditioned stimulus until the conditioned stimulus no longer elicits the conditioned response.

(8) 2. Given the following information, specify operant and respondent behaviors: A man gets in his car and drives home. As he walks through his front door, the aroma of dinner cooking makes his mouth water. He runs to the kitchen, and when he arrives there, panting, he kisses his wife and sits down at the table.

Answers:

Operant behaviors: Gets in his car, drives home, walks into the house, runs to the kitchen, kisses his wife, and sits down

Respondent behaviors: Mouth waters and panting

(1) 3. Explain the persistence of emotional respondent behavior in the absence of identifiable reinforcing consequences for the individual.

Answer: Respondent behaviors are not controlled by their consequences as are operant behaviors. They are controlled by antecedents and, therefore, persist regardless of consequences, as long as the conditioned stimulus is occasionally paired with the unconditioned stimulus.

(2) 4. What are the two measures of response strength for a classically conditioned response?

Answers:

A. Magnitude

B. Latency

Criterion score: 11

Chapter 12: Generalization and Maintenance of Behavior Change

(2) 1. You are treating an alcohol-abusing client. As part of the treatment program to decrease his drinking, you suggest several nondrinking behaviors that would be appropriate in the social situations in which he usually drinks. These behaviors are new to him, but he agrees to try them.

A. What is the most likely obstacle to success for this part of therapy?

Answer: He is unlikely to perform these nondrinking behaviors in social situations either because he has never been reinforced for them or because he does not have the skills required to perform them.

B. What can you do to counteract this effect or to plan for this problem?

Answer: You can use behavioral rehearsal; that is, you can have the client practice and receive reinforcement for nondrinking behaviors in the treatment setting. You can also use behavioral assignments to maximize successful generalization of the nondrinking behaviors practiced in the treatment setting to the client's natural environment.

(1) 2. Using the information in Case Example 6 (p. 271), describe how Bill's therapist and group used behavioral rehearsal with Bill to facilitate generalization of appropriate responses to correction.

Answer: The therapist and group members showed Bill how to make appropriate responses to criticism by conducting role plays of situations in which Bill was criticized by his employer. The therapist and group members praised Bill for performing appropriately in these role plays.

(1) 3. Behavioral assignments are given for which of the following reasons? (Circle the correct answer[s].)

A. To structure the client's activities between therapy sessions

B. To help the client apply in his or her natural environment what he or she has learned in treatment

C. To provide feedback to the client from the therapist based on a specific behavior the client has attempted to perform

D. All of the above

(1) 4. It is usually more difficult for a desired behavior to generalize beyond the practice setting when more than one therapist is involved in developing the behavior. (Circle one.)

A. True

(B.) False

(3) 5. Turn to Case Example 4 (p. 269). State three ways in which you could maximize successful generalization of Leon's speech.

Answers: Any three of the following are acceptable:

A. By providing positive reinforcement to unit staff for reinforcing Leon's speech on the unit

B. By shifting reinforcement for Leon's speech from continuous reinforcement to an intermittent reinforcement schedule

C. By having the therapist reinforce Leon's speech on the unit

D. By using more than one therapist to reinforce Leon's speech in the treatment setting

E. By conducting additional sessions in the treatment setting to maintain Leon's speech at a high level after Leon has achieved criterion performance in speaking about the slides

F. By having unit staff reinforce Leon's speech in the treatment setting

Criterion score: 7

Chapter 13: Behavioral Assessment

(2) 1. Rewrite the following sentences so that the strength of the response is stated in measurable terms.

Criteria for correct answers: Each sentence must include information on the frequency/time (rate), duration, or intensity of the response.

A. Hortense has repeatedly phoned the adoption agency.

Sample answer: Hortense phoned the adoption agency 10 times this month.

B. Roger rarely kisses his wife.

Sample answer: Roger kissed his wife two times last week.

(2) 2. In Case Example 2 (p. 268), what were the behavioral excesses shown by Bella and Cliff?

Answers:

A. Bella and Cliff asked questions and made comments that were unrelated to the topics being discussed.

B. Bella and Cliff talked continuously for 5 minutes or more without pausing for responses from others.

(2) 3. What were the negative consequences of Bella and Cliff's behavioral excesses?

Answers:

A. Bella and Cliff were ridiculed.
B. Bella and Cliff were excluded from many conversations.

(3) 4. From the information given in the following paragraph, identify Henry's target responses, the antecedent, and the negative consequences.

> When someone comes over to talk to Henry or ask him a question, he mutters and speaks in a low voice so that the person has difficulty hearing what he is saying. Typically, individuals who approach Henry stop talking and walk away from him soon after he begins to mutter.

Answers:

A. *Henry's target responses:* Henry mutters and speaks in a low voice.
B. *Antecedent:* Someone starts talking to Henry or asks him a question.
C. *Negative consequences:* The person stops talking to Henry and walks away.

(2) 5. What are two questions that a practitioner should ask about a client's problems in establishing priorities for treatment.

Answers: The practitioner should ask the following four questions in establishing priorities for problem treatment:

A. Which problem is of immediate concern to the client, significant others, or both?
B. Which problem has the most severe aversive or negative consequences for the client, significant others, or society if not handled immediately?
C. Which problem requires handling before other problems can be treated?
D. Which problem can be corrected most quickly, considering resources and obstacles?

(2) 6. How is behavioral reenactment used in behavioral assessment?

Answers:

A. It is used in role plays to obtain RAC-S assessment information on the client's target behaviors in the problematic situation.
B. It is especially useful for validating the accuracy of a client's verbal report of the target behaviors and their controlling conditions.

Criterion score: 12

Chapter 14: Goal Setting, Intervention Planning, and Evaluation

(1) 1. What does the term *informed consent* refer to in the context of a behavioral change program?

Answer: Informed consent refers to the client's having received all the information he or she needs to understand the proposed intervention and to the client's voluntary agreement to participate.

(1) 2. An intervention plan for teaching an individual with mental retardation self-care skills could include which of the following? (Circle one.)
   A. Covert sensitization and modeling
   B. Positive reinforcement and systematic desensitization
   Ⓒ Positive reinforcement, shaping, and chaining
   D. None of the above

(3) 3. State three ways of evaluating a client's progress.

   Answers: Any three of the following are acceptable:

   A. Through observation of behavioral changes in the desired direction from baseline measures
   B. Through the client's subjective perceptions of improved circumstances
   C. Through reports by significant others of improvement in the client's target behaviors
   D. Through the client's report of satisfaction with practitioner services

(2) 4. What is the purpose of a treatment contract?

   Answer: The purpose of a treatment contract is to make explicit the client's expectations for service and the practitioner's assessment of what is required of the client and significant others to achieve treatment success.

Criterion score: 6

Chapter 15: Intervention Techniques

(1) 1. Which of the following intervention techniques is *not* used to decrease anxiety?
   A. Systematic desensitization
   B. Flooding
   Ⓒ Covert sensitization
   D. In vivo desensitization

(1) 2. Covert sensitization is most appropriate for which one of the following purposes?
   A. To decrease anxiety to a feared stimulus
   B. To treat adolescent panic disorder
   Ⓒ To develop alternative behaviors to overeating
   D. To treat the negative effects of depression

(1) 3. Cognitive restructuring is used for which of the following purposes?
  A. To extinguish delinquent behavior among high school dropouts
  B. To substitute effective covert behaviors for self-defeating cognitions
  C. To shape successive approximations to nondrinking behaviors
  D. To reinforce the performance of desired overt behaviors

(2) 4. Give two examples of problem behaviors that can be treated with thought stopping.

  Criteria for correct answers: Correct answers indicate recurring negative or self-defeating thoughts.

  Sample answers:

  "I can't do anything right."
  "I'll never be attractive to another man."
  "I'll never find the right job."

(1) 5. Panic control treatment includes breathing retraining, cognitive therapy, and exposure to physiological components of panic. (Circle one.)
  A. True
  B. False

Criterion score: 5

Appendix 4

Chapter Posttest Questions

Chapter 1: Specifying Behavior

(10) 1. A. Indicate with a plus sign (+) which of the following statements are written in behaviorally specific terms, and indicate with a minus sign (−) the statements that are vague and require further specification.

   B. After completing question 1A, rewrite in specific terms only those statements in which the responses are not described behaviorally.
   a. Eddie took two cans of beer from the refrigerator.
   b. Johnny expressed his feelings of inadequacy at the ball game.
   c. Norman showed hostile feelings toward his probation officer this week.
   d. Mr. Smith asserted his authority over use of the car.
   e. He thinks of his girlfriend often.
   f. Mr. Foster said, "I can't earn enough money to make you happy."

(1) 2. In Case Example 1 (p. 267), Robert's teacher described him as having "low self-esteem." Specify a behavior that might have led the teacher to describe Robert in this way.

(1) 3. Rewrite the following statement to include a measure of response strength: Dan drinks at the bar.

Chapter 2: Positive Reinforcement

(2) 1. Define the positive reinforcement procedure and its effect on the strength of a response.

(2) 2. Give one example of an object or event that you think acts as a positive reinforcer for you. State your proof.

(3) 3. Using the information in Case Example 1 (p. 267), draw a diagram showing how positive reinforcement could be used to increase the rate of Robert's

completing his class assignments; label each component of your diagram. What evidence could be used to evaluate the effect of this procedure?

(4) 4. Rewrite the following statements so that they specify target behaviors and indicate baseline rates:
A. Hank is always annoying his brother.
B. Mary was often depressed.

(2) 5. Rewrite the following statements so that they describe situations in which the effectiveness of the positive reinforcers is maximized:
A. Mrs. Jones gave Edward a candy bar and asked him to take her dog for a walk.
B. Harvey washed his father's car, and 3 weeks later his father took him to the movies.

(1) 6. Lillian goes shopping immediately after she completes her housework. How could you use baseline data to determine whether going shopping serves as a positive reinforcer for Lillian's doing housework?

Chapter 3: Extinction

(3) 1. Describe the procedure for extinguishing a response and give an example in which you specify the response, its reinforcer, and the effect.

(3) 2. After you have observed a mother hugging her son when he cried, what would you do to determine whether the mother's hugging serves as a positive reinforcer for the child's crying?

(1) 3. Describe the effects of extinction on the rate of a target response.

(2) 4. Using the information in Case Example 3 (p. 268), indicate how positive reinforcement played a part in the following:
A. Increasing the rate of an undesired behavior
B. Increasing the rate of a desired behavior

(1) 5. How is spontaneous recovery considered in a treatment plan?

Chapter 4: Positive Reinforcement Contingencies

(2) 1. State a positive reinforcement contingency related to Case Example 1 (p. 267) that you could use to help Robert complete his class assignments. Specify a reinforcer and a response.

(2) 2. As described in this chapter, self-control reinforcement contingencies are more desirable than accidental contingencies. What is the difference between an accidental contingency and a self-control reinforcement contingency?

(3) 3. Define the Premack Principle and give an example of its use and effect.

(1) 4. What evidence indicates that intermittent reinforcement makes a response more resistant to extinction than does continuous reinforcement?

(3) 5. Using the information in Case Example 4 (p. 269), how could you schedule reinforcement to maintain Leon's increased vocalizations after session 15?

Chapter 5: Shaping and Response Differentiation

(4) 1. Define a response class and give an example of one, describing two of its members.

(7) 2. The seven steps involved in shaping a behavior are listed below. Fill in the specific responses or reinforcers, or both, related to each step, using your own example of shaping a motor (nonverbal) behavior.

	Fill in with examples
1. Specify the target response.	1.
2. Specify reinforcer(s).	2.
3. Specify initial and intermediate responses.	3.
4. Reinforce initial response each time it is performed until it occurs consistently.	4.
5. Shift criterion for reinforcement to intermediate responses.	5.
6. Continue the procedure of differential reinforcement and shift the criterion for reinforcement to intermediate responses that successively approximate the target response.	6.
7. Reinforce the target response.	7.

(2) 3. Two second-grade students hit each other whenever they are together in school. Describe how a DRO procedure can be used to decrease the rate of their hitting behavior.

(3) 4. Give an example of response differentiation, specifying a response class, the differentiated response, and the reinforcer.

Chapter 6: Stimulus Control

(3) 1. Using the information in Case Example 5 (p. 269), do the following:
   A. Describe the discrimination training procedure that was used.

      B. Describe how reinforcement and extinction were involved in this procedure.

      C. Describe the effects of this procedure.

(2) 2. In Case Example 4 (p. 269), what two functions did the green light serve?

(5) 3. Describe a procedure for establishing a discrimination. In your example, include one S^D, one S^Δ, and one response. Specify the reinforcer. How do you know when stimulus control has been achieved?

(2) 4. Give an example of stimulus generalization.

Chapter 7: Conditioned Reinforcement and Chaining

(2) 1. A social worker gave Ben, a resident of a skilled nursing facility, some coins to determine whether money would serve as a reinforcer for Ben's performing personal hygiene tasks. Ben dropped one of the coins on the floor and left the rest on the table. The social worker concluded that money did not function as a generalized conditioned reinforcer for Ben in the way that it does for most adults in our society. What could the social worker do to establish money as a generalized conditioned reinforcer for Ben?

(3) 2. You are a social worker in a community setting, and adolescents who have had one or two contacts with the police and juvenile authorities are referred to you. You station yourself in the socioeconomically disadvantaged neighborhood in which these youths live because you plan to engage a group of them in activities that will help them stay out of trouble with the law, improve their academic performance, interview for and successfully hold jobs, and solve various interpersonal and family difficulties. Give two examples that describe how you could establish yourself as a generalized conditioned reinforcer.

(2) 3. State two advantages of using generalized conditioned reinforcers rather than primary reinforcers in behavioral change programs.

(4) 4. Give an example of a problem that can be analyzed as a stimulus-response chain. Draw the stimulus-response chain; include at least two stimulus-response units and label each component.

Chapter 8: Modeling and Imitation

(3) 1. Give an example of a modeling plus reinforcement procedure to develop and strengthen a response.

(4) 2. Give an example of the use of modeling in developing assertive behaviors in a group setting.

(4) 3. Describe the use of a modeling procedure with prompts, reinforcement, and fading, given the following information: A social worker is trying to teach a child with mental retardation to answer questions about his family. When the social worker asks the child, "How many brothers do you have?" the child does not answer. The child can talk and can say all the words necessary to answer the question.

Chapter 9: Punishment

(3) 1. Give an example of each of the two types of punishment procedures and indicate how you would evaluate the effectiveness of each procedure.

(2) 2. Give an example that compares extinction with negative punishment.

(5) 3. Give an example of how a practitioner could maximize the effectiveness of punishment with a child who exhibits self-injurious behavior.

(2) 4. Using the information in Case Example 7 (p. 271), name the punishment procedure administered to Stephen by his father. Give an example of an incident that would lead Stephen's father to use this procedure.

(1) 5. Give an example of punishment applied in a self-control contingency.

Chapter 10: Negative Reinforcement

(2) 1. Give an example that compares the effects of punishment with the effects of negative reinforcement. Specify relevant responses and stimuli involved in each procedure.

(3) 2. Give an example of escape behavior developed by negative reinforcement. Label relevant responses and stimuli.

(2) 3. Using the information in Case Example 3 (p. 268), describe the interaction between Carla and her mother (Juanita) in terms of positive and negative reinforcement prior to the social worker's intervention.

(4) 4. Sylvia told Harold, "Buy me a new car or I'll leave you." Harold bought Sylvia a new car, and she stopped threatening to leave him. Draw a diagram that describes the avoidance behavior and label all relevant components.

Chapter 11: Respondent Conditioning

(3) 1. Using the information in Case Example 5 (p. 269), state one operant behavior and two possible respondent behaviors involved in Pat's being "upset."

(7) 2. The following examples include operant and respondent behaviors. Place an O next to those in which the behaviors appearing in italics are operant and an R next to those that are respondent:
    A. 1. _____ A teenager in a treatment group *swears* at another boy.
       2. _____ The second boy's face *turns* red.
    B. 1. _____ You *ask* a client a question about his brother, and
       2. _____ you observe that his breathing *quickens* and
       3. _____ perspiration *appears* on his forehead.
    C. 1. _____ You *give* Janet a piece of candy for completing her assignment.
       2. _____ Carol observes this and starts *whining*.

(3) 3. Draw a diagram showing respondent conditioning of the following phobia: A child is afraid of dentists. When he approaches a dentist's office, he begins to tremble, turns pale, breathes rapidly, and then turns and runs away. This child has dental problems that must be taken care of soon or he may lose many of his teeth.

(1) 4. Describe the procedure for extinguishing a classically conditioned response.

Chapter 12: Generalization and Maintenance of Behavior Change

(4) 1. State four obstacles to generalization of desired responses from the practice setting to the client's natural environment.

(1) 2. In Case Example 4 (p. 269), Leon's speech was developed in a laboratory-like situation. State one reason his speech might not generalize from the treatment setting to the unit.

(4) 3. State four ways in which the therapist could maximize successful generalization of Leon's speech.

(2) 4. In Case Example 5 (p. 269), what are two behavioral assignments that the marriage counselor gave to Pat?

(2) 5. State two reasons for using behavioral assignments in implementing a behavioral change program.

(1) 6. In Case Example 2 (p. 268), how was behavioral rehearsal used to help Bella and Cliff converse appropriately with their peers?

(1) 7. What is the rationale for using behavioral rehearsal?

Chapter 13: Behavioral Assessment

(2) 1. Give an example of a behavioral deficit and an example of a behavioral excess.

(4) 2. A caseworker tells her supervisor that a client is always late for his appointments.

    A. Which of the following questions should the supervisor ask the caseworker to obtain baseline measures of the complaint? (Circle the correct answer[s].)

      1. Why do you think the client is always late?

      2. How many minutes late is the client?

      3. How many times has the client been late this month?

      4. What do you think the client's lateness means?

    B. Give one hypothetical answer to each of the questions you chose above that would provide baseline data on the target behavior.

(2) 3. Using the information about Denice's case in Chapter 13 (p. 203), state two of Denice's target behaviors.

(1) 4. Specify one antecedent related to Denice's problematic interaction with her coworkers.

(2) 5. State two negative consequences of Denice's target responses.

(2) 6. State two possible reinforcers for Denice's target responses.

(1) 7. State one hypothesis regarding the conditions that exerted control over Denice's target behaviors.

(1) 8. Using the information in Case Example 1 (p. 267), state a possible reinforcer maintaining Robert's drug use.

Chapter 14: Goal Setting, Intervention Planning, and Evaluation

(3) 1. Using the information in Case Example 8 (p. 272), state an intermediate behavioral change goal for Bruce, specifying (a) a desired response, (b) a relevant antecedent, and (c) a possible reinforcer.

(2) 2. State one possible resource and one possible obstacle to goal attainment for Bruce, given the following behavioral change goal: Bruce assertively asks his employer for a salary increase.

(4) 3. Using information from Chapter 14, develop an intervention plan for teaching Tim how to shave (see p. 223). He has never been observed to shave. Include two behavioral techniques and outline the procedure you would follow to achieve the goal.

(3) 4. State three evaluation criteria a practitioner could use to determine whether marital arguments have been treated effectively.

(2) 5. Using the information in Case Example 8, describe a method for evaluating the effectiveness of an assertiveness training procedure that could be used with Bruce.

Chapter 15: Intervention Techniques

(4) 1. Describe how covert sensitization can be used in the treatment of a sex offender who targets children.

(6) 2. Using the following example, describe how thought stopping can be used to decrease undesired thoughts: Jill's fiancé just broke off their engagement, and Jill is having persistent thoughts of how unattractive she is to men and that she will never marry and have children.

(3) 3. Compare the uses of systematic desensitization, in vivo desensitization, and flooding in the treatment of phobias.

(3) 4. Stan complains of panic attacks while driving on the freeway and thinks that he will have a heart attack and die in his car. How could a therapist use panic control treatment to decrease the panic attacks Stan has while driving?

Appendix 5

Chapter Posttest Answers

Chapter 1: Specifying Behavior

(10) 1. A. Indicate with a plus sign (+) which of the following statements are written in behaviorally specific terms, and indicate with a minus sign (−) the statements that are vague and require further specification.

Criteria for correct answers: Responses describe what the person says or does in positively stated, observable terms. Responses stated negatively are incorrect. Sample answers follow those statements that require further specification.

   B. After completing question 1A, rewrite in specific terms only those statements in which the responses are not described behaviorally.

   + a. Eddie took two cans of beer from the refrigerator.
   − b. Johnny expressed his feelings of inadequacy at the ball game.

   Sample answer: After striking out, Johnny threw down his bat and ran home.

   − c. Norman showed hostile feelings toward his probation officer this week.

   Sample answer: Every time Norman's probation officer asked him a question about school, Norman said, "Mind your own business."

   − d. Mr. Smith asserted his authority over use of the car.

   Sample answer: Mr. Smith kept both sets of keys to the car in his pocket.

   − e. He thinks of his girlfriend often.

   Sample answer: Every evening he says to himself, "I wish Linda were here."

   + f. Mr. Foster said, "I can't earn enough money to make you happy."

(1) 2. In Case Example 1 (p. 267), Robert's teacher described him as having "low self-esteem." Specify a behavior that might have led the teacher to describe Robert in this way.

Criterion for correct answer: A correct answer states a measurable behavior performed by Robert.

Sample answers:

Robert says, "I'm not too smart."
Robert buys drugs and gives them to his friends.
Robert tells himself, "No one wants to be my friend."

(1) 3. Rewrite the following statement to include a measure of response strength: Dan drinks at the bar.

Criterion for correct answer: A correct answer states the number of times Dan drank at the bar within a specified time period or the number of drinks Dan drank at the bar within a specified time period.

Sample answers:

Dan drank six drinks at the bar in 45 minutes.
Dan drank one drink at the bar in the past 6 hours.
Dan finished two drinks in 20 minutes.

Scoring: The total point value of this test is 12 (each question's point value appears in parentheses before the question number). Score 1 point for each correctly identified statement in question 1A, 1 point for each correctly written statement in question 1B, 1 point for a correct answer to question 2, and 1 point for a correct answer to question 3. (For guidelines on scoring your answers, see pp. xix-xx.)

Criterion score for this test is 11. If your score is at least 11, you have mastered key concepts in this chapter and can go on to Chapter 2. If your score is less than 11, review the chapter until you can answer the questions correctly.

Chapter 2: Positive Reinforcement

(2) 1. Define the positive reinforcement procedure and its effect on the strength of a response.

Answer: The positive reinforcement procedure consists of the presentation of a stimulus contingent on performance of a response; the effect of this procedure is an increase in the strength of that response.

(2) 2. Give one example of an object or event that you think acts as a positive reinforcer for you. State your proof.

Criteria for correct answer: A correct answer may specify any object or event as long as evidence is given that the response increases in strength after presentation of the stimulus.

Sample answer: I go to a new hairstylist to get my hair cut. I am pleased with the results. I now go only to this hairstylist to have my hair cut once a month.

Response: Going to new hairstylist

Positive reinforcer: Hair cut the way I like it

Baseline rate of going to this hair stylist: 0 times/month

Current rate: Once a month for the past 8 months

(3) 3. Using the information in Case Example 1 (p. 267), draw a diagram showing how positive reinforcement could be used to increase the rate of Robert's completing his class assignments; label each component of your diagram. What evidence could be used to evaluate the effect of this procedure?

Criteria for correct answer: A correct answer gives the positive reinforcement diagram, specifying the reinforcer used. Each component of the diagram is labeled as shown in the following sample answer. Evidence for the reinforcement effect shows that the rate of the response increased over its baseline rate.

Sample answer:

R $\longrightarrow$ S^{r+}

Robert shows	is followed by	Robert receives
his mother one		television privileges
completed assignment		for the evening

Watching television serves as a positive reinforcer if the rate of Robert's completing his assignments increases over the baseline rate.

(4) 4. Rewrite the following statements so that they specify target behaviors and indicate baseline rates:

Criteria for correct answers: Correct answers specify behaviors in positively stated, measurable terms and include a baseline measure of response rate (frequency/time).

A. Hank is always annoying his brother.

Sample answer: Three times last week, Hank read the newspaper aloud while his brother practiced the violin.

Target behavior: Reading the newspaper aloud

Baseline measure: Three times last week

B. Mary was often depressed.

Sample answer: Mary cried alone in her room four nights this week.

Target response: Cried alone in her room

Baseline measure: Four nights this week

(2) 5. Rewrite the following statements so that they describe situations in which the effectiveness of the positive reinforcers is maximized:

A. Mrs. Jones gave Edward a candy bar and asked him to take her dog for a walk.

Sample answer: As soon as Edward returned from walking her dog, Mrs. Jones gave Edward a candy bar.

B. Harvey washed his father's car, and 3 weeks later his father took him to the movies.

Sample answer: Harvey washed his father's car, and immediately after he finished his father took him to the movies.

(1) 6. Lillian goes shopping immediately after she completes her housework. How could you use baseline data to determine whether going shopping serves as a positive reinforcer for Lillian's doing housework?

Answer: One could compare the baseline rate of Lillian's doing housework (without going shopping) with the rate of her doing housework and going shopping immediately afterward. If shopping is a positive reinforcer for housework, Lillian will do housework more frequently than during a baseline period when housework is not followed by going shopping.

Criterion score: 13

Chapter 3: Extinction

(3) 1. Describe the procedure for extinguishing a response and give an example in which you specify the response, its reinforcer, and the effect.

Criteria for correct answer: A correct answer states a measurable response and a specific reinforcer and also states that this reinforcer is withheld each time the response is performed.

Sample answer:

Response: The client stares at the ceiling while talking to you.

Positive reinforcer: Attention in the form of conversing with the client, looking at the client, and smiling.

Extinction procedure: Each time the client stares at the ceiling while talking to you, you remain silent—that is, you withhold your attention (conversing, looking at, smiling).

Effect: The rate of the client's staring at the ceiling while talking to you decreases.

(3) 2. After you have observed a mother hugging her son when he cried, what would you do to determine whether the mother's hugging serves as a positive reinforcer for the child's crying?

Answer: Take the following steps:

A. Determine the rate of the child's crying.

B. Tell the mother to refrain from hugging the child each time he cries. If the child's crying decreases (even after an initial increase), it is likely that the mother's hugging serves as a positive reinforcer for her son's crying.

C. If it is important to demonstrate that the hugging does reinforce the crying, the mother could reinstate hugging her son when he cries. If the crying increases again, it is likely that the mother's hugging serves as a positive reinforcer for her son's crying.

(1) 3. Describe the effects of extinction on the rate of a target response.

Answer: There is usually an initial increase or burst in the rate of responding and then a gradual decrease in the rate of the target response to its baseline rate or to a prespecified rate.

(2) 4. Using the information in Case Example 3 (p. 268), indicate how positive reinforcement played a part in the following:
A. Increasing the rate of an undesired behavior

Answer: Juanita provided positive reinforcement—she promised to buy new clothes and put the toys away—for Carla's undesired behavior of screaming when told to put her toys away.

B. Increasing the rate of a desired behavior

Answer: Juanita provided positive reinforcement—praise, gum, and cookies— for the desired behavior of Carla's putting her toys away.

(1) 5. How is spontaneous recovery considered in a treatment plan?

Answer: The behavior modifier can anticipate the possible recurrence of the target response at a later date when the client is in a situation that is similar to the one in which the target response was reinforced. The behavioral practitioner, client, and significant others can then arrange for reinforcement to be withheld consistently should the target behavior recur.

Criterion score: 9

Chapter 4: Positive Reinforcement Contingencies

(2) 1. State a positive reinforcement contingency related to Case Example 1 (p. 267) that you could use to help Robert complete his class assignments. Specify a reinforcer and a response.

Criteria for correct answer: A correct answer specifies the amount of schoolwork that Robert must complete to receive a specified positive reinforcer. The answer states the response and reinforcer in positive terms.

Sample answer: You could tell Robert, "After you complete one of your assignments, you can play your stereo for half an hour."

(2) 2. As described in this chapter, self-control reinforcement contingencies are more desirable than accidental contingencies. What is the difference between an accidental contingency and a self-control reinforcement contingency?

Answer: In a self-control reinforcement contingency, the individual arranges conditions so that his or her behavior is predictably followed by reinforcement. The reinforcer is made available contingent on performance of the response. In an accidental contingency, an individual makes a response that is followed by a noncontingent reinforcer that coincidentally strengthens the response.

(3) 3. Define the Premack Principle and give an example of its use and effect.

Answer: The Premack Principle states that a response that occurs more frequently (high-probability response) than another response can serve as a reinforcer for the response that occurs less frequently (low-probability response).

Criteria for correct example: A correct example specifies two responses, one occurring with greater frequency than the other. The high-probability response is made contingent on performance of the low-probability response. The effect is an increase in strength of the low-probability response.

Sample answer: Lenora frequently invites her friends over for coffee in the morning but rarely makes breakfast for her children. She can increase the rate of making breakfast for her children if inviting her friends over is made contingent on her making breakfast for her children. The effect of using the Premack Principle is an increase in the rate of Lenora's making the children's breakfast.

(1) 4. What evidence indicates that intermittent reinforcement makes a response more resistant to extinction than does continuous reinforcement?

Answer: If a response is maintained on an intermittent reinforcement schedule, an individual will perform a greater number of responses during extinction than if the response had been maintained on a continuous schedule of reinforcement.

(3) 5. Using the information in Case Example 4 (p. 269), how could you schedule reinforcement to maintain Leon's increased vocalizations after session 15?

Criteria for correct answer: A correct answer includes the following three points:

A. After a consistent rate is established on a continuous reinforcement schedule, shift to a small fixed-ratio (FR) schedule (e.g., FR 2).

B. Gradually shift from FR 2 to progressively larger schedules, such as FR 3, FR 4, FR 6, and FR 8.

C. Gradually shift from FR to variable-rate (VR) schedules (VR 4, VR 7, VR 10, and so on) to approximate reinforcement availability in the natural environment.

Criterion score: 10

Chapter 5: Shaping and Response Differentiation

(4) 1. Define a response class and give an example of one, describing two of its members.

Criterion for correct answer: In a correct answer, members of the response class specified have the same or similar effect on the environment.

Sample answer:

Response class: Joe's talking about sports topics

Effect: Father talks with him about sports.

Members of response class: For example, explaining a player's batting style and describing a touchdown pass

(7) 2. The seven steps involved in shaping a behavior are listed below. Fill in the specific responses or reinforcers, or both, related to each step, using your own example of shaping a motor (nonverbal) behavior.

	Fill in with examples
1. Specify the target response.	1. A child with autism throws a ball.
2. Specify reinforcer(s).	2. Raisins and praise ("Good") are reinforcers.
3. Specify initial and intermediate responses.	3. Responses include the following: movement toward the ball with any part of the body, touching the ball with the hands, holding the ball in the hands, and moving the ball around in the air.
4. Reinforce initial response each time it is performed until it occurs consistently.	4. Any movement toward the ball with any part of the body was reinforced.

(Continued)

(Continued)

5. Shift criterion for reinforcement to intermediate responses.	5. Reinforcement was given only when the child was touching the ball with her hands.
6. Continue the procedure of differential reinforcement and shift the criterion for reinforcement to intermediate responses that successively approximate the target response.	6. When the child was consistently touching the ball with her hands, the criterion for reinforcement was shifted and given only when the child was holding the ball in her hands. The criterion for reinforcement was again shifted and given only when the child moved the ball around in the air.
7. Reinforce the target response.	7. Give praise and raisins when the child throws the ball.

(2) 3. Two second-grade students hit each other whenever they are together in school. Describe how a DRO procedure can be used to decrease the rate of their hitting behavior.

Answer: Reinforcement is given only when the students are doing something other than hitting. The teacher praises the students and gives them extra privileges for interacting in a positive manner, for doing their schoolwork while sitting next to each other, and for any other behaviors except hitting. The teacher ignores the students when they hit. Thus hitting is extinguished while other appropriate behaviors are strengthened.

(3) 4. Give an example of response differentiation, specifying a response class, the differentiated response, and the reinforcer.

Criteria for correct answer: A correct answer includes (a) a class of responses whose members can be reinforced, (b) a specific response in the class that has been selectively reinforced compared to the others and is performed at a higher rate, and (c) the specific reinforcer involved.

Sample answer: When Joe tried to talk to his stepfather about his problems, his stepfather turned on the television and looked away from Joe. When Joe talked about sports, however, his stepfather looked at him, listened to him, and discussed the topic with him.

Response class: Talking to his stepfather

Differentiated response: Talking about sports

Reinforcer: Stepfather's attention—looking at Joe, listening to him, and discussing sports with him

Criterion score: 14

Chapter 6: Stimulus Control

(3) 1. Using the information in Case Example 5 (p. 269), do the following:

    A. Describe the discrimination training procedure that was used.

    Answer: In Case Example 5, the counselor employed a discrimination training procedure with Pat in which List A topics functioned as S^Ds and List B topics were S^Δs.

    B. Describe how reinforcement and extinction were involved in this procedure.

    Answer: In role plays in the counselor's office, the counselor reinforced Pat's talking about List A topics with praise. Pat's talking about topics on List B was extinguished by the counselor's looking away and not replying (withholding reinforcement).

    C. Describe the effects of this procedure.

    Answer: Pat's rate of talking about topics on List A increased, and her rate of talking about List B topics decreased.

(2) 2. In Case Example 4 (p. 269), what two functions did the green light serve?

    Answer: When the green light was on, it served as an S^D for Leon's speech, indicating that his speaking during that time would be reinforced. When the green light was off, it served as an S^Δ for Leon's speech, indicating that his speaking during that time would be extinguished.

(5) 3. Describe a procedure for establishing a discrimination. In your example, include one S^D, one S^Δ, and one response. Specify the reinforcer. How do you know when stimulus control has been achieved?

    Criteria for correct answer: A correct answer specifies a response, an S^D, an S^Δ, and the reinforcer. The procedure consists of reinforcing the response in the presence of the S^D and allowing the response to be performed initially in the presence of the S^Δ while withholding reinforcement. Stimulus control is achieved when the response is performed in the presence of the S^D and not in the presence of the S^Δ. An additional characteristic of stimulus control is that the latency between the S^D and the response is short.

    Sample answer: The procedure is teaching a small child to call his father "Daddy" and not to call his uncle "Daddy." The father is the S^D for the child's saying "Daddy," a response that leads to reinforcement, such as the father saying "Good" or hugging the child. The uncle is an S^Δ for the child's saying "Daddy." Reinforcement is withheld when the child says "Daddy" upon seeing the uncle. When the child calls his father (S^D) "Daddy" immediately upon seeing him and does not call his uncle (S^Δ) "Daddy," stimulus control has been achieved.

(2) 4. Give an example of stimulus generalization.

Sample answer: Last year, Sue received help for her problems from a female therapist. This year, Sue moved to a different city, where she chose a female therapist as well as a female dentist and a female physician.

Criterion score: 11

Chapter 7: Conditioned Reinforcement and Chaining

(2) 1. A social worker gave Ben, a resident of a skilled nursing facility, some coins to determine whether money would serve as a reinforcer for Ben's performing personal hygiene tasks. Ben dropped one of the coins on the floor and left the rest on the table. The social worker concluded that money did not function as a generalized conditioned reinforcer for Ben in the way that it does for most adults in our society. What could the social worker do to establish money as a generalized conditioned reinforcer for Ben?

Criteria for correct answer: A correct answer describes a procedure in which the social worker pairs money with the delivery of known reinforcers.

Sample answer: The social worker showed Ben a variety of items placed on a table, including chewing gum, magazines, and cookies. He told Ben to point to an item he would like to have. After Ben pointed to an item, the social worker gave Ben a coin (S^D) and asked Ben to hand him the coin (R). The social worker gave Ben the item Ben had pointed out (S^{r+}) as soon as Ben gave him the coin. The social worker repeated this procedure until Ben took the money each time it was offered and exchanged it for selected items.

(3) 2. You are a social worker in a community setting, and adolescents who have had one or two contacts with the police and juvenile authorities are referred to you. You station yourself in the socioeconomically disadvantaged neighborhood in which these youths live because you plan to engage a group of them in activities that will help them stay out of trouble with the law, improve their academic performance, interview for and successfully hold jobs, and solve various interpersonal and family difficulties. Give two examples that describe how you could establish yourself as a generalized conditioned reinforcer.

Criteria for correct answer: A correct answer includes examples that show your arrangement of conditions in which you are associated with a variety of unconditioned and conditioned positive reinforcers.

Sample answer: You could invite the youths to meetings at which you would provide a variety of refreshments, such as soft drinks, cookies, and popcorn. The only behavior you would require of the youths is attendance at the meetings. You could also take them for rides in the agency's van and to activities such as bowling. Through your association with these reinforcers, you would become a conditioned social reinforcer who can increase the youths' desired behaviors.

(2) 3. State two advantages of using generalized conditioned reinforcers rather than primary reinforcers in behavioral change programs.

Answers:

A. The individual is less likely to satiate on a generalized conditioned reinforcer.
B. Generalized conditioned reinforcers are more abundantly available contingent on appropriate behaviors than primary reinforcers. Generalization of desired behaviors is, therefore, more likely to occur the more similar the reinforcers in the treatment environment are to reinforcers in the client's natural environment.

(4) 4. Give an example of a problem that can be analyzed as a stimulus-response chain. Draw the stimulus-response chain; include at least two stimulus-response units and label each component.
Criteria for correct answer: A correct answer includes a series of behaviors linked by conditioned reinforcers that also serve as S^Ds for the responses that follow and a final reinforcer that maintains the chain.

Sample answer: At parties, Joe is often either drinking or getting himself a drink. Some behaviors in this chain are shown in Figure A.1.

Criterion score: 10

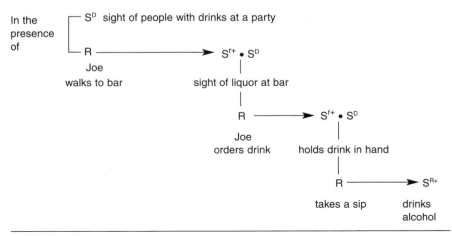

In the presence of

S^D sight of people with drinks at a party

R ⟶ $S^{r+} \cdot S^D$
Joe
walks to bar | sight of liquor at bar

R ⟶ $S^{r+} \cdot S^D$
Joe
orders drink | holds drink in hand

R ⟶ S^{R+}
takes a sip | drinks alcohol

(Continued)

(Continued)

Effect: When Joe is at a party where people are drinking alcohol, he is likely to perform the sequence of behaviors in the chain that leads to his drinking alcohol. Each response in the chain is strengthened. When any S^D in the chain is presented, the rest of the chain will follow. This same chain can be initiated by the S^D of Joe having an empty glass in his hand.

S^D = discriminative stimulus

S^{R+} • S^D = conditioned positive reinforcer that also serves as the discriminative stimulus for the following response

R = response

S^{R+} = positive reinforcer that terminates the chain

Figure A.1   Stimulus-Response Chain of Joe's Drinking

Chapter 8: Modeling and Imitation

(3) 1. Give an example of a modeling plus reinforcement procedure to develop and strengthen a response.

   Criteria for correct answer: A correct answer includes the following elements: (a) a model who demonstrates the behavior (S^m), (b) a person who performs an imitative response (R), and (c) a reinforcer delivered contingent on appropriate imitation.

   Sample answer: In Case Example 6 (p. 271), Bill observed group members role-playing him and demonstrating appropriate responses to criticism. These models demonstrated responses that served as S^{m}s (modeled stimuli) for Bill to imitate. When Bill imitated these behaviors in role plays, group members and the therapist gave him positive reinforcement in the form of praise and encouragement.

(4) 2. Give an example of the use of modeling in developing assertive behaviors in a group setting.

   Criteria for correct answer: A correct answer includes the following elements: (a) specification of target assertive responses, (b) the use of a group member as a model who demonstrates assertive responses (S^m), (c) performance of an imitative response (R) by the client, and (d) a reinforcer presented by group members contingent on appropriate imitation.

   Sample answer: Neil has a hard time asking women to go out with him. He typically approaches them with statements such as "You wouldn't like to go to the movies Saturday night, would you?" and "I have two tickets to a play, if you wouldn't mind going." In addition, Neil speaks in a pleading, whining voice. These underassertive behaviors were observed by group members during a behavioral reenactment of Neil's last attempt to get a date. The therapist asked Nick, another group member, to model assertive responses for Neil. Neil imitated the behaviors that Nick demonstrated and gradually learned to perform assertive behaviors in a variety of role plays. Group members reinforced Neil with praise for appropriate imitation.

(4) 3. Describe the use of a modeling procedure with prompts, reinforcement, and fading, given the following information: A social worker is trying to teach a child with mental retardation to answer questions about his family. When the social worker asks the child, "How many brothers do you have?" the child does not answer. The child can talk and can say all the words necessary to answer the question.

Criteria for correct answer: A correct answer includes the following points: (a) The social worker models the correct response; (b) if the child still does not respond, the social worker models the correct response and prompts the child; (c) a specific reinforcer is given when the child correctly imitates the model; and (d) the prompt is faded out when the child answers on his own.

Sample answer: The social worker asks the child, "How many brothers do you have?" When the child does not answer, the social worker models the correct response—"I have four brothers." If the child still does not respond, the social worker models the correct answer again and prompts the child, "Now you say it, Tony." When the child imitates the model (S^m), the social worker gives the child a raisin and praises him, saying "That's good, Tony." Gradually, the social worker fades out the prompt by saying it in a softer voice each time until the child says, "I have four brothers" in response to the question "How many brothers do you have?"

Criterion score: 10

Chapter 9: Punishment

(3) 1. Give an example of each of the two types of punishment procedures and indicate how you would evaluate the effectiveness of each procedure.

Criteria for correct answer: In a correct answer, one example specifies a punishing stimulus that is presented contingent on performance of a response (positive punishment), and the other example specifies the withdrawal of a positive reinforcer contingent on performance of a response (negative punishment). In both cases, you can evaluate the effectiveness of punishment by observing a decrease in the strength of the punished response.

Sample answers:

Example 1: Mrs. Jones said to Mr. Jones, "You spend all your money on booze." Mr. Jones slapped Mrs. Jones across the face.

Effect: Mrs. Jones stopped complaining to Mr. Jones about his spending money on liquor.

Example 2: During the past 2 weeks, Bert came home 30 to 40 minutes late five times. His mother then told him he could not drive the car for 3 days.

Effect: Since his mother took away his driving privileges, Bert has come home on time.

(2) 2. Give an example that compares extinction with negative punishment.

Criteria for correct answer: A correct answer includes the following points: (a) Punishment is the removal of a reinforcer other than that which maintains the target response, whereas extinction is the withdrawal of the positive reinforcer maintaining the target response; and (b) punishment results in a rapid decrease or suppression of the target response, whereas extinction results in a gradual decrease in strength of the target response.

Sample answer: Fred criticized his wife, Sally, for being overweight when she undressed at bedtime.

Punishment: After Fred criticized Sally, she refused to have sex with him.

Effect: Fred stopped criticizing Sally about her weight.

Extinction: When Fred criticized Sally at bedtime, she turned away from him and stopped speaking to him that evening.

Effect: After three incidents during the past week, Fred stopped criticizing Sally about her weight.

(5) 3. Give an example of how a practitioner could maximize the effectiveness of punishment with a child who exhibits self-injurious behavior.

Criteria for correct answer: A correct answer includes the following elements: (a) delivery of a punisher immediately after self-injurious behavior, (b) delivery of punisher each time self-injury occurs, (c) punisher of sufficient intensity to suppress self-injury, (d) specification of alternative appropriate behaviors, (e) positive reinforcement of appropriate behaviors, (f) removal of reinforcement for undesired behavior, and (g) arrangement of the punishment contingency so that escape is not possible.

Sample answer: A child with mental retardation scratched himself so much that his body was covered with sores. Each time he scratched himself, a mild nonharmful electric shock was delivered to the child's hand. The shock suppressed the scratching after three trials and was discontinued. The practitioner then specified appropriate behavior for the child to engage in, such as picking up a puzzle piece and fitting it into a puzzle. When the child responded appropriately to the instructions, he received a piece of cereal and praise ("Good boy!").

(2) 4. Using the information in Case Example 7 (p. 271), name the punishment procedure administered to Stephen by his father. Give an example of an incident that would lead Stephen's father to use this procedure.

Answers:

A. The procedure used was time-out, a form of negative punishment.
B. Example of an incident that would lead Stephen's father to use this procedure: When Dianne made faces at Stephen and Stephen hit Dianne, the father took Stephen to the laundry room (time-out).

(1) 5. Give an example of punishment applied in a self-control contingency.

Criteria for correct answer: A correct answer includes self-administered punishment, either presentation of a punishing stimulus (positive punishment) or removal of a positive reinforcer (negative punishment).

Sample answers:

If I smoke more than one pack of cigarettes this week, I will send $50 to the American Cancer Society (removal of a positive reinforcer, or negative punishment).

An individual carries an electronic cigarette case that is set to deliver a slight shock if it is opened at intervals of less than 30 minutes (presentation of a punishing stimulus, or positive punishment).

Criterion score: 12

Chapter 10: Negative Reinforcement

(2) 1. Give an example that compares the effects of punishment with the effects of negative reinforcement. Specify relevant responses and stimuli involved in each procedure.

Criteria for correct answers: A correct answer demonstrates the effect of punishment in decreasing the strength of the punished response and the effect of negative reinforcement in increasing the strength of the escape or avoidance response.

Sample answers:

Punishment: A program evaluator requested data on client outcomes from treatment staff (R). They told him that they were too busy to get the data for him (S^{r-}). The program evaluator stopped asking for the data.

Negative reinforcement: A program evaluator repeatedly requested data on client outcomes from treatment staff (S^{r-}). They finally gave her the data she requested (R), thus terminating the requests ($\cancel{S^{r-}}$). The likelihood is increased that the staff will comply with similar requests in the future.

(3) 2. Give an example of escape behavior developed by negative reinforcement. Label relevant responses and stimuli.

Criteria for correct answer: A correct answer includes the following elements: (a) presentation of a negative reinforcer; (b) a response that terminates, removes, or reduces its effect; and (c) evidence that the strength of the escape response increases.

Sample answer: Pat nagged and criticized her husband, Dick (S^{r-}). Dick left the house (R) more often, which removed him from the nagging and criticism ($\cancel{S^{r-}}$).

(2) 3. Using the information in Case Example 3 (p. 268), describe the interaction between Carla and her mother (Juanita) in terms of positive and negative reinforcement prior to the social worker's intervention.

Answers:

Positive reinforcement for Carla: Juanita put the toys away and promised to buy Carla new clothes.

Negative reinforcement for Juanita: Carla screamed (S^{R-}) until Juanita put the toys away and promised to buy Carla new clothes (R)—the responses that terminated Carla's screaming ($\cancel{S^{R-}}$).

(4) 4. Sylvia told Harold, "Buy me a new car or I'll leave you." Harold bought Sylvia a new car, and she stopped threatening to leave him. Draw a diagram that describes the avoidance behavior and label all relevant components.

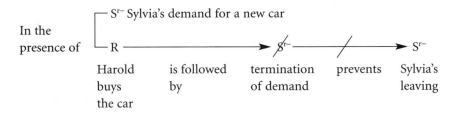

In the presence of
┌ S^{r-} Sylvia's demand for a new car
└ R ——————→ $\cancel{S^{r-}}$ ———— ╱ ————→ S^{r-}

Harold   is followed   termination   prevents   Sylvia's
buys   by   of demand   leaving
the car

Criterion score: 10

Chapter 11: Respondent Conditioning

(3) 1. Using the information in Case Example 5 (p. 269), state one operant behavior and two possible respondent behaviors involved in Pat's being "upset."

Answers:

Operant behaviors: (a) Pat's running into the bedroom and (b) her locking the door.

Possible respondent behaviors: (a) Pat's hands trembling, (b) her heart rate increasing, and (c) her crying.

(7) 2. The following examples include operant and respondent behaviors. Place an O next to those in which the behaviors appearing in italics are operant and an R next to those that are respondent:

   A. 1. __O__ A teenager in a treatment group *swears* at another boy.

       2. __R__ The second boy's face *turns* red.

   B. 1. __O__ You *ask* a client a question about his brother, and

       2. __R__ you observe that his breathing *quickens* and

       3. __R__ perspiration *appears* on his forehead.

   C. 1. __O__ You *give* Janet a piece of candy for completing her assignment.

       2. __O__ Carol observes this and starts *whining*.

(3) 3. Draw a diagram showing respondent conditioning of the following phobia: A child is afraid of dentists. When he approaches a dentist's office, he begins to tremble, turns pale, breathes rapidly, and then turns and runs away. This child has dental problems that must be taken care of soon or he may lose many of his teeth.

   Criteria for correct answer: A correct answer includes a diagram that shows the pairing of a painful stimulus (US) with a previously neutral stimulus (dentist's office) until the neutral stimulus acquires the ability to elicit anxiety (conditioned response [CR]).

   Sample answer: A diagram showing respondent conditioning of the child's fear of dentists appears as follows:

I. Before conditioning

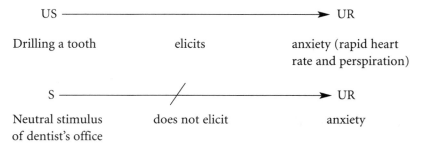

US		UR
Drilling a tooth	elicits	anxiety (rapid heart rate and perspiration)

S		UR
Neutral stimulus of dentist's office	does not elicit	anxiety

II. During conditioning

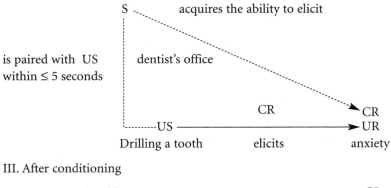

S .... acquires the ability to elicit

is paired with US
within ≤ 5 seconds

dentist's office

CR

CR

----US ——————————————→ UR

Drilling a tooth   elicits   anxiety

III. After conditioning

S = CS ————————————————————→ CR

Dentist's office   elicits   anxiety

(1) 4. Describe the procedure for extinguishing a classically conditioned response.

Answer: Present the conditioned stimulus (CS) repeatedly until it no longer elicits the CR.

Criterion score: 13

Chapter 12: Generalization and Maintenance of Behavior Change

(4) 1. State four obstacles to generalization of desired responses from the practice setting to the client's natural environment.

Answers:

A. Lack of similarity between antecedent stimuli (S^Ds and CSs) in the practice setting and the client's environment
B. Reinforcement of undesired responses in the natural environment
C. Lack of reinforcement for desired responses in the client's environment
D. Insufficient practice of desired responses in the practice setting

(1) 2. In Case Example 4 (p. 269), Leon's speech was developed in a laboratory-like situation. State one reason his speech might not generalize from the treatment setting to the unit.

Answer: Leon's speech might not generalize from the treatment setting to the unit for any of the following reasons:

A. If unit staff do not reinforce Leon's speech, his speaking will be extinguished.

B. S^Ds for speech on the unit might be different from S^Ds for speech in the treatment setting (e.g., there is no green light for speaking on the unit).

C. Unit staff might reinforce quiet, inactive patient behaviors performed by Leon.

D. Leon might not have had sufficient practice at speaking in the treatment setting.

(4) 3. State four ways in which the therapist could maximize successful generalization of Leon's speech.

Answers: Any four of the following are acceptable:

A. The therapist could reinforce the unit staff for reinforcing Leon's speech on the unit.

B. The therapist could shift reinforcement for Leon's speech from a continuous to an intermittent schedule.

C. The therapist could reinforce Leon's speech on the unit.

D. More than one therapist could be used to reinforce Leon's speech in the treatment setting.

E. The therapist could conduct additional sessions to maintain Leon's speech at a high level after Leon has achieved criterion performance in speaking about the slides.

F. The therapist could have the unit staff reinforce Leon's speech in the treatment setting.

(2) 4. In Case Example 5 (p. 269), what are two behavioral assignments that the marriage counselor gave to Pat?

Answers: The counselor gave Pat the following behavioral assignments:

A. Make two lists of topics: one to discuss with her husband, Dick (List A), and the other not to discuss with Dick (List B).

B. Kiss Dick when he comes home from work and ask him how his day has gone.

(2) 5. State two reasons for using behavioral assignments in implementing a behavioral change program.

Answers: Any two of the following are acceptable:

A. To give the client opportunities to try out behaviors discussed and rehearsed in the practice setting

B. To direct the client's activities between meetings toward performance of desired behaviors and attainment of behavior change goals

C. To promote generalization of desired responses from the practice setting to the client's natural environment

D. To give the client homework to perform, with the results reported to the practitioner and used to evaluate the client's progress toward goal achievement

(1) 6. In Case Example 2 (p. 268), how was behavioral rehearsal used to help Bella and Cliff converse appropriately with their peers?

Answers: The social worker required Bella and Cliff to make appropriate statements during the group conversation exercise. They were reinforced with praise for doing so, and they were corrected and instructed to try again when they made inappropriate statements.

(1) 7. What is the rationale for using behavioral rehearsal?

Answer: Behavioral rehearsal allows the client to become more skilled in performing appropriate behaviors in a supportive environment. Behavioral rehearsal also promotes generalization of desired responses from the practice setting to the client's natural environment by ensuring that the desired behaviors are first well learned in the practice setting.

Criterion score: 14

Chapter 13: Behavioral Assessment

(2) 1. Give an example of a behavioral deficit and an example of a behavioral excess.

Criteria for correct answers: Behavioral deficits refer to the absence or low rates of appropriate behaviors. Behavioral excesses refer to high rates of inappropriate behaviors.

Sample answers:

Behavioral deficits:

When someone compliments Joy, she says, "I don't deserve it" in a very low voice.
A 10-year-old child with mental retardation speaks only three words.

Behavioral excesses:

Bill, a 9-year-old, throws rocks at other children.
Carol runs away from home when she is disciplined.

(4) 2. A caseworker tells her supervisor that a client is always late for his appointments.
   A. Which of the following questions should the supervisor ask the caseworker to obtain baseline measures of the complaint? (Circle the correct answer[s].)
      1. Why do you think the client is always late?
      2. How many minutes late is the client?
      3. How many times has the client been late this month?
      4. What do you think the client's lateness means?

B. Give one hypothetical answer to each of the questions you chose above that would provide baseline data on the target behavior.

Criteria for correct answers: Correct answers provide specific data on the rate of the target behavior, the duration of the target behavior, or both.

Sample answer to question 2: He is 15 minutes late each time.

Sample answer to question 3: She has been late for three out of four appointments this month.

(2) 3. Using the information about Denice's case in Chapter 13 (p. 203), state two of Denice's target behaviors.

Answers: Any two of the following are acceptable:

A. Shouted
B. Clenched her fists
C. Frowned
D. Moved her arms rapidly up and down

(1) 4. Specify one antecedent related to Denice's problematic interaction with her coworkers.

Answer: Any one of the following is acceptable:

A. The coworker made a suggestion about how Denice could improve her work performance.
B. Denice said to herself, "I don't deserve criticism from my coworker" and "He thinks I can't do my job."
C. Denice said she felt very anxious about her ability to do her job.

(2) 5. State two negative consequences of Denice's target responses.

Answers: Any two of the following are acceptable:

A. Denice's boss criticized Denice's shouting.
B. Denice's boss warned Denice that she could lose her job.
C. Denice felt anxious.

(2) 6. State two possible reinforcers for Denice's target responses.

Answers:

A. Denice's coworker stopped giving her suggestions.
B. Denice's coworkers left her alone.

(1) 7. State one hypothesis regarding the conditions that exerted control over Denice's target behaviors.

Answer: Denice's shouting at coworkers was reinforced and maintained by negative reinforcement (Denice's anxiety decreased, her coworker stopped giving her suggestions about how to do her job, and other coworkers left her alone).

(1) 8. Using the information in Case Example 1 (p. 267), state a possible reinforcer maintaining Robert's drug use.

Answer: Any one of the following is acceptable:

A. He listens to music with his friends.
B. He spends time with his girlfriend.
C. He avoids doing his homework.
D. He avoids the nagging of his parents.

Criterion score: 14

Chapter 14: Goal Setting, Intervention Planning, and Evaluation

(3) 1. Using the information in Case Example 8 (p. 272), state an intermediate behavioral change goal for Bruce, specifying (a) a desired response, (b) a relevant antecedent, and (c) a possible reinforcer.

Criteria for correct answers: Correct answers indicate that Bruce makes an alternative response in the presence of an antecedent that previously led to nonassertive behaviors. This response is less difficult for Bruce to perform than his target behavior. A reinforcer is delivered after performance of the desired behavior.

Sample answers:

Intermediate goal for a date: Bruce talks about a topic of mutual interest with his date.

>   *Desired response:* Bruce speaks to his date in a pleasant tone of voice about a topic of mutual interest, such as a recent movie they have both seen.

>   *Relevant antecedent:* Bruce has coffee in a restaurant with a woman.

>   *Possible reinforcer:* The woman responds favorably to Bruce; she smiles at him and talks with him.

Intermediate goal with employer: Bruce makes a legitimate request of his employer, such as asking for time off to visit a sick relative.

>   *Desired response:* Bruce looks directly at his employer, speaks in a pleasant tone of voice, and clearly states his request.

>   *Relevant antecedent:* In his employer's office, Bruce sits across the desk from his employer.

>   *Possible reinforcer:* Bruce's employer agrees to Bruce's stated request or acknowledges the legitimacy or reasonableness of the request.

(2) 2. State one possible resource and one possible obstacle to goal attainment for Bruce, given the following behavioral change goal: Bruce assertively asks his employer for a salary increase.

Answers:

Possible resources: Bruce's stated cooperation and desire to improve his situation, possible support from his male friend, and Bruce's favorable employment record with the company

Possible obstacles: Bruce's high anxiety in interpersonal situations, Bruce's negative self-statements that have been reinforced by his boss, and Bruce's reluctance to make an appointment to meet with his employer

(4) 3. Using information from Chapter 14, develop an intervention plan for teaching Tim how to shave (see p. 223). He has never been observed to shave. Include two behavioral techniques and outline the procedure you would follow to achieve the goal.

Criteria for correct answer: A correct answer includes behavior change techniques (selected from those in Table 14.1) that can (a) develop a new response and (b) maintain the response. A correct answer also describes the procedure for implementing the techniques.

Sample answer: Modeling and positive reinforcement are behavior change techniques that could be used. The staff would demonstrate shaving to Tim and tell him to do it the same way. When Tim picked up the shaver, he would be reinforced with a token. The staff would continue to model each step of shaving and reinforce Tim for correct imitative responses. Shaping could also be used in conjunction with modeling. In this case, Tim would be reinforced for any approximations he made to the modeled stimulus. Standing near the sink, reaching for the shaver, and putting the shaver up to his face are approximations that would be reinforced. The reinforcement would be shifted from one approximation to the next until Tim is shaving himself. Another technique that could be used in conjunction with modeling and positive reinforcement is chaining or backward chaining.

(3) 4. State three evaluation criteria a practitioner could use to determine whether marital arguments have been treated effectively.

Answers: Any three of the following are acceptable:

A. The number of arguments decreases.
B. The duration of arguments decreases.
C. The intensity of arguments decreases.
D. The spouses report greater satisfaction with the marriage.

(2) 5. Using the information in Case Example 8, describe a method for evaluating the effectiveness of an assertiveness training procedure that could be used with Bruce.

Criteria for correct answer: A correct answer describes an evaluation method that includes a measure of the strength of social skills before, during, and after treatment, both in the practice setting and in the client's environment.

Sample answer: One way to obtain an objective measure of behavior change would be for Bruce to role-play a situation with the therapist. The therapist would observe Bruce's social skills and include those observations in his or her evaluation of the effectiveness of the intervention program. The second source of such information would be data provided by Bruce before, during, and after treatment concerning his rate of performing social skills in his natural environment.

Criterion score: 13

Chapter 15: Intervention Techniques

(4) 1. Describe how covert sensitization can be used in the treatment of a sex offender who targets children.

Criteria for correct answer: A correct answer includes the following: (a) a detailed description of the maladaptive behavior; (b) the client's imagined performance of the maladaptive behavior, which is then paired with highly aversive stimuli that elicit anxiety-conditioned responses; (c) repeated pairings of these two scenes in the client's imagination; and (d) specification of escape and avoidance responses that are negatively reinforced by removal of the imagined aversive stimuli.

Sample answer: The client has a history of approaching young boys and enticing them into having sex with him. The client is instructed to imagine the following scenario: He approaches a young boy. As he does, he feels nauseated, and an overwhelming urge to vomit overtakes him. He cannot stop it. He vomits all over himself, the young boy, and the street. People are staring at him. The stench is disgusting. As he turns away from the boy, he begins to feel better. He walks away from the boy and continues to feel better. This procedure of imagining the inappropriate sexual partner paired with the nausea and anxiety of vomiting in public is repeated. Covert negative reinforcement (removal of the anxiety and nausea by turning away from young boys) is used to provide appropriate escape and avoidance responses.

(6) 2. Using the following example, describe how thought stopping can be used to decrease undesired thoughts: Jill's fiancé just broke off their engagement, and Jill is having persistent thoughts of how unattractive she is to men and that she will never marry and have children.

Criteria for correct answer: A correct answer includes specification of the negative thoughts and a description of the procedure in which (a) as the client verbalizes the thoughts, the therapist shouts "Stop!" to block the undesired thoughts and redirect the client's attention; (b) the client concentrates on the thoughts and signals the therapist when they begin; (c) the therapist shouts "Stop!" to disrupt the thoughts; (d) the therapist gradually fades out the shouting of "Stop!" as the client takes over saying "Stop!" first aloud and then to him- or herself; and (e) the client redirects his or her thoughts to positive, self-reinforcing self-statements incompatible with the unwanted thoughts.

Sample answer: The following are Jill's negative thoughts: "I'm unattractive to men. I'll never have a good relationship, and I'll never find anyone to marry me." As she begins to speak these thoughts aloud, the therapist loudly shouts "Stop!" The therapist then instructs Jill to think the negative thoughts and to signal the therapist by raising her finger when they begin. When Jill raises her finger, the therapist shouts "Stop!" and discusses with Jill the effect of the shout in disrupting the thought. This procedure is repeated, with the therapist fading out shouting "Stop!" as Jill takes over saying "Stop!" first aloud and then to herself. When the undesired cognition has been disrupted, Jill redirects her thoughts to positive ones, such as "I have a lot of friends who like to spend time with me."

(3) 3. Compare the uses of systematic desensitization, in vivo desensitization, and flooding in the treatment of phobias.

Answer: All three are exposure techniques used for treating phobias. Systematic desensitization uses an imaginal graduated hierarchy of anxiety-evoking stimuli. In vivo desensitization is a graduated exposure technique that is used to treat phobias in the actual problematic situations. Flooding is a technique that uses intense, prolonged exposure, either imaginally or in actual problematic situations.

(3) 4. Stan complains of panic attacks while driving on the freeway and thinks that he will have a heart attack and die in his car. How could a therapist use panic control treatment to decrease the panic attacks Stan has while driving?

Answer: Stan's treatment would include the following components: (a) breathing retraining, relaxation training, or both; (b) cognitive therapy to restructure Stan's belief that he will have a heart attack and die while driving; and (c) interoceptive exposure in which the therapist exposes Stan to physical sensations (e.g., dizziness, heart racing) that elicit or trigger the panic symptoms. The therapist would remain in the situation with Stan until his panic symptoms decrease or extinguish.

Criterion score: 14

Appendix 6

Course Posttest Questions

Questions for Case Example 1 (p. 267)

(3) 1. Specify three antecedents to Robert's drug and alcohol consumption.

(2) 2. State two negative consequences related to Robert's drug and alcohol consumption.

(4) 3. State four negative consequences of Robert's failing grades.

(2) 4. Specify two measures that could be used to evaluate movement toward Robert's behavior change goals.

(3) 5. State three possible reinforcers (positive or negative) maintaining Robert's drug and alcohol consumption.

Questions for Case Example 2 (p. 268)

(5) 1. Specify the target behaviors and their negative consequences for Bella and Cliff.

(3) 2. State three measurable goals of the procedure carried out by the social worker.

(2) 3. Describe two behavioral techniques that the social worker could use to help Bella and Cliff generalize appropriate verbal behavior outside the group.

(2) 4. Describe (a) a reinforcer that was given in the group to Bella and Cliff contingent on appropriate speech and (b) a possible reinforcer that could maintain Bella's and Cliff's appropriate speech outside the group.

Questions for Case Example 3 (p. 268)

(2) 1. Specify the two measures used to determine movement toward behavior change goals.

(4) 2. Describe the interactions between Carla and Juanita in terms of positive reinforcement and in terms of negative reinforcement. Draw diagrams of the interactions and label each component.

(2) 3. Name the operant procedure used to decrease Carla's screaming when she was asked to put her toys away. Describe how it was implemented—that is, to which of Juanita's actions does the procedure refer?

(1) 4. What was the social worker's rationale for instructing Juanita to praise Carla for putting her toys away?

Questions for Case Example 4 (p. 269)

(2) 1. In this case example, no goal is explicitly stated for treatment. State a possible behavior change goal for Leon and specify a measure that could be used to determine whether it was achieved.

(1) 2. What data should Leon's therapist collect before implementing the intervention described in the case example?

(3) 3. Describe the function of the green light. Name and briefly state the purpose of the operant procedure involving the green light.

(2) 4. Apply the concept of conditioned reinforcement to explain how Leon's speech could have generalized to the unit from the treatment setting even though the unconditioned reinforcer (candy) was not given to him on the unit. What specifically did the psychologist do to promote the generalization of Leon's speech to the unit?

Questions for Case Example 5 (p. 269)

(4) 1. State four possible desired behaviors that could be included in treatment goals for Pat, and indicate what measures could be used to evaluate movement toward those goals.

(2) 2. In behavioral terms, describe the rationale for the procedure of having Pat draw up two lists of topics.

(2) 3. State two measures that could be used to evaluate the effectiveness of the discrimination training procedure employed by the counselor.

(1) 4. How was Dick's leaving the house negatively reinforced?

Questions for Case Example 6 (p. 271)

(2) 1. What inappropriate behaviors did Bill emit during criticism?

(3) 2. How could a modeling plus reinforcement procedure have been used to help Bill obtain a new job?

(2) 3. What reinforcement was arranged for Bill in the treatment situation, and what were the conditions for its delivery?

(4) 4. List Bill's respondent behaviors elicited by criticism.

(2) 5. Identify the behavioral procedures that were used to promote generalization of desired behavior change from the group treatment setting to Bill's natural environment.

Questions for Case Example 7 (p. 271)

(5) 1. List five contingencies that Edward carried out with Stephen and Dianne.

(3) 2. Name the behavioral principle that was the basis for the punishment administered to Stephen and Dianne. Name the reinforcers involved for Stephen and Dianne.

(2) 3. The therapist told Edward to spend time with Stephen in the evenings and to play cards with him. The goal was to increase social behaviors performed by father and son that would be positively reinforced by each other. Describe two possible situations that would indicate that this goal was being achieved.

(6) 4. Describe a shaping procedure that Edward could have used to establish cooperative play behaviors between Stephen and Dianne.

Questions for Case Example 8 (p. 272)

(2) 1. State two desired behaviors that could be included in behavior change goals related to Bruce's problem of nonassertiveness.

(2) 2. Describe two role-playing techniques that could be used as part of Bruce's treatment if he were participating in group therapy.

(2) 3. Describe a procedure that Bruce could use to establish himself as a conditioned reinforcer for his dates.

Appendix 7

Course Posttest Answers

Answers for Case Example 1 (p. 267)

(3) 1. Specify three antecedents to Robert's drug and alcohol consumption.

Answers:

A. Friends invite Robert over to listen to music and drink beer.
B. Robert is with his girlfriend at her home.
C. Robert is home alone and looks in his notebook for his assignments. (Chapter 13)

(2) 2. State two negative consequences related to Robert's drug and alcohol consumption.

Answers: Any two of the following are acceptable:

A. He fails to complete class assignments.
B. He is unprepared for class.
C. He receives failing grades. (Chapter 13)

(4) 3. State four negative consequences of Robert's failing grades.

Answers:

A. He is grounded by his parents.
B. His parents nag him.
C. He is denied certain privileges, such as watching television and going out with his friends.
D. His parents withhold his allowance. (Chapter 13)

Note: The chapter numbers in parentheses following the answers in this appendix indicate the chapters in which the preceding material is discussed.

(2) 4. Specify two measures that could be used to evaluate movement toward Robert's behavior change goals.

Answers: Any two of the following are acceptable:

A. Robert turns in an increased number of complete assignments.
B. Robert decreases the frequency of his drug consumption, his alcohol consumption, or both.
C. Robert decreases the amount of his drug consumption, his alcohol consumption, or both. (Chapter 13)

(3) 5. State three possible reinforcers (positive or negative) maintaining Robert's drug and alcohol consumption.

Answers: Any three of the following are acceptable:

A. He spends time with his girlfriend (positive reinforcer).
B. He avoids doing his homework (negative reinforcer).
C. He escapes the nagging of his parents (negative reinforcer).
D. He listens to music and spends time with his friends (positive reinforcer). (Chapters 10 and 13)

Answers for Case Example 2 (p. 268)

(5) 1. Specify the target behaviors and their negative consequences for Bella and Cliff.

Answers:

Target behaviors: (a) asking questions unrelated to topics being discussed, (b) making comments unrelated to topics being discussed, and (c) talking continuously for 5 minutes or more without pausing for others to respond.

Negative consequences: (a) ridicule and (b) exclusion from conversations held by other group members. (Chapter 13)

(3) 2. State three measurable goals of the procedure carried out by the social worker.

Answers: Any three of the following are acceptable:

A. To decrease inappropriate questions and comments
B. To increase Bella's and Cliff's appropriate speech during conversations
C. To decrease the amount of time each spoke without a pause
D. To increase Bella's and Cliff's participation in appropriate conversations with staff and others. (Chapter 13)

(2) 3. Describe two behavioral techniques that the social worker could use to help Bella and Cliff generalize appropriate verbal behavior outside the group.

Answers: The social worker could give Bella and Cliff behavioral assignments in which they would be required to practice the desired verbal behaviors outside the group setting; behavioral rehearsal could also be used in the group setting to allow Bella and Cliff to practice appropriate verbal behavior with reinforcement. (Chapter 12)

(2) 4. Describe (a) a reinforcer that was given in the group to Bella and Cliff contingent on appropriate speech and (b) a possible reinforcer that could maintain Bella's and Cliff's appropriate speech outside the group.

Answers:

A. The social worker and group members complimented and praised Bella and Cliff when they made appropriate statements during the conversation exercise.
B. Reinforcers outside the group could include other persons involving Bella and Cliff in their conversations and staff or relatives reinforcing appropriate speech with praise, attention, and interest. (Chapters 2 and 12)

Answers for Case Example 3 (p. 268)

(2) 1. Specify the two measures used to determine movement toward behavior change goals.

Answers:

A. The decrease in the duration of Carla's screaming when told to put her toys away
B. The increase in the rate of Carla's putting her toys away. (Chapter 14)

(4) 2. Describe the interactions between Carla and Juanita in terms of positive reinforcement and in terms of negative reinforcement. Draw diagrams of the interactions and label each component.

Answers: Carla's screaming was positively reinforced by Juanita's putting the toys away and promising to buy Carla new clothes. Juanita's responses of putting the toys away and promising to buy Carla new clothes were negatively reinforced by the removal of Carla's screaming. (Chapters 2 and 10)

Diagrams:

Positive Reinforcement for Carla

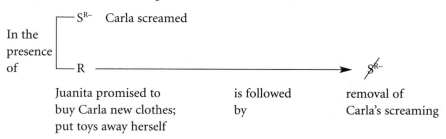

(2) 3. Name the operant procedure used to decrease Carla's screaming when she was asked to put her toys away. Describe how it was implemented—that is, to which of Juanita's actions does the procedure refer?

Answers: Juanita used an extinction procedure to decrease Carla's screaming. When Carla screamed about putting her toys away, Juanita walked away from her. Juanita also refrained from making promises to buy Carla new clothes and from putting Carla's toys away herself. (Chapter 3)

(1) 4. What was the social worker's rationale for instructing Juanita to praise Carla for putting her toys away?

Answer: In situations in which undesired behaviors are decreased, it is important to establish and increase desired behaviors that are incompatible with the undesired behaviors. Therefore the social worker instructed Juanita to praise and reinforce Carla when she put her toys away. (Chapter 3)

Answers for Case Example 4 (p. 269)

(2) 1. In this case example, no goal is explicitly stated for treatment. State a possible behavior change goal for Leon and specify a measure that could be used to determine whether it was achieved.

Criterion for correct answer: The behavior change goal indicates that Leon speaks according to a specific, measurable criterion.

Sample answers: The following are possible behavior change goals: (a) Leon speaks five complete sentences during a 30-minute session, and (b) Leon responds to five of six questions asked of him by the psychologist during a 20-minute session. (Chapter 5)

(1) 2. What data should Leon's therapist collect before implementing the intervention described in the case example?

Answer: The therapist should obtain a baseline indicating the rate of Leon's speech in the treatment setting and on the unit. (Chapter 1)

(3) 3. Describe the function of the green light. Name and briefly state the purpose of the operant procedure involving the green light.

Answers: When on, the green light served as an S^D for verbal responses that would be reinforced. When the green light was off, it served as an S^Δ during which time speech was not reinforced. The psychologist used the discrimination training procedure to teach Leon to speak only when the green light was on. (Chapter 6)

(2) 4. Apply the concept of conditioned reinforcement to explain how Leon's speech could have generalized to the unit from the treatment setting even though the unconditioned reinforcer (candy) was not given to him on the unit. What specifically did the psychologist do to promote the generalization of Leon's speech to the unit?

Answers: Leon's speech was probably maintained by conditioned reinforcers on the unit, such as people responding to his speech, staff praising him for speaking, and other residents commenting favorably on his speech. By saying "Good," the psychologist was using a conditioned reinforcer (praise) with the primary reinforcer (candy) to promote the shifting from unconditioned to conditioned reinforcers more readily available in Leon's natural environment. (Chapters 7 and 12)

Answers for Case Example 5 (p. 269)

(4) 1. State four possible desired behaviors that could be included in treatment goals for Pat, and indicate what measures could be used to evaluate movement toward those goals.

Answers: Any four of the following are acceptable:

A. An increase in frequency of Pat's making breakfast for Dick
B. A decrease in frequency of Dick's going out with his friends
C. An increase in the frequency of Pat and Dick's going to movies or other entertainment together
D. An increase in the frequency of Dick's accompanying Pat on shopping trips
E. A decrease in the intensity of arguments between Pat and Dick
F. A decrease in the frequency of arguments between Pat and Dick

G. An increase in the frequency of pleasant conversation between Pat and Dick

H. An increase in the amount of time Dick spends with Pat and the children watching television, going on trips, or talking with one another. (Chapters 13 and 14)

(2) 2. In behavioral terms, describe the rationale for the procedure of having Pat draw up two lists of topics.

Answer: Pat made a list of topics to discuss with Dick (S^D) and a list of topics not to discuss with Dick (S^Δ). Items on the S^D list (List A) were S^Ds for Pat's speaking that were reinforced by the counselor in role-play situations. Pat's speaking about items on the S^Δ list (List B) was not reinforced by the counselor. The counselor used a discrimination training procedure to teach Pat to talk only about S^D topics to increase the frequency of pleasant conversation with Dick and to decrease the frequency of arguments involving List B topics. (Chapter 6)

(2) 3. What are two measures that could be used to evaluate the effectiveness of the discrimination training procedure employed by the counselor?

Answers:

A. An increase in frequency of Pat's speaking about List A topics

B. A decrease in frequency of Pat's speaking about List B topics. (Chapters 6 and 14)

(1) 4. How was Dick's leaving the house negatively reinforced?

Answer: By leaving the house, Dick removed Pat's nagging and criticizing. Thus his response of leaving the house was negatively reinforced. (Chapter 10)

Answers for Case Example 6 (p. 271)

(2) 1. What inappropriate behaviors did Bill emit during criticism?

Answers: Bill (a) rapped his knuckles against each other and (b) made excuses. (Note: The other behaviors were elicited from Bill, not emitted by him.) (Chapters 1 and 11)

(3) 2. How could a modeling plus reinforcement procedure have been used to help Bill obtain a new job?

Answer: Group members could have modeled appropriate behaviors for Bill in role plays of job interviews. When Bill imitated these appropriate behaviors in role plays, the group members and therapist would give him positive reinforcement in the form of praise. (Chapter 8)

(2) 3. What reinforcement was arranged for Bill in the treatment situation and what were the conditions for its delivery?

Answer: The therapist and group members praised Bill as soon as he responded appropriately in role plays. (Chapter 2)

(4) 4. List Bill's respondent behaviors elicited by criticism.

Answers:

A. His hands trembled.
B. His breathing became rapid.
C. He perspired heavily.
D. His face turned red. (Chapter 11)

(2) 5. Identify the behavioral procedures that were used to promote generalization of desired behavior change from the group treatment setting to Bill's natural environment.

Answers:

A. Behavioral rehearsal was used in the group treatment setting to provide Bill with an opportunity to become more skillful in performing appropriate behaviors.
B. Behavioral assignments were given to Bill so that he would practice appropriate behaviors that he learned in the group in his natural environment. (Chapter 12)

Answers for Case Example 7 (p. 271)

(5) 1. List five contingencies that Edward carried out with Stephen and Dianne.

Answers:

A. If Dianne teased or made faces at Stephen, she would lose privileges, such as watching television and having a bedtime snack.
B. If Stephen hit Dianne, he was told to go to the laundry room.
C. If Stephen refused to go to the laundry room, Edward would physically move Stephen to the laundry room, where he was to remain for 10 minutes.
D. If Stephen kicked or cursed Edward, his time in the laundry room was extended by 5 minutes.
E. If Stephen screamed or made loud noises while in the laundry room, his time there was extended by 5 minutes. (Chapters 4 and 9)

(3) 2. Name the behavioral principle that was the basis for the punishment administered to Stephen and Dianne. Name the reinforcers involved for Stephen and Dianne.

Answers: Both procedures involved negative punishment (response cost). The positive reinforcers for Stephen were Edward's attention and Dianne's crying when Stephen hit her. The positive reinforcers for Dianne were privileges such as television and bedtime snacks. (Chapter 9)

(2) 3. The therapist told Edward to spend time with Stephen in the evenings and to play cards with him. The goal was to increase social behaviors performed by father and son that would be positively reinforced by each other. Describe two possible situations that would indicate that this goal was being achieved.

Criteria for correct answers: Correct answers include information that some behaviors related to time spent together by Edward and Stephen have increased compared with their previous rate. The behaviors should be positive or rewarding, in contrast to the verbal reprimands and physical punishment by Edward and the cursing and kicking by Stephen that characterized their past interactions.

Sample answers:

Edward reports that Stephen is telling him many things about his school activities that he never talked about before.
Stephen asks Edward to read to him.
Edward reports speaking in a mild tone of voice to Stephen more often.
Edward reports that he puts his arm around Stephen more often. (Chapter 9)

(6) 4. Describe a shaping procedure that Edward could have used to establish cooperative play behaviors between Stephen and Dianne.

Criteria for correct answer: A correct answer includes the following steps of a shaping procedure: (a) specification of the target behavior, (b) specification of reinforcers, (c) specification of initial and intermediate responses, (d) reinforcement for performance of initial response until it is performed consistently, (e) shifting criteria for reinforcement to next intermediate response, (f) continued reinforcement of one response during shifting of criteria to next intermediate response until the target behavior is achieved, and (g) reinforcement of the target behavior.

Sample answers: The target behavior is that Stephen and Dianne play a game together for 15 minutes without physical or verbal attacks. Reinforcers are pennies and gumdrops. The initial response is Stephen and Dianne sitting in the same room engaged in separate activities. Intermediate responses include their sitting next to each other playing different games, one of them asking to play a game together, and both of them agreeing to play a game. Initially, Edward would reinforce Stephen and Dianne when they were both in the same room doing different things. When these responses occurred consistently, Edward would shift the criterion for reinforcement to the next intermediate response. This procedure of reinforcing one response until it occurs consistently and then shifting the criterion for reinforcement to the next intermediate response would continue until the target behavior is performed. The target behavior would then be reinforced. (Edward could also model appropriate behaviors or use verbal instructions in conjunction with the shaping procedure.) (Chapter 5)

Answers for Case Example 8 (p. 272)

(2) 1. State two desired behaviors that could be included in behavioral change goals related to Bruce's problem of nonassertiveness.

Answers: Any two of the following are acceptable:

A. Bruce asks his boss for a raise.
B. Bruce states his opinion to his boss.
C. Bruce speaks to his boss in a clear, firm voice, with his hands at his sides.
D. Bruce speaks to a woman in a clear, firm voice, with his hands at his sides.
E. Bruce appropriately defends his rights in a conversation with his boss. (Chapter 13)

(2) 2. Describe two role-playing techniques that could be used as part of Bruce's treatment if he were participating in group therapy.

Answers: Any two of the following are acceptable:

A. Modeling: A group member demonstrates appropriate behaviors in role plays of problematic situations; Bruce appropriately imitates the modeled behaviors and is positively reinforced.
B. Role reversal: Bruce plays the part of his boss, for example, and another group member plays Bruce to demonstrate appropriate behaviors and to demonstrate how Bruce's nonassertive behaviors serve as antecedents for his boss's responses.
C. Behavioral rehearsal: Bruce practices appropriate social skills in role plays of problematic situations and is reinforced by the therapist and group members for appropriate performance. (Chapter 8)

(2) 3. Describe a procedure that Bruce could use to establish himself as a conditioned reinforcer for his dates.

Criteria for correct answer: A correct answer shows Bruce's arrangement of conditions so that he is associated with a variety of unconditioned and conditioned positive reinforcers delivered noncontingently to his dates.

Sample answer: Bruce could invite a woman out for dinner, bring her flowers or candy, talk about her interests during the meal, and take her dancing afterward. He does these things noncontingently—that is, the woman does not have to perform any specific behaviors to obtain these things other than accepting them from Bruce. As these items appear to be reinforcing to the woman, Bruce becomes associated with their delivery. Bruce thus begins to acquire reinforcing value for the woman. (Chapter 7)

Total possible points: 87

Criterion score: 78

Appendix 8

Notational Symbols and Diagrams

Notational Symbols

R	=	response
S	=	stimulus
S^{R+}	=	presentation of an unconditioned positive reinforcer
S^{r+}	=	presentation of a conditioned positive reinforcer
S^{R-}	=	presentation of an unconditioned punisher or an unconditioned negative reinforcer
S^{r-}	=	presentation of a conditioned punisher or a conditioned negative reinforcer
US	=	unconditioned stimulus
UR	=	unconditioned response
CS	=	conditioned stimulus
CR	=	conditioned response
→	=	is followed by (operant)
→	=	elicits (respondent)
↛	=	is not followed by (operant)
↛	=	does not elicit (respondent)
[	=	in the presence of
S^D	=	discriminative stimulus signaling reinforcement (pronounced *ess-dee*)
S^Δ	=	discriminative stimulus signaling nonreinforcement (pronounced *ess-delta*)
S^m	=	modeled stimulus
$\cancel{S}^{R+}$	=	removal of an unconditioned positive reinforcer
$\cancel{S}^{r+}$	=	removal of a conditioned positive reinforcer

$\cancel{S}^{R-}$ = termination, removal, or reduction of an unconditioned negative reinforcer

$\cancel{S}^{r-}$ = termination, removal, or reduction of a conditioned negative reinforcer

Behavioral Diagrams

1. *Procedure:* Positive reinforcement
   Effect: Increase in strength of R

   R ⟶ S^{R+}

2. *Procedure:* Extinction
   Effect: Decrease in strength of R

   R ⟶ / ⟶ S^{R+}

3. *Procedure:* Discrimination training
   Effect: Increase in strength of R in the presence of S^D; decrease in strength of R in the presence of S^Δ

   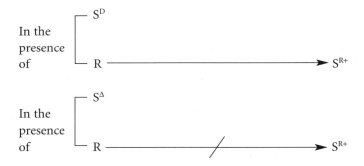

   In the presence of
   ⌐ S^D
   └ R ⟶ S^{R+}

   In the presence of
   ⌐ S^Δ
   └ R ⟶ / ⟶ S^{R+}

4. *Procedure:* Stimulus generalization
   Effect: Increase in strength of R_1 in the presence of S^{D1}; increase in the likelihood of R_1 occurring in the presence of S^{D2}, S^{D3}, and S^{D4}

   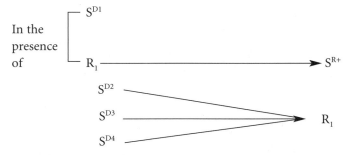

   In the presence of
   ⌐ S^{D1}
   └ R_1 ⟶ S^{R+}

   S^{D2}
   S^{D3} ⟶ R_1
   S^{D4}

5. *Procedure:* Positive punishment
   Effect: Decrease in strength of R

   R ⟶ S^{R-}

6. *Procedure:* Negative punishment; response cost
   Effect: Decrease in strength of R

7. *Procedure:* Negative reinforcement; escape conditioning
   Effect: Increase in strength of the escape response, R

8. *Procedure:* Negative reinforcement; avoidance conditioning
   Effect: Neutral stimulus, S, becomes a conditioned negative reinforcer; increase in strength of the avoidance response, R

   Step 1: Escape condition

   Step 2: Avoidance condition

9. *Procedure:* Respondent conditioning
   Effect: Neutral stimulus becomes a conditioned stimulus capable of eliciting a conditioned response

   I. Before conditioning

   II. During conditioning

   Is paired
   with US within
   ≤5 seconds

   S ········· acquires the ability to elicit

   ········· US ⟶ UR
   ⟶ CR

   III. After conditioning

   S = CS ⟶ CR

Glossary

ABAB design; reversal design   A single-subject research design (SSRD) used to evaluate the effectiveness of an intervention in producing behavior change. The first A refers to baseline, the first B indicates introduction of an intervention, the second A indicates return to baseline, and the second B refers to reintroduction of the intervention. The baseline and treatment phases are alternated to demonstrate that the intervention was responsible for the behavior change.

Accidental reinforcement contingency   A coincidental relationship between a response and a reinforcer. The response is strengthened by an unplanned or noncontingent reinforcer. The likelihood that the response will recur under similar conditions is increased. Superstitious behavior is established under this contingency.

Antecedent   An event that precedes or accompanies a response and could influence its occurrence.

Anxiety   An intense emotional response frequently characterized by physiological changes such as increased heart rate, perspiration, rapid breathing, and subjective statements of unease or fear. Anxiety may generate escape or avoidance behaviors.

Assertiveness training   A behavioral change procedure for teaching individuals how to state and express their opinions and rights without abusing the rights of others. This usually involves instructions, role playing, modeling, behavioral rehearsal, behavioral assignments, and reinforcement. Relaxation training techniques may also be used to decrease anxiety related to underassertive or overassertive behaviors. Assertiveness training can help an individual decrease behaviors such as mumbling, looking at the floor when conversing, and inappropriately agreeing with someone as well as increase appropriate behaviors such as speaking in a clear voice, looking at the person to whom one is speaking, and stating divergent views or opinions.

Aversion therapy   An intervention technique used to treat behavioral excesses, such as drug addiction, alcoholism, and sexual deviations. An aversive stimulus (US/CS) is presented that competes with the inappropriate stimulus to inhibit the undesired response (UR/CR). Operant escape and avoidance responses are also developed to negatively reinforce desired behaviors.

Aversive stimulus   An object or event identified as unpleasant, annoying, or painful; when given the opportunity, the individual will usually escape or avoid such a stimulus. Aversive stimuli can be used as punishers, negative reinforcers, conditioned stimuli, and unconditioned stimuli.

Avoidance behavior   A behavior that results in removal or reduction of a negative reinforcer and prevents the onset of a second established negative reinforcer.

Backward chaining   A behavioral change technique used to teach a complex series or sequence of behaviors. The last stimulus-response unit of the chain is established first, and the other units are added in reverse order until the desired chain is complete.

Baseline data   Measures of response strength recorded prior to intervention, including rate, duration, intensity, latency, and magnitude. Response rate or frequency per time unit is the most common measure recorded.

Baseline rate; baseline level   The strength of a behavior prior to intervention or modification as measured by rate, duration, intensity, latency, or magnitude.

Behavior; response   Any observable or measurable movement or activity of an individual. The terms *behavior* and *response* are used interchangeably throughout this text. Covert behaviors are unobservable but can be reported as self-statements or measured with instrumentation.

Behavior change approach; behavior modification   The application of principles and techniques derived from the experimental analysis of behavior to human problems. This approach emphasizes the methods of applied behavior analysis, the principles of operant and respondent conditioning, and observational learning. The goals of the approach are to improve the human condition and to advance the scientific knowledge base concerning human behavior. Basic features of the approach include (a) specificity in describing problems, goals, and interventions; and (b) systematic planning, implementation, and evaluation of interventions and behavior change programs.

Behavior therapy   The provision of behavior modification services to individuals in a client-therapist setting. This term is generally used synonymously with *behavior change approach* and *behavior modification*. Historically, the term *behavior therapy* has been used to refer to treatment methods based primarily on classical conditioning.

Behavioral assessment   The method used to analyze a client's problem or circumstances; provides the basis for the formulation of behavior change goals and the development of an appropriate intervention plan.

Behavioral assignment   A specific task involving behaviors to be performed by the client outside the practice setting between treatment sessions.

Behavioral contingency   A statement that specifies the behaviors to be performed for certain consequences to follow.

Behavioral contract   An agreement between two or more individuals in which the expected behaviors of each are specified along with the consequences for their performance and nonperformance.

Behavioral deficit   The absence or low frequency of appropriate behaviors.

Behavioral diagram   A stimulus-response model using notational symbols to depict relationships between stimuli and responses.

Behavioral excess   High frequency of inappropriate behaviors.

Behavioral medicine   An interdisciplinary field that applies behavioral analysis and technology to problems of physical health, such as asthma, headaches, insomnia, and hypertension.

Behavioral reenactment   A role-playing technique used to obtain RAC-S information regarding the client's behaviors in the problematic situation by observing him or her role-play an incident that simulates the problem.

Behavioral rehearsal   A role-playing technique in which the client practices desired behaviors that have been suggested or demonstrated by the therapist or by the client's fellow group members in a structured situation with feedback.

Behavioral trap   Naturally occurring reinforcers in a client's environment that maintain behaviors developed through a behavior change program.

Biofeedback   A process that allows an individual to monitor and influence his or her physiological responses using auditory, visual, or other sensory feedback regarding physiological states, such as heart rate, muscle tension, brain waves, and skin temperature. Biofeedback is used in the operant control of autonomic functions and is often applied in conjunction with self-control procedures and relaxation training techniques.

Chains   See *Stimulus-response chains.*

Classical conditioning; respondent conditioning   The development or establishment of a response through the pairing of a neutral stimulus (S) with an unconditioned stimulus (US) until the neutral stimulus acquires the ability to elicit a conditioned response (CR).

Cognitions   See *Covert responses.*

Cognitive behavior therapy; cognitive behavior modification   A behavior change approach that attempts to modify private events or cognitions (covert behaviors) as well as overt behavior.

Cognitive behavior rehearsal   A covert intervention technique to facilitate the client's transfer of instructional control from overt external instructions to covert self-instructions by saying the instructions aloud and then covertly.

Cognitive restructuring   An intervention technique that identifies self-defeating thoughts and negative self-statements and substitutes positive, adaptive self-statements and coping thoughts.

Conditioned aversive stimulus   An unpleasant, annoying, or painful stimulus that has acquired these properties through pairing or association with an established aversive stimulus. When given the opportunity, the individual will usually escape or avoid such a stimulus.

Conditioned negative reinforcer   A stimulus that signals an escape or avoidance response that removes or reduces the effect of the stimulus. The removal of the stimulus increases the likelihood that the escape or avoidance response will be performed again. The conditioned negative reinforcer acts in this way through pairing or association with an established negative reinforcer.

Conditioned positive reinforcer   A stimulus that increases the strength of a response it follows because of its association with other positive reinforcers.

Conditioned punisher   A stimulus that decreases the strength of a response it follows because of its association with other punishers.

Conditioned response (CR)   In respondent conditioning, a measurable activity elicited by a conditioned stimulus (CS). The CR is similar to the unconditioned response (UR).

Conditioned stimulus (CS)   In respondent conditioning, a previously neutral event that acquires the ability to elicit a conditioned response through pairing with an unconditioned stimulus (US).

Consequence   A stimulus that follows a behavior and can influence the future likelihood of the behavior. Consequences can be reinforcing, punishing, or neutral.

Contingency   See *Behavioral contingency.*

Contingency contracting   The practice of establishing behavioral contingencies or contracts between individuals.

Continuous reinforcement (CRF) schedule   A reinforcement schedule in which a reinforcer is delivered each time the response is performed.

Covert responses   Private or unobservable events that can be cognitive, emotional, or physiological. Cognitive behaviors include thoughts, perceptions, attitudes, and beliefs.

Covert sensitization   An anxiety-eliciting intervention technique that employs respondent pairing of imagined aversive stimuli with behavioral excesses to weaken the behavioral excesses. The client is often instructed to make appropriate escape and avoidance responses that can be negatively reinforced by termination of the imagined aversive stimuli.

Deprivation   A condition in which a reinforcer has not been available to or experienced by an individual for an extended period of time. A reinforcer is most effective in increasing the strength of a response when a high level of deprivation exists.

Differential reinforcement   A procedure in which one response is reinforced while reinforcement is withheld from other responses. When the reinforced response occurs frequently, to the exclusion of responses from which reinforcement is withheld, the response has become differentiated.

Discrimination training   A behavioral procedure in which a response is reinforced in the presence of the S^D and extinguished in the presence of the S^Δ. Results in stimulus control; the response occurs during S^D and never or rarely during S^Δ.

Discriminative stimulus, S^D   An antecedent stimulus that signals or sets the occasion for a response made in its presence to be followed by a reinforcer.

Discriminative stimulus, S^Δ   An antecedent stimulus signaling that a response made in its presence will not be followed by a reinforcer.

DRA   Differential reinforcement of alternative behaviors. Decreases the rate of a target behavior by reinforcing behaviors that are alternatives to the target response.

DRI   Differential reinforcement of incompatible behaviors. Decreases the rate of a target behavior by reinforcing behaviors that interfere with performance of the target response.

DRO   Differential reinforcement of behaviors other than the target behavior. Used to decrease the rate of a target behavior by reinforcing any behavior other than the target response.

Duration   A measure of response strength; the length of time a response occurs.

Escape behavior   Behavior that results in the removal or reduction of a negative reinforcer. Removal of the negative reinforcer increases the strength of this behavior.

Ess-dee (S^D)   See *Discriminative stimulus, S^D*.

Ess-delta (S^Δ)   See *Discriminative stimulus, S^Δ*.

Evidence-based practice (EBP)   Mental health practice based on the best scientific evidence available in providing efficacious and effective interventions for clients.

Extinction   *Operant extinction:* The positive reinforcer for a response is withheld each time the response occurs until the response decreases in strength to zero or a prespecified rate. *Respondent extinction:* The conditioned stimulus is presented repeatedly, without the unconditioned stimulus, until the conditioned stimulus no longer elicits the conditioned response.

Fading   See *Stimulus fading.*

Fixed-duration (FD) schedule   An intermittent reinforcement schedule in which reinforcement is presented after a response has occurred continuously for a specified period of time.

Fixed-interval (FI) schedule   An intermittent reinforcement schedule in which reinforcement becomes available when a response is made after the passage of a specified period of time.

Fixed-ratio (FR) schedule   An intermittent reinforcement schedule in which a prescribed number of responses must be performed for a reinforcer to be presented.

Flooding   An intense, prolonged exposure technique for treating phobias by extinction of avoidance responses. Flooding consists of exposing the individual—directly or in imagination—to the phobic stimulus for a prolonged period of time while preventing any escape or avoidance responses.

Frequency   The number of times a response is performed. Frequency per time interval or time unit (response rate) is the most common measure used in recording response strength.

Functional analysis; functional assessment   A method for analyzing a client's problem or circumstances by identifying controlling antecedents and consequences. Functional analysis has also been defined as the manipulation of antecedents and consequences to determine their role in maintaining the target response.

Functional communication training   A DRA procedure in which a client is taught to obtain a reinforcer by performing a desired behavior instead of the undesired behavior that produced the reinforcer.

Generalized conditioned reinforcer   A previously neutral or nonreinforcing stimulus that has acquired the ability to increase response strength through association with established reinforcers; usually an object that can be exchanged for a variety of conditioned or unconditioned reinforcers, such as money.

Imitative response   A response an individual performs after observing a modeled stimulus. The imitative response is physically similar to the modeled stimulus with regard to an observable property, such as form, position, or movement.

Intensity   A measure of response strength that is expressed in units such as grams, pounds, or decibels; indicates the severity of an operant response.

Intermittent reinforcement   Any schedule of reinforcement that is less than continuous. A response is reinforced on some occasions, and reinforcement for that response is withheld on other occasions.

Intervention plan; treatment plan   The product of intervention planning; delineates the behavior change program and specifies the behavioral and cognitive interventions and procedures to be applied in the behavior change program.

Intervention planning; treatment planning   The process of developing a strategy to formulate a behavior change program based on the behavioral assessment and behavior change goals.

In vivo desensitization   An intervention technique for treating phobic behaviors; similar to systematic desensitization except that the client progresses through the hierarchy in real-life situations rather than in imagination.

Latency   A measure of response strength of a classically conditioned response; the interval between presentation of the US or CS and elicitation of the UR or CR, respectively. In operant conditioning, a measure of stimulus control; the interval between presentation of a stimulus and performance of the response.

Magnitude   A measure of the strength of a classically conditioned response; usually obtained through the measurement of secretion of a gland or contraction of a muscle or blood vessel.

Matching law   A law that states that individuals will perform concurrently available responses according to the relative frequency of reinforcement for each response. The reinforcement schedule can be altered to increase the likelihood of performance of a desired response over an undesired response.

Model   An individual whose behavior is imitated.

Modeled stimulus (S^m)   The behavior of a model presented to influence performance of an imitative response.

Modeling procedure; model presentation   The presentation of a modeled stimulus to influence performance of an imitative response. The imitative response is similar to the modeled stimulus.

Natural environment   The physical and social surroundings in which the target behavior was reinforced and in which behavioral changes are designed to be performed and maintained.

Negative reinforcement   The strengthening of a response through escape or avoidance conditioning. *Escape conditioning:* A procedure in which a response that removes or reduces the effect of an aversive stimulus is strengthened. *Avoidance conditioning:* A procedure in which a response is strengthened when it removes or reduces the effect of a conditioned negative reinforcer and prevents the onset of a second negative reinforcer.

Negative reinforcement contingency   A statement that specifies the response that must be performed to remove or reduce the effect of an aversive stimulus.

Negative reinforcer   An aversive stimulus whose removal or reduction increases the strength of an escape or avoidance response.

Neutral stimulus   *Operant conditioning:* A stimulus that neither increases nor decreases the strength of a response it follows. *Respondent conditioning:* An antecedent stimulus that does not elicit a UR or a CR.

Operant behavior   Behavior that is controlled by its consequences.

Operant conditioning   The individual operates or acts on the environment to produce consequences that influence the strength of a response.

Overcorrection   A punishment procedure used to decrease undesired behaviors while at the same time providing S^{D}s and reinforcers for desired behaviors. *Restitutional overcorrection:* Restoring the environment to its condition before the inappropriate act was committed and then improving it even further. *Positive practice overcorrection:* Instructing the individual to perform desired behaviors that are incompatible with undesired behaviors and to practice them repeatedly.

Phobia   Maladaptive anxiety or fear attached to a specific object; involves a conditioned avoidance response.

Positive reinforcement   A procedure to increase the strength of a response by presenting a reinforcer contingent on performance of the response.

Positive reinforcement contingency A statement or condition indicating the behavior that must be performed for a positive reinforcer to be delivered.

Positive reinforcer A stimulus presented after a response that increases the strength of that response and the likelihood that it will be performed again.

Premack Principle A positive reinforcement contingency, named for its originator, that states that a higher-probability behavior can reinforce a lower-probability behavior. That is, a behavior occurring more frequently than another behavior can serve as a reinforcer for the behavior that occurs less frequently.

Primary aversive stimulus See *Unconditioned aversive stimulus.*

Primary negative reinforcer See *Unconditioned negative reinforcer.*

Primary positive reinforcer See *Unconditioned positive reinforcer.*

Primary punisher See *Unconditioned punisher.*

Prompt A discriminative stimulus that helps initiate a response. Verbal cues, instructions, physical guidance, and gestures can serve as prompts to increase the likelihood that a response will be performed.

Punisher; punishing stimulus A stimulus presented after a response that suppresses or decreases the strength of the response. Removal of a positive reinforcer contingent on a response is also referred to as a punisher or punishing stimulus.

Punishment Procedures applied to suppress or decrease the strength of behaviors. *Positive punishment:* Response-contingent presentation of a punisher. *Negative punishment:* Response-contingent removal of a positive reinforcer. See *Response cost.*

Punishment contingency A statement or condition indicating the response that must be performed for positive or negative punishment to be delivered.

RAC-S Acronym for *response, antecedents, consequences, strength;* the framework for behavioral assessment used in this book.

Rate The most common measure of response strength; response frequency per time unit.

Reinforcer A stimulus whose presentation or removal contingent on a response increases the strength of that response and the likelihood that it will be performed again. See *Positive reinforcer; Negative reinforcer.*

Reinforcer sampling Giving an individual a small amount of a reinforcer to encourage further consumption of that reinforcer, such as free samples of a product.

Resistance to extinction The number of responses performed after reinforcement has been discontinued. The greater the number, the higher the resistance.

Respondent behavior Behavior that is elicited by a preceding or antecedent stimulus.

Respondent conditioning; classical conditioning Development or establishment of a response by pairing a neutral stimulus (S) with an unconditioned stimulus

(US) until the neutral stimulus acquires the ability to elicit a conditioned response (CR).

Response; behavior   Any observable or measurable movement or activity of an individual.

Response class   A group of behaviors of which each member or response produces the same or similar effect on its environment.

Response cost   The punishment technique of removing or withdrawing a positive reinforcer contingent on performance of the target response. Also called *negative punishment.*

Response differentiation   The refinement of a response or the narrowing of a response class through differential reinforcement.

Response priming   A technique used to help initiate early responses in a chain, when the responses have a low probability of performance.

Response rate   See *Frequency.*

Response strength   For operant behavior, measured by (a) frequency per time unit (rate), (b) duration, and (c) intensity. For respondent behavior, measured by (a) latency and (b) magnitude.

Reversal design   See *ABAB design.*

Reward   An object or event that is identified as pleasant, satisfying, or desirable, or one that an individual will seek out or approach. A reward may or may not act as a positive reinforcer.

Role reversal   A role-play technique in which the client role-plays the part of another person while the therapist or one of the client's fellow group members role-plays the client's part.

Satiation   A condition in which an individual has consumed or experienced a reinforcer until it has lost its reinforcing effect.

Schedule of reinforcement   A contingency that specifies the conditions under which reinforcement is delivered for a response. Types of reinforcement schedules include continuous, fixed interval, fixed ratio, variable interval, variable ratio, fixed duration, and variable duration.

S-dee (S^D)   See *Discriminative stimulus, S^D.*

S-delta (S^Δ)   See *Discriminative stimulus, S^Δ.*

Secondary aversive stimulus   See *Conditioned aversive stimulus.*

Secondary negative reinforcer   See *Conditioned negative reinforcer.*

Secondary positive reinforcer   See *Conditioned positive reinforcer.*

Secondary punisher   See *Conditioned punisher.*

Self-control reinforcement contingency   A situation in which an individual arranges conditions so that the desired response is followed by self-administered reinforcement.

Self-instruction training   A cognitive-behavioral intervention technique that teaches individuals how to give themselves instructions to cope effectively with difficult situations.

Self-statements   Statements that individuals say to themselves, either aloud or covertly.

Shaping with successive approximations   A behavioral procedure used to develop a new behavior or one that rarely occurs. Differential reinforcement is used to strengthen members of one response class. When these responses are performed consistently, the criterion for reinforcement is shifted to the next response class. Each successive response class more closely approximates the desired target response until the target response is performed and reinforced.

Simple conditioned reinforcer   A previously neutral or nonreinforcing stimulus that has acquired the ability to increase response strength through pairing or association with one particular established reinforcer.

Social reinforcer   A reinforcing stimulus that becomes available through interaction with another individual; examples include attention, praise, and approval.

Social skills training   A behavioral procedure for teaching individuals effective ways of interacting in social situations; includes model presentation, behavioral rehearsal, coaching and prompting, behavioral assignments, and positive reinforcement.

Social validity   Evaluation of the social significance of behavior change programs by the program's consumers; includes evaluation of training objectives, training procedures, and treatment outcomes.

Spontaneous recovery   The recurrence of an extinguished response when stimulus conditions are similar to those in which the response was reinforced.

Stimulus (plural, stimuli)   Any measurable object or event. Stimuli can include physical features of the environment, an individual's behavior, or the behavior of others and may be discriminative, eliciting, reinforcing, punishing, or neutral.

Stimulus control   A condition in which a response occurs in the presence of S^D and never or rarely in the presence of S^Δ. In addition, the interval between presentation of the S^D and the occurrence of the response (latency) is short.

Stimulus fading   A procedure used to transfer stimulus control of a behavior from an original S^D to a novel stimulus. The S^D is gradually altered along one dimension (e.g., size, form) until it resembles the new stimulus. The individual responds appropriately and is reinforced in the presence of S^D throughout its changes with no errors or responses to S^Δ.

Stimulus generalization   A response reinforced in the presence of one stimulus—S^D, US, or CS—is subsequently performed or elicited in the presence of other similar stimuli.

Stimulus-response chains   Units of stimuli and responses that constitute complex sequences or patterns of behavior. Each unit consists of an S^D, a response, and a conditioned reinforcer that also serves as the S^D for the next response. The chain terminates with delivery of a reinforcer that maintains the entire chain.

Straining the ratio   A phenomenon that occurs when a fixed-ratio schedule of reinforcement is increased too rapidly. A response will extinguish if the number of responses required for reinforcement is increased too rapidly.

Stress inoculation training   A technique for teaching physical and cognitive coping skills in response to stressful situations by rehearsing the skills in the presence of stressors.

Superstitious behavior   The result of an accidental contingency. Behavior is strengthened by a noncontingent reinforcer that follows it. See *Accidental reinforcement contingency*.

Systematic desensitization   A respondent procedure for treating phobias that involves systematic and gradual pairing of relaxation stimuli in the client's imagination with phobic stimuli until the phobic stimuli no longer elicit anxiety. A hierarchy of items related to the feared stimulus is constructed, and the client is presented with the items on the hierarchy, from the least anxiety-eliciting item to the most anxiety-producing item, until no or minimal anxiety is elicited.

Target behavior; target response   The behavior or response to be observed and measured; the behavior selected for analysis or modification.

Time-out   A form of negative punishment in which the individual is removed from the reinforcing situation immediately after the target behavior is performed and placed for a brief period in an environment with minimal availability of reinforcement.

Token economy   A planned reinforcement program in which individuals earn tokens or points for performing desired behaviors. The tokens or points can be exchanged for a variety of objects or privileges that serve as *backup reinforcers* for the tokens.

Transfer of behavior change   The generalization of behavior change from the practice setting to the client's natural environment.

Treatment contract   A written or verbal statement of commitment between the practitioner and client that defines the roles of the client and practitioner so that each agrees to perform certain activities that can lead to attainment of the client's goals.

Treatment planning   See *Intervention planning*.

Unconditioned aversive stimulus   A stimulus that is identified as unpleasant, annoying, or painful. Pairing or association with another stimulus is not required for the stimulus to possess these properties. When given the opportunity, the individual will usually escape or avoid the stimulus.

Unconditioned negative reinforcer   A stimulus that signals an escape or avoidance response that removes or reduces the effect of the stimulus. The removal of this stimulus increases the likelihood that the escape or avoidance response will be performed again. The unconditioned negative reinforcer acts this way without requiring prior pairing or association with another negative reinforcer.

Unconditioned positive reinforcer   A stimulus whose presentation contingent on a response increases the strength of that response without requiring prior pairing or association with another reinforcing stimulus.

Unconditioned punisher   A stimulus whose presentation contingent on a response suppresses or decreases the strength of that response without requiring prior pairing or association with another punishing stimulus.

Unconditioned response (UR)   In respondent conditioning, the response that is elicited by an unconditioned stimulus.

Unconditioned stimulus (US)   In respondent conditioning, an object or event that elicits an unconditioned response without requiring prior pairing or association with another stimulus.

Variable-duration (VD) schedule   An intermittent reinforcement schedule in which reinforcement is presented after a response has occurred continuously for an amount of time that is varied around a mean.

Variable-interval (VI) schedule   An intermittent reinforcement schedule in which a reinforcer is presented contingent on performance of a response after an average (mean) amount of time has passed. The interval is randomly varied around a given time value.

Variable-ratio (VR) schedule   An intermittent reinforcement schedule in which a reinforcer is delivered after an average number of responses is performed. The ratio is randomly varied around a given value.

Author Index

Subject Index

About the Authors

Martin Sundel, President of Sundel Consulting Group, is a behavior change consultant and practitioner. He is a Charter Clinical Fellow of the Behavior Therapy and Research Society. He was the Dulak Professor of Social Work at the University of Texas at Arlington, and also served on the faculties of the University of Michigan, the University of Louisville, and Florida International University. He holds professional degrees in social work and psychology from the University of Michigan and was a postdoctoral fellow at the Laboratory of Community Psychiatry at Harvard Medical School. He has published extensively on the application of behavioral science knowledge to the helping professions. His publications include *Assessing Health and Human Service Needs, Be Assertive, Individual Change Through Small Groups* (2nd edition), *Midlife Myths,* and *Women at Midlife.*

Sandra S. Sundel is Executive Director of Jewish Family Service of Broward County, Florida. She was formerly a professor of social work at Florida Atlantic University. She has taught courses in social work practice, behavior therapy, interpersonal communication, and group work, and has conducted numerous workshops and seminars on these topics. She has consulted with corporations, government agencies, and nonprofit organizations on organizational behavior management and interpersonal communication in the workplace. She is coauthor of *Be Assertive* and *Women at Midlife* and has published many book chapters and journal articles. She specializes in behavior therapy with women and families.